# The Founders' Second Amendment

**The INDEPENDENT INSTITUTE**

THE INDEPENDENT INSTITUTE is a non-profit, non-partisan, scholarly research and educational organization that sponsors comprehensive studies of the political economy of critical social and economic issues.

The politicization of decision-making in society has too often confined public debate to the narrow reconsideration of existing policies. Given the prevailing influence of partisan interests, little social innovation has occurred. In order to understand the nature of and possible solutions to major public issues, the Independent Institute adheres to the highest standards of independent inquiry, regardless of political or social biases and conventions. The resulting studies are widely distributed as books and other publications, and are publicly debated in numerous conference and media programs. Through this uncommon depth and clarity, the Independent Institute expands the frontiers of our knowledge, redefines the debate over public issues, and fosters new and effective directions for government reform.

THE INDEPENDENT INSTITUTE
100 Swan Way, Oakland, California 94621-1428, U.S.A.
Telephone: 510-632-1366 • Facsimile: 510-568-6040
Email: info@independent.org • Website: www.independent.org

# The Founders' Second Amendment

ORIGINS OF THE RIGHT TO BEAR ARMS

## Stephen P. Halbrook

*Ivan R. Dee*

CHICAGO 2008

PUBLISHED IN ASSOCIATION WITH THE INDEPENDENT INSTITUTE

www.ivanrdee.com

Library of Congress Cataloging-in-Publication Data:

Halbrook, Stephen P.

  The founders' Second Amendment : origins of the right to bear arms / Stephen P. Halbrook.

    p. cm.

  Includes bibliographical references and index.

  ISBN-13: 978-1-56663-792-3 (cloth : acid-free paper)

  ISBN-10: 1-56663-792-9 (cloth : acid-free paper)

  1. United States. Constitution. 2nd Amendment—History 2. Firearms—Law and legislation—United States—History. 3. Constitutional history—United States. I. Title.

KF3941.H349 2008a

344.7305'33—dc22                                                           2008001451

# Contents

# Preface

THIS IS THE FIRST book-length account of the
nature of the Second Amendment right of the people to
keep and bear arms during the generation of the Founders of the American
republic. This period spans from the last years of British rule and the American Revolution through the adoption of the Constitution and Bill of Rights
and the passing away of the Founders' generation. Those years began in 1768,
when Redcoats first occupied Boston, and ended when Thomas Jefferson and
John Adams died on July 4, 1826.

"Marshaling an impressive array of historical evidence," writes Supreme
Court Justice Clarence Thomas, "a growing body of scholarly commentary
indicates that the 'right to keep and bear arms' is, as the Amendment's text
suggests, a personal right." [1] He cited two books, Joyce Lee Malcolm's *To Keep
and Bear Arms: The Origins of an Anglo-American Right*—the preeminent study
of the English beginnings of the right—and this author's *That Every Man Be
Armed: The Evolution of a Constitutional Right*—which traces the right from
its Greco-Roman origins through modern American jurisprudence.

Few contributions to Second Amendment scholarship existed until the
1980s. Today, journal articles on the amendment abound. [2] This author also

published books on how the right to keep and bear arms was perceived in the original thirteen states[3] and on the treatment of this right during Reconstruction as a civil right won by freedmen.[4]

Yet perhaps the most important piece of the puzzle is missing—a truly comprehensive treatment of the views of the Founders, from the pre-Revolutionary days through the passing of that generation. This book seeks to fill that void.[5]

It would be difficult to acknowledge every person who assisted in preparation of this work. The author, while solely responsible for any deficiencies, thanks the many scholars over the years who, in one way or another, contributed toward a critique of the theses of this book. Special thanks for their critical perusal of the manuscript are due to Forrest McDonald, Distinguished University Professor, University of Alabama; Joyce Lee Malcolm, Professor of Law, George Mason University; Nelson Lund, Patrick Henry Professor of Constitutional Law and the Second Amendment, George Mason University; and Alexander Tabarrok, Research Director, the Independent Institute. There were several anonymous peer reviewers whose challenges, on points great and small, invariably made this a better book. Also helpful, in many contexts, were the contributions of William Van Alstyne, David Kopel, Robert Dowlet, Richard Gardiner, Don Kates, David Caplan, George Knight, Eugene Volokh, Akhil Amar, Robert Cottrol, and Glenn Reynolds.

Appreciation must also be expressed to those who pored through obscure eighteenth-century documents or otherwise assisted in the research for this book, including Heather Barry, David Fischer, Patrick Halbrook, Oliver Harriehausen, Jordan Jackson, and Suzanne Anglewicz. Editorial assistance was provided by Lisa Halbrook and Jennifer Gordon. For preparation of the manuscript, the assistance of Gail Saari, Megan Whitson, and Alyson Nolan must be acknowledged. Special thanks are due to David J. Theroux, President of the Independent Institute, for tirelessly sponsoring and moving the publication of this book forward.

# The Founders' Second Amendment

# Introduction

THE FOUNDERS of the American republic sought to guarantee what they termed "the right of the people to keep and bear arms" as a fundamental liberty. Hotly debated and sometimes denigrated today, the Second Amendment to the U.S. Constitution somewhere along the way became a controversial enigma. But what did it mean to the Founders? What perceived violations of their rights prompted them to insert this provision into the Bill of Rights? What was the history of how this right found its way into that esteemed charter of liberties?

The amendment states: "A well regulated Militia, being necessary to the security of a free State, the right of the people to keep and bear Arms, shall not be infringed." A long-standing interpretation is that individuals have a right to possess and carry firearms and that an armed populace constitutes a militia that secures a free country. In recent decades the view has become prominent that the Amendment guarantees a "collective right" of the states to maintain militias free of federal control, or, in a more sophisticated version, that individuals have a "right" to bear arms in militia service, but not otherwise.

This work seeks to present the views of the Founders who actually created the Second Amendment. It is based on their own words as found in newspapers, correspondence, debates, and resolutions. Generous quotations from the

Founders are used to allow them to speak for themselves, thereby avoiding the appearance of re-characterization of their views.

The "Founders" were the generation of Americans in the eighteenth century who suffered in the final stages of British colonialism, fought the Revolution and won independence, debated and adopted the Constitution and Bill of Rights, and established the republic. The members of that generation passed away by the early nineteenth century, but their constitutional legacy is, if not immortal, a singular triumph in the history of human freedom.

The story begins in 1768 when the Redcoats are sailing to occupy Boston, and the patriots are spreading the alarm that, among other deprivations, the inhabitants are to be disarmed. The presence of a standing army quartered within the population, Chapter 1 shows, led the colonists vigorously to assert their rights as Englishmen. The tragedy of the Boston Massacre only solidified the patriots' commitment to protect themselves, by arms if need be.

From the Boston Tea Party through the Powder Alarm, a period taking place in the months just before through just after 1774, repressive measures against the increasingly troublesome Americans sharply escalated. The Royalist-imposed government in Boston—the radicals called it "the Divan" after an institution of Turkish despotism—debated a prohibition on all private arms. General Thomas Gage's troops seized the gunpowder in the powder houses, cutting off the supply of that essential commodity. Searches and seizures, including alleged entrapment, were instituted against those attempting to obtain and distribute arms. Chapter 2 describes these events.

Well aware that the colonists were making every effort to arm themselves, George III sought to cut off all arms and ammunition at the source, by prohibiting the export of these articles from Britain and elsewhere (particularly Holland) and the import thereof into the colonies. As Chapter 3 recounts, this arms embargo was combined with stepped-up search-and-seizure operations in Boston, particularly at the Neck, the narrow strip of land where patriots were smuggling large quantities of munitions to the countryside.

The "shot heard 'round the world" at Lexington and Concord in 1775 involved the Redcoats' attempted seizure of arms being hoarded by militiamen and the repulse of these troops by the local citizens armed with their own muskets and sporting arms. This led General Gage, as detailed in Chapter 4, to impose the confiscation of all firearms from Boston's civilians, under the promise that those in compliance could depart the besieged city. After seizing the arms, "the perfidious Gage" held the townsfolk as hostages.

During these years, history was not standing still in the other colonies. However, the patriots in such colonies as Virginia, Pennsylvania, and New York were being radicalized because of events in Boston, and the British authorities saw Boston as the root of all evil in the colonies. Accordingly, the above chapters focus on Boston, where the patriot–British conflict spiraled out of control. The Boston experience showed that many colonists were armed or sought to obtain arms and that Gage's successful and unsuccessful attempts to disarm them constituted yet more proof of the Crown's objective to destroy their rights as Englishmen.

The above were key events that led the Founders to adopt the Second Amendment. A tyrannical government supported by a standing army had sought to disarm a people through various artifices. It took these repressive measures against both citizens organized as militia and against citizens as individuals. The patriots then exercised their right to keep and bear arms to protect both this right and their many other rights.

The Revolution had now been sparked. Its philosophy, as expressed in the Declaration of Independence, was that the people must endure some amount of injustice, but they may wage armed resistance when injustice becomes tyranny. The ramifications of this republican doctrine are presented in Chapter 5.

Beginning in 1776 and continuing during the War for Independence, the states took measures to provide for their own governance. Virginia was the first state to adopt a declaration of rights, which included the admonition for "a well regulated Militia, composed of the Body of the People." And Pennsylvania was the first to declare that "the people have a right to bear arms for the defence of themselves, and the state." These principles were held dear in all of the states, as Chapters 6 and 7 detail, without regard to whether they adopted a bill of rights. Skeptics deemed it unnecessary to list the many rights of mankind in a formal instrument.

With independence won and rights vindicated, the next phase of the Second Amendment's saga begins with the drafting of the Constitution at the Philadelphia convention in 1787. Its lack of a bill of rights was defended in *The Federalist Papers* and attacked by the antifederalists. But both sides agreed, as explained in Chapter 8, with the ideal of an armed populace.

The proposed constitution was then considered by the state conventions, largely in 1788. In the initial phase, those demanding a bill of rights protecting free speech or any other right could not muster a majority in any convention. However, the Pennsylvania minority proposed that "the people have a right to bear arms" to defend themselves, the state, and the United States, as well as for hunting. In the Massachusetts convention, Samuel Adams proposed that "peaceable citizens" have a right to keep "their own arms." Finally, as Chapter 9 explains, the New Hampshire convention became the first to propose a bill of rights, including that "Congress shall never disarm any citizen" unless in rebellion.

It was now Virginia's turn. Patrick Henry argued "that every man be armed," and George Mason drafted a declaration of rights, including a guarantee of "the right of the people to keep and bear arms." James Madison and his federalist colleagues reached the great compromise with the antifederalists: Virginia would ratify the Constitution without a bill of rights, but would propose one and urge its prompt adoption. How Virginia tipped the scale in favor of a declaration of rights is described in Chapter 10.

In the remaining state conventions, the majority in favor of a bill of rights had become irresistible. New York demanded one, and North Carolina refused to ratify the Constitution until a bill of rights had been introduced in Congress. Chapter 11 explains these developments, which included significant mention of the right to bear arms.

James Madison lived up to his promise and introduced what became the Bill of Rights in the first session of Congress in 1789. The Second Amendment was interpreted, as federalist Tench Coxe expressed it, to guarantee the right of the people to keep and bear "their private arms." The Senate rejected restricting the right to bear arms to "the common defence" and also rejected a proposed state power to maintain a militia. These developments are described in Chapter 12.

The proposed Bill of Rights was then considered for adoption by the states. No record exists of any criticism of "the right of the people to keep and bear arms," although the militia clause was taken to task for not actually doing anything. The Bill of Rights, as explained in Chapter 13, was finally adopted in 1791.

Meanwhile, the nature of a well regulated militia was debated in Congress. The Militia Act of 1792 would require that all able-bodied white males enroll in the militia and provide their own arms. Both the power of the states to maintain militias and the right of individuals to have arms for self-defense, as Chapter 14 shows, were considered basic.

"Old soldiers never die, they just fade away"—the same could be said for the Founders, as detailed in Chapter 15. The first commentary on the Constitution, by St. George Tucker, posited that the Second Amendment protects individual rights and that legislative infringement was subject to judicial review. George Washington and John Adams both exposited and exercised the right to bear arms. Thomas Jefferson loved and collected good books, good wines, and good firearms. Their generation, but not their constitutional ideals, faded away.

What does the Second Amendment say? This is the subject of the Conclusion, which engages in a linguistic analysis as informed by the Founders' usage of terms. The terms "right of the people" as used in the First, Second, and Fourth Amendments are contrasted with such phrases as "the militia, when in actual service" in the Fifth Amendment and with the powers "reserved to the states respectively" in the Tenth Amendment.

A lively debate has erupted in recent times on the meaning of the Second Amendment.[1] Under the "collective rights" view, the Amendment protects state powers to maintain militias, not an individual to keep and bear arms.[2] A hybrid version argues that it protects a "civic right" to bear arms in the militia.[3] Other studies focus on the extent of firearm ownership in the Founders' generation.[4]

The historical evidence set forth in this work suggests that the Founders had a predilection for both a well regulated militia and an individual right to have arms, and that they envisioned that the two clauses of the Amendment would complement rather than be in tension with each other. Colonial newspapers, forgotten diaries, and related sources have been exhaustively examined for insights into what the Founders viewed as violations of the right to bear arms. The history of how demands for a bill of rights came to develop has been enhanced by publication of numerous additional volumes of *The Documentary History of the Ratification of the Constitution*.

But that is getting ahead of the story, which is far richer than any modern legal controversy. The Crown's attempts to disarm the colonists as a contributing grievance in the chain of events leading to the American Revolution and the imperative of guaranteeing the right to have arms in bills of rights are themes that pervade the thinking of the Founders' generation. This book seeks to interweave expressions of concern for that right and other liberties which found expression in bills of rights with contemporaneous developments leading to the founding of the constitutional republic. The meaning and scope of the Second Amendment may be fully comprehended only in the context of the Founders' understanding of what is necessary to guarantee, as the amendment itself states, "the security of a free State."

A bill of rights is intended not only to instruct government on its limits, but also to "giv[e] information to the people," wrote St. George Tucker in 1803. Every man, even the most humble, thereby "may learn his own rights, and know when they are violated."[5] Ferreting out the Founders' conceptions of the right to have arms side-by-side with an array of other substantive rights contributes to a broader understanding of the Bill of Rights as a whole.

# Disarming the Colonists

## CHAPTER I

# "The Inhabitants to Be Disarmed"

A S BRITISH OCCUPATION TROOPS were about to land in Boston, an anonymous patriot signing his name only as "A.B.C." issued the following dire warning in the *Boston Gazette* on September 26, 1768, which would be repeated throughout the colonies:

> It is reported that the Governor has said, that he has Three Things in Command from the Ministry, more grievous to the People, than any Thing hitherto made known. It is conjectured 1st, that the Inhabitants of this Province are to be disarmed. 2d. The Province to be governed by Martial Law. And 3d, that a Number of Gentlemen who have exerted themselves in the Cause of their Country, are to be seized and sent to Great-Britain.

> Unhappy America! When thy Enemies are rewarded with Honours and Riches; but thy Friends punished and ruined only for asserting thy Rights, and pleading for thy Freedom.[1]

The most influential patriotic newspaper in the colonies, the *Boston Gazette*'s chief contributor was Samuel Adams—a likely suspect as author of the above lines—and its other distinguished writers included James Otis, Josiah Quincy, and John Adams.[2] While the seeds of the Revolution had been sown with the

Stamp Act crisis of 1765 and Parliament's subsequent claim that it could bind the colonies "in all cases whatsoever,"[3] it was in 1768 that the patriots began to charge that the Ministry intended to disarm the inhabitants.

This warning foreshadowed what would come to fruition over a half decade later, in 1774–75, when the Crown, imposing martial law, did indeed seek to disarm the inhabitants and to seize and send "traitors" to England. For all the patriots knew, however, the Royal government could take such drastic measures sooner rather than later.

On September 8, Governor Francis Bernard leaked information that British troops were sailing to Boston.[4] In response to the above charges of "A.B.C.," Bernard evasively explained: "My Apprehensions that some of his Majesty's Troops are to be expected in Boston, arise from Information of a private Nature: I have received no public Letters, notifying to me the coming of such Troops, and requiring Quarters for them; Whenever I do, I shall communicate them to his Majesty's Commands."[5] Actually, as explained below, the governor himself had requested troops to enforce British tax collection in the colonies.

After Governor Bernard refused demands that he convene a general assembly of the populace, enraged patriots plotted resistance. On the evening of September 11, James Otis, Samuel Adams, and other popular leaders met at the house of Joseph Warren to draft resolutions to be presented at a town meeting planned for the next morning.[6]

The greater part of Boston's populace turned out for the stormy meeting that would take place on September 12–13. They met in Faneuil Hall and its surrounding square—the marketplace and town hall that still stand today.[7] Rousing speeches were made and resolutions were adopted deploring taxation and standing armies. Four hundred muskets that belonged to the town lay exposed on the floor.[8] Hotheads demanded that the muskets be distributed to the people then and there, but James Otis, who presided over the meeting, persuasively argued: "There are the arms; when an attempt is made against your liberties, they will be delivered . . . ."[9] Instead, the assembly considered and passed the following prepared resolution admonishing every man to provide arms for himself:

Upon a Motion made and seconded, the following vote was passed by a very great Majority, *viz.*

whereas, by an Act of Parliament, of the first of King *William* and Queen *Mary*, it is declared, that the Subjects being Protestants, may have arms for their Defence; It is the Opinion of this town, that the said Declaration is founded in Nature, Reason and sound Policy, and is well adapted for the necessary Defence of the Community.

*And Forasmuch*, as by a good and wholesome Law of this Province, every listed Soldier and other Householder (except Troopers, who by Law are otherwise to be provided) shall always be provided with a well fix'd Firelock, Musket, Accouterments and Ammunition, as in said Law particularly mentioned, to the Satisfaction of the Commission Officers of the Company; and as there is at this Time prevailing Apprehension, in the Minds of many, of an approaching War with France: In order that the Inhabitants of this Town may be prepared in Case of Sudden Danger: voted, that those of the Inhabitants, who may at present be unprovided, be and hereby are requested duly to observe the said Law at this Time.[10]

Parliament had indeed, in the English Bill of Rights of 1689, declared certain "true, ancient and indubitable rights," including: "That the Subjects which are Protestants, may have Arms for their Defence suitable to their Condition, and as are allowed by Law." This stemmed from the grievance that James II had attempted to subvert "the Laws and Liberties of this Kingdom," in part "By causing several good Subjects, being Protestants, to be disarmed, at the same Time when Papists were both armed and employed, contrary to law."[11]

While disingenuous, the alleged apprehensions about a war with France provided an urgent reason to admonish every man who was not already armed to obtain a firearm, as required by the cited law. The real reason for strict compliance could hardly be stated publicly—that the people should arm themselves for protection against the approaching British troops.

As far back as 1645, Massachusetts law had required "that all inhabitants . . . are to have armes in their houses fit for service."[12] British member of Parliament William Gerard Hamilton, who opposed taxing the American colonies, warned in 1767 about the colonists:

There are, in the different provinces, about a million of people, which we may suppose at least 200,000 men able to bear arms; and not only able to bear arms, but having arms in their possession, unrestrained by any iniquitous

Game Act. In the Massachusetts government particularly, there is an express law, by which every man is obliged to have a musket, a pound of powder, and a pound of bullets by him . . . .[13]

A general militia composed of all citizens capable of bearing arms was seen as superior to a select militia consisting of a selective group, which bordered on a standing army, the bane of liberty. The English Bill of Rights of 1689 had also accused James II of subverting liberty in part "By raising and keeping a Standing Army within the Kingdom in Time of Peace, without Consent of Parliament, and quartering Soldiers contrary to Law." It accordingly declared "That the raising or keeping a standing Army within the Kingdom in Time of Peace, unless it be with Consent of Parliament, is against Law."[14]

The above would be reflected in one of the resolutions adopted by the above Boston assembly, which met on September 12–13, as follows:

> And whereas in the aforesaid Act of Parliament it is declared, That the raising or keeping a standing Army, within the Kingdom in Time of Peace, unless it be with the Consent of Parliament, is against Law: It is the Opinion of this Town, that the said Declaration is founded in the indefeasible Right of the Subjects to be consulted, and to give their free Consent, in Person, or by Representatives of their own free Election, to the raising and keeping a standing Army among them; And the Inhabitants of this Town, being free Subjects have the same Right, derived from Nature and confirmed by the British Constitution, as well as the said Royal Charter; and therefore the raising or keeping a standing Army, without their Consent, in Person or by Representatives of their own free Election, would be an Infringement of their Natural, Constitutional and Charter Rights; and the employing such Army for the enforcing of Laws made without the consent of the People, in Person, or by their Representatives, would be a Grievance.[15]

The assembly also decided that the selectmen of Boston—the town's elected councilmen—should send a circular letter to the selectmen of several other local towns, calling for a convention to meet on September 22. The letter recited the following allegations: "The concern and perplexity into which these things have thrown the people, have been greatly aggravated, by a late declaration of his Excellency governor Bernard, that one or more regiments may soon be expected in this province. The design of these troops is, in every one's apprehension, nothing short of enforcing by military power the execution of acts of parliament . . . ."[16]

The letter was well received, and delegates from nearly two hundred towns in Massachusetts arrived at Faneuil Hall on the appointed morning. Furious, Governor Bernard ordered them to disperse immediately. The delegates replied with a letter explaining the reasons for the assembly, but the governor refused to receive it and again declared that the assembly was illegal.[17] The selectmen remained to finish their business, adopting declarations and describing their grievances in a letter to the king.[18]

The colonists felt that they had inherent rights as Englishmen. These rights included not just keeping and bearing arms and jury trial by one's peers but also the right to petition for redress of grievances and the right of representation—which extended not just to the ever-present issue of taxation but also whether a standing army would be allowed. The right against searches and seizures without a warrant, the sanctity of the home, and many other rights must be counted among the rights of an Englishman that the Americans felt they inherited.[19]

It was in these days of escalating conflict that "A.B.C." wrote in the *Boston Gazette*, as quoted at the beginning of this chapter, that the governor had received three commands from the ministry "more grievous to the People, than any Thing hitherto made known": that "the Inhabitants of this Province are to be disarmed," "the Province to be governed by Martial Law," and patriots "are to be seized and sent to Great-Britain."[20]

The troops, some seven hundred infantrymen from Halifax, Nova Scotia, actually landed on October 1.[21] They took over key points in Boston, including Faneuil Hall.[22] Richard Draper, official printer to the Royal governor,[23] advised the public to remain calm and denied A.B.C.'s charges. "We are authorized to inform the Publick, that the Article of the Report of the Sayings of the Governor . . . is an infamous Lye, invented for the wicked Purpose of raising groundless Fears of, and creating an unnatural Disaffection to his Majesty and his Government."[24] A.B.C. shot back:

> I observe Mr. Draper in his last paper says he is authorized to assure the Publick, that the Reports mentioned in your Paper of September 26, was an infamous Lie. . . . Mr. Draper (as he was about the Town, and these Reports were the subject of much Conversation) must have known he was publishing a Falsehood . . . . When an armed Force is bro't in upon a peaceable Country against their Consent, and in Violation of their Rights as Men and British subjects, we have Reason to believe that soon unheard of Oppressions are coming upon us.[25]

Relations between Britain and her American colonies, which had been simmering for some time, were reaching a new level of conflict, the beginning of a spiral that would eventually push the colonists toward independence. The underlying basis of the conflict culminating in the above events concerned taxation. In February 1768, the Massachusetts House of Representatives had circulated a letter of grievances to other representatives throughout the colonies, condemning unjust taxation while still asserting their loyalty to the king.[26] The source of their woes was the Townshend Acts, particularly the Revenue Act, which imposed customs duties on imported glass, lead, paints, paper, and tea.

The letter was received with sympathy and agreement but caused great insult to Lord Hillsborough, secretary of state for colonial affairs. Hillsborough wrote to the colonial governors, advising them to quell any support their assemblies would give to the letter, and demanded that the Massachusetts House of Representatives rescind its proceedings.[27] It refused, and Governor Bernard dissolved the House. When they reconvened in May, as required by their charter, they were again requested to rescind their previous resolutions. Instead of doing so, the House made a failed attempt to impeach Bernard, after which it was once again dissolved.[28]

In the meantime, the assemblies of the other colonies adopted resolutions agreeing that the British taxes were illegal and sent petitions to the Crown and Parliament.[29] The escalating trouble spearheaded by Boston prompted Lord Hillsborough on June 8 to write an instruction to General Thomas Gage, commander in chief of the British army in North America, to send "such Force as You shall think necessary to Boston, to be Quartered in that Town, and to give every legal assistance to the Civil Magistrate in the Preservation of the Public Peace; and to the Officers of the Revenue."[30]

Tensions between the colonists and the Crown escalated further as a result of the abrupt seizure on June 10 of *Liberty*, John Hancock's ship, which allegedly had imported more wine from Madeira than the volume declared for payment of the duty.[31] As Mercy Otis Warren later recounted, "The mode of seizure appeared like a design to raise a sudden ferment, that might be improved to corroborate the arguments for the necessity of standing troops to be stationed within the town."[32] Some mischief followed, resulting in broken windows of the custom house office and perhaps the threatening of the officers' lives. Hotheads dragged one of the collector's boats through town and set it ablaze.[33] The riot gave Bernard the much-desired excuse to call for troops to be stationed in Boston and prompted Hillsborough to order General Gage to strengthen the British garrison there.[34]

As a protest against the Townshend Act duties, on August 1 some sixty Boston merchants agreed that they would not, at the start of the new year, import any tea, paper, glass, or painters' colors until the duties on these articles were repealed; further, they would import nothing from Great Britain except salt, coal, and a handful of other critical items—including "bar-lead and shot."[35] "Bar-lead" was melted and molded into musket balls, and "shot" consisted of smaller balls for firing from fowling pieces, as shotguns were called in those days. Over the following months, similar nonimportation agreements were adopted in most of the other colonies.[36]

Lord Hillsborough's June 8 order to call in the troops was received by General Gage by August 31, when Gage sent his aide-de-camp to confer with Governor Bernard concerning the number of troops needed.[37] Gage sent for two regiments from the Halifax garrison, one of which would be quartered in Boston and the other at Castle William.[38] Thereafter, Bernard leaked the news that troops were coming, "A.B.C." stirred the pot with charges that the inhabitants would be disarmed and martial law declared, and the rest of the uproar described at the beginning of this chapter occurred.

Once the troops had arrived in Boston, any pleas that the colonists made to the king to reconsider the troops' unpopular presence fell upon deaf ears.[39] Such was the subject of an article by "A North-American," who decried Parliament's disregard for the colonists' basic rights as set forth in numerous petitions and the fact that "the most vigorous measures are pursuing to inforce obedience, and non-resistance to them by the dint of military power."[40] That author also found the reasons given for the British troops' presence to be highly implausible:

> The Pretence for a Military Establishment on this Continent, was for its Protection and Defence.—But the mask is now taken off, and the cat let out of the bag entirely,—witness the warlike preparations and threats against our brethren of Boston, for having dared, with a modest freedom, and becoming firmness, to assert their inestimable and indefeasible rights . . . .
>
> An Act of Parliament was passed full as oppressive as the Stamp-Act . . . . But now the detestable Purpose is known (tho' before only suspected) for which a large Standing Army is quartered in America.—That they may be ready on

all occasions to dragoon us into any measures, which the arbitrary tools of Ministerial Power may think fit to impose.[41]

Reports of acts of violence by the soldiers against civilians began to appear. The following accounts gave details of abuses but did not identify the victims:

> The inhabitants of this town have been of late greatly insulted and abused by some of the officers and Soldiers, several have been assaulted on frivolous Pretences, and put under Guard without any lawful Warrant for so doing. A Physician of the Town walking the Streets the other Evening, was jostled by an Officer, when a Scuffle ensued, he was afterwards met by the same Officer in Company with another . . . who repeated his blows, and as is supposed gave him a stroke with a pistol, which so wounded him as to endanger his life. A Tradesman of this town . . . in his way home, had a thrust in the breast with a bayonet from a soldier; another person passing the street was struck with a musket, and the last evening a Merchant of the Town was struck down by an officer who went into the Coffee-House . . . . [A] little Time will discover whether we are to be governed by the Martial or the Common Law of the Land.[42]

However, the patriotic press found a hidden irony in the quartering of troops among the populace: It would expose civilians to the soldiers' methods of training with firearms. One article opined: "Some of the Consequences of bringing the Troops into this Town, in direct violation of the Act of Parliament, . . . instead of Quartering them in the Barracks on Castle Island, are likely to be the scattering proper Tutors through the Country, to instruct the Inhabitants in the modern Way of handling the Firelock and exercising the Men . . . ."[43] Actually, the Quartering Act required the colonies to provide the funds necessary to quarter the soldiers, but the Massachusetts House of Representatives refused, calling the tribute illegal.[44]

The British "tutors" would increase with the arrival in mid-November of five hundred soldiers from Ireland, bringing the total to some 1,200 men. This was a sizable force, given that Boston's population was only 20,000.[45]

But the colonists, according to a report from London, needed little instruction with firearms: "The total number of the Militia, in the large province of New-England, is upwards of 150,000 men, who all have and can use arms, not only in a regular, but in so particular a manner, as to be capable of shooting a

Pimple off a man's nose without hurting him."[46] The legend of the American sharpshooter was already widespread, even though obviously exaggerated, as was the readiness of the militia.

Friends of the ministry, speaking in the Parliament, were determined to suppress the unruly colonists. They "spoke with great respect of Governor Bernard," who was hampered by the constitution of the Massachusetts Bay Colony. This was because the Massachusetts council, "which was intended to support Government," became "the Means of weakening it, in Consequence of their being elected by a popular Assembly; and the juries being often an instrument of faction, instead of a check upon it, because returned by the towns, and not by the sheriffs." Members of the ministry also expressed "a determination not to repeal the last Revenue Law, at least till America had submitted." At bottom, "if the troops were withdrawn, the tumults would be renewed; but an effort of faction perfectly quelled would strengthen the Hands of Government."[47]

Following on the heels of the occupation of Boston came the newspaper column "Journal of the Times," which became the most widely circulated pre-Revolutionary writing after John Dickinson's *Letters from a Pennsylvania Farmer*. The column was written in Boston, covertly sent to New York and published in the *New York Journal*, and then reprinted in newspapers all over the colonies and even in England. Its anonymous authors probably included Samuel Adams, John Adams, Josiah Quincy, and various editors, the same likely suspects who wrote for the *Boston Gazette*.[48]

The king's speech of November 8, 1768, at the opening of a new session of Parliament, and related orations in the Houses of Lords and Commons, questioned the loyalty of the colonists. King George III averred that the inhabitants of Boston were "in a state of disobedience to all law and government" and had "a disposition to throw off their dependence on Great Britain."[49] The House of Lords singled out Boston's resolutions of September 12 (among others) as "illegal and unconstitutional, and calculated to excite sedition and insurrections in his Majesty's province of Massachusetts Bay."[50] Those were the above-quoted resolutions that included the admonition that every man provide himself with arms and that denounced standing armies.[51]

These Parliamentary speeches prompted the writers of the "Journal of the Times" to defend the Boston vote that called upon each citizen to arm and the assembly that adopted the vote. Samuel Adams, author of the following editorial, argued:

> For it is certainly beyond human art and sophistry, to prove the British sub-jects, to whom the *privilege* of possessing arms is expressly recognized by the Bill of Rights, and, who live in a province where the law requires them to be equip'd with *arms*, &c. are guilty of an *illegal act*, in calling upon one another to be provided with them, as the *law directs*. . . . One man has as good reason to affirm, that a few, in calling for a military force under *pretence* of supporting civil authority, *secretly* intended to introduce a general massacre, as another has to assert, that a number of loyal subjects, by calling upon one another to pro-vided with arms, *according to law*, intended to bring on an insurrection.
>
> It will be equally difficult to prove it *illegal*, for a number of British subjects, to invite as many of their fellow subjects as they please, to convene and consult together, on the most prudent and constitutional measures for the redress of their grievances . . . .[52]

Adams thus appealed, as had the Boston resolution passed the previous September, to the right to have arms as guaranteed in the English Bill of Rights as well as the duty under Massachusetts law to be armed. An intent to engage in insurrection could not be inferred from the citizens lawfully provid-ing themselves with arms and assembling to consult together respecting their grievances. These were rights of Englishmen, which the colonists held dear.

Just after Adams' editorial was published, it was reported in February 1769 that the inhabitants of Boston were being disarmed. After noting that "part of the troops had been quartered in the castle and barracks, and the remainder of them in some old empty houses," the report continued: "That the inhabitants had been ordered to bring in their arms, which in general they had complied with; and that those in possession of any after the expiration of a notice given them, were to take the consequences."[53] The report did not disclose who is-sued the order or where the surrender of arms allegedly took place. Perhaps this incident actually occurred, perhaps it was patriot propaganda, or perhaps the facts lie somewhere in between.

It is difficult to imagine much compliance with such an order, which would have provoked widespread protests. However, disarming the colonists was clearly being contemplated if not executed, and it was discussed on both sides of the Atlantic. The previous fall, news from London included the claim that "orders will soon be given to prevent the exportation of either naval or military stores, gun-powder, &c. to any part of North-America."[54]

The colonists perceived a disarmed populace as typical of the world's most notorious despotisms, such as that of Turkey. The following illustrates this perception:

> Some time ago the Grand Seignior ordered all his subjects to give up the arms they were possessed of, in order to be publically sold; in consequence of which, great quantities of these arms have been brought to market but they were for the most part in very bad condition. We learn upon this occasion that the Greeks, who inhabit some islands in the Archipelago, refuse to comply with this order, alleging that they want their arms for their own defence.[55]

In asserting their right to keep and bear arms, the colonists were well aware of the dangers and risks. As with other types of accidents, mishaps involving firearms were reported. In one tragedy, the wind blew open shutters in a window, knocking over a loaded gun that discharged and killed a 13-year-old girl.[56] In another incident, a soldier grabbed a pistol from an African American who was loading it, causing it to fire the ramrod "into the Belly of a young Lad that was passing," which the jury ruled to be accidental.[57] In yet another misfortune, "a Number of Persons had been shooting at Marks" (target shooting) when a 13-year-old—thinking a gun was unloaded—fired it at a girl to frighten her but shot and killed the wife of the gun's owner.[58]

Meanwhile, the British stranglehold on Boston continued to tighten. A meeting of the selectmen of Boston on February 16, 1769—whose attendees included Joshua Henshaw, Joseph Jackson, John Ruddock, John Hancock, John Rowe, Samuel Pemberton, and Henderson Inches—led to the drawing up of an address to be presented to Governor Bernard:

> To behold this Town surrounded with ships of war; and military troops even in a time of peace, quartered in its very bowel; exercising a discipline, with all the severity which is used in a garrison, and in a state of actual war, is truly alarming to a free people. And what still heightens the misfortune is, that our gracious sovereign and his ministers have formed such an idea of the present state of the town, as to induce a necessity of this naval and military force, for the aid of the civil magistrate in the preservation of its peace and good order.[59]

In the face of these grievances, the colonists continued to rely on their right to have arms to protect themselves. In an article he signed "E.A.," Samuel Adams published perhaps the most remarkable analysis of the right to keep and bear arms in the pre-Revolutionary era. He recalled the absolute English monarchs, with their doctrines of nonresistance and divine right, and traced the reigns of "a race of kings, bigoted to the greatest degree to the doctrines of *slavery* and regardless of the *natural, inherent, divinely hereditary* and *indefeasible* rights of their subjects."[60] Quoting freely from William Blackstone, Adams assessed the results of the Glorious Revolution of 1688:

> At the revolution, the British Constitution was again restor'd to its original principles, declared in the bill of rights; which was afterwards pass'd into a law, and stands as a bulwark to the natural rights of subjects. "To vindicate these rights, says Mr. *Blackstone*, when actually violated or attack'd, the subjects of England are entitled first to the regular administration and *free course of justice* in the courts of law—next to the right of *petitioning the King* and parliament for redress of grievances—and lastly, to the right of *having and using arms for self-preservation and defence.*" These he calls "auxiliary subordinate rights, which serve principally as *barriers* to protect and maintain inviolate the three great and primary rights of *personal security, personal liberty* and *private property*": And that of *having arms for their defence* he tells us is "a public allowance, under due restrictions, of the *natural right of resistance and self-preservation,* when the sanctions of society and laws are found *insufficient* to restrain the *violence of oppression.*"—How little do those persons attend to the rights of the constitution, if they know anything about them, who find fault with a late vote of this town, calling upon the inhabitants to *provide themselves with arms for their defence* at any time; but more especially, when they had reason to fear, there would be a necessity of the means of self preservation against the *violence of oppression.*[61]

The individual right to have arms for self-defense was a bulwark to guarantee personal security and liberty. This right extended not just to individual preservation but also to collective resistance to oppression. Adams continued even more explicitly as follows:

> Everyone knows that the exercise of the military power is forever *dangerous* to civil rights . . . . But there are some persons, who would, if possibly they could,

perswade the people *never to make use* of their *constitutional* rights or terrify them from doing it. No wonder that a resolution of this town to *keep arms* for its own defence, should be represented as having at bottom a *secret intention* to oppose the landing of the King's troops: when those very persons, who gave it this colouring, had before represented the peoples petitioning their Sovereign, as proceeding from a *factious* and *rebellious* spirit . . . .[62]

The only anticipated source of oppression was, of course, the king's troops, who were quartered in Boston to back up the king's tax collectors. But Adams rested on the constitutional and legal right of the colonists to arm themselves defensively, and his argument was a sound account of this traditional right as explained by Blackstone, England's leading legal scholar.

Letters from London arriving by vessels in this period recount a debate in the House of Commons that discouraged "the least possible hope in America of a repeal of the late Duty Act, until the duty is submitted to," and made manifest that "the billeting soldiers in the colonies, by act of Parliament, would never be receded from." Once again, the September 1768 resolution of Boston was attacked: "The invitation to the inhabitants of Massachusetts to provide themselves with arms, &c. from an apprehension of an approaching war with France, was urged to be treason against the state in the persons voting that request."[63]

In yet another installment, the "Journal of the Times" authors continued to defend the private right to have arms and were more explicit that military oppression could be rightfully resisted:

> Instances of the licentious and outrageous behavior of the *military* conservators of the peace still multiply upon us, some of which are of such a nature, and have been carried to so great lengths, as must serve fully to evince that a late vote of this town, calling upon the inhabitants to provide themselves with arms for their defence, was a measure as prudent as it was *legal*; such violences are always to be apprehended from military troops, when quartered in the body of a populous city; but more especially so, when they are led to believe that they are *become necessary to awe a spirit of rebellion*, injuriously said to be existing therein. It is a natural right which the people have reserved to themselves, confirmed by the Bill of Rights, to keep arms for their own defence; and as Mr. Blackstone observes, it is to be made use of when the sanctions of society and law are found insufficient to restrain the violence of oppression.[64]

As the days of occupation turned to months, incidents of violence by soldiers against civilians allegedly increased. In April, the Council and selectmen of Boston represented that "the Troops, and Commissioners of Customs, are by sundry violences grieving and irritating the people."[65] The following accounts of attacks on women, whether true or not, undoubtedly fanned the flames of outrage:

> Two Women the other Evening, to avoid the Solicitations and Insults of a Soldier, took Refuge in a House, at the South End of the Town; the Soldier was so audacious, as to enter with them: the Cries of Distress, brought the Master of the Family into the Entry with a Candle; and before he could know the Occasion of the Noise, he received, a Stroke from the Soldier with his Cutlass, which brought him to the Ground, where he lay Senseless for some Time, and suffered the loss of a Quart of his Blood.—Another Woman not happening to please some Soldiers, received a considerable Wound on her Head with a Cutlass; and a 3rd. Woman presuming to scream when laid hold of by a Soldier, had a Bayonet run through her Cheek.[66]

Some reports of this type may have been either exaggerated or invented.[67] One clash, however, was real and had legal consequences. On April 19, 1769, a British impressment gang boarded the American brig *Pitt Packet* as she neared her home port of Marblehead, Massachusetts. In the course of attacking the seamen on board, a British officer fired his pistol at, but missed, Michael Corbet, the sailors' leader. Corbet harpooned the officer in the throat, killing him.[68]

Charged with murder, Corbet and three mates were defended by John Adams and James Otis, two of the colony's ablest lawyers. Adams argued that the attempted impressment was illegal and that the crew had a right to defend themselves from attack: "Self Preservation is first Law of Nature . . . . This Right and Duty, are both confirmed by the municipal Laws of every civilised Society."[69] When the officer fired his pistol in Corbet's face, the seaman "had an undoubted Right . . . to have darted a Harpoon, a dagger thro the Heart of every Man in the whole Gang."[70] Adams quoted Sir William Hawkins' adage that "the killing of dangerous Rioters, by any private Persons, who cannot otherwise suppress them, or defend themselves from Them, inasmuch as every private Person seems to be authorised by the Law to arm himself for the Purposes aforesaid."[71]

The case had the potential of sparking dangerous rioting—the defendants were denied a trial by jury, and impressment was especially hated. However, a clash between the authorities and the colonists was averted when the court, on June 17, acquitted all of the defendants on the basis that the press gang had no impressment warrant, and thus the killing was justifiable homicide in self-defense.[72]

Three weeks before the verdict was handed down, a new session of the House of Representatives of the Massachusetts Bay Colony convened in Boston. Its first act was to demand that Governor Bernard order the removal of the British troops surrounding the State House. Bernard responded that he had no authority to remove the troops, thereby suggesting to the patriots that the military held sway over the civil authority.[73] The House replied that a standing army quartered among the loyal subjects of Boston was "contrary to act of Parliament, and to every principle of reason, justice and equity," and that a military execution of the laws was "inconsistent with the Spirit of a free Constitution." Such a military execution of laws was unnecessary:

> for the body of the people, the Posse Comitatus will always aid the magistrate in the execution of such laws as ought to be executed carries with it the strongest presumption that it is an unjust law; at least that it is ensalutary.—It cannot be their law; for by the nature of a free Constitution, the people must consent to laws, before they can be obliged in conscience to obey them.[74]

In short, a law based on the consent of the people could and would be enforced, if necessary, by the *posse comitatus*, the armed populace. A law requiring enforcement by a standing army was not based on the consent of the people.

The House refused to carry on its business while the troops remained. After several weeks, Bernard adjourned the assembly to Cambridge, where the session finally began. But tensions continued to escalate until Bernard abruptly canceled the session and dissolved the House. He then sailed to England, never to return.[75]

In September an attempt was made to assassinate James Otis, one of Boston's most influential patriots. Otis had published a scathing criticism of the commissioners of customs in the *Boston Gazette*. John Robinson, one of the commissioners Otis had denounced, allegedly led a gang of hooligans with swords and clubs in an assault on Otis in a coffeehouse.[76] Otis barely escaped with his life but suffered a sword wound to his head and was left mentally incapacitated.[77]

There were clashes between colonists and Redcoats, including occasional deaths, in the fall and winter of 1769–1770, and they took place not just in

Boston but also in New York City.[78] The violence reached a head in the Boston Massacre of March 5, 1770.

The trouble began when a sentry at the Customs House struck a troublesome boy with his gun. A crowd gathered and, shouting "kill him," began pelting the guard with snowballs and other objects. Captain Thomas Preston and seven soldiers from the nearby Main Guard station came to the rescue. Thereupon Crispus Attucks, described as a "mulatto," led the growing crowd in an attack on the Redcoats with snowballs, ice, oyster shells, and sticks. Yelling "you lobster scoundrels, fire if you dare," some struck at the solders with clubs and a cutlass. The soldiers then fired, killing Attucks and four others and wounding six more.[79]

The next day, a body of citizens appointed a committee, led by Samuel Adams, to demand that the governor, Thomas Hutchinson, order the immediate removal of the troops. Hutchinson responded that he had no such authority. However, Colonel Dalrymple recognized the explosive situation for what it was and decided to remove his troops under his own authority. Within four days, the Redcoats had all been evacuated from Boston and quartered at Castle William.[80] The soldiers, General Gage candidly quipped to Lord Hillsborough, "were of no other use in the Town of Boston, for the People were as Lawless and Licentious after the Troops arrived, as they were before."[81]

It befell John Adams and Josiah Quincy, the colony's ablest lawyers, to defend the British soldiers who were charged with unlawful homicide. Adams began his celebrated opening argument with the words: "I am for the prisoners at the bar, and shall apologise for it only in the words of the Marquis *Beccaria*: 'If I can but be the instrument of preserving one life, his blessings and tears of transport, shall be sufficient consolation to me, for the contempt of all mankind.'"[82]

Both prosecution and defense attorneys stipulated that the Bostonians had the right to arm themselves for self-defense. The issue was whether the inhabitants or the soldiers were the aggressors.[83] Crown prosecutor Robert Treat Paine argued that due to the long-term abusive conduct of the soldiers, "the most peaceable among us had . . . found it necessary to arm themselves with heavy Walking Sticks or Weapons of Defence when they went abroad."[84] Similarly, co-prosecutor Samuel Quincy contended that when the soldiers sallied out "with clubs, cutlasses, and other weapons of death; this occasioned a general alarm; every man therefore had a right, and very prudent it was to endeavor to defend himself if attacked; this accounts for the reason of Dr. *Young* or any one inhabitant of the town having a sword that evening . . . ."[85]

The right of citizens to arm themselves against abusive soldiers was also enunciated in the press. Samuel Adams argued that the slain Mr. Attucks "was leaning upon his stick when he fell, which certainly was not a *threatening* posture: It may be supposed that he had as good right, *by the law of the land*, to carry a stick for his own and his neighbor's defence, in a time of danger, as the Soldier who shot him had, to be arm'd with musket and ball, for the defence of himself and his friend the Centinel."[86]

As for the soldiers, John Adams upheld the right of "Self Defence, the primary Canon of the Law of Nature." As to the populace, Adams conceded on the authority of Hawkins, the great English jurist: "Here every private person is authorised to arm himself, and on the strength of this authority, I do not deny the inhabitants had a right to arm themselves at that time, for their defence, not for offence . . . ."[87]

The court's charge to the jury asserted the traditional duty of private persons to respond to the hue and cry and to carry arms: "It is the duty of all persons (except women, decrepit persons, and infants under fifteen) to aid and assist the peace officers to suppress riots & c. when called upon to do it. They may take with them such weapons as are necessary to enable them effectually to do it."[88]

The evidence showed that Preston never fired a shot but was in conflict on whether the sergeant ordered his men to fire. Preston was tried first and was acquitted of murder. The other soldiers were tried separately, and all were likewise acquitted, except that the soldier who shot Mr. Attucks was convicted of manslaughter.[89] While this only fanned the flames kept up by the hotheads, the spectacle of the Boston Massacre trial posed ironies. Patriot lawyers prosecuted the soldiers on behalf of the Crown, and other patriot lawyers defended the soldiers. Citizens of Boston had been slain, but Boston juries acquitted all the soldiers of murder.

While this was the leading criminal trial of the epoch, the right to have arms for self-defense was also enunciated in other trials of the period. Defending an assault case in 1771, James Otis (co-counsel with Adams and Quincy) relied on "Orat[ion] pro Milone beginning."[90] This referred to the following passage from Cicero's defense of Titus Annius Milo in ancient Rome on murder charges: "When arms speak, the laws are silent; they bid none to await their word . . . . And yet most wisely, and, in a way, tacitly, the law authorises self-defence . . . . The man who had employed a weapon in self-defence was not held to have carried that weapon with a view to homicide."[91]

The early 1770s emerged as the quiet before the storm. There was more saber rattling than actual conflict. The major Townshend Act duties except that on tea were repealed in 1770, leading to a relatively calm period of three years. Passage of the Tea Act in 1773 led to renewed rumblings.[92] Reportedly "Governor Hutchinson, in order to enforce the maxims of administration, had recourse to the military; and that the House of Representatives, in behalf of the people, resolved such a step to be rebellion against their constitutional rights and privileges, and determined to oppose force by force, by ordering out the Militia." A commentator in the newspaper wrote that this assertion was "intended to show the true spirit of the contending parties in America, rather than the truth of Fact." But it could be prophetic, given the course of events: "It is a common proverb, that many true words are spoken in jest, and it may be relied upon by all slave makers, that the people of this province are too enlightened and spirited, much longer to submit to Tyrants."[93]

But there are two sides to every controversy. Governor Thomas Hutchinson has been described as following moderate policies which appeased neither the Ministry nor the American radicals.[94]

The colonists continued to speak about armed resistance, and not necessarily in a veiled fashion. "Massachusettensis," pseudonym of Daniel Leonard, a prominent Massachusetts lawyer, penned several essays pleading America's cause. While he would soon transform into a Tory, as a Whig he made the following inflammatory remarks:

Men combined to subvert our civil government, to plunder and murder us, can have no right to protection in their persons or properties among us; they have by their attempts upon our liberty, *put themselves in a state of war with us*, as Mr. Locke observes, and being the aggressors, if they perish, the fault is their own. "If any person in the best condition of the state, demands your purse at the muzzle of his pistol, you have no need to recur to law, you cannot give, i.e. immediate security against your adversary; and for that reason, viz. because the law cannot be applied to your relief, you make your own defence on the principles of natural law, which is now your only rule, and his life is forfeited into your hands, and you indemnified if you take it, because he is the first and a dangerous aggressor." This rule applies itself to states, and to those employed by them to distress, rob or enslave other states; and shall property be secure where even life is forfeited?[95]

This analogy from John Locke was unmistakable in distinguishing the British highwayman from the innocent colonist who would resist.

A common thread that runs through the above events and the related expression of patriotic opinion is that the citizen has a right to bear arms in self-defense and in defense of the Commonwealth. Reverend Simeon Howard, a Harvard graduate and minister, enunciated these concepts from the pulpit in his celebrated sermon to the Ancient and Honourable Artillery Company in Boston in June of 1773.

The universal principle of self-preservation, Reverend Howard averred, "allows of every thing necessary to self-defence, opposing force to force, and violence to violence."[96] Christianity is fully consistent with this fundamental law:

> Defending ourselves by force of arms against injurious attacks is a quite different thing from rendering evil for evil. The latter implies doing hurt to another, because he has done hurt to us; the former implies doing hurt to another, if he is hurt in the conflict, only because there is no other way of avoiding the mischief he endeavours to do us: the *one* proceeds from malice and revenge; the *other* merely from self-love, and a just concern for our own happiness, and argues no ill will against any man.[97]

Given that it is right and necessary for citizens to defend themselves, they must acquire the means to do so: "A people who would stand fast in their liberty, should furnish themselves with weapons proper for their defence, and learn the use of them."[98] No matter how numerous a people may be, "if they are unskilled in arms, their number will tend little more to their security, than that of a flock of sheep does to preserve them from the depredations of the world."[99]

Not surprisingly, Howard asserted the superiority of a militia to a standing army. Standing armies "propagate corruption and vice where they reside, they frequently insult and abuse the unarmed and defenceless people: Where there is any difference between rulers and subjects, they will generally be on the side of the former, and ready to assist them in oppressing and enslaving the latter . . . ." He continued:

But rulers of arbitrary disposition, have ever endeavoured to have a standing
army at their command, under a pretence indeed, of being for the safety of the
state, though really with a view of giving efficacy to their orders. . . . To have
an army continually stationed in the midst of a people, in time of peace, is a
precarious and dangerous method of security.[100]

Far safer "is to have the power of defence in the body of the people, to
have a well regulated and well-disciplined militia." If the people themselves
are armed, they will defend their country. A force made up of men of property, who have always worked, "will generally equal the best veteran troops, in
point of strength of body and firmness of mind, and when fighting in defence
of their religion, their estates, their liberty, and families, will have stronger
motives to exert themselves, and may, if they have been properly disciplined,
be not much inferior to them in the skill of arms."[101]

Even so, Howard insisted that caution "be used in constituting a militia,
that it may answer the end for which it is designed, and not be liable to be
made an instrument of tyranny and oppression." The state would have the
power to call out the militia, if the safety of the people compelled it. "But this
power should be so limited and restrained, as that it cannot call it unneces-
sarily, oblige it to commit violence or oppression upon any of the subjects."[102]
The capacity for evil is inherent in mankind, although some institutions promote it and others minimize it.

As the above demonstrates, the people of Boston experienced during
1768–1773 the initial shock of invasion by military force, followed by escalating violence culminating in the Boston Massacre, and then a period of uncertain but false respite. The right of the inhabitants to be armed was perceived
to be in peril, but the conflict had not escalated to a consummation of their
disarming. The year 1774 would open a new chapter in what appeared to be
escalating into an irresistible conflict between the colonists and the Crown.

## CHAPTER 2

# From the Tea Party to
# the Powder Alarm

O N DECEMBER 16, 1773, patriots disguised as Mohawk Indians gathered at Boston harbor, boarded three
vessels, broke open 342 chests, and dumped the contents—forty-five tons of
tea—into the ocean. The whooping "Indians" were "cloath'd in Blankets with
the head muffled, and copper color'd countenances, being each arm'd with
a hatchet or axe, and pair pistoles," wrote Boston merchant John Andrews.[1]
Andrews had written two weeks before the Tea Party that the inhabitants
unanimously opposed the landing of the tea, and "'twould puzzle any person
to purchase a pair of p——ls [pistols] in town, as they are all bought up, with
a full determination to repel force by force."[2]

The raid, thought to have been led by John Hancock, was in protest of the
recently passed Tea Act, which sought to give the British East India Company
a monopoly on the tea trade and to suppress importation of the highly taxed
Dutch tea, which most colonists consumed and which was widely smuggled.
The Sons of Liberty depicted the scheme as yet another instance of taxation
without representation.

Parliament responded to the Boston Tea Party by enacting the Intolerable
Acts. The Boston Port Act closed Boston's port altogether until the colonists

paid full reparations for the destroyed tea. Under the Quartering Act, British troops returned to Boston—they had been removed from the town after the 1770 massacre—and British ships blockaded the harbor. The Massachusetts Regulating Act revoked the Massachusetts Province Charter of 1691 and gave the colonial governor unprecedented powers, including absolute authority over all judicial and official appointments and removals. The town selectmen, who were traditionally elected by the populace, could no longer call a meeting at any time, but must instead get the governor's permission. Jurors, formerly selected by freeholders and inhabitants of the towns, were now selected by sheriffs, who were in turn appointed by the governor.[3]

The Crown would appoint the Massachusetts Council in lieu of the former council elected by the legislature. Thirty-six men were appointed by "mandamus"—an order commanding a supposed legal duty—to serve in this council, but many of them refused, and others were persuaded or intimidated into resigning.[4] These "Mandamus Counselors" became known to the patriots as "the Divan," after the privy council of the Ottoman Empire. These Turkish rulers were considered perhaps the world's most absolute despots.

To heap coals on the fire, Thomas Hutchinson resigned as governor and into his shoes stepped General Thomas Gage, the commander in chief of the British Army in North America. William Legge, Earl of Dartmouth, secretary of state for America, informed Gage of his appointment as captain general and governor in chief of His Majesty's Province of Massachusetts Bay. Lord Dartmouth stressed the imperative of enforcing the Boston Port Act, adding with typical British understatement:

> [Y]our Authority as the first Magistrate, combined with your Command over the King's Troops, will, it is hoped, enable you to meet every opposition, and fully to preserve the public peace, by employing those Troops with Effect, should be madness of the People on the one hand, or the timidity or want of Strength of the peace officers on the other hand, make it necessary to have recourse to their assistance.[5]

Four regiments were ordered from England and Ireland to Boston, and Gage was authorized to declare martial law and to "repel force and violence by every means within his reach."[6] Regarding the Regulating Act, Dartmouth explained to Gage:

The Act for better Regulation of the Government of the Province of Massachusetts Bay, provides, that from the first of August next, all Elections of the Council under the Authority of the Charter, shall be void, and that for the future the Council shall be appointed by the King.

In consequence of that Provision, His Majesty has, with the Advice of His Privy Council, nominated thirty-six persons, qualified as the Act directs, to be the Council of Massachusetts Bay, from & after the time limited for the Continuance of the present Council, and inclosed herewith I send you His Majesty's additional Instruction, under the Sign Manual, authorising and requiring you to assemble the said Council, and containing such further Directions as are thought necessary and incident to this new Establishment, and as correspond with the Provisions of the Act in relation thereto.[7]

Together with his soldiers and his "Divan" Gage would take the repressive measures that united the other colonies with Massachusetts Bay and hastened the Americans' march toward revolution. Not the least of these measures was the disarming of the inhabitants. It was no secret that the people were arming themselves. That could be surmised in newspaper advertisements, such as an early 1774 notice in the *Boston Gazette* that a merchant "has just imported for sale, a neat assortment of guns, complete with bayonets, steel rods and swivels, a few neat fowling pieces, pocket pistols."[8]

Moreover, this armed populace was being arrayed into militia. John Hancock averred in his oration on the fourth anniversary of the Boston Massacre: "From a well regulated militia we have nothing to fear. . . . They fight for their houses, their lands, for their wives, their children, for all who claim the tenderest names, and are held dearest in their hearts, they fight *pro aris & focis*, for their liberty, and for themselves, and for their God." Hancock added that "no militia ever appear'd in more flourishing condition, than that of this province now doth . . . ."[9]

The same theme resounded in newspaper commentary: "The establishment of a militia, which is putting arms in the hands of the people, for their defence, was a point which the patriots lately carried in the mother country, and contended for, as essential to the preservation of their liberties."[10]

General Gage was greeted by a component of this American militia when he arrived in Boston to assume his powers as governor. For his official transfer of power to Gage on May 17, 1774, Governor Hutchinson "ordered the Regiment of the Militia of the Town, the Company of Cadets, and the Troop of Horse Guards to appear in arms," after which a public dinner with invited guests would be served.[11] John Andrews wrote:

> Our Militia was yesterday muster'd for the reception of General Gage, who was proclaim'd Governor, amid the acclamations of the people. He express'd himself as sensible of the unwelcome errand he came upon, but as a servant of the Crown, he was obliged to see the Act put in execution: but would do all in his power to serve us.[12]

Gage thereby extended an olive branch at a time when the militia could still muster. However, his sword began to be drawn in June and July, when several regiments and warships arrived to execute the Boston Port Act and the Massachusetts Regulating Act.[13]

Meanwhile, the colonists were stockpiling large quantities of arms and ammunition. Countless barrels of gunpowder were imported, stored in powder houses, and then distributed as merchants and provincial authorities made withdrawals. General Gage began to restrict the distribution of this stored gunpowder. Redcoats were also beginning to seize firearms. Boston merchant John Andrews noted in a July 22 letter about an incident at the Boston Neck, the only access to the town by land and that was, in those days, only 120 yards wide:

> Its reported for fact, both last evening and this morning, that a country team was stopped by ye. Guards upon the Neck and riffled of two firelocks that they were carrying into the country. Certain I am that the Governor has order'd the Keeper of the Province's Magazine not to deliver a kernel of powder (without his express order) of either public or private property: which is attended with great inconvenience to the dealers in that article, as he is, for the most part of his time, at Salem, and a personal attendance is necessary to procure an order.[14]

Circumstances changed before Andrews could send the letter. He added that "Gov. [Gage] previous to his going out of town, yesterday morning delivered up the keys of the Powder House [on Boston Common] to Slyde again, with liberty to deliver as usual, but not in such enormous quantities as about a month since; being inform'd that he deliver'd near two thousand barrels in ye course of about a fortnight, which gave some alarm to the troops . . . ."[15]

While Gage was prepared drastically to reduce the supply of gunpowder, he was not yet ready directly and lawlessly to disarm the inhabitants by force. On August 1, John Andrews referred to his previous letter, which

> mention'd a waggon's being riffled of four firelocks by the Centinel on guard upon ye. Neck, which I have since been inform'd is a fact, and that the officer of the day return'd them and pleaded much with the party injur'd not to prosecute the matter, as it might be consider'd as a military robbery: which leads me to think that notwithstanding their hostile preparations and formidable appearance, they as yet esteem themselves as liable to the civil law; whether their dispositions when the two infernal acts arrive, with the royall assent, I can't say.[16]

It is significant that military personnel still considered themselves to be subordinate to the civil power. Just as the civil courts tried soldiers after the Boston Massacre, this suggests that seizure of a firearm would have been considered robbery. This deference to the civil law would not last much longer.

The colonists saw the handwriting on the wall. None other than Paul Revere engraved a plate diagramming how to refine saltpeter, an essential component in the making of gunpowder. It was published in August 1774 in the *Royal American Magazine*, the unlikely title for a magazine published by Isaiah Thomas, a member of the Sons of Liberty.[17]

The prospect of the use of military force to enforce the Intolerable Acts galvanized the other colonies as never before. An assembly of inhabitants in Lancaster County, Pennsylvania, bluntly resolved: "That in the event of Great Britain attempting to force unjust laws upon us by the strength of arms, our cause we leave to heaven and our rifles."[18] "A Carolinian" wrote under the sarcastic title "Some of the Blessings of military Law, or the Insolence of governor gage" as follows:

> With all the plausible Pretences to Protection and Defence, a standing Army is the most dangerous Enemy to the Liberties of a Nation that can be thought of. . . . It is much better, with a well regulated Militia, to run the Risk of a foreign Invasion, than, with a Standing Army, to run the Risk of Slavery. . . . When an Army is sent to enforce Laws, it is always an Evidence that either the Law makers are conscious that they had no clear and indisputable Right to make those Laws, or that they are bad and oppressive. Wherever the People themselves have

had a Hand in making Laws, according to the first Principles of our constitution, there is no Danger of Non-submission, nor can there be Need of an Army
to enforce them.[19]

The Royalists saw the colonists as traitors, but the latter saw themselves as
loyal to the law. "Massachusettensis," aka Daniel Leonard—although quickly
transforming himself from a Whig to a Tory—still had the gumption to say:
"The man who arms himself in defence of his Life, Liberty, Fortune, Laws
and Constitution of his Country, can never be accounted a Rebel by any but
a Banditti of villains . . . ."[20]

In Gage's perception, the Boston radicals were spreading their subversion
throughout Massachusetts and into Connecticut. Among other instances he
cited in a letter to Dartmouth dated August 27 was the following:

> In Worcester they keep no Terms, openly threaten Resistance to Arms, have
> been purchasing Arms, preparing them, casting Ball, and providing Powder,
> and threaten to attack any Troops who dare to oppose them. . . . I apprehend
> that I shall soon be obliged to march a Body of Troops into that Township, and
> perhaps into others, as occasion happens, to preserve the Peace.[21]

Just two days before, Gage had sent two companies of Redcoats to dissolve
an illegal town meeting in Salem. The soldiers backed down when swarms of
armed patriots began to appear. John Andrews confided about the affair:

> there was upwards of three thousand men assembled there from the adjacent
> towns, with full determination to rescue the Committee if they should be sent
> to prison, even if they were oblig'd to repel force by force, being sufficiently
> provided for such a purpose; as indeed they are all through the country—every
> male above the age of 16 possessing a firelock with double the quantity of pow-
> der and ball enjoin'd by law.[22]

In the midst of this unrest the Massachusetts Council, consisting of the
Mandamus Counselors, met at the Council Chamber in Boston on August
31, 1774. The minutes reflect that Governor Gage presided and that fifteen
counselors attended. Gage discussed "the very great tumults and disorders
prevailing in many parts of the Province, tending to the intire subversion of
Government, and particularly the attacks made upon divers Members of this
Board (residing in the Country) . . . ." He then inquired "what they thought

expedient and proper for him to do in this exigency of affairs, and whether they would advise to the sending of any troops into the County of Worcester, or any other County in the Province, for the protection of the Judges and other Officers of the Courts of Justice."[23]

In response, "several Gentlemen of the Council expressed their Opinions, that inasmuch as the opposition to the execution of any part of the late Acts of Parliament relating to this Province, was so general, they apprehended it would not be for His Majesty's service to send any Troops into the interior parts of the Province . . . ."[24] Instead, "the main body [should] continue in the Town of Boston, which might be strengthened by the addition of other Troops," and there those who found it necessary would find "a place of safe retreat." The Council unanimously approved.[25]

Apparently part of the discussion about making Boston "safe" was a proposal to ban firearms. The *Boston Gazette* reported that the Council considered the following:

> Tis said an article deliberated upon by the Divan last Wednesday [August 31] was the disarming of the town of Boston, and as much of the province as might be, to which sundry new counsellors advised. Was this also for the good of your country, Gentlemen!
>
> Governor Gage has at length laid his hand on private property, so far as to deny one cask of powder to be delivered out of the powder house whatever.[26]

The above was one of two accounts of the proposed firearms ban to be widely reprinted in colonial newspapers. (Its reference to Gage's ban on transfer of gunpowder from the powder house is explained below.) The other account of the debate in the Divan included the following details:

> It is said, it was proposed in the Divan last Wednesday, that the inhabitants of this Town should be disarmed, and that some of the new-fangled Counsellors consented thereto, but happily a majority was against it.—The report of this extraordinary measure having been put in Execution by the Soldiery was propagated through the Country, with some other exaggerated stories, and, by what we are told, if these Reports had not been contradicted, we should by this date have had 40 or 50,000 men from the Country (some of whom were on the march) appear'd for our Relief.[27]

A majority of the Divan may have felt that a firearms ban would be unenforceable at that time. But the rumor that the disarming measure was actually being enforced by the Redcoats sparked widespread protest and led the patriots to escalate their intimidation of the counselors. Some counselors wrote accounts of how literally thousands of patriots, at times led by militia officers and in some cases armed, assembled at their houses and intimidated them into resigning. Others recorded how mobs appeared at their houses, but they were able to flee to Boston and be protected by Gage's forces.[28] Such accounts filled the newspapers.

The perpetrators of the Crown's repressive measures were referred to as the "imperial Divan" and as "his most exalted Highness, the most potent, the most omnipotent Bashaw Thomas [Gage], lately appointed by the illustrious Sultan Selim [George] III to the subduction of the military province of B [Boston]."[29]

Colonist opposition effectively rendered the Council into a paper tiger. After all the ruckus caused by the very existence of the Council and by its above meeting, Gage called no more meetings. As Lieutenant Governor Oliver wrote to Secretary Dartmouth the following December, "the People have so far put an end to all law and order," that Gage had governed "rather in the line of a General than that of a Governor." If the Council met under these circumstances, "the prejudices of the People would only tend to encrease their violences."[30] The Council would not meet again until July 17, 1775,[31] by which time the Revolutionary War had isolated the British in Boston and the Council was rendered meaningless.

While the Council's rule was effectively ended just as it started, Gage's own actions fanned the flames. If the Council could not recommend a decree disarming the people, Gage was planning to cut off the colonists' ammunition supply by forbidding deliveries from, and actually seizing the gunpowder at, the powder houses, which were essentially safe warehouses for importation, storage, and distribution of powder. Gunpowder was imported in large quantities and then, at least in some areas, stored in powder houses, specially built structures located away from other buildings. Merchants stored reserve quantities in powder houses,[32] as did the province and the towns.

The black gunpowder of that age was far more volatile than modern smokeless powder. As a fire prevention measure, in 1736 the General Court had provided for the building of a powder house.[33] Partly as a result of a 1771 petition by patriots such as John Hancock, Sam Adams, and Paul Revere, a new powder house was built on the west side of Boston, by the Charles River and just above the Common, safely away from populated areas to the east.[34]

With scattered powder houses throughout Massachusetts, the question became whether the patriots or the agents of the Crown would seize the powder first. Apparently referring to an incident in August, it was reported: "The Selectmen of Wrentham have published a notification, offering a reward of Sixty Dollars for the discovery of the person who, about five weeks past, broke open the Powder-house there, and carried off six half-barrels of powder, about 1300 flints, and a quantity of lead."[35]

On September 1, the day after the Council debated the disarming of the inhabitants, Gage took decisive action in what came to be known as the Powder Alarm. On August 27, Brigadier William Brattle wrote to Gage about the Massachusetts Provincial Powder House in Charlestown: "This morning the Select Men of Medford came and received their Town stock of powder which was in the Arsenal, on Quarry Hill. So there is now therein the King's powder only, which shall remain there as a sacred Depositum till ordered out by the Capt. General."[36]

The patriots did not regard the remaining powder as belonging to the king. Brattle's message became known to the public on August 31, when it is said that Gage himself dropped the letter on a Boston street. As John Andrews interpreted it, Brattle "was apprehensive the Province Powder was in danger; all other either belonging to particular towns, or individuals, had been withdrawn. It being private property, he could not do otherwise than deliver it, and as a friend to good government he should do his utmost endeavour to preserve that as a sacred depositum."[37]

Alarmed by the withdrawals of gunpowder, and aware that the patriots could not be trusted to regard the remaining powder as belonging to the king, Gage decided to seize it. Before daybreak on September 1, some 260 soldiers from Castle William sailed to a point on the Mystic River and then marched ashore to the powder house on Quarry Hill, which may still be seen today. While the town slept, the Redcoats seized between 250 half-barrels and 300 barrels of gunpowder.[38]

After Brigadier Brattle's letter to Gage become known, an assembly of perhaps 4,000 "country people" surrounded his Cambridge home. Brattle fled to Castle William. The patriots also visited other Tories and pressured Royal counselors to resign.[39] John Andrews wrote from Boston on September 2:

But a report having prevail'd through the country (by reason of the seizure of the powder yesterday) that ye. same game had been play'd here, and ye. inhabitants disarm'd has rais'd such a spirit as will require the utmost prudence to allay; for they are in arms at all quarters, being determin'd to see us redress'd. At eight o'clock this morning there were about three thousand under their regular leaders at Cambridge common, and continually increasing; had left their arms at a little distance . . . .[40]

According to another report, on the evening of September 1 the inhabitants of Middlesex County "began to collect in large bodies, with their arms, provisions, and ammunition, determining by some means to give a check to a power which so openly threatened their destruction, and in such a clandestine manner rob them of the means of their defence." The next morning "some thousands of them had advanced to Cambridge, armed only with sticks, as they had left their fire-arms, &c., at some distance behind them."[41]

News that the army was approaching against them reached the crowd gathered at Cambridge, according to Andrews, "which set the people in a prodigious ferment (who before were become quite calm and compos'd) and every one retir'd to Watertown, where they had left their arms, and return'd to take the Common fully equipp'd and well dispos'd to make a tryal of skill."[42] But the Redcoats did not come, and the situation was diffused.

Meanwhile, reported Andrews from Boston, "a Guard of Soldiers is set upon the Powder house at the back of ye. Common, so that people are debar'd from selling their own property; and the Guard upon the Neck is doubled . . . ."[43] By preventing merchants from withdrawing their gunpowder from the powder house, Gage could reduce the ammunition available to the inhabitants.

According to a newspaper account, "Your Excellency has been pleased to order the powder from the magazine in Charlestown, to forbid the delivery of the powder in the magazine of Boston, to the legal proprietors, to seize the cannon at Cambridge, and bring a formidable number from Castle William, which are now placed at the entrance to town of Boston."[44]

The Crown forcibly purchased arms and ammunition held in the inventory of merchants, and an order went out that the inhabitants must turn in their arms.[45] Thus, despite the Council's failure officially to adopt the latter measure, Gage apparently decreed the same result—albeit without necessarily trying to enforce it.

New England patriots hastened toward Boston. A Connecticut patriot named McNeil reported on September 2 how women and children were fully engaged in supporting the men:

All along were armed men rushing forward—some on horseback. At every house, women and children making cartridges, running [i.e., casting molten lead into] bullets, making wallets, baking biscuits, crying and bemoaning and at the same time animating their husbands and sons to fight for their liberties, though not knowing whether they should ever see them again.[46]

Probably out of breath, Gage reported few details to Dartmouth, noting that a crowd assembled at the house of Lieutenant Governor Oliver partly "on Account of some Ammunition belonging to the Province in the Arsenal in Cambridge, which I had before sent a Detachment to secure, and lodged it in Castle William."[47] (The Charlestown powder house was actually located between that town and Cambridge.[48])

Both the Redcoats and the patriots reacted to each others' escalating actions, spiraling tensions upward. John Andrews wrote on September 5 that "The alarm caus'd by the movement of the country has induc'd the Governor to order a number of field pieces up to the neck guard, and this morning has got a number of workmen there, to build blockhouses and otherways repair the fortification." The next day, Andrews continued, "Its allowed, by the best calculations, that at least a hundred thousand men were equipt with arms, and moving towards us from different parts of the country."[49]

Numerous accounts of the powder seizure with varied allegations were published throughout the colonies. One report stated:

General Gage seized the public Stock of Gunpowder in the Magazine at Cambridge, about 250 Quarter Barrels, . . . ordered it to the Castle, and a Detachment of his Troops were proceeding to Medford, a Town adjoining Charlestown, for the same Purpose. This Measure gives great Umbrage to the People (it is said they were armed) gathered at Cambridge last week; the Report here yesterday Morning was, that there were 30,000 of them, but the latest Accounts bring them down to 1500; that upon hearing the Resignation of several of the Counselors they said they were satisfied, and retired to their respective Homes.[50]

Another account alleged that 250 British troops seized the powder and that 30 other Redcoats seized two field pieces belonging to the Cambridge militia:

> The Report of this Maneuver, exaggerated no Doubt in the Country, brought this Morning [September 2], on Cambridge Common, at least 3000 People from different Parts of the Country, in Order to learn the Truth of the Matter. They were unarmed, and demanded the public Resignation of two Counselors, Inhabitants of Cambridge, which was complied with; and after choosing several Persons to stop the great Numbers coming in from the distant Parts, said to be many Thousands, and being satisfied that the Governor had seized only the King's Powder, they peaceably dispersed.[51]

The alarm spread into Connecticut, whose patriots were prepared to relieve their brethren in Boston. "It is said the Governor [Gage] is determined not to risk any Troops in the Country, till he is reinforced, being apprehensive of their loss, from the amazing number and fury of our People, who are all provided with Arms and Ammunition, &c."[52]

Rumors abounded in this highly charged atmosphere. The Continental Congress had just convened in Philadelphia for the first time, where on September 6 Patrick Henry of Virginia insisted "that by the oppression of Parliament all Government was dissolved, and that we were reduced to a State of Nature."[53] As if to buttress his speech, an express arrived with intelligence "that the soldiers had seized the powder in one of the Towns near Boston, That a party was sent to take this, and that six of the Inhabitants had been killd in the skirmish, That all the Country was in arms down to [blank] in Connecticut, That the cannon fired upon the Town the whole Night."[54] Fortunately, the accounts of deaths and cannon fire were baseless rumors. As John Adams, a delegate at the Congress, wrote in his diary two days later: "The happy news were brought us from Boston, that *no blood had been spilled*, but that General Gage had taken away the provincial powder from the magazine at Cambridge."[55]

There would be more happy news from Adams' hometown of Braintree, located 10 miles southeast of Boston. Abigail Adams wrote to her husband John that the patriots had seized the gunpowder from the powder house and that they had jokingly offered her some:

> In consequence of the powders being taken from Charlstown, a general alarm spread thro many Towns and was caught pretty soon here. . . . [A]bout 8 o clock

a Sunday evening there passed by here about 200 men, preceeded by a horse cart, and marches down to the powder house from whence they took the powder and carried it into the other parish and there secreeted it. I opened the window upon there return. They pass'd without any noise, not a word among them till they came against this house, when some them perceiving me, askd me if I wanted any powder. I replied not since it was in so good hands. The reason they have for taking it, was that we had so many Tories here they dare not trust us with it.[56]

During this period, Gage had under two thousand soldiers in Boston "to control a well-armed population of about fifteen thousand," not to mention that "the country people conducted militia drills in deadly earnest and squirreled away a growing stockpile of arms and ammunition."[57] John Andrews wrote on September 12 that many inhabitants wanted to leave Boston, anticipating that Gage—despite assurances to the contrary—would confine them in the town once it was sufficiently fortified. "But if they should come to disarming the inhabitants, the matter is settled with the town at once; for blood and carnage must inevitably ensue—which God forbid! should ever take place."[58]

What Andrews described as "the County Committee" met with Gage, who asked them to "make yourselves easy, and I'll be so." The general grilled them, "What is the reason that the cannon were remov'd from Charlestown?—And why do the country people go in and out of the town arm'd?" The committee promised to respond in writing the next day. Andrews commented: "In regard to the people coming in arm'd, I never understood that they did; but as to their going out so is very common, for every man in the country not possess'd of a firelock making it a point to procure one, so that I suppose for a month past, or more, not a day has pass'd but a hundred or more are carried out of town by'em."[59]

Lord Hugh Percy, of His Majesty's forces, also wrote a letter on September 12, deploring that "the People here openly oppose the New Acts. They have taken up arms in almost every part of this Province, & have drove in the Govr & most of the Council." Percy groused about his superior Gage: "The General's great lenity and moderation serve only to make them more daring & insolent." Percy then added:

What makes an insurrection here always more formidable than in other places, is that there is a law of this Province, wh[ich] obliges every inhabitant to be furnished with a firelock, bayonet, & pretty considerable quantity of ammuni-

tion. Besides wh[ich], every township is obliged by the same law to have a large
magazine of all kinds of military stores.

They are, moreover, trained four times in each year, so that they do not make
a despicable appearance as soldiers, tho' they were never yet known to behave
themselves even decently in the field.[60]

Percy was particularly peeved that Gage had not clamped down on the citizens who were carrying arms: "The Gen[era]l has not yet molested them in
the least. They have even free access to and from this town, tho' armed with
firelocks, provided they only come in small nos."[61]

Yet Gage was no pansy. He had already incensed the colonists by seizing
large quantities of ammunition from the powder houses. Cutting off arms and
ammunition at the source was a superior strategy to singling out individuals
carrying arms and seizing them, thereby violating the guarantee in the English
Bill of Rights "That the Subjects which are Protestants, may have Arms for their
Defence suitable to their Condition, and as are allowed by Law."[62] As governor,
Gage could not just ignore this act of Parliament, any more than the Council
could repeal it. But he was well aware of the seriousness of the situation, writing to Dartmouth the same day (or perhaps that night by candlelight):

> The Country People are exercising in Arms in this Province, Connecticut, and
> Rhode Island, and getting Magazines of Arms and Ammunition in the Coun-
> try, and such Artillery, as they can procure good and bad. They threaten to
> attack the Troops in Boston, and are very angry at a Work throwing up at the
> Entrance of the Town . . . .[63]

While Gage's troops could shut down the powder houses, no pretense yet
existed to seize lawfully imported gunpowder from abroad. John Andrews
noted on September 21: "Captain Scott arriv'd yesterday at Salem in 7 weeks
from London. He has brought a quantity of powder, which comes very season-
ably at this time, as it's now five or six weeks since the Governor has allow'd
any to be taken out of the magazine here, whereby for some weeks there has
not been a pound to be sold or bought in town."[64]

Gage, still trying to bring Dartmouth up to date, wrote of the alarming
situation, both in terms of the spread to other colonies of the armed insubor-
dination to authority and the more drastic solution being proposed:

We hear of Nothing but Extravagancies in some Part or other, and of military Preparations from this place to the Province of New York, in which the whole seems to be united. Upon a Rumour propagated with uncommon Dispatch thro' the Country, that the Soldiers had killed six People, and that the Ships and Troops were firing upon Boston, the whole Country was in Arms, and in Motion, and numerous Bodies of the Connecticut People had made some Marches before the Report was contradict'd. From present Appearances there is no Prospect of putting the late Acts in Force, but by first making a Conquest of the New-England Provinces.[65]

Gage did not reckon well, in the words of historian David Hackett Fischer, that "the people of New England were jealous of their liberties, including their liberty to keep and bear arms."[66] Gage's deprivation of privately owned gunpowder became a major complaint of the Suffolk County Resolutions of September 6, which were widely published and acclaimed throughout the colonies. (Boston was the county seat of Suffolk County.) In a series of charges penned by Dr. Joseph Warren, the patriot doctor who carried pistols when making his rounds,[67] the Suffolk delegates resolved in part: "That the Fortifications begun and now carrying upon Boston Neck are justly alarming to this County, and give us reason to apprehend some hostile intention against that town, more especially as the Commander in Chief has in a very extraordinary manner removed the powder from the magazine at Charlestown, and has also forbidden the keeper of the magazine at Boston to deliver out to the owners the powder which they had lodged in said magazine."[68]

Paul Revere rushed copies of the Suffolk Resolutions to the Continental Congress in Philadelphia, which had just assembled for the first time the day before and which unanimously denounced "these wicked ministerial measures."[69] In a letter to Dartmouth that would be published in the proceedings of Parliament, Gage responded to the Suffolk allegations, noting: "No private Property has been touched, unless they mean an order to the Storekeeper not to deliver out any Powder from the Magazine, where the Merchants deposit it, which I judged a very Necessary and prudent Measure in the present Circumstances, as well as removing the Ammunition from the Provincial Arsenal at Cambridge."[70]

The Suffolk delegates sent a committee led by Dr. Joseph Warren to meet with Gage. The committee's list of grievances, dated September 9, included the charge that "the ferment now excited in the minds of the people, is occasioned" in part "by withholding the powder lodged in the magazine of the town of Boston, from the legal proprietors, insulting, beating, and abusing passengers to and from the town of Boston, by the soldiery . . . ." Ignoring the accusations, Gage responded with a countercharge: "I would ask what occasion there is for such numbers going armed in and out of the Town, and through the country in an hostile manner? or why were the guns removed privately in the night, from the battery at Charlestown?"[71]

There is another account of Warren meeting with Gage, although it is unclear if it was the same meeting or a subsequent one on behalf of the Committee of Correspondence, of which Warren was president. Warren demanded an explanation for the fortifications and for Gage's recent purchase of a large quantity of military stores from a private vendor (to which the patriots strongly objected). Gage responded that "the country people were all armed, and collecting cannon and military stores from all quarters, which, as they were not soldiers by profession, or under the least apprehension of any invasion, could indicate nothing but their intention of attacking his Majesty's forces in that town . . . ." Gage added that the fortifications were defensive, and the inhabitants had not been annoyed. However, Gage insisted, "it is notorious that many cannon have been conveyed, notwithstanding the works, from thence; and arms are carried out openly by every man that goes out of Boston without molestation."[72]

However, the Boston Committee of Correspondence charged that "a number of Cannon, the property of a private gentleman, were a few days ago seized and taken from his wharf by order of the General . . . ."[73] Moreover, despite the Mandamus Counselors having found an official ban on firearms temporarily impolitic, Gage's forces had begun to seize them without lawful authority. Dr. Warren wrote to Samuel Adams on September 29:

> The troops are availing themselves of every opportunity to make themselves more formidable, and render the people less able to oppose them. They keep a constant search for every thing which will be serviceable in battle; and whenever they espy any instruments which may serve or disserve them,—whether they are the property of individuals or the public is immaterial,—they are seized, and carried into the camp or on board the ships of war.[74]

As an example, Warren noted that "Mr. Samuel Phillips, jun., of Andover, was this day carrying about a dozen fire-arms over Charleston ferry. The sloop-of-war lying in the river dispatched a boat, and seized them."[75] Boston merchant John Andrews wrote in more detail that this ship:

> seiz'd a parcell of Merchandize to the amount of about fifty pounds, lawful money, which were a dozen firelocks, the property of Mr. Phillips of Andover. He waited on Captain Bishop to obtain a release of them; but most people would be glad to have the matters come to a tryal, in order to have it determin'd whether they have a right to seize any article, transported across the harbour, or not.[76]

But military rule may have by now precluded intervention by the courts to challenge seizures of private arms. And given that the courts were either filled with the Crown's appointees or were not open because the patriots had pressured Crown judges to resign, a test case was most improbable.

An apologist for Gage wrote to Peyton Randolph, president of the Continental Congress, denying that the general had seized private property. A commander of one of His Majesty's ships, not Gage, had seized several cannon, because they were water-borne and intended to be smuggled. No one had claimed them in the Court of Admiralty. Regarding the merchants' gunpowder, the writer conceded that "the General did, for a short time, very wisely and prudently prohibit the Keeper of the Magazine from delivering out any Powder—but this is, at most, only in the nature of an embargo, and is no more an invasion of private property than an embargo on ships is."[77]

The patriots were more likely to challenge the Redcoats in places outside the courts. But nonjudicial test cases were at hand. John Andrews recorded an incident in which soldiers were shooting at a target in a stream at Boston Common. A countryman standing by laughed when the whole regiment could not hit the target. The officer in charge challenged the man to shoot better. He did so repeatedly, hitting the target exactly where the officer directed him. Andrews noted:

> The officers as well as the soldiers star'd, and tho't the Devil was in the man. Why, says the countryman, I'll tell you *naow*. I have got a *boy* at home that will toss up an apple and shoot out all the seeds as its coming down.[78]

The country people were not only honing up their sharpshooter skills, they were organizing their own militias from the bottom up rather than the top down. John Andrews commented:

> The Country towns, in general, have chose their own officers, and muster for exercise once a week at least—when the parson as well as the Squire stands in the Ranks with a firelock.—In particular at Marblehead, they turn out three or four times a week, when Col. Lee as well as the Clergy men there are not asham'd to appear in the ranks, to be taught the manual exercise, in particular.[79]

While Massachusetts was the hotbed of the trouble, the people of other colonies were arming themselves too. Gage noted in a missive to Dartmouth that "they talk even in that Province [Pennsylvania] of taking Arms with an Indifference, as if it was a Matter of little Importance. I don't suppose People were ever more possessed with Zeal and Enthusiasm."[80]

By now the Redcoats had instituted a general policy of searching places for arms and seizing them, which only induced the populace to arm themselves further. The address from Worcester County presented to General Gage stated:

> This County are constrained to observe, they apprehend the People justified in providing for their own Defence, while they understood there was no passing the Neck without Examination, the Cannon at the North-Battery spiked up, & many places searched, where Arms and Ammunition were suspected to be; and if found seized; yet as the People have never acted offensively, nor discovered any disposition so to do, as above related, the County apprehend this can never justify the seizure of private Property.[81]

Gage denied any hostile intent, but as usual, refused to respond to the specific charges.[82] The same day as the above was published, Gage wrote privately to Dartmouth, enclosing the Worcester address and similar resolves:

> The above relate to Works I have been making at the Entrance of the Town, at which they pretend to be greatly alarmed, least the Inhabitants of the Town should be enslaved, and made Hostages of, to force the Country to comply with the late Acts; a Scheme which they know is not feasible; but I believe the Works have hitherto obstructed some pernicious Projects they have had in View, which has determined me to refuse all Applications for their Demolition.[83]

Meanwhile, when the Massachusetts Assembly convened, Gage denounced it as an illegal assembly. Undeterred, its members renamed themselves as the Provincial Congress. Presided over by John Hancock, the Provincial Congress resolved on October 26, 1774, that Gage's military rule was subversive of the constitution of the province, having "thus greatly endangered the lives, liberties, and properties of its suppressed citizens:——Invaded private property, by unlawfully seizing and retaining large quantities of ammunition in the arsenal at Boston, and sundry pieces of ordnance in the same town—committed to the custody of his troops the arms, ammunition, ordnance and warlike stores of all sorts, provided at the public expense for the use of the province." It admonished that militia companies organize and elect their officers, and that at least a quarter of them must "equip and hold themselves in readiness to march at the shortest notice." The Provincial Congress further resolved:

> That as the security of the lives, liberties and properties of the inhabitants of this province depends under providence on their knowledge and skill in the art military, and in their being properly and effectually armed and equipt; if any of said inhabitants are not provided with arms and ammunition according to law, they immediately provide themselves forthwith; and that they use their utmost diligence to perfect themselves in military skill . . . .[84]

Gage declared the Provincial Congress to be an unlawful assembly and ordered it to disperse. The Congress ignored the order and continued to meet through December. A patriot with a sense of humor responded with a poem:

> Since an Assembly most unlawful,
> At Cambridge met in Congress awful,
> October last, did then presume,
> The Powers of Government t' assume;
> And slighting British Administration,
> Dar'd rashly seek their own Salvation;
> By ordering every sturdy Farmer,
> To be prepar'd with proper Armour.
> ('Tis what indeed the Law requires,
> But different quite from our Desires.)[85]

Having the militiamen elect their own officers meant that those appointed by the Royal governor would be thrown out. The Provincial Congress further usurped the Crown's militia power by appointing a Committee of Safety that could call out the militia when necessary.[86] Gage remarked to Dartmouth about this democratization of the militia:

> The Officers of the Militia have in most Places been forced to resign their Commissions, And the Men choose their Officers, who are frequently made and unmade; and I shall not be surprized, as the Provincial Congress seems to proceed higher and higher in their Determinations, if Persons should be Authorised by them to grant Commissions and Assume every Power of a legal Government, for their Edicts are implicitly obeyed throughout the Country.[87]

Gage brooded that "the whole Country [is] in a Ferment, many parts of it, I may say, actually in Arms, and ready to unite. Letters from other Provinces tell us they are violent every where, and that no Decency is observed in any Place by New-York."[88]

Gage had good intelligence: Activities encouraging the organization of militia and accumulation of arms were taking place everywhere, from Connecticut, Rhode Island, and New Hampshire, to Maryland, South Carolina, and Virginia. These militias were independent companies that no longer recognized the authority of their former officers who had been appointed by the Crown's governors.[89]

While assuring the authorities of their loyalty, the patriots made thinly veiled threats concerning their prowess with firearms. The *Boston Gazette* declared: "Besides the regular trained militia in New-England, all the planters sons and servants are taught to use the fowling piece from their youth, and generally fire balls with great exactness at fowl or beast."[90] Reiterating complaints about seizures of gunpowder stores, both public and private, the *Gazette* added: "But what most irritated the People next to seizing their Arms and Ammunition, was the apprehending six gentlemen, select men of the town of Salem, who had assembled a Town meeting. . . ."[91] (That late August incident is mentioned above.)

While some Tories scoffed at the colonists as boastful cowards who would run in a fight, Gage took the phenomenon of the increasingly armed populace very seriously. He recommended to Dartmouth a powerful army to disarm and crush the rebels:

> If Force is to be used at length, it must be a considerable one, and Foreign Troops must be hired, for to begin with Small Numbers will encourage Resis-

tance and not terrify; and will in the End cost more Blood and Treasure. An Army on Such a Service should be large enough to make considerable Detachments to disarm and take in the Counties, procure Forrage Carriages & ca and keep up Communications, without which little Progress could be made in a Country, where all are Enemies.[92]

Orders to confiscate arms arrived from London, but the job was easier said than done. Lord Dartmouth, secretary of state for America, urged General Gage in a letter dated October 17 to consider disarming the most rebellious Americans, but only if practicable:

> Amongst other things which have occurred on the present occasion as likely to prevent the fatal consequence of having recourse to the sword, that of disarming the Inhabitants of the Massachusetts Bay, Connecticut and Rhode Island, have been suggested. Whether such a Measure was ever practicable, or whether it can be attempted in the present state of things you must be the best judge; but it certainly is a Measure of such a nature as ought not to be adopted without almost a certainty of success, and therefore I only throw it out for your consideration.[93]

Gage received the letter on December 3 and replied on the 15th (the same day Gage also acknowledged notice of the related ban on arms imports[94]), noting: "Your Lordship's Idea of disarming certain Provinces would doubtless be consistent with Prudence and Safety, but it neither is nor has been practicable without having Recourse to Force, and being Masters of the Country."[95] This letter would later be read in the House of Commons[96] and summarized in the colonial press as proof of the Crown's ill intentions: "General Gage's Letters being read in the House of Commons, it appears from one of them that it had been recommended to him by Lord Dartmouth to disarm some of the Colonies, which in his Opinion, was not practicable, till he was Master of the Country."[97]

Every day that passed, however, it became less likely that Gage's forces would "become masters of the country" and be able to "disarm certain provinces." Colonists were arming themselves and organizing into independent militias to oppose the standing force. Josiah Quincy's celebrated tome referred to "a well regulated militia composed of the freeholders, citizens, and husbandmen, who take up arms to preserve their property as individuals, and their rights as freemen."[98] He asked: "Who can be surprised, that princes and their subalterns discourage a martial spirit among the people, and endeavour to render useless and contemptible the militia, when this institution is the natural strength, and only stable safeguard, of a free country?"[99] After all, "the supreme power is ever possessed by those who have arms in their hands, and are disciplined to the use of them."[100]

Other popular works of the day similarly emphasized the Americans' affinity for popular armed self-defense. Daniel Dulany of Maryland referred to "democratical governments, where the power is in the hands of the people and where there is not the least difficulty or jealousy about putting arms into the hands of every man in the country."[101] The Americans "have several hundred thousands and perhaps near a million men capable of bearing arms in their own defence . . . ."[102] In an oration "humbly dedicated" to the Earl of Dartmouth, John Allen warned that

> you will find, my Lord, that the Americans will not submit *to be* slaves, they
> know the use of the gun, and the military art, as well as any of his Majesty's
> troops at St. James's; and where his Majesty has one soldier, who art in general
> the refuse of the earth, America can produce fifty free men, and all volunteers,
> and raise a more potent army of men in three weeks, than England can in three
> years. But God forbid that I should be thought to aim at rousing the Americans
> to arms, without their rights, liberties and oppression call for it.[103]

For his own part, Dartmouth heard rumors that Gage was being too soft on the Boston militia. The secretary admonished the general that "upon no account suffer the Inhabitants of at least the Town of Boston, to assemble themselves in arms on any pretence whatever, either of Town guard or Militia duty; and I rather mention this, as a Report prevails that you have not only indulged them in having such a Guard, but have also allowed their Militia to train and discipline in Faneuil Hall."[104] Actually, Gage did make "proposals for maintaining good order and harmony between the soldiers and town people," but he did not state that the "guards" and "marshals" that would help keep order would be militia and did not authorize militia training.[105]

Moreover, the Redcoats did seek to suppress militia activities in Boston, albeit not necessarily with success. In a December incident, it was reported that

> a party of the militia being at exercise on Boston common, a party of the army
> surrounded them and took away their fire arms; immediately thereupon a larger

party of the militia assembled, pursued the Army, and retook their fire arms. Whereupon the Governor ordered the man of war to fire upon the Town, which was instantly obeyed; several houses were damaged, and only 6 people killed.[106]

While the allegation about deaths proved to be false, the obvious point of the story was that the militia could and would retain their arms against attempted seizure by the standing army. And the cancer had spread to the other colonies. Virginia's Governor Dunmore wrote to Dartmouth on Christmas Eve that every county "is now arming a Company of men, whom they call an Independent Company, for the avowed purpose of protecting their Committees, and to be employed against Government, if occasion require." These independent companies were "universally supported" and "set themselves up superiour to all other authority, under the auspices of their Congress."[107]

As is usual in police search and seizure operations, a cat-and-mouse game was played in which the searchers and the searchees exchanged charges and countercharges. A Tory queried, "who carried cannon off privately in a boat to a mill-pond, and when detected declared it to be nothing but a boat-load of *old iron?*"[108] A patriot—whose comrades were arming themselves as rapidly as possible—depicted them as penmen:

> We are told, that it is an undoubted act, that the supposed boxes of small arms, lead, & c. which were lately seized by the custom-house officers at New York, and caused so much disturbance there, *turns out* to be—What?—Why only a few boxes of *Printing Types*! Aye, says a wag, and what was the Gun-Powder?— Why truly, nothing but two cakes of Printing Ink![109]

For the Loyalists, the troublemakers were smugglers feigning innocence. By contrast, the patriots depicted themselves as victims of repressive measures executed by overzealous soldiers assigned to ferret out any potential violation, yielding only innocent objects.

Still, there is no denying that the patriots sought to scare the British with talk about the colonists' expertise with arms. A pamphlet printed all over the colonies and even England credited with convincing the British of this expertise was written by Charles Lee, who was influential in the Continental Congress.[110] A key passage states: "The Yeomanry of America have, besides infinite advantages, over the peasantry of other countries; they are accustomed from their infancy to fire arms; they are expert in the use of them:—Whereas the lower and middle people of England are, by the tyranny of certain laws, almost as ignorant in the use of a musket, as they are of the ancient Catapulta."[111]

Lee had served in the British army, and Dartmouth wrote Gage to keep an eye on him and obstruct his efforts, explaining: "I am told that Mr Lee, a Major upon half pay with the rank of Lieutenant Colonel, has lately appeared at Boston; that he associates only with the Enemies of Government; that he encourages the discontents of the people by harangues and publications; and even advises to Arms."[112] After the War for Independence began, Lee would be appointed second major-general in the Continental army.

None other than John Adams expanded on the theme of the armed citizen in his influential *Novanglus* series, a refutation of former Whig and now Tory "Massachusettensis" (Daniel Leonard), who argued that Parliament's authority extended to the colonies. In response to the suggestion that the colonies could not defend themselves, partly because the colonies south of Pennsylvania had no men to spare, Adams wrote:

> But we know better; we know that all those colonies have a back country, which is inhabited by a hardy, robust people, many of whom are emigrants from New England, and habituated, like multitudes of New England men, to carry their fuzees[113] or rifles upon one shoulder, to defend themselves against the Indians, while they carry their axes, scythes, and hoes upon the other, to till the ground.[114]

Those same colonies (except Maryland) furnished men in the French and Indian War—one Virginia regiment was "equal to any regular regiment in the service"—and would exert themselves all the more in an "unnatural, horrid war" against them waged by the Crown. Adams proceeded to the next objection:

> But, "have you arms and ammunition?" I answer, we have, but if we had not, we could make a sufficient quantity of both. . . . We have many manufacturers of fire-arms now, whose arms are as good as any in the world. Powder has been made here, and may be again, and so may saltpetre. . . . We have all the materials in great abundance, and the process is very simple. But if we neither had them nor could make them, we could import them.[115]

Actually, the colonists imported most gunpowder but made it in smaller quantities by older and simpler, albeit less safe, methods. These methods required that the ingredients be pounded while kept moist, particularly with alcohol and urine (preferably that of wine consumers).[116]

As for the Crown's embargo against import of arms into the colonies, Adams averred that it took many ships just to blockade Boston harbor, yet the American coastline had countless bays, harbors, creeks, and inlets. "Is it to be supposed, then, that the whole British navy could prevent the importation of arms and ammunition into America, if she should have occasion for them to defend herself against the hellish warfare that is here supposed?"[117]

And then there was the armed populace, organized in decentralized militia rather than as a force under the tutelage of the Royal government:

> "The new-fangled militia," as the specious Massachusettensis calls it, is such a militia as he never saw. They are commanded through the province, not by men who procured their commissions from a governor as a reward for making themselves pimps to his tools, and by discovering a hatred of the people, but by gentlemen, whose estates, abilities, and benevolence have rendered them the delight of the soldiers . . . . The plausibly Massachusettensis may write as he will, but in a land war, this continent might defend itself against all the world.[118]

In the following issues of *Novanglus*, John Adams refuted the Tory claim that the colonists were engaged in rebellion. "Opposition, nay, open, avowed resistance by arms, against usurpation and lawless violence, is not rebellion by the law of God or the land."[119] Relying on the natural rights philosophy, Adams averred that "there are tumults, seditions, popular commotions, insurrections, and civil wars, upon just occasions as well as unjust."[120] He quoted Hugo Grotius' dictum that "it is not repugnant to the law of nature, for any one to repel injuries by force."[121] "A tyrant . . . may lawfully be dethroned by the people," according to Samuel von Pufendorf.[122] And Algernon Sidney affirmed: "Neither are subjects bound to stay till the prince has entirely finished the chains which he is preparing for them, and put it out of their power to oppose."[123] This classic Whig theory would find expression the following year in the Declaration of Independence.

There was no denying that the American Whigs were arming themselves for what they considered to be just resistance to tyranny. Peter Oliver, a prominent Tory and former Chief Justice of the Massachusetts Superior Court, recalled: "The People began now to arm with Powder & Ball, and to discipline their

Militia. Genl. Gage, on his Part, finding that Affairs wore a serious Aspect, made Preparations for Defence." He added, "The People were continually purchasing Muskets, Powder & Ball in the Town of Boston, & carrying them into the Country; under the Pretence that the Law of the Province obliged every Town & Person to be provided with each of those Articles. They urged another also, that there was Danger of a French War, which put them upon their Guard." Oliver described Gage's reaction as follows:

> A Person who was more than stark Blind might have seen through such pitifull Evasions. Genl. *Gage* therefore took wise Precautions; he put a Stop to the carrying off any more; & as all warlike Stores, except private Property, are vested in the King, the Govr. therefore seized upon some of the Magazines, & secured the Powder under the Protection of his Troops. This provoked the People, & some of the Smuglers sent to the Dutch at Eustatia, & got a Recruit of Powder. They also secured Cannon from Vessells, & some of the Kings Forts, & acted with great Vigour in all their Preparations; & thus passed the Remainder of the Year 1774, in Offence on one Side & in Defence on the other.[124]

As noted in the January 31 diary entry of Lieutenant Frederick MacKenzie of the Royal Welch Fusiliers, "the people are evidently making every preparation for resistance. They are taking every means to provide themselves with Arms; and are particularly desirous of procuring the Locks of firelocks, which are easily conveyed out of town without being discovered by the Guards."[125] In those days, a firearm (or firelock) was referred to as having a "lock, stock, and barrel"—the lock being the ignition device that shot sparks into the charge in the barrel to ignite the powder, expelling the ball.

Lieutenant MacKenzie wrote the next day: "A Garrison Court Martial assembled this day for the trial of some Soldiers for selling firelocks, and locks to the Country people."[126] One verdict was: "A Soldier of the 4th Reg[imen]t who was tried a few days ago for disposing of Arms to the towns people, has been found guilty and sentenced to receive 500 lashes." This may have been a slip of the pen or a misprint, as fifty lashes would have been a cruel but not unusual punishment, but 500 lashes may have killed the defendant. MacKenzie also noted: "A serjeant and two Soldiers of the 38th Reg[imen]t tried for the same crime, have been acquitted."[127]

Gage perceived and foretold a great decentralized force of American marksmen waging guerrilla warfare, which would be most difficult to repress. He wrote to Dartmouth on March 4:

The most natural and eligible mode of attack on the part of the people is that of detached parties of bushmen who from their adroitness in the habitual use of the firelock suppose themselves sure of their mark at a distance of 200 rods [*sic*—yards or meters?]. Should hostilities unhappily commence, the first opposition would be irregular, impetuous, and incessant from the numerous bodies that would swarm to the place of action, and all actuated by an enthusiasm wild and ungovernable.[128]

The annual memorial of the Boston Massacre of 1770 was held on March 6, MacKenzie noted in his diary. Joseph Warren gave the address from the pulpit from which hung a black cloth. He was "attended by all the most violent fellows in town, particularly Hancock, the Adams's, Church, Cooper, and the rest of the Select Men."[129] Warren's words were restrained, although hissed at by British officers in attendance. "The towns people certainly expected a Riot, as almost every man had a short stick, or bludgeon, in his hand; and it was confidently asserted that many of them were privately armed."[130] Fortunately, no violence erupted.

Search and seizure for contraband goes hand-in-hand with entrapment, and the colonial epoch was no exception. The diary entry for March 9 by Boston merchant John Rowe stated: "This morning a Country Fellow who had Bought a Gun from one of the Soldiers was punished by them in the Modern Taste of Tarring & Feathering & carried in a Cart through the main Streets of the Town."[131] The patriot version of the incident ran thus: "An honest countryman . . . was inquiring for a firelock; a soldier heard him, and told him, he had one which he would sell; away goes the Ignoramus, and after paying the soldier very honestly for the gun, (which was an old one without a lock) & was walking off, when half a dozen seized him, & hurried the poor fellow away under guard, for a breach of the act against trading with soldiers . . . ."[132]

Thomas Ditson, the country boy in question, affirmed in an affidavit, "I enquired of some Townsmen who had any Guns to sell; one of whom I did not know, replied he had a very fine Gun to sell."[133] Since the one who offered the gun was a soldier, Ditson continued:

I asked him if he had any right to sell it, he reply'd he had, and that, the Gun was his to dispose of at any time; I then ask'd him whether he tho't the Sentry would not take it from me at the Ferry, as I had heard that some Persons had their Guns taken from them, but never tho't there was any law against trading

with a Soldier; . . . I told him I would give four Dollars if there was no risque in
carrying it over the Ferry; he said there was not . . . . I was afraid . . . that there
was something not right . . . and left the Gun, and coming away he followed me
and urg'd the Gun upon me . . . .[134]

When he finally paid money to the soldier, several other soldiers appeared and
seized Ditson, whom they proceeded to tar and feather.

The soldier swore in his affidavit, however, that it was a case of a rebel
trying to obtain arms and urging a soldier to desert. The citizen said "that
he would buy more Firelocks of the Deponent, and as many as he could get
any other Soldier to sell him . . . ."[135] Lieutenant Frederick MacKenzie noted
in his diary:

A Country fellow was detected this day in buying arms from a Soldier of the
47[th] Reg[imen]t. The men of that Regiment immediately secured him, and having provided the proper materials, they stripped, and then Tarred & feathered
him, and setting him upon a Truck, in the manner paraded him, in the afternoon through most parts of the town, to The Neck. This matter was done with
the knowledge of the Officers of the Regiment, altho they did not appear in it,
and it gave great Offence to the people of the town, and was much disapproved
of by General Gage. Arms of all kinds are so much sought after by the Country
people, and that they use every means of procuring them; and have been successful amongst the Soldiers, several of whom have been induced to dispose of
Arms or such parts of Arms, as they could come at. Perhaps this transaction
may deter the Country fellows from the like practices in future.[136]

The incident created another *cause célèbre* for the patriots. Samuel Adams
described the Ditson affair in a letter as follows:

A simple Country man was inveigled by a Soldier to bargain with him for a
Gun; for this he was put under Guard and the next day was tarred and feathered by the Officers and Soldiers of the 47. . . . We are at a Loss to account for
this Conduct of a part of the Army in the face of the Sun unless there were
good Assurances that the General [Gage] would connive at it. However, he *says*
he is very angry at it.[137]

In a letter to Richard Henry Lee dated March 21, Adams suggested that
Gage "is afraid of displeasing his Officers & has no Command over them."[138]
The Committee of Correspondence was enquiring into the Ditson incident

and other abuses. To Adams, it was another episode in the scheme to disarm the colonists, as was the following event:

> Last Saturday a Waggon going from this Town into the Country was stopped by the Guards on the Neck, having Nine Boxes of Ball Cartridges which were seisd by the Troops. Application has been made to the General, by a private Gentleman who claimd them as his property. The General told him that he would order them to be markd as such, but they could not then be delivrd.[139]

While that allegation was consistent with Gage's policies to search for and seize arms and ammunition, it is doubtful that a general of Gage's caliber would have countenanced the particularly unsoldierly treatment of Ditson, a breach of discipline that would only create friction with the populace. Gage explained in a missive to Dartmouth:

> A Man from the Country who says he was seduced into the Quarters of the 47th Regiment to purchase some of their old Cloaths and Arms, but accused by the Regiment to have artfully mingled with the Soldiers to buy their Arms and Ammunition and tempt them to dessert, was Seized by Order of the Commanding Officer, tarred feathered and carried thro' some of the Streets. The Moment it was known I sent to stop them and release the Man, for I could not look upon the Proceeding, so below the Character of Soldiers, without expressing the highest Indignation at it. The Town of Belerica, of which the Man is an Inhabitant, has sent me a very insolent and threatening Remonstrance upon the Subject, and it will create a good deal of Work for the Courts as Soon as they are Open.[140]

However, events were moving too fast for the courts to administer justice for a long time—several years to be sure. The years 1774 and early 1775 followed a familiar pattern. In the aftermath of the Boston Tea Party and the subsequent Intolerable Acts, the British ministry sent General Gage to restore order. While the Divan debated the disarming of the inhabitants, Gage seized their gunpowder. This prompted the colonists to arm themselves even more, while the soldiers executed search-and-seizure operations to confiscate firearms.

Instead of a return to normalcy in which the colonists would once more be dutiful subjects of His Majesty, the Americans were only becoming more rebellious. The time had come to cut off the supply of all arms and ammunition.

## CHAPTER 3

# The Arms Embargo and
# Search and Seizure at the Neck

MEANWHILE, the British ministers undertook to cut off firearms and ammunition from their source. News traveled slowly from England across the Atlantic, but in December 1774 the colonists learned that two months before, King George and his ministers had decreed a ban on importation of firearms into the colonies. Present at the Court at St. James on October 19 were "The King's most excellent Majesty in Council," including the Earl of Rockford, Lord Viscount Townshend, the Earl of Dartmouth, Lord Mansfield, the Earl of Suffolk, and Lord North. The ministers decreed:

> whereas an Act of Parliament has passed in the Twenty Ninth Year of the Reign of his late Majesty King George the Second, intitled, "An Act to empower his Majesty to prohibit the Exportation of Saltpetre, and to enforce the Law for im-powering his Majesty to prohibit the Exportation of Gunpowder, or any sort of Arms or Ammunition, and also to empower his Majesty to restrain the carrying coastways of Saltpetre, Gunpowder, or any sort of Ammunition."[1]

> And His Majesty judging it necessary to prohibit the Exportation of Gun-powder, or any sort of Arms or Ammunition, out of this Kingdom, doth there-fore, with the advice of his Privy Council, hereby order, require, prohibit and

command that no Person or Persons Whatsoever (except the Master General of the Ordnance for his Majesty's Service) do, at any time during the space of Six Months from the date of this Order in Council, presume to transport into any parts out of this Kingdom, or carry coastways any Gunpowder, or any sort of Arms or Ammunition, on board any Ship or Vessel, in order to transporting the same to any part beyond the Seas or carrying the same coastways, without Leave and Permission in that behalf, first obtained from his Majesty or his Privy Council, upon Pain of incurring and suffering the respective Forfeitures and Penalties inflicted by the aforementioned Act. . . .[2]

In addition, the Crown dispatched orders to the colonial governors and British navy to halt the importation of arms and ammunition into the colonies.[3] Dartmouth wrote to Gage:

His Majesty having thought fit, by His Order in Council this Day, to prohibit the Exportation from Great Britain of Gunpowder, or any sort of Arms or Ammunition, I herewith inclose to you a Copy of the Order, and it is His Majesty's Command that you do take the most effectual Measures for arresting, detaining & securing any Gunpowder, or any Sort of Arms or Ammunition, which may be attempted to be imported into the Province under your Government, unless the Master of the Ship, having such Military Stores on board, shall produce a Licence from His Majesty, or the Privy Council for the Exportation of the same from some of the Ports of this Kingdom.[4]

Dartmouth enclosed secret papers with the orders, explaining: "That you may be fully informed of the Motives for the Caution we have used, and the Steps We have taken for guarding against an Importation into the Colonies of Gunpowder, Arms & Ammunition, I think fit to send you in Confidence, & for your own Information, the inclosed Copies of such Papers as have passed upon that Occasion."[5]

The enclosures were letters from Sir Joseph Yorke to Lord Suffolk, and from Suffolk to Dartmouth.[6] Yorke, the British ambassador to The Hague,[7] sounded the alarm during August–October 1774 about American procurement of arms and gunpowder. While calling the notorious contraband trade between Holland and North America in teas and linens unworthy of note, Yorke warned that "the Polly, Capt. Benjamin Broadhelp bound to Nantucket in the province of New York, . . . has shipped on board a considerable quantity of gunpowder." Among other firms, Amsterdam's House of Crommelin was a chief culprit in exports to the colonies.[8]

Yorke next reported the alarming intelligence "that the quantity of gunpowder shipped for New York on board the [vessel?] formerly mentioned amounts, as I am positively assured, to three hundred thousand pounds." That enormous quantity seems exaggerated. Yorke continued: "The Dutch export likewise a pretty large quantity from their Island of St. Eustatia, which is the center of all contraband in that part of the world." Artillery was also being distributed from that Caribbean island.[9]

The Earl of Suffolk forwarded the letters to Lord Dartmouth, describing them as concerning "large quantities of gunpowder which are said to be purchased in Holland, shipped for some of the ports in North America."[10] Yorke later wrote the earl:

> I am informed from Amsterdam that an English brigantine [ship] of 60 tons burthen called the Smack (or some such name) commanded by Benjamin Page was arrived there from Rhode Island, addressed to Mr. Hodgson on a merchant [ship], sent expressly to load different sorts of firearms; and that Hodgson had already in execution of his commission put on board about 40 small pieces of cannon.[11]

Benjamin Page's name had previously surfaced as a suspect in Britain's investigation of an attack in 1772 on the British armed schooner *Gaspee* as it enforced the revenue laws against Rhode Island shippers.[12] At any rate, Suffolk lost no time in transmitting Yorke's latest intelligence to Dartmouth.[13]

This was the complete correspondence that Dartmouth forwarded to Gage regarding the decision to prohibit export of arms and gunpowder to the American colonies. It illustrates how the perceived right of the colonists to keep and bear arms to protect their liberties depended on commercial intercourse in arms and ammunition and how the Crown would seek to repress such trade to maintain its power. Interestingly, none other than Benjamin Franklin appears to have orchestrated the export of arms and ammunition from Holland, France, and Spain on behalf of the patriots.[14]

While not the subject of the correspondence sent to Gage, Ambassador Yorke unsuccessfully sought to persuade Dutch authorities to suppress the export of munitions to America. But an armed British cutter anchored near Amsterdam and blockaded the Rhode Island ship *Polly* and others bound with munitions for America.[15] Yorke eventually pressured the Dutch officially to restrict the export of arms and ammunition to America, but the lively commerce continued to thrive.[16] When the British sailed away from Amsterdam the following April, the Americans recommenced their gunrunning.[17]

Responding to Dartmouth's correspondence in a letter dated December 15, Gage acknowledged receipt of the above orders on December 3 and confirmed that he distributed them to the other colonial governors:

> Your Lordship's Circular Letter of the 19th of October, inclosing an Order
> of the King in Council to prohibit the Exportation of Arms Gun-Powder or
> other Military Stores from Great-Britain is duely received. And I have con-
> certed Measures with the Admiral and the Commissioners of the Customs for
> Stopping and Securing all Military Stores that shall be attempted to be im-
> ported into this Province except by Licence from His Majesty or the Council.
>
> The Circular Letters for the other Governors have been forwarded.[18]

Gage also acknowledged receipt of a copy of Sir Joseph Yorke's Letter to the Earl of Suffolk, which "confirms the Report spread here of Peoples sending to Europe for all kinds of Military Stores. I hope this intelligence is received in time to give a Chance of intercepting the Brigantine from Rhode Island with the 40 small Pieces of Ordnance on Board."[19] Gage sought immediate implementation of the prohibition on import of arms into the colonies.

The Royal instructions and the secret letter from Lord Dartmouth to the colonial governors prohibiting the importation of firearms and ammunition into America was quickly revealed by the governor of Rhode Island, and copies of those dispatches leaked to the patriots. Before Gage had a chance even to confirm receipt of the order, the *Boston Gazette* reported this new violation of the colonists' rights as follows:

> We learn from undoubted Authority, that Lord Dartmouth, Secretary of State,
> has wrote a circular Letter to the Governors upon this Continent, informing
> them, That his Majesty has thought fit, by his Order in Council, dated the 19th
> October 1774, to prohibit the Exportation from Great Britain, of Gun Powder
> or any Sort of Arms or Ammunition, and has signified to them his Majesty's
> Command, that they do take the most effectual Measures for arresting, detain-
> ing and securing any Gun Powder or any Sort of Arms or Ammunition, which
> may be attempted to be imported into the Province over which they respectively

preside, unless the Masters of the Ship having such Military Stores on Board shall produce a License from his Majesty or the Privy Council for the Exportation of the same from some of the Ports of Great-Britain.[20]

Upon receiving word of the arms embargo, the Boston Committee of Correspondence sent the news by Paul Revere to their friends in New Hampshire, warning them that two British ships would be proceeding to Fort William and Mary at Portsmouth to secure the Crown's materiel. On December 14, some 400 armed men approached the fort by boat and overran it.[21]

That same day New Hampshire Governor John Wentworth wrote an urgent missive informing General Gage of the attack, noting that the intruders "by violence carried away upwards of 100 barrels of powder belonging to the King, deposited in the castle." Wentworth learned that they would be back the next day to seize the remaining arms unless Gage could send help. He added: "This even too plainly proves the imbecility of this government to carry into execution his Majesty's order in council, for seizing and detaining arms and ammunition imported into this province, without some strong ship of war in this harbour . . . ."[22]

The rebels returned the next day, as Governor Wentworth predicted, and took away "many cannons, &c., and about sixty muskets." (Lord Percy wrote that they seized "1500 stand of small arms."[23]) On the third day of the disturbances, Wentworth further informed Gage—who had not sent help—that "the town is full of armed men who refuse to disperse," although "the people abstain from private or personal injuries . . . ."[24]

A New Hampshire patriot justified this action, describing the import ban as a violation of the right to keep and bear arms. "A Watchman" recalled the lesson of the ancient Carthaginians, who complied with the demand "that they must deliver up all their Arms to the Romans," only to be slain. He continued:

> Could they [the Ministry] not have given up their Plan for enslaving America without seizing . . . all the Arms and Ammunition? and without soliciting and finally obtaining an Order to prohibit the Importation of warlike Stores in the Colonies? . . . And shall we like the Carthaginians, peaceably surrender our Arms to our Enemies, in Hopes of obtaining in Return the Liberties we have so long been contending for? . . .

I . . . hope that no Person will, at this important Crisis, be unprepared to act in his own Defence, should he by Necessity be driven thereto. And I must here beg Leave to recommend to the Confederation of the People of this Continent, Whether, when we are by an arbitrary Decree prohibited *the having* Arms and Ammunition by Importation, we have not by the Law of Self Preservation, a Right to seize upon all those within our Power, in order to *defend the* liberties which GOD and Nature have given us . . .?[25]

More information on what precipitated the import ban was published in London and reprinted in the colonial newspapers. Exaggerated accounts of armed struggle in the colonies had reached England. One such account stated:

An order of the council, dated the 19th inst. is published in this night's Gazette, prohibiting the exportation of gun powder and arms, from any point of the kingdom. . . .

By a letter received by a merchant in this city from New York . . . [the ship left New York in mid-September] the Captain says an express was just mailed there from Boston, with an account that there had been an engagement between the troops and the Bostonians; the Troops set fire to the town, which was all in flames when the express came away. What gives the greatest credit to this account is, the entire prohibition of gunpowder, and all sorts of arms and ammunition.

Notwithstanding the ministerial accounts from America are kept a profound secret the late embargo on gunpowder proves their fears respecting that country to be very great. Great quantities of nitre and salt-petre just shipped, are again disembarking in consequence of Saturday night's Gazette.[26]

While the above correspondence Dartmouth shared with Gage stressed the Dutch connection, English gun makers had been receiving orders for vast numbers of arms from the Americans. As was originally published in a London newspaper:

Saturday's proclamation, it is said, was occasioned by intelligence received from Sheffield and Birmingham of amazing quantities of fire arms, & c. being nearly ready to be sent to America, in consequence of an order received from thence some time since.

Two vessels, laden with gun-powder and other military utensils, bound for the other side of the Atlantic, were stopped at Gravesend on Monday by the out clearers, in consequence of the King's Proclamation inserted in Saturday night's Gazette. . . .

A letter received in town from an English Gentleman at Brest says, that a French frigate and a snow lately sailed from that port for America, laden with firelocks, gunpowder, & c. . . .

The letters received for Friday from Boston, dated the 21st of September, are of the most alarming nature. They assert, that the inhabitants of Boston, and of the province of Massachusetts Bay are now in arms. . . .[27]

As noted, the Royal proclamation immediately halted arms shipments bound for America. "Some ships fitting out at Liverpool could not have permission to take on board any gun-powder, guns, or swords, . . . which . . . proves the fears of the ministry, respecting America, to be very great."[28] An American sympathizer in England predicted that "the proclamation against sending guns and gun powder out of this kingdom will be of very little use or effect, because the Americans will certainly procure whatever quantity of them they want from Holland, France, and Spain . . . ."[29]

British authorities anticipated that, and "orders have been given for the seizing every ship, of what nation soever, that are employed in conveying arms or ammunition to the Americans. This, 'tis thought, will be the cause of some serious disputes."[30] Indeed, "immediately after the King's proclamation issued prohibiting the exportation of arms and ammunition from Great-Britain, two men of war were ordered to the Texel, in Holland, in order to prevent the transportation of those articles in English bottoms to America." The same report referred to "the late Seizure of Arms, Lead and Powder, made by the Collector of this Port [New York]."[31] A letter from Bristol dated the day after Christmas reported that "orders are given for several frigates to be fitted out immediately to sail for America, to be stationed there in order to cruise along the coasts, to prevent any ammunition or arms being sent to the Americans by any foreign power."[32]

The merchants and people of Liverpool reportedly "were heartily disposed in favor of America," and "Sir William Meredith declared openly, before and at his election for Liverpool, his sentiments against the measures of administration toward the colonies: that the order of his Majesty in council, prohibiting the exportation of gun powder or armies had stopped ten or fifteen large ships there, almost ready for the sea, bound to the coast of Africa."[33]

But the Americans claimed to have the practical ability to arm themselves. A Philadelphian wrote to a member of Parliament on Christmas Eve:

> The late Proclamation forbidding the exportation of gun-powder and firearms to America seemed intended to take away from the colonies the power of defending themselves by force. I think it my duty to inform you that the said proclamation will be rendered ineffectual by a manufactory of gunpowder, which has lately been set on foot in this Province, the materials of which may be procured in great perfection, and at a easier rate than they can be imported from Great Britain, among ourselves. There are, moreover, gunsmiths enough in this Province to make one hundred thousand stands of arms in one year, at twenty-eight shillings sterling apiece, if they should be wanted. It may not be amiss to make this intelligence as public as possible, that our rulers may see the impossibility of enforcing the late Acts of Parliament by arms.[34]

A vocal minority of members of Parliament sympathized with the Americans regarding the arms embargo and other grievances. On March 22, 1775, Parliament debated Edmund Burke's Resolutions for Conciliation with America, which proposed that the colonies not be taxed and which, not surprisingly, failed. In the course of his eloquent speech, Burke pointed out that some of the same injustices the Americans were suffering had been committed before in Wales:

> Sir, during that state of things, Parliament was not idle. They attempted to subdue the fierce spirit of the Welsh by all sorts of rigorous laws. They prohibited by statute the sending all sorts of arms into Wales, as you prohibit by proclamation (with something more of doubt on the legality) the sending arms to America. They disarmed the Welsh by statute, as you attempted, (but still with more question on the legality) to disarm New England by an instruction. They made an Act to drag offenders from Wales into England for trial, as you have done (but with more hardship) with regard to America.[35]

A perhaps typical example of the seizure of imported arms and powder took place in the port of New York City in late December 1774. Several containers of arms and a barrel of powder were seized for lack of cockets (receipts for payment of duties). The containers were taken to the Custom House, and then, after

someone attempted to retrieve them, to a man-of-war. The powder was lodged in
the Powder House. Andrew Elliot, the customs collector, received a letter dated
the 27th purportedly signed by "the Mohawks and River Indians" stating:

> A number of Fire-arms of British manufacture, legally imported, having been
> lately seized by your orders and conveyed on board the Man-of-War, by which
> arbitrary steps you have declared yourself and inveterate enemy to the liberties
> of North America; in this light we view you, and from you we shall demand
> these Arms whenever they are wanted, which is probable will be soon. You will
> therefore, if you have the least regard to the safety of yourself or your servants,
> who seized them, be careful to prevent their being sent away, as you may de-
> pend upon answering for a contrary conduct with a vengeance.[36]

The collector responded with a letter denying any illegal conduct in the
seizure, and had it posted at the Coffee House, apparently a place where the
alleged smugglers would learn of it.[37] In response, a handbill was "secretly conveyed into almost every house in Town" imploring whether, "when Slavery is
clanking her infernal chains, . . . will you supinely fold your arms, and calmly
see your weapons of defence torn from you, by a band of ruffians?" It asked
whether the readers would be "robbed of your Arms, by a few petty Custom
House Officers, with impunity?" The missive continued:

> your country has been basely robbed by the Officers of the Customs, of a con-
> siderable number of Arms, which were legally exported from Great Britain,
> and imported here, in the Ship Lady Gage, and therefore not liable to a seizure,
> upon any pretence whatsoever, as they are actually the manufacture of Eng-
> land. Those Arms I am credibly informed, are now on board the Man-of-War,
> and are in a few days to be sent to General Gage, and of consequence are to be
> used for your destruction.[38]

The handbill urged that the people assemble before the collector, "insist
upon the Arms being relanded," or face the consequences. It concluded: "It is
not a season to be mealy-mouthed, . . . and we do not know but that the Arms
may be wanted to-morrow."[39] It seems doubtful that the arms and powder were
ever returned to the owners.

Domestically, Gage may have extended his seizure of powder to shops and
other private places, for it was reported in December "that General Gage has
taken possession of all the gunpowder he could discover [in Boston], which is

proof that the new Governor thinks there is something to be feared from the virtuous spirit of the Americans."[40]

A political satire had General Gage averring: "The inhabitants of the province of Massachusetts Bay, have not only thrown off the jurisdiction of the British Parliament, but they are disaffected to the British Crown. . . . They have even provided themselves with arms and ammunition, and have acquired a complete knowledge of the military exercises, in direct opposition to my proclamations."[41] However, the statement sounds more like reality than satire.

The freeholders and other inhabitants of Boston met at Faneuil Hall on December 30, with Samuel Adams in the chair. The gathering's resolutions recounted the seizures of gunpowder and militia cannon, dispersal of peaceable assemblies, and military occupation, which "at length roused the people to think of defending themselves and their property by arms, if nothing less could save them from violence and rapine." And contrary to Gage's assertion "that no man's property has been seized or hurt, except the King's," the resolutions averred: "We need not enumerate all the instances of property seized; it is enough to say, that a number of Cannon, the property of a respectable Merchant of this Town, were seized and carried off by force."[42]

Meanwhile, the Provincial Congress in Cambridge urged the Minutemen and other militiamen to perfect their military discipline and resolved to promote gun making. The Congress sought to encourage "such persons, as are skilled in the manufacturing of fire arms and bayonets, diligently to apply themselves thereto, for supplying such of the inhabitants as shall be deficient." It promised to purchase "so many effective arms and bayonets as can be delivered in a reasonable time upon notice given to this congress at its next session."[43]

The colonists often repeated points of political philosophy from their Whig brethren across the Atlantic. The Freeman's *Dublin Journal* offered a typical example, stating that "the instant a king violates his part of the contract, . . . a Whig thinks that the *legislative power of course naturally returns to the people*, and that they are at full liberty to take arms, and drive the tyrant from the throne."[44] Scottish Whig James Burgh's *Political Disquisitions* (1774)—"a book which ought to be in the hands of every American who has learned to read," according to John Adams[45]—was frequently quoted, particularly the following:

> The confidence, which a standing *army* gives a minister, puts him upon carrying things with a higher hand, than he would attempt to do, if the people

were armed, and the court unarmed, that is, if there were no land-force in the
nation, but a militia. Had we at this time no standing army, we should not
think of *forcing* money out of the pockets of three millions of our subjects. . . .
[Burgh goes on to list deprivation of jury trial, lack of representation, and other
grievances of the Americans.] There is no end to observations on the difference
between the measures likely to be pursued by a minister backed by a standing
*army*, and those of a court awed by the fear of an *armed people*.[46]

Opposing the armed patriots were the Royal militias buttressed by the
Redcoats: "It is said that orders are given for his Majesty's militias stationed in
North America to be immediately reinforced by several detachments of land
forces from Great-Britain and Ireland."[47]

Bloodshed was barely avoided on February 27, when British forces landed
at Salem, Essex County, to seize the colonists' growing stock of munitions.
A rider warned, "The Regulars are coming after the guns and are now near
Malloon's Mills!" The people swarmed out of the churches and dragged off
cannon and other weapons into the woods. Militiamen from the vicinity
filled the town. After a standoff, confrontation was avoided, and the troops
left empty-handed.[48]

While Massachusetts took the center stage, the other colonies were preparing for the worst. Patrick Henry's "liberty or death" oration on March 23,
1775, to the Convention of Delegates of Virginia in Richmond, directly con-
fronted the political import of an armed versus a disarmed populace. Henry
implored:

> They tell us . . . . that we are weak—unable to cope with so formidable an
> adversary. But when shall we be stronger? . . . Will it be when we are totally dis-
> armed, and when a British guard shall be stationed in every house? . . . Three
> million people, armed in the holy cause of liberty . . . are invincible by any force
> which our enemy can send against us.[49]

Among the resolutions that Henry proposed and the convention adopted
was the following: "That a well regulated Militia, composed of Gentlemen and
Yeomen, is the natural Strength, and only Security, of a free Government."[50]
The militia rendered unnecessary the standing army, which is "always subversive of the quiet, and dangerous to the liberties of the people." The militia
would "secure our inestimable rights and liberties from those further violations with which they are threatened." Such luminaries as Patrick Henry,

Richard Henry Lee, George Washington, and Thomas Jefferson formed "a committee to prepare a plan for the embodying, arming, and disciplining such a number of men as may be sufficient" to protect the colony.[51] The convention also recommended "that every Man be provided with a good Rifle" and "that every Horseman be provided . . . with Pistols and Holsters, a Carbine, or other Firelock."[52]

Meanwhile, patriots were smuggling quantities of arms and gunpowder out of Boston, and searches and seizures, some yielding massive supplies, were being stepped up. Boston merchant John Andrews wrote on March 18:

> Our provincial congress is to meet next month at Concord, when, I am told, there is to be an army of observation incamp'd, consisting of twenty thousand men. Am also inform'd that the congress have expended near a million in our Old tenor for ammunition and provisions. This I know, that they have had upwards of fifty ton of shot, shell, &ca., cast, besides an innumerable number of Musket balls. Have seen twenty load cover'd with dung go out of town myself, but lately all carts have been searched by the Guards, and unluckily last Saturday evening a load of cartridges were seiz'd pack'd in candle boxes, consisting of 13,500 besides 4 boxes balls. The countryman struggled hard before he would deliver'em, and received two or three bad wounds.[53]

This seizure, with a higher estimate of cartridges, was noted by Lieutenant Frederick MacKenzie of the Royal Welch Fusiliers in his diary entry on the same date:

> A country man was Stopped at the Lines, going out of town with 19,000 ball Cartridges, which were taken from him. When liberated, he had the insolence to go to Head quarters to demand the redelivery of them. When asked who they were for, he said they were for his own use; and on being refused them, he said he could not help it, but they were the last parcel of a large quantity which he had carried out at different times. Great numbers of Arms have been carried out of town during the Winter; and if more strict search had been made at the Lines, many of them, and much Ammunition might have been seized.[54]

The owner was Robert Pierpont of Roxbury, Suffolk County, whose "insolence" must have stemmed from being so Americanized—his apparent namesake ancestor sailed from England and established the family in Roxbury a century before.[55] Pierpont gave a detailed deposition about the seizure and his

petition to Gage for return of his property, explaining that on the afternoon
of March 10:

> on a cart of mine drove by one Hugh Floud while at the Neck, it was stopped
> by a number of soldiers, who having searched the cart and finding thirteen
> boxes containing cartridges & bullets for muskets, they took the same from
> the cart who they kept under guard for sometime and then permitted him to
> depart with his cart, whereupon I this morning waited upon General Gage,
> having before acquainted him with their stoppage, and claimed the boxes of
> shot & cartridges as my property. Upon this his Excellency reply'd, that he'd
> opposed the Errand I was upon before this time, for two Custom house officers
> had gone up to them, and that I could not have them at present, but that they
> should be marked and put in a safe place.[56]

Gage was personally willing to hear Pierpont's petition, perhaps not so
much to be a caring governor but to gain intelligence about such smuggling.
While the above wording is somewhat unclear, it seems that the Customs House
officers may have suspected that the huge quantity of ammunition had been
imported in violation of the ban, and the soldiers thus seized it as smuggled
goods. This would justify indefinite detention of the seized items.

Pierpont sought the legal basis for the seizure—Gage cited none, at least
in this account—and argued the legitimacy of supplying the populace with
ammunition as follows:

> I then asked his Excellency by what Authority he detained my Goods—he an-
> swered, that it was not allowed in any Nation to transport such articles at par-
> ticular times. I observed upon it, that there was a plain law of the Province that
> every Man should be Equipt with a certain quantity of Powder and Ball, and
> that now the time of year was come about to review arms; his Excellency then
> asked me by what authority they viewed arms, and who was their commanding
> officer, I answered the Law of the Province required it, and I further told him
> that being acquainted with the Country People, I had orders and letters, for
> sending large quantities and that I had carried out of Town about forty load,
> the Winter past, and that this near the last load I had to send, that I knew of,
> upon which he said that he wished the Laws of the Province were in force. I
> agreed with his Excellency in this, and said I wished it with all of my heart that
> they were observed.[57]

While Governor Gage would have been familiar with any law of the province requiring every man to be armed and to muster periodically, one detects a note of sarcasm in his wish that the laws were in force—Gage would have preferred the laws of the Crown over those of the province. His eyes must have rolled at Pierpont's audacity in volunteering that he had successfully taken forty loads of ammunition out of Boston that winter. Of course, the patriots wished to dissuade any coercive military measures by creating the impression that they were well armed. In any event, Pierpont concluded his deposition thus:

> I again requested that I might have an order for the forementioned articles, and he told me that they should be kept safe and it was likely I should have them again, I then said to his Excellency that, if I could not now have an order, I must seek any recompense in some other way, upon which I left his Excellency.[58]

Pierpont's threat to take legal action to recover his property or to seek damages would hardly have left Gage shaking in his boots, for his will was by then the law. Not surprisingly, despite his assurances, no record exists that Gage ever returned Pierpont's (or anyone else's) seized ammunition. To the contrary, Gage was only weeks away from launching an expedition to seize the colonists' arms in the countryside that would spark the Revolutionary War.

The patriot press made the most of the seizure, emphasizing that there was nothing unlawful about the owner's possession of ammunition, regardless of the amount. One account stated: "The Neck Guard seized 13,425 musket cartridges with ball, (we suppose through the information of some dirty scoundrel, of which we have now many among us) and about 300 lb. of ball, which we were carrying into the country—this was private property.—The owner applied to the General first, but he absolutely refused to deliver it—they abused the teamster very much, and ran a bayonet into his neck."[59]

In an open letter to General Gage, another writer linked this illegal seizure to the Crown's decree banning import of arms (also of dubious lawfulness) as follows:

> It is said that the troops, under your command, have seized a number of cartridges which were carrying out of the town of Boston, into the country; and as you were pleased to deny that you had meddled with private property, to the President of the Continental Congress, I would gladly be informed on what different pretence you now meddled with those cartridges. . . . I cannot con-

ceive you will urge the late ridiculous proclamation [banning export of arms and ammunition to America] in defence of the action. That creature, absurd and strained as it is, can have no reference to the carriage of powder and shot from any one inland place to another. But admitting it had, are Royal Proclamations again to be forced upon us for laws? I can, indeed, Sir, account for your conduct in this and many other instances, upon no other footing than that of an actual conspiracy to overthrow the laws and constitution of the country you are sworn to protect . . . .[60]

When governments conduct police actions involving searches and seizures for contraband, many items go undetected for every successful seizure. The arms seized were only the tip of the iceberg. The patriots acquired, moved, and secreted many more firearms and ammunition than were ever detected and confiscated. In one incident, "three teams, loaded with three tons of gun powder, made up in cartridges, came out of Boston; two of them passed over the Neck unsuspected, but the last were stopped by the centinels; who being immediately reinforced by a party of solders, seized that load of powder."[61] John Andrews mentioned that "the Commissioners have appointed an officer, under pretence of searching for contraband goods, who inspects every Cask that is carried out of the town by opening and boring, so that the waggons are detain'd sometime by him."[62]

Although not subjected to the same intense repression as New England, the other colonies saw the arms import ban as violating the right to keep and bear arms. The General Committee, South Carolina's patriotic governing body, found that

by the late prohibition of exporting arms and ammunition from England, it too clearly appears a design of disarming the people of America, in order the more speedily to dragoon and enslave them; it was therefore recommended, to all persons, to provide themselves immediately, with at least twelve and a half pounds of powder, with a proportionate quantity of bullets.[63]

The colonists armed themselves from all possible sources. It was reported from Newport in early 1775 that "powder bears a very good Price in this Town; the People from all parts of the Country, the Fall past, having bought up almost all there was, to defend themselves against Wolves, and other Beasts of prey."[64] If such tongue-in-cheek satire was to be believed, it was as if there had recently been an invasion of wild animals.

There was no similar satire in the resolution of the Provincial Congress, "That it be strongly recommended, to all the inhabitants of this colony, to be diligently attentive to learning the use of arms . . . ."[65] A letter from an American sympathizer in London warned that Gage was being reinforced to suppress the American rebels, and that British warships were coming "to obstruct the American trade, and prevent all European goods from going there; particularly arms and ammunition, which makes it expedient, without a moment's delay, to be provided with such things as you may want."[66]

General Gage indeed received the ministry's directive on April 14 to suppress the rebellion, in part through organization of a Tory corps. Dartmouth wrote: "The violence committed by those, who have taken up arms in Massachusetts . . . have appeared to me as the acts of a rude rabble, without plan, without concert, without conduct, and therefore I think that a small force now, if put to the test, would be able to encounter them, with greater probability of success, than might be expected of a large army . . . ."[67] The ministry ignored the warnings of moderates such as the Duke of Manchester, who in Parliamentary debate "cautioned the House to proceed with deliberation, as America had now three millions of people, and most of them were trained to arms, and he was certain they could now produce a stronger army than Great-Britain."[68]

At the same time, George III extended the ban on export of arms: "His Majesty's order in Council for prohibiting the exportation of gunpowder, or any sort of arms or ammunition, expiring on the 19th [of April] insists his Majesty hath been further pleased to command the said order to be continued for six months longer."[69] The Crown also persuaded the States General of Holland to join in the embargo. Writing from Whitehall on April 5, John Pownall notified the colonial governors:

> As it may be of use that His Majesty's subjects in America should be informed of the Proclamation issued by the orders of the States General, prohibiting the exportation of Arms and Ammunition from their Dominions, in British Ships, or in their own Ships, without leave of their College of Admiralty, I am directed by Lord Dartmouth to transmit to you the enclosed Gazette, containing the said Proclamation, which you will cause to be printed and published in such manner as you shall think fit.[70]

Gage acknowledged receipt on June 3 from Pownall of "the Gazette containing the Proclamation issued by Order of the State's General, prohibiting the exportation of Arms and Ammunition to British America, which I shall cause to be made as Public as possible."[71] But that would be easier said than done. Amsterdam merchants evaded the restrictions, shipping large amounts of gunpowder disguised as tea chests and rice barrels to the Caribbean island of St. Eustatia and from there to America.[72]

It is worth pausing to note that, in the worldview of the patriots, possession of arms by the populace was necessary for both individual and common defense. This fundamental value was not questioned by the occurrence of random, tragic incidents, such as the two men who made a suicide pact and killed themselves with pistols, or the father who murdered his three daughters with a knife.[73] Moreover, British authorities sought to disarm the colonists in order to dominate them politically, economically, and militarily, not as a purported safety measure to protect the colonists from themselves.

In the first quarter of 1775, the Crown sharply turned the screws against the Americans. To cut off the colonists' ability to resist at the source, George III decreed a ban on export of arms and ammunition to America, with orders to his Royal governors to prohibit the import thereof into the colonies. At the same time, General Gage instituted general searches and seizures for arms and gunpowder, particularly at Boston Neck, the only access by land with the rest of Massachusetts. The patriots did everything in their power to evade the arms embargo and to smuggle arms and ammunition out of Boston.

For the ministry, the Americans could be put in their place only if completely disarmed. The shooting was about to begin.

## CHAPTER 4

# A Shot Heard 'Round the World
# and "a Cruel Act of Perfidy"

D ISPERSE YOU REBELS —Damn you, throw down your Arms and disperse!" shouted British Major John Pitcairn at the militiamen who were assembled on Lexington's common. "Upon which the Troops huzz'd, and immediately one or two Officers discharged their Pistols, which were instantaneously followed by the Firing of four or five of the Soldiers, then there seemed to be a general discharge from the whole Body."[1] So went a widely published American account of that fateful day of April 19, 1775.

The skirmish gave rise to numerous statements of eyewitnesses. John Robbins, one of the Lexington militiamen, would testify:

the company under Captain John Parker, being drawn up . . . on the green or common, . . . there suddenly appeared a number of the King's troops, about a thousand as I thought, at the distance of about 60 or 70 yards from us, with three officers in their front on horseback and on full gallop towards us, the foremost of which cried, throw down your arms, go willing ye rebels, upon which said company dispersing, the foremost of the three officers ordered their men saying fire . . . .[2]

Still another patriot account claimed: "The regulars demanded their arms, which being refused, they fired and killed 7. The fire was returned by the brave survivors."[3] By contrast, Major Pitcairn wrote that, when his troops arrived and observed some 200 militiamen filing off toward some stone walls, "I instantly called to the Soldiers not to Fire, but to surround and disarm them, and after several repetitions of those positive Orders to the men, not to Fire etc., some of the Rebels who had jumped over the Wall, Fired Four or Five shott at the Soldiers," wounding a soldier and the major's horse. "At the same time several Shott were fired from a Meeting House on our Left—upon this, without any order or Regularity, the Light Infantry began a scattering Fire . . . ."[4]

The militiamen of Lexington and Concord consisted of all able-bodied males aged 16 through 60, from its gentlemen and yeomen to its laborers and apprentices, excluding the town's Harvard students and a dozen African American slaves. All provided their own arms except for a few poor men who had to borrow them.[5] One of the wounded at Lexington was listed as "Prince Easterbrooks (a Negro-Man)."[6]

Women and children assisted the militiamen in preparing for conflict. On the eve of the clash, Militia Colonel James Barrett's 15-year-old granddaughter Meliscent taught the other young women of the town how to assemble cartridges. On an earlier occasion, when a British officer asked her how the colonists could resist without being able to make cartridges, she responded "that they would use powder horns and bullets—just as they shot bear."[7]

The patriots had accumulated vast stores of arms and ammunition, secreting them at some thirty private homes and farms in Concord. General Gage sent two officers disguised as farmers to gain intelligence regarding the places of storage and the mood of the country.[8] Other informers, their identities unknown, reported intelligence to Gage about arms stored at the houses of named individuals.[9] "The policy of disarming the people had been acted on, though it had not been followed up very energetically," Richard Frothingham later noted. "The indications now were, that this policy would be carried out in earnest."[10]

On April 18, Gage appointed Lieutenant Colonel Francis Smith of the Tenth Regiment to head an expedition, with Major Pitcairn second in command, of some 700 soldiers to carry out the following orders:

Having received Intelligence, that a Quantity of Ammunition, Provision, Artillery, Tents and small Arms, having been collected at Concord, for the Avowed Purpose of raising and supporting a Rebellion against His Majesty, you will March with the Corps of Grenadiers and light Infantry, put under your Command, with the utmost expedition and Secrecy to Concord, where you will seize and destroy . . . [them]. . . .

You have a Draught of Concord, on which is marked the Houses, Barns, etc. which contain the above Military Stores.[11]

The patriots got wind of the expedition—General Gage's American wife has always been a suspect—and agreed on the signal "one if by land, two if by sea." After the Charlestown patriots saw the two lights burning in the church steeple across the water, they knew the Redcoats were coming from Boston across the Back Bay to Cambridge. Paul Revere saddled up, leaving his pistol at home.[12] When Revere (along with several lesser-known colleagues) made his famous midnight ride to warn the countryside that the Redcoats were coming, he was seized by British troops. Major Edward Mitchell of the 5th Foot ordered that Revere be searched for arms, but none were found. The officer put a pistol to Revere's head, threatening to blow his brains out unless information was given. Revere warned them not to go to Lexington, where extreme danger awaited.[13] Revere later escaped, renewing his call to arms, and the undeterred Redcoats continued to march to Lexington, where just hours later the shot heard 'round the world was fired.

The main British troops marched in the darkness, little knowing that the country people were feverishly preparing. In one instance, soldiers saw a light on in a house and knocked on the door. The lady of the house claimed to be brewing herb tea, but in fact she and her husband were melting pewter dishes into bullets. In another house, an 11-year-old girl later recalled that she and her sisters "were set to work making cartridges."[14]

Anne Hulton, "A Loyalist Lady," wrote a letter to a friend in England describing the combat between the "banditti" and Lord Hugh Percy. She observed that "The People in the Country (who are all furnished with Arms and have what they call Militia Companies in every Town ready to march on any alarm) had a signal . . . so that before daybreak the people in general were in Arms & on their March to Concord."[15]

At Lexington, Brigade Commander Lord Percy routed the Americans with cannon and musket fire, burning several houses to prevent militiamen from using them for cover.[16] They dispersed the Americans sufficiently at Concord to execute search-and-seizure operations.

The British had a map, prepared by one of their spies, showing suspected places where arms and stores were secreted, and they proceeded to search numerous farms and houses for the contraband. They discovered 500 pounds of musket balls and dumped them into the mill pond. Major Pitcairn seized and disabled a cannon, which Ephraim Jones, the town jailer and an innkeeper, had hidden; the major manhandled and threatened Jones and then ate breakfast at his inn, paying the tab. In other incidents, Concord's women persuaded soldiers not to search certain rooms of houses where supplies were hidden.[17] Most of the stores went undiscovered.[18]

According to an account by an officer of one of the British flank companies,[19] troops secured two bridges "to prevent the Rebels from interrupting the troops while they were destroying those Military Stores at Concord, which it was the object of the Expedition to effect . . . . The houses at Concord were now searched, and some pieces of Cannon, Carriage-wheels, Ammunition, & flour, found."[20] But when the Redcoats began their withdrawal back to Boston, the officer noted that the Americans ambushed them from houses and from behind walls and hedges. Some of the rebels would ride horses to get ahead of the troops, find a hiding spot, and take a shot—then repeat the maneuver to fire again. The officer conceded, "These fellows were generally good marksmen, and many of them used long guns made for Duck-Shooting."[21] This attested to the shooting skills of the colonists and indicated that private arms designed for hunting were in common use.[22]

Other accounts indicate that a number of militiamen carried arms that were designed for hunting or were obsolete. A man from Lynn bore a "long fowling piece, without a bayonet, a horn of powder, and a seal-skin pouch, filled with bullets and buckshot." "Here an old soldier carried a heavy Queen's arm . . . while by his side walked a stripling boy with a Spanish fussee not half its weight and calibre . . . while not a few had old French pieces . . . ."[23]

Some of the firearms used at Lexington and Concord are still extant, including Ezekiel Rice's fowling piece and Captain John Parker's musket.[24] Parker commanded the militiamen at Lexington. His musket, "an icon of American freedom," hangs today in the Massachusetts Senate Chamber.[25]

The hunting culture, as the above indicates, was responsible in part for some being in possession of arms and having the experience to use them effectively. Some also had experience in guerrilla warfare dating back to the French and Indian War. Describing the patriots' hit-and-run tactics, Lord Percy noted:

> They have men amongst them who know very well what they are about, having been employed as Rangers against the Indians & Canadians, & this country being much covered with woods, and hilly, is very advantageous for their method of fighting.

> Nor are several of their men void of a spirit of enthusiasm, as we experienced yesterday, for many of them concealed themselves in houses, & advanced within 10 yards to fire at me & other officers, tho' they were morally certain of being put to death themselves in an instant.[26]

In the account of Tory Peter Oliver, the conflict began when "the commanding Officer ordered the armed Rabble to disperse, upon which some of the armed Rabble returned an Answer from their loaded Muskets." After fighting the entire day, British troops had expended most of their ammunition and would have been captured had not reinforcements arrived with cannon. "The Cannon checked the Progress of the Rebels; who kept at a greater Distance, & chiefly fired from Houses, & from behind Hedges, Trees, and Stone Walls."[27] Oliver described the following extraordinary event:

> There was a remarkable Heroine, who stood at an House Door firing at the Kings Troops; there being Men within who loaded Guns for her to fire. She was desired to withdraw, but she answered, only by Insults from her own Mouth, & by Balls from the Mouths of her Muskets. This brought on her own Death, & the Deaths of those who were within Doors.[28]

Another contemporary verified that "even women had firelocks. One was seen to fire a blunderbuss between her father and husband from their windows."[29]

As the militiamen marched off, some women armed themselves with guns, axes, and pitchforks. Some patrolled the roads. Prudence Cummings Wright organized a women's guard and captured a Tory with incriminating papers.[30]

Boys on horseback resupplied the militia.[31] Militiamen on the way to Lexington and Concord stopped at a farm in Braintree, Massachusetts. To their amusement, 8-year-old John Quincy Adams, son of Abigail and John Adams, was executing the manual of arms with a musket taller than he was.[32]

British troops, according to a patriot account, "pillaged almost every house they passed by, breaking and destroying floors, windows, glasses, & c. and carrying off clothing and other valuable effects. . . . Not content with shooting down the unarmed, aged, and infirm, they disregarded the cries of the wounded, killing them without mercy . . . ."[33] In his diary, British Lieutenant John Barker admitted: "Our Soldiers . . . were so wild and irregular, that there was no keeping 'em in any order; by their eagerness and inattention they kill'd many of our own People; and the plundering was shameful; many hardly thought of anything else; what was worse they were encouraged by some Officers."[34]

Lieutenant Frederick MacKenzie recorded that, having been fired at from the houses along the roadside, and several of the soldiers having been killed, "the soldiers were so enraged at suffering from an unseen Enemy, that they forced open many of the houses from which the fire proceeded, and put to death all those found in them."[35] Aside from that, "Our men had very few opportunities of getting good shots at the Rebels, as they hardly ever fired but under cover of a Stone wall, from behind a tree, or out of a house; and the moment they had fired they lay down out of sight until they had loaded again, or the Column had passed."[36] MacKenzie verified that "Many houses were plundered by the Soldiers . . . . By all accounts some Soldiers who staid too long in the houses, were killed in the very act of plundering by those who lay concealed in them."[37]

The British ran low on ammunition as they retreated back to Boston. To resupply them, Gage sent two ammunition wagons with an officer and thirteen soldiers. However, a group of patriots who were too old for the formal militia, led by David Lamson, a "mulatto," attacked a body of Redcoats. The elderly men killed, wounded, or captured all the soldiers.[38]

At the end of the day, the Americans would be victorious. While most British soldiers made good their retreat back to Boston, they gained a grudging respect for those previously regarded as an armed rabble. A sympathetic if embellished account averred:

> The British officers and soldiers have done ample justice to the bravery and conduct of the Massachusetts Militia;—they say that no troops ever behaved with more resolution;—a soldier who had been in the action, being congratulated by a fellow solder on his safe return to Boston, declared, "That the Militia

had fought like bears, and that he would as soon attempt to storm hell, as to fight against them a second time.—We are likewise further informed that the two brigades, consisting of 1800 men . . . were attacked and routed by only 500 of the Militia."[39]

The patriots made good many shots at various distances. The Redcoats fired more rounds per hit than did the Americans.[40] Some 50 Americans were killed, 39 wounded, and 5 missing, for a total of 94 casualties. According to Gage, the Redcoats suffered 65 killed, 157 wounded, and 27 missing, for a total of 272 casualties.[41] The patriots exhibited excellent marksmanship for shooting flintlocks in anger, many for the first time in their lives. By comparison, U.S. forces in Vietnam expended 50,000 rounds to cause a single enemy casualty.[42]

General Gage, in a letter to Dartmouth, explained the expedition from beginning to end, and his account is worth quoting in full:

I am to acquaint your Lordship having received Intelligence of a large Quantity of Military Stores being collected at Concord, for the avowed Purpose of Supplying a Body of Troops to act in opposition to His Majesty's Government, I got the Grenadiers and Light Infantry out of Town under the Command of Lieut Col Smith of the 10th Regt and Major Pitcairne of the Marines with as much Secrecy as possible, on the 18th at Night and with the Orders to destroy the said Military Stores; and Supported them the next Morning by Eight Companys of the 4th the same Number of the 23d, 47th and Marines, under the Command of Lord Percy. It appears from the Firing of Alarm Guns and Ringing of Bells that the March Lieutenant Colonel Smith was discovered, and he was opposed by a Body of Men within Six Miles of Concord; Some few of whom first began to fire upon his advanced Companys which brought on a Fire from the Troops that dispersed the Body opposed to them; and they proceeded to Concord where they destroyed all the Military Store they could find, on the Return of the Troops they were attacked from all Quarters where any Cover was to be found, from whence it was practicable to annoy them, and they were so fatigued with their March that it was with Difficulty they could keep out their Flanking Partys to remove the Enemy to a Distance, so that they were at length a good deal pressed. Lord Percy then Arrived opportunely to their Assistance with his Brigade and two Pieces of a Cannon, and Notwithstanding a continual Skirmish for the Space of Fifteen Miles, receiving Fire from every

Hill, Fence, House, Barn, &ca. His Lordship kept the Enemy off, and brought the troops to Charles-Town, from whence they were ferryed over to Boston.[43]

The British attempt to disarm the militiamen and other inhabitants at Lexington and Concord could be regarded as a milestone in Second Amendment historiography. It undoubtedly helped inspire recognition of the right to keep and bear arms. Indeed, virtually every citizen was a militiaman who owned and kept his firearms at home, and the British sought to seize these private arms, as well as the stores of gunpowder and cannon held by the towns or controlled by committees of safety.

But what transpired *after* the day of the shot heard 'round the world was perhaps more significant in some respects. That event was General Gage's attempt to confiscate the arms of all the inhabitants of Boston. Disarming the militiamen in the countryside had a plausible purpose—the Crown was the "legitimate" government and the militiamen were engaged in rebellion. But to disarm every peaceable inhabitant of Boston without those inhabitants having committed any unlawful act or threatening any transgression was conclusive evidence to the colonists, including many not committed to fight for either side, that their fundamental rights as Englishmen were being destroyed.

Historians and Second Amendment scholars alike have all but ignored the disarming of the people of Boston. The following provides a detailed account of this episode and its perceived significance throughout the colonies.

Boston's citizens well anticipated that they would pay a price for Lexington and Concord. John Rowe noted in his diary on April 21: "This afternoon Several Gentlemen met with the Selectmen to Consult on Our Situation & chose a Committee to draft a Memorial to Gen Gage—vizt—The Selectmen, James Bowdoin, Henderson, Inches, Alex Hill, Edward Payne & Jos Barrett—they adjourn'd until tomorrow Ten of Clock."[44]

The next day, Rowe recorded the following entry: "The Same Company met & Reported upon which the Inhabitants were called together. After much Debate & some Amendments they Passed two Votes which were presented to the General by the same Committee & on delivery they asked the General to Grant their Prayer—he in some measure Complyed but made some other Proposalls."[45]

The official proceedings of the meeting with Gage reveal little, other than Gage's statement to Boston's selectmen that "there was a large body of men in arms" hostilely assembled and that the inhabitants could be injured if the soldiers attacked.[46] But Gage's fears included Boston's inhabitants, as suggested by historian Allen French: "knowing that many of the Boston householders had arms, he was afraid the town would rise at his back."[47]

Gage reported to Dartmouth that same day: "The whole Country was assembled in Arms with Surprizing Expedition, and Several Thousand are now Assembled about this Town threatning an Attack, and getting up Artillery. And we are very busy in making Preparations to oppose them."[48] Not the least of those preparations would be the disarming of the inhabitants of Boston.

Gage promised to the town committee at their meeting the next day, April 23, "that upon the inhabitants in general lodging their arms in Faneuil Hall, or any other convenient place, under the care of the selectmen, marked with the names of the respective owners, that all such inhabitants as are inclined, may depart from the town . . . . And that the arms aforesaid at a suitable time would be return'd to the owners."[49] This benign promise that the confiscated arms would be subject only to temporary safekeeping, if sincere, was utterly naive and must have been greeted with skepticism.

Yet many of the inhabitants yearned to flee Boston, given the flare up of hostilities, the military occupation, and the scarcity of provisions—Boston was then cut off from the countryside. Gage calculated that by offering release from being held essentially as hostages, the inhabitants would have the incentive to surrender their arms, which would supposedly be carefully secured for their owners.

The committee recommended "that the town accept of his excellency's proposal, and will lodge their arms with the Selectmen accordingly," the minutes relate.[50] "The town unanimously accepted of the foregoing report, and desired the inhabitants would deliver their arms to the Selectmen as soon as may be."[51]

John Rowe added more details about the events of April 23 in his diary: "The Inhabitants met again this morning & after some Debate they came into the Generall's Measures—which was to deliver up their Arms to be deposited in the hands of the Select Men & such of the Inhabitants as had a mind to leave the Town might go with their Effects."[52] Similarly, John Andrews wrote in a missive the next day: "Yesterday, though Sunday, we have town meetings all day, and finally concluded to deliver up all our Arms to the Selectmen, on condition that the Governor would open the avenues to the town, which is to be comply'd with tomorrow when if I can escape with the skin of my teeth, shall be glad, as I don't expect to be able to take more than a change of apparell with me . . . ."[53]

While the agreement called for the temporary safekeeping of the arms in the hands of the selectmen, Gage planned all along to have his soldiers seize them. British Lieutenant John Barker recorded in his diary on April 27, the day the arms were surrendered:

> The Townspeople have to day given up their Arms to the Select Men, who are to deliver them over to the Gen[era]l. I fancy this will quiet him a little for he seemed apprehensive that if the Lines shou'd be attack'd the Townspeople wou'd raise and assist; they wou'd not give up their Arms without the Gen[era]l promising that they shou'd have leave to quit the Town as many as pleased.[54]

The patriots outside Boston indeed considered the townspeople to be their comrades. One wrote from Roxbury the day after the arms surrender that Gage and his troops were trapped in Boston but lamented that "our friends are entrapped by them. We have some hopes they will be liberated this day. General Gage has proposed, upon their surrendering their arms, that they march out. They surrendered their arms yesterday."[55]

Gage promised the people of Boston, commented one writer, "that if the inhabitants of Boston would give up their arms and ammunition, and not assist against the King's troops, they should immediately be permitted to depart with all their effects, merchandise included; finally, the inhabitants gave up their arms and ammunition—to the care of the Selectmen: the General then set a guard over the arms . . . ." Having seized the arms, Gage refused to let the inhabitants and merchandise leave Boston.[56] In reaction, "the same day a town meeting was to be held in Boston, when the inhabitants were determined to demand the arms they had deposited in the hands of the select men, or have liberty to leave town."[57]

How many and what types of arms were confiscated? John Rowe wrote in his diary: "This day the Inhabitants carried in their Arms. The number 2674 . . . ."[58] According to Richard Frothingham, "the people delivered to the selectmen 1778 fire-arms, 634 pistols, 973 bayonets, and 38 blunderbusses."[59] The "fire-arms" were muskets (to which the bayonets attached) and other shoulder arms, with pistols being listed separately. "Blunderbusses" were short-barreled shotguns.

Frothingham's figures show a total of 2,450 firearms of all kinds seized, that is, one for every 5.6 inhabitants of the town population of 15,000.[60] Using a slightly different estimate of the number of people in Boston, historian Page Smith commented that these quantities of arms surrendered "were a very substantial armory for a city of some 16,000, many of whom were women and children. If we take into account those weapons that had already been taken out of the city by patriots, it is probably not far off the mark to say that every other male Bostonian over the age of eighteen possessed some type of firearm."[61] Even this estimate was probably low, because the above statistics reflect only the numbers of arms actually surrendered; it cannot be determined how many arms were hidden.

The recorded lists of names of persons who surrendered arms and the descriptions of the arms are not known to be extant.[62] Many inhabitants may have feigned compliance by turning in obsolete or inoperable arms while secreting their valuable weapons.

On the same day as the arms surrender, Bostonians were told at a town meeting that Gage would permit them to leave by land or sea and that they must apply to General Robertson for passes.[63] A sample of one of the passes reads: "Boston, May, 1775. Permit [name illegible], together with his family, consisting of seven persons, and their effects, to pass over the lines between sunrise and sunset. By order of his Excellency the Governor. No arms nor ammunition is allowed to pass nor merchandize."[64]

Procuring passes was difficult from the beginning. John Rowe noted in his diary on April 27: "The General has given Leave for All People to leave the Town that Choose with their Effects." But the very next day he wrote: "This day I apply'd to get a Pass to go out with my Effects but could not prevail."[65]

Americans were reminded of Gage's confiscation of arms some fourteen years later, when adoption of the Bill of Rights was pending. In 1789, Dr. David Ramsay published his *History of the American Revolution*. A prominent federalist, Ramsay wrote this work while he was a member of the Continental Congress in the 1780s.[66] He also served as a delegate to the South Carolina convention that ratified the federal Constitution in 1788. James Madison, who served with Ramsey in the Continental Congress, was aware of the book.[67] Ramsey's account of grievances leading to the Revolution was apropos, particularly in regard to what became the Second Amendment:

To prevent the people within Boston from co-operating with their countrymen without in case of an assault which was now daily expected, General Gage agreed with a committee of the town, that upon the inhabitants lodging their arms in Faneuil-hall or any other convenient place, under the care of the select-men, all such inhabitants as were inclined, might depart from the town, with their families and effects. In five days after the ratification of this agreement, the inhabitants had lodged 1778 fire arms, 634 pistols, 273 bayonets and 38 blunderbusses. The agreement was well observed in the beginning, but after a short time obstructions were thrown in the way of its final completion, on the plea that persons who went from Boston to bring in the goods of those who chose to continue within the town, were not properly treated. Congress remonstrated on the infraction of the agreement, but without effect.[68]

Frothingham had reported confiscation of 973 bayonets, while Ramsay put the figure at 273; otherwise the weapon types and quantities are the same. The original documents from which this information was taken are unknown. The referenced remonstrance of the Continental Congress was its Declaration of Causes of Taking Up Arms of July 6, 1775, which decried Gage's seizure of the arms that had been turned in to the selectmen under false pretenses and his reneging on his promise that the inhabitants could leave Boston.[69] The Declaration is discussed below.

Gage was not so gullible as to believe that the inhabitants turned in all of their arms and used such assumed failure to comply as an excuse to prevent the inhabitants from departing Boston. Ramsay noted:

The select-men gave repeated assurances that the inhabitants had delivered up their arms, but as a cover for violating the agreement, general Gage issued a proclamation, in which he asserted that he had full proof to the contrary. A few might have secreted some favourite arms, but nearly all the training arms were delivered up.[70]

The "training arms" were military muskets with bayonets used for militia exercises. These arms were quite large and would have been harder to hide than smaller shoulder arms and especially pistols.

All manner of alarm, rumor, and exaggeration abounded throughout the colonies. The following was printed in a Pennsylvania newspaper, datelined New York, quoting letters from Connecticut, about events in Boston:

We hear there are letters in this town, from Connecticut, which say that the number of men lately assembled at Boston, including those from Connecticut and Rhode-Island amounted to 600,000; that they are mostly returned to their respective homes, leaving an army of 15,00 [*sic*] to watch General Gage who we are told, has given the inhabitants of Boston permission to leave the town on condition they left their arms behind them. . . .

A letter from Boston, dated last Monday night, and received since writing the above paragraph says: "The communications between this town and country is entirely stopped up, and not a soul permitted to go in or out without a pass. This day, the Governor has disarmed all the inhabitants, after giving his word and honour that solders should not molest or plunder them . . . .[71]

Had 600,000 men really assembled in Boston, they would have constituted perhaps nearly half of the entire adult male citizen population of all the colonies!

The agreement that citizens could leave Boston after surrendering their firearms may have affected unrelated plans of the Provincial Congress to facilitate the exchange of British for American prisoners. Referring to previous communications on the prisoner exchange, the Congress wrote to Stephen Hopkins on April 27:

The above is a copy of an order and letter which passed this Congress yesterday, since which we have received from Boston copies of sundry votes of that town to general Gage, upon the subject of a licence [for the inhabitants] to remove, with their effects, into the country; and by his answers it appears that he has consented to suffer such inhabitants as have inclination therefor, to leave the place, with all their effects, excepting fire arms, which are to be delivered at Faneuil hall to the selectmen of the town, and the names of the owners to be placed on them; and the general expects, on the other hand, a proclamation from Congress, giving liberty to all inhabitants of the colony, having inclination therefore, to remove, with their effects, into Boston. Some of the inhabitants have already left the town, by permission of the general; and under these circumstances, should we issue the order which has passed in Congress, it may put a stop to this unexpected favorable event, and prevent the emancipation of many thousands of friends to America. We, nevertheless, purpose to detain the prisoners of war; and if the general should not forfeit his plighted faith, to use all expedition in getting out families and the effects of our friends from Boston, that we may be at liberty to use our prisoners, and every other means in our power, for the release of Mr. Brown, as was intended.

P.S.—We have just heard the passages from Boston are again stopped, but the occasion of this extraordinary manévre we cannot yet learn.[72]

On April 30, the Provincial Congress adopted a resolution proposed by the Committee of Safety that implemented the above plan to allow inhabitants of Boston—Whigs and their sympathizers—to leave the city while also allowing unarmed Tories to pass unmolested into Boston:

> Whereas, an agreement has been made between general Gage and the inhabitants of the city of Boston, for [the] removal of the persons and effects of such of the inhabitants of the town of Boston as may be so disposed, excepting their fire arms and ammunition, into the country:
>
> *Resolved*, That any of the inhabitants of this colony, who may incline to go into the town of Boston with their effects, fire arms and ammunition excepted, have toleration for that purpose; and that they be protected from any injury and insult whatsoever in their removal to Boston, and that this resolve be immediately published.
>
> P.S.-Officers are appointed for giving permits for the above purposes; one, at the sign of the Sun, at Charlestown; and another, at the house of Mr. John Greaton, Jun., at Roxbury.[73]

On that same date, the committee of Selectmen who had continued to meet with Gage reported to the town: "The committee waited on his Excellency General Gage with the papers containing the account of the arms delivered to the selectmen, and the return made to them by the constables of the town relative to the delivery of the arms in their respective wards."[74] Gage now had both lists of the firearms and their owners, as well as possession of the firearms.

Meanwhile, some Tories were fleeing to Boston and leaving their property behind. To accommodate them, the Provincial Congress on May 2 passed the following to allow the Loyalists to send out servants to retrieve their property outside of Boston:

> *Resolved*, That such inhabitants of this colony, as have repaired to the town of Boston, there to take up their residence, and have effects in the other towns of

this government, be permitted, each of them, to send out a servant, or other person, without arms, to put up and transport, into the said town of Boston, any such goods or effects, excepting arms and ammunition; and that the officers appointed for granting permits, at Roxbury and Charlestown, be, and hereby are, directed to provide a suitable attendant to each person so sent out, whose business it shall be to continue with him till he returns, and that permits . . . be granted.[75]

The Provincial Congress apparently hoped that by facilitating the removal of Tories to Boston, Gage would do the same for Bostonians wishing to depart. Gage probably saw little advantage to such a respite, as few Tories may have wished to move to a possible war zone with few provisions for civilians, while Bostonians who departed might join the patriotic cause.

Indeed, passes to leave issued by Gage quickly dried up. John Andrews wrote on May 6 that he and two others chartered a vessel to convey them to Halifax, "but the absolute refusal of the Governor to suffer any merchandize to be carried out of the town, has determin'd me to stay and take care of my effects . . . ." He continued: "Near half the inhabitants have left the town already, and another quarter, at least, have been waiting for a week past, with earnest expectation of getting papers, which have been dealt out very sparingly of late, not above two or three procur'd of a day, and those with the greatest difficulty." Even that statement was outdated before the ink was dry, as Andrews added the postscript that "no person who leaves the town is allow'd to return again, and this morning an order from the Governor has put a stop to any more papers at any rate, not even to admit those to go who have procur'd 'em already."[76]

The Provincial Congress sent the following angry but polite protest to Gage on May 10, complaining that the agreement between Gage and the selectmen that the inhabitants could leave Boston was not being followed:

We think it our duty to remonstrate to your excellency, that, from the papers communicated to us by the said selectmen, it appeared, that the inhabitants were promised, upon surrendering their arms, that they should be permitted to leave the town, and carry with them their effects. The condition was immediately complied with, on the part of the people; since which, though a number of days have elapsed, but a very small proportion of the inhabitants have been allowed to take the benefit of your covenant.

We would not affront your excellency by the most distant insinuation, that you intended to deceive and disarm the people, by a cruel act of perfidy. A regard to your own character, as well as the fatal consequences which will necessarily result from the violation of your solemn treaties, must [suggest] sufficient reasons, to deter a gentleman of your rank and station from so injurious a design. But your excellency must be sensible, that a delay of justice is a denial of it, and extremely oppressive to the people now held in duress.[77]

Gage saw the world quite differently. After all, he was governor of Massachusetts and commander of the British forces, which were besieged in Boston by armed rebels. He explained to Dartmouth in a May 13 letter:

Ever since the Skirmish of the 19th Ultimo the Avenues to this Town have been possessed by large Bodys of Men from all Places in this Province, Connecticut, New Hampshire &ca and they have collected Artillery and Military Stores that had been deposited in various parts of the Country. All Supplys from the Country have been stopped, and the Inhabitants of the Town desired to remove out with their Effects, which was consented to, but it was demanded that they should immediately deliver up their Arms; This was approved at first by all, for there would be fewer Mouths left to be fed, and the Danger from Enemies within removed. It has Since occasioned great Clamour amongst some People who say that none but the ill inclined will go out, and when they are Safe with their Effects, the Town will be set on Fire, and there is a Demurr about the Meaning of the Word Effects, Whether Mechandize is therein included.[78]

While even Gage discounted the paranoid Tory rumor that the rebels would be arsonists, the rebels did discuss decisive action. Since the men, women, and children of Boston were being held hostage, some patriots contemplated taking British officials hostage and then offering an exchange. Dr. Joseph Warren suggested decisive action by the Provincial Congress in a letter to Samuel Adams on May 14:

General Gage, I fear, has trepanned the inhabitants of Boston. He has persuaded them to lay down their arms, promising to let them remove with their effects; but he suffers them to come out but very slowly, contriving every day new excuses for delay. It appears to me, that a spirited remonstrance from your congress, and a recommendation forthwith to seize all crown officers on the continent, would be the most effectual method of liberating our friends in Boston.[79]

While no such scheme materialized, after several months food shortages at last forced the British to allow Bostonians to leave. Mercy Otis Warren, a literary figure who was the wife of Provincial Congress President James Warren (cousin of Joseph Warren), explained in her history of the Revolution:

> The insulted people of Boston, after performing the hard conditions of the contract, were not permitted to depart, until after several months of anxiety had elapsed, when the scarcity and badness of provisions had brought on a pestilential disorder, both among the inhabitants and the soldiers. Thus, from a reluctance to dip their feebler connexions were exposed, this unfortunate town, which contained near twenty thousand inhabitants, was betrayed into a disgraceful resignation of their arms, which the natural love of liberty should have inspired them to have held for their own defence, while subjected to the caprice of an arbitrary master. After their arms were delivered up and secured, general Gage denied the contract, and forbade their retreat; afterwards obliged to a partial compliance, by the difficulty of obtaining food for the subsistence of his own army. On certain stipulated gratuities to some of his officers, a permit was granted them, to leave their elegant houses, their furniture, and goods, and to depart naked from the capital, to seek an asylum and support from the hospitality of their friends in the country.[80]

A Bostonian lamented that numerous town meetings and conferences with Gage had resulted in the agreement that "the inhabitants should deliver up all their arms to the Selectmen" in exchange for being able to leave. The arms surrender "was generally done, though it took up some days." However, "the arms being delivered," Gage ordered that persons in compliance must "give in their names to the Selectmen, to be by them returned to the Military Town Major, who was then to write a pass for the person or family applying, to go through the lines, or over the ferry . . . ." At first only merchandise was forbidden, which was soon extended to all provisions and medicine. "Guards are appointed to examine all trunks, boxes, beds, and every thing else to be carried out; these have proceeded to such extremities, as to take from the poor people a single loaf of bread, and half pound of chocolate . . . ."[81]

Needless to say, Gage saw things differently. To the General, the Crown's lawful forces were surrounded by an armed, traitorous populace. In response to an enquiry from Connecticut Governor Jonathan Trumbull, Gage replied: "You ask why is the town of Boston now shut up? I can only refer you, for an answer, to those bodies of armed men, who now surround the town, and prevent all access to it. . . . I am surrounded by an armed country . . . ."[82]

None other than Benjamin Franklin verified Gage's description as the general condition of the colonies. Arriving at Philadelphia from London, Franklin "was highly pleased to find the Americans arming and preparing for the worst events, against which he thinks our spirited exertions will be the only means under God to secure us."[83]

Indeed, Pennsylvania patriots were typically admonished to "put your Militia into good order. . . . Arm yourselves and be ready at all times, for while I know, that it will prevent bloodshed;—but if you sit tamely and silent, you will not only be cut off, but despised by all good men."[84]

The Massachusetts Provincial Congress warned her sister colonies to do just that. On its behalf Josiah Warren wrote on May 26, 1775, to the Provincial Congress of New York, describing "the breach of a most solemn treaty with respect to the inhabitants of Boston when they had surrendered their arms and put themselves wholly in the power of a military commander," who then "suffered only to scatter from their prison a few in a day . . . ." Warren advised to avail "yourselves of every article which our enemies can improve with the least advantage to themselves for effecting the like desolation, horrors and insults on the inhabitants of your city and Colony, or which might enable you to make the most effectual defence." The alternatives were either to grab the weapons for yourselves, or allow your enemies to use them against you: "If you should delay securing them until they should be out of your power, and within a few days you should behold these very materials improved in murdering you, and yourselves perishing for the want of them, will not the chagrin and regret be intolerable."[85]

During this period, the colonists sought allies from any quarter, reaching out to friendly Native Americans. The address of Massachusetts to the Mohawk and other eastern tribes drafted by Samuel Adams and dated May 15, 1775, used simplified language in perhaps one of the most concise and forceful renditions of the American cause:

> brothers: the great, wickedness of such as should be our friends, but are our enemies, we mean the ministry of Great Britain, has laid deep plots to take away our liberty and your liberty, they want to get all our money; make us pay it to them, when they never earned it; to make you and us their servants; and let us

have nothing to eat, drink, or wear, but what they say we shall; and prevent us from having guns and powder to use, and kill our deer, and wolves, and other game, or to send to you, for you to kill your game with, and to get skins and fur to trade with us for what you want: but we hope soon to be able to supply you with both guns and powder, of our own making.[86]

The ministry's aim to "prevent us from having guns," whether through such actions as the import ban or direct seizure, had the purpose of allowing the British to deprive the colonists of their liberty and property. But it had a further pernicious effect, which the Mohawk would have understood better than the urban white man—depriving the people of guns interfered with subsistence hunting. As General Gage had noted years before, Native Americans "are disused to the Bow, and can neither hunt nor make war, without Fire-Arms, Powder and Lead."[87] For many rural whites, too, firearms were used to put food on the table. Adams' above message made clear that the colonists saw hunting as a significant purpose of the right to keep and bear arms.

In times of repression, when anyone who possesses arms is suspect, those in power use the arms scare to suppress their political enemies. While Gage had imposed no prior restraints on the press, Admiral Samuel Graves of the Royal navy sent sailors to arrest John Gill and Peter Edes of the *Boston Gazette*, the leading patriot newspaper, on bogus charges of having firearms. Edes escaped and published the *Gazette* in Watertown.[88]

Gage received a letter from Dartmouth on May 25 from the hands of General Howe, who with Generals Clinton and Burgoyne had just arrived in Boston with fresh troops from England, "to prevent the Abettors of Rebellion in their dangerous designs of leading forth the People, in the four New England Governments, to oppose in Arms the Restoration of the Public Tranquility & Constitutional Authority of Government." In addition to securing all forts that the rebels might attack, Dartmouth ordered:

That all Cannon, Small Arms, and other military Stores of every kind that may be either in any public Magazine, or secretly collected together for the purpose of aiding Rebellions, should also be seized and secured, and that the persons of all such as, according to the Opinions of His Majesty's Attorney and Solicitor General, have committed themselves in Acts of Treason & Rebellion, should be arrested & imprisoned.[89]

This was an order to seize both public and private arms to prevent use thereof by the rebels, who must also be apprehended. Gage knew this to be easier said than done. On June 12, he wrote to Dartmouth: "The Skirmish that happened on the 19th of April, has shewn the general Disposition of the Provinces in a Manner not to be mistaken. All have armed, and tho' there are people no doubt in all, who disapprove of Violent Measures, and some who would join Government had they Opportunitys, they are now borne down by Force and Numbers."[90]

Based on that candid assessment, Gage could not have been too optimistic about compliance with his proclamation that same day of martial law and his offer of a pardon to all who would lay down their arms except Samuel Adams and John Hancock.[91] The decree, suggested in Dartmouth's above directive, was drafted by General Burgoyne.[92] The proclamation described the events at Lexington and Concord as an ambush in which thousands "of armed persons, . . . from behind walls and lurking holes, attacked a detachment of the king's troops, who . . . made use of their arms only in their own defence."[93] It continued:

> I avail myself of the last effort within the bounds of my duty to spare the effusion of blood, to offer, and I do hereby, in his majesty's name, offer and promise his most gracious pardon to all persons who shall forthwith lay down their arms, and return to the duties of peaceable subjects: excepting only from the benefit of such pardon, Samuel Adams and John Hancock, who offences are of too flagitious a nature to admit of any other consideration than that of condign punishment.
>
> And, to the end, that no person within the limits of this proffered mercy, may plead ignorance of the consequence of refusing it, I, by these presents, proclaim, not only the persons above named and excepted, but also all their adherents, associates and abettors; meaning to comprehend in these terms, all and every person, and persons, of what class, denomination, or description soever, who have appeared in arms against the king's government, and shall not lay down the same as before mentioned; and likewise all such as shall so take arms after the date hereof, or shall, in any wise, protect or conceal such offenders, or assist them with money, provision, cattle, arms, ammunition, carriages, or any other necessary for subsistence, or offence; or shall hold secret correspondence with them, by letter, message, signal, or otherwise; to be rebels and traitors, and as such to be treated.[94]

An angry patriot shot back, "are you not ashamed to throw out such an insult upon human understanding, as to bid people disarm themselves till you and your butchers murder and plunder them at pleasure! We well know you have orders to disarm us, and what the disposition of the framers of these orders is, if we may judge from the past, can be no secret."[95] An American in a more humorous mood offered a widely published poem entitled "Tom Gage's Proclamation," which told how the general had sent an expedition "the men of *Concord* to disarm" and how he afterwards reflected:

Yet e'er I draw the vengeful sword
I have thought fit to send abroad
This present gracious Proclamation,
Of purpose mild the demonstration;
That whosoe'er keeps gun or pistol,
I'll spoil the motion of his systole;
Or, whip his breech, or cut his weason
As has the measure of his Treason:—
But every one that will lay down
His hanger bright, and musket brown,
Shall not be beat, nor bruis'd, nor bang'd,
Much less for past offences, hang'd,
But on surrendering his toledo,
Go to and fro unhurt as we do:—
But then I must, out of this plan, lock
Both SAMUEL ADAMS and JOHN HANCOCK;
For those vile traitors (like debentures)
Must be tuck'd up at all adventures;
As any proffer of a pardon,
Would only tend those rogues to harden:—
But every other mother's son,
The instant he destroys his gun,
(For thus doth run the King's command)
May, if he will, come kiss my hand. . . .
Meanwhile let all, and every one
Who loves his life, forsake his gun. . . .[96]

The references to several types of arms in the above poem, as well as those turned in to selectmen in Boston, warrant explanation. What types of arms did the colonists believe they had a right to keep and bear?

The arms the people of Boston surrendered to their selectmen, as discussed above, included "firearms" (muskets and other shoulder weapons), pistols, blunderbusses, and bayonets.[97] The above poem mentions "gun or pistol" separately, for as stated in America's first dictionary: "the smaller species [of guns] are called muskets, carbines, fowling pieces, &c. But one species of fire-arm, the pistol, is never called a gun."[98] The poem also refers to a "musket brown," meaning a Brown Bess musket, which was used with a bayonet. This musket was the official British infantry weapon, a number of which Americans bought, captured, or otherwise obtained from Redcoats.[99] The colonists imported other military muskets from France and made highly accurate, long-range Pennsylvania rifles (owned mostly by civilians) locally.[100]

The carbine is a short-barreled shoulder weapon designed to fire a single projectile. The blunderbuss is a short-barreled shotgun designed to fire multiple projectiles and was popular with civilians for defense against highwaymen or intruders attacking a house.[101] Civilians in urban areas and travelers commonly carried pocket pistols, and larger pistols were widely used for military purposes.[102]

The poem mentions two types of swords: the hanger (a short military sword) and the Toledo, named after its place of production in Spain.[103] The small sword was the popular civilian design in America.[104]

Such was the array of firearms and edged weapons that the colonists owned and believed they were entitled to keep and bear.[105] Seizure of these arms from the peaceable citizens of Boston who were not even involved in hostilities sent a message to all of the colonies that fundamental rights were in grave danger.

The colonists' skills in hunting and target shooting combined with their militia experience to create good marksmen. David Ramsay's 1789 history of the American Revolution avers: "All their military regulations were carried on by their militia, and under the old established laws of the land. For the defence of the colonies, the inhabitants had been, from their early years, enrolled in companies, and taught the use of arms."[106] He added: "Europeans, from their being generally unacquainted with fire arms are less easily taught the use of them than Americans, who are from their youth familiar with these instruments of war . . . ." Of the battle of Bunker Hill, which took place on June 17, 1775, Ramsay wrote:

> None of the provincials in this engagement were riflemen, but they were all good marksmen. The whole of their previous military knowledge had been derived from hunting, and the ordinary amusements of sportsmen. The dexterity which by long habit they had acquired in hitting beasts, birds, and marks, was fatally applied to the destruction of British officers.[107]

The day after Bunker Hill, John Hancock wrote to Joseph Warren—not knowing that he had been killed in the battle—that the Continental Congress had ordered ten companies of riflemen from Pennsylvania, Maryland, and Virginia to join the army near Boston. "These are the finest Marksmen in the world. They do Execution with their Rifle Guns at an Amazing Distance."[108] Similarly, John Adams wrote to James Warren: "They are the most accurate Marksmen in the World; they kill with great Exactness at 200 yards Distance; they have Sworn certain death to the ministerial officers."[109]

"Courage I know we have in abundance, conduct I hope we shall not want, but powder—where shall we get a sufficient supply?" asked Abigail Adams in a letter to her husband John.[110] Due to the shortage of gunpowder, the Revolutionary leaders encouraged the colonists to confine their target shooting to human targets in red coats. While the New England militia previously engaged in regular target practice,[111] Ramsey noted: "The public rulers in Massachusetts issued a recommendation to the inhabitants, not to fire a gun at beast, bird or mark, in order that they might husband their little stock for the more necessary purpose of shooting men."[112]

In a letter to Dartmouth, Gage paid tribute to American marksmanship and martial discipline at Bunker Hill as follows:

> The Number of the killed and wounded is greater than our Force can afford to lose, the Officers who were obliged to exert themselves have suffered very much, and we have lost some extraordinary good Officers. The Tryals we have had shew that the Rebels are not the despicable Rabble too many have supposed them to be, and I find it owing to a Military Spirit encouraged amongst them for a few years past, joined with an uncommon Degree of Zeal and Enthousiasm that they are otherwise. Wherever they find Cover they make a good Stand, and the Country, Naturaly Strong, affords it them, and they are taught to assisst it's Natural Strength by Art, for they entrench and raise Batterys.

Your Lordship will perceive that the Conquest of this Country is not easy and can be effected only by Time and Perseverance, and Strong Armys attacking it in various Quarters; and dividing their Forces. Confining Your Operations on this Side only is attacking in the strongest part, and you have to cope with vast Numbers.[113]

Evidently, a certain American tradition of civil disobedience to firearms prohibitions was well entrenched in 1775. As noted above, General Gage issued a proclamation on June 19, 1775, two days after Bunker Hill, charging:

Whereas notwithstanding the repeated assurances of the selectmen and others, that all the inhabitants of the town of Boston had *bona fide* delivered their fire arms unto the persons appointed to receive them, though I had advices at the same time of the contrary, and whereas I have since had full proof that many had been perfidious in this respect, and have secreted great numbers: I have thought fit to issue this proclamation, to require of all persons who have yet fire arms in their possession immediately to surrender them at the court house, to such persons as shall be authorised to receive them; and hereby declare that all persons in whose possession any fire arms may hereafter be found, will be deemed enemies to his majesty's government.[114]

This was yet another proclamation declaring firearm owners to be "enemies to his majesty's government." Of course, Gage's allegations that arms were being clandestinely retained were true. The surrender of arms voluntarily would have been considered highly unpatriotic, not to mention indiscreet for a person wishing only to be armed for self-protection. Gage's new decree illustrated the futility of issuing a second proclamation requiring that firearms be surrendered when the first proclamation did not work.

The patriots continued to brag about how well they could shoot British soldiers and did not meekly whisper how they should surrender their firearms. On the same day Gage issued his latest proclamation, James Madison wrote to William Bradford an encouraging note about Virginia's sharpshooters:

The strength of this Colony will lie chiefly in the rifle-men of the Upland Counties, of whom we shall have great numbers. You would be astonished at the perfection this art is brought to. The most inexpert hands rec[k]on it an indifferent shot to miss the bigness of a man's face at the distance of 100 Yards.

I am far from being among the best & should not often miss it on a fair trial at that distance. If we come into an engagement, I make no doubt but the officers of the enemy will fall at the distance before they get within 150 or 200 Yards. Indeed I believe we have men that would very often hit such a mark 250 Yds. Our greatest apprehensions proceed from the scarcity of powder but a little will go a great way with such as use rifles.[115]

That last remark of Madison reflected that the highly accurate rifles had a smaller bore and used less powder than the less accurate smooth-bore muskets of the day.

There were so many volunteers eager to join a rifle company in Virginia's back country that the commander held a shooting match to determine who were the best shots. A witness described the scene:

He took a board of a foot square and with chalk drew the shape of a moderate nose in the center and nailed it up to a tree at one hundred and fifty yards distance, and those who came nighest the mark with a single ball was to go. But by the first forty or fifty that fired, the nose was all blown out of the board, and by the time his company was up, the board shared the same fate.[116]

"General Gage, take care of *your* nose," joked the *Virginia Gazette* about this episode.[117]

Tales of the American riflemen found their way across the Atlantic. A Philadelphian wrote to a gentleman in London that the Americans were "determined to submit to no infringement on their constitutional rights" and so "have taken arms to oppose the despotick system of an infamous Administration."[118] The Continental Congress ordered the raising of "one thousand more marksmen, or, as we call them, Riflemen," who were to be "divided in small parties, and scattered through the Army, for the purpose of removing the officers." A party of them had recently "placed their balls in poles of seven inches diameter, fixed up for the purpose, at the distance of two hundred and fifty yards." Even the Quakers had "taken arms."[119]

Echoing similar sentiments, a London newspaper reported: "This province [Pennsylvania] has raised 100 rifle-men, the worst of whom will put a ball into a man's head at a distance of 150 or 200 yards, therefore advise your officers who shall hereafter come out to America, to settle their affairs in England before their departure."[120]

The Continental Congress itself adopted a petition to the king on July 8, 1775, averring that "your Ministers (equal Foes to British and American freedom) have added to their former Oppressions an Attempt to reduce us by the Sword to a base and abject submission," with the following consequences:

> On the Sword, therefore, we are compelled to rely for Protection. Should Victory declare in your Favour, yet Men trained to Arms from their Infancy, and animated by the Love of Liberty, will afford neither a cheap or easy Conquest. Of this at least we are assured, that our Struggle will be glorious, our Success certain; since even in Death we shall find that Freedom which in Life you forbid us to enjoy.[121]

Despite all of the above talk about Americans shooting General Gage's nose in target form and British officers in human form, the ordinary Bostonians whose arms Gage would seize had expressed no rebellious sentiments. Attacking "the perfidious, the truce-breaking Thomas Gage," an anonymous patriot harped back on the disarming of the inhabitants of Boston, seething:

> But the single breach of the capitulation with them, after they had religiously fulfilled their part, must brand your name and memory with eternal infamy— the proposal came from you to the inhabitants by the medium of one of your officers, through the Selectmen, and was, *that if the inhabitants would deposit their fire-arms in the hands of the Selectmen, to be returned to them after a reasonable time, you would give leave to the inhabitants to remove out of town with all their effects, without any lett or molestation.* The town punctually complied, and you remain an infamous monument of perfidy, for which an Arab, a Wild Tartar or Savage would dispise [*sic*] you!!![122]

The Continental Congress would adopt very similar, albeit less rustic, language in the Declaration of Causes of Taking Up Arms of July 6, 1775,[123] which made clear that Gage's disarming of the inhabitants was a justification for armed resistance. Drafted by Thomas Jefferson and John Dickinson, the Declaration protested in part about Gage's seizure of the firearms of Boston's inhabitants:

> The inhabitants of Boston being confined within that town by the General their Governor, and having, in order to procure their dismission, entered into a treaty with him, it was stipulated that the said inhabitants having depos-

ited their arms with their own magistrates, should have liberty to depart, taking with them their other effects. They accordingly delivered up their arms, but in open violation of honor, in defiance of the obligation of treaties, which even savage nations esteem sacred, the Governor ordered the arms deposited as aforesaid, that they might be preserved for their owners, to be seized by a body of soldiers; detained the greatest part of the inhabitants in the town, and compelled the few who were permitted to retire, to leave their most valuable effects behind.[124]

The language in the above that "the Governor ordered the arms deposited as aforesaid, that they might be preserved for their owners, to be seized by a body of soldiers," appeared in John Dickinson's draft of the Declaration.[125] Jefferson's earlier drafts stated that "their arms, deposited with their own magistrates to be preserved as their property, were immediately seized by a body of armed men under orders from the said General . . . ."[126] Under both versions, it is clear that the arms being seized were the individual private property of the owners.

Gage informed Dartmouth about the Declaration, "Copys of which will no doubt be sent to England from Philadelphia. They pay little Regard to Facts, for the Contents of it is as replete with Deceit and Falsehood as most of their Publications."[127] Although the Declaration had accused Gage of a number of horrible acts, its claims about his treatment of the inhabitants of Boston insulted him the most, for it was the only specific allegation he mentioned to Dartmouth:

> Nor has the Continental Congress scrupled to publish to the World the most Notorious Falsehoods; amongst others that I had broke My Faith in not suffering the Inhabitants of Boston to depart the Town, that I had ordered a Detachment of Troops to seize their Arms when delivered up, contrary to Agreement, and that I had even Seized the Donations of the poor. These Assertions forged to delude and deceive on both sides the Atlantick can only Serve the Purpose of a Day, of their Forgery. I am to hope from the Affection I bear my Country that no Man in Great-Britain or Ireland will be longer deceived by false Professions and Declarations; but see through all the Disguise, that this is no sudden Insurrection of America, but a preconcerted Scheme of Rebellion, hatched years ago in the Massachusetts Bay, and brought to this perfection by the help of Adherents on both Sides the Atlantick.[128]

The Continental Congress adopted an address "To the People of Ireland" on July 28, 1775, which complained in part that "the citizens petitioned the General for permission to leave the town, and he promised, on surrendering their arms, to permit them to depart with their other effects; they accordingly surrender their arms, and the General violated his faith . . . ."[129]

Individual patriots were making their case internationally. John Zubly's pamphlet *Great Britain's Right to Tax . . . By a Swiss*, published in London and Philadelphia, indicted Gage for "detaining the inhabitants of Boston, after they had, in dependence on the General's word of honour, given up their arms, to be starved and ruined . . . ."[130] Zubly, a member of the Continental Congress from Georgia, noted that "in a strong sense of liberty, and the use of fire-arms almost from the cradle, the Americans have vastly the advantage over men of their rank almost every where else." In fact, "every child unborn will be impressed with the notion: It is slavery to be bound at the will of another in all cases whatsoever," and children were "shouldering the resemblance of a gun before they are well able to walk."[131] "The Americans will fight like men, who have everything at stake," and their motto was "DEATH OR FREEDOM."[132]

The colonists believed that Boston was only the first step and that the ministry's intention was generally to disarm the Americans. Even before the above two declarations were adopted by the Continental Congress, patriot newspapers throughout the colonies had begun to publish the following intelligence from London: "It is reported, that on the landing of the General Officers, who have sailed for America, a proclamation will be published throughout the provinces inviting the Americans to deliver up their arms by a certain stipulated day; and that such of the colonists as are afterwards proved to carry arms shall be deemed rebels, and be punished accordingly."[133] Such reports could have only prompted more colonists to take up arms and join the resistance.

Patriots throughout the colonies were inflamed by the facts and rumors being reported as taking place in Massachusetts. But the basic political value judgment that the individual should be armed for defense went unquestioned, even if it meant private seizure of the public arms. A letter from New York City dated April 24 noted:

> The city was alarmed yesterday by a report from the eastward, that the King's troops had attacked the Massachusetts Bay people . . . . Towards evening they [the people] went and secured about half the city arms, a guard of 100 men

I am told was to be placed at the city hall to secure the rest of the arms, and another hundred at the powder house, this was not done by the magistrates, but by the people . . . .

Tuesday last [April 18], . . . pursuant to public notice, there was a meeting of near eight thousand of the inhabitants of the city, to consider of the measures to be pursued in the present situation of America. The business was opened with several eloquent and patriotic speeches, and the company unanimously agreed to associate, for the purpose of defending with Arms, their Property, Liberty, and Lives against all attempts to deprive them of them.[134]

But the British had other ideas. Due to its geographic location, suggested a patriot, New York "is to be a place of arms, and provisions are to be provided there for supplies of the [British] army in New England."[135] To prevent such incursion, as reported elsewhere, "the inhabitants there are arming themselves, have shut up the port, and got the keys of the Custom-House."[136] It was claimed that "the whole city and province are subscribing an association, forming companies, and taking every method to defend our rights. The like spirit prevails in the province of New Jersey, where a large and well disciplined militia are now fit for action." The New York General Committee resolved "that it be Recommended to every Inhabitant, to perfect himself in Military Discipline, and be provided with Arms, Accoutrements, and Ammunition, as by Law directed."[137] Similarly, the freeholders and inhabitants of Morris County, New Jersey, recommended "to the inhabitants of this country, capable of bearing arms, to provide themselves with arms and ammunition, to defend their country in case of any invasion."[138]

On May 10, Ethan Allen led his fellow Vermonters to capture Fort Ticonderoga. Ira Allen, his brother, described this feat of armed citizens as follows:

Thus, in a few days, at the commencement of hostilities between the British and the Americans, two hundred undisciplined men, with small arms, without a single bayonet, made themselves masters of the garrisons of Ticonderoga, Crown Point, and St. Johns . . . to the honour of the *Green Mountain Boys*. It is to be remembered, that this was the first offensive part taken against Great Britain in the American revolution.[139]

Trouble was brewing in both the northern and southern colonies. Gage informed Dartmouth: "This Province [Massachusetts,] Connecticut, and

Rhode Island are in open Rebellion and I expect the same Accounts of New-Hampshire. They are arming at New-York and as we are told, in Philadelphia, and all the Southern Provinces . . . ."[140]

On the night of April 21, 1775, Royal authorities secretly removed twenty barrels of gunpowder from the public magazine at Williamsburg, Virginia. They also stripped the public arms of their locks, making the guns unusable. The Virginia House of Burgesses complained to Governor Dunmore, who was also the military commander in chief, declaring:

> The inhabitants of this country, my Lord, could not be strangers to the many attempts in the northern colonies to disarm the people, and thereby deprive them of the only means of defending their lives and property. We know, from good authority, that the like measures were generally recommended by the Ministry, and that the export of pow[d]er from Great Britain had been prohibited. Judge then how very alarming a removal of the small stock which remained in the public magazine, for the defence of the country, and the stripping of the guns of their locks, must have been to any people, who had the smallest regard for their security.[141]

Similarly, the mayor and other civil authorities—all "his majesty's dutiful and loyal subjects"—protested to Governor Dunmore that "the inhabitants of this city were this morning exceedingly alarmed by a report that a large quantity of gun powder was in the preceding night, while they were sleeping in their beds, removed from the public magazine, in this city, and conveyed under an effort of marines, on board one of his majesty's armed vessels, lying off a ferry on James River." They asserted that "this magazine was erected at the public expense of this colony, and appreciated to the safe keeping of such ammunition as should be there lodged from time to time, for the protection and security of the country, by arming thereout such of the militia as might be necessary in cases of invasions and insurrections . . . ." They demanded that the powder be returned.[142]

But Dunmore was well aware of the recent events in Massachusetts Bay and Virginia itself and had taken preemptive action. He responded orally to the above:

> That, hearing of an insurrection in a neighbouring county, he had removed the powder from the magazine, where he did not think it secure, to a place of per-

fect security; and that, upon his word and honour, whenever it was wanted on any insurrection, it should be delivered in half an hour; that he had removed it in the night time to prevent any alarm . . .; he was surprised to hear the people were under arms on this occasion, and that he should not think it prudent to put powder into their hands in such a situation.[143]

Yet the governor could not muster the regular Williamsburg militia against the Hanover Independent Militia Company led by Patrick Henry, who, although unable to recapture the powder, had forced restitution for it.[144] Lord Dunmore complained that Henry and his followers "have taken up arms and styling themselves an Independent Company, have . . . put themselves in a posture for war."[145] The governor soon saw it necessary to generalize this complaint in a letter to the British colonial minister: "Every County is now Arming a Company of men whom they call an independent Company for the avowed purpose of protecting their Committee, and to be employed against Government if occasion require."[146]

Before long, Henry and his militia struck back in Williamsburg. "Some people privately entered the public magazine in this city and took a great number of guns, cartouch boxes, swords, canteens, &c. for which his Excellency the Governor has ordered a diligent search to be made."[147]

Further south, North Carolina's Colonial Governor Martin proclaimed against those "endeavouring to engage the People to subscribe papers obliging themselves to be prepared with Arms, to array themselves in companies, and to submit to the illegal and usurped authorities of Committees."[148] "The Inhabitants of this County on the Sea Coast," he wrote on May 18, "are . . . arming men, electing officers and so forth. In this little town [Newburn] they are now actually endeavouring to form what they call independent Companies under my nose."[149]

In a widely published message to the committees of safety, Richard Caswell, William Hooper, and Joseph Hewes, North Carolina's members of the Continental Congress, stated:

> It is the Right of every English Subject to be prepared with Weapons for his Defense. We conjure you . . . to form yourselves into a Militia . . . .
>
> Carefully preserve the small quantity of Gunpowder which you have amongst you, it will be the last Resource when every other Means of Safety fails you;

Great-Britain has cut you off from further supplies . . . . We cannot conclude without urging again to you the necessity of arming and instructing yourselves, to be in Readiness to defend yourselves against any Violence that may be exerted against your Persons and Properties.[150]

Incidentally, the same issue of the *North Carolina Gazette* that published the above also reported an incident in which "a Demoniac being left in a Room, in which were 18 loaded Muskets," shot three men and wounded another with a sword, "upon which the People present, without further Ceremony, shot him dead."[151] For the Founders, the right of the subject to be armed for defense of self and the community was necessary to suppress such tragedies—they never imagined a world in which they would be disarmed for the supposed benefit of preventing access to weapons by madmen.

Governor Martin issued a "Fiery Proclamation" deploring the above message by Hooper, Hewes, and Caswell, "the preposterous enormity of which cannot be adequately described and abhor'd . . . [I]t proceeds upon these false and infamous assertions and forgeries to excite the people of North Carolina to usurp the prerogative of the Crown by forming a Militia and appointing officers thereto and finally to take up arms against the King and His Government."[152] Governor Martin warned that all "persons who hath or have presumed to array the Militia and to assemble men in Arms within this Province without my Commission or Authority have invaded His Majesty's just and Royal Prerogative and violated the Laws of their Country to which they will be answerable for the same."[153]

The governor's threats failed to deter the North Carolinians. Beginning with their personal right to have weapons for defense, they asserted a right to associate in militia companies independent of the government and to use those arms against despotism. A typical committee of safety resolution of the time referred to "the painful necessity of having recourse to Arms for the preservation of those rights and Liberties which the principles of our Constitution and the Laws of God, Nature, and Nations have made it our duty to defend."[154] This reference to "our Constitution" meant the colonial charter that protected all of the rights of Englishmen.

On November 9, Joseph Hewes wrote from Philadelphia that arms and ammunition "are very scarce throughout all the Colonies, I find on enquiry that neither can be got here, all the Gunsmiths in the Province are engaged and cannot make Arms near so fast as they are wanted."[155] He reported that "I have furnished myself with a good musket and Bayonet."[156] Yet arms remained scarce, due to the British embargo. "Americans ought to become industrious in making those articles at home, every Family should make saltpetre, every Province have powder Mills and every colony encourage the making of Arms."[157]

The pattern was the same elsewhere. The Address and Declaration of the Provincial Congress of South Carolina implored, "solely for the Preservation and in Defence of our Lives, Liberties, and Properties we have been impelled to associate, and to take up Arms . . . Our taking up Arms is the Result of dire Necessity, and in compliance with the first Law of Nature."[158]

The epoch was expressed perhaps best in a letter from a Virginia gentleman to a friend in Scotland dated September 1 as follows:

> We are all in arms, exercising and training old and young to the use of the gun. No person goes abroad without his sword, or gun, or pistols. . . . Every plain is full of armed men, who all wear a hunting shirt, on the left breast of which are sewed, in very legible letters, *Liberty or Death.*"[159]

By the end of 1775, the British were destroying whole towns for refusing to surrender their arms. Admiral Graves ordered the burning of all seaports north of Boston.[160] In Falmouth (now Portland), Maine, a town committee went on board a British man-o-war to try to save the town. "Captain [Henry] Mowat informed the Committee at Falmouth, there had arrived orders from England about ten days since, to burn all the sea port towns on the continent, that would not lay down and deliver up their arms, and give hostages for their future good behaviour . . . ." They promised to spare the town if "we would send off four carriage guns, deliver up our small arms, ammunition, & c. and send four gentleman of the town as hostages, which the town could not do." So the British ship fired on Falmouth all day and destroyed it. General George Washington personally requested newspapers to publish this information so that the colonists could see the lengths to which the British were willing to go.[161]

Further details of the above incident were set forth in a letter dated October 21, 1775, concerning the plight of towns along the Massachusetts coast as follows:

An express came to general Washington, yesterday from Portsmouth, with advice that a naval force from Boston appeared off Falmouth, Casco Bay, and
demanded of the inhabitants the surrender of their arms and hostages for their
future good behaviour. He offered, upon this delivering up part of their arms
the same evening, to allow them to the next day to consider of the demands.
They accordingly delivered him eight muskets. The next day a very heavy firing
was heard upon Falmouth. The commander of the fleet showed his orders to
the committee, which were to destroy the town, and Portsmouth, in case they
should refuse to comply with the demand. To me it appears highly probably
that Newport and the other sea-port towns, may soon expect a similar treatment.[162]

These experiences demonstrate how the encroachments of the Crown on
the liberties of the subjects would later influence adoption of the Bill of Rights,
particularly the Second Amendment. The mere possibility in 1768 that the
Crown's authorities would seize arms gave rise to a robust philosophical defense of what was considered a fundamental right. When in 1774 the rulers of
Boston dared even to consider disarming the inhabitants, thousands of armed
citizens felt justified in assembling and marching into town to demonstrate
their opposition. The Founders considered a ban on importation of firearms
and ammunition to violate the right to obtain and possess arms. Imposition
of martial law only exasperated the belief that they must keep and bear arms
for parity against an oppressive standing army.

The patriots' aversion to the governmental policy of searching persons,
places, and houses and seizing firearms demonstrates the close connection
between the Second Amendment right to keep arms and the Fourth Amendment prohibition on warrantless searches and seizures. Gage's trickery in in-
ducing the inhabitants to turn in their arms for "temporary safekeeping" and
then in seizing those arms, never to be returned, gave rise to the traditional
American skepticism toward benevolent rulers who promise only limited infringements on their rights.

The dogs of war were now unleashed. For the Crown, this was an imperial war to be waged by a standing army and mercenaries against a colonial
populace. But for the Americans, this was a revolutionary war of the armed
people for independence.

# Of Revolution and Rights

## CHAPTER 5

# "Times That Try Men's Souls"

W E HOLD THESE TRUTHS to be self-evident, that all men are created equal, that they are endowed by their Creator with certain unalienable rights, that among these are life, liberty and the pursuit of happiness." These immortal words of the Declaration of Independence, written by Thomas Jefferson and signed by the members of the Continental Congress on July 4, 1776, expressed a political philosophy based on the right of the people to assert and reclaim their own sovereignty over an oppressive government.[1] As the Declaration proceeds to aver:

> That to secure these rights, governments are instituted among men, deriving their just powers from the consent of the governed. That whenever any form of government becomes destructive to these ends, it is the right of the people to alter or to abolish it, and to institute new government, laying its foundation on such principles and organizing its powers in such form, as to them shall seem most likely to effect their safety and happiness.

To be sure, governments should not be changed "for light and transient causes," and the people "are more disposed to suffer, while evils are sufferable," than to abolish the government. "But when a long train of abuses and usurpations, pursuing invariably the same object evinces a design to reduce them under absolute despotism, it is their right, it is their duty, to throw off such government, and to provide new guards for their future security." Inherent in this philosophy is the right of the people to keep and bear arms in order that they may do just that. Indeed, ideally the mere existence of this right provides the kind of balance in a polity that precludes the development of despotism and thus the need "to throw off such government."

Noting that the colonists had patiently suffered, the Declaration proclaimed: "The history of the present King of Great Britain is a history of repeated injuries and usurpations, all having in direct object the establishment of an absolute tyranny over these states." A list of grievances, some very general and others narrow, follow. Several charges relate to the violation of the right of representation in legislative bodies, interference with beneficial lawmaking, and causing judges to be dependent on the king's will alone. The Crown had sent both bureaucrats and soldiers to oppress the populace:

> He has erected a multitude of new offices, and sent hither swarms of officers to harass our people, and eat out their substance.

> He has kept among us, in times of peace, standing armies without the consent of our legislature.

> He has affected to render the military independent of and superior to civil power.

Several further charges particularized the above grievances concerning economic and military exploitation. The Declaration alleged that the king caused enactment of the following "pretended legislation":

> For quartering large bodies of armed troops among us:

> For protecting them, by mock trial, from punishment for any murders which they should commit on the inhabitants of these states:

> For cutting off our trade with all parts of the world:

> For imposing taxes on us without our consent:

> For depriving us in many cases, of the benefits of trial by jury . . . :

> For suspending our own legislatures, and declaring themselves invested with power to legislate for us in all cases whatsoever.

He has abdicated government here, by declaring us out of his protection and waging war against us.

He has plundered our seas, ravaged our coasts, burned our towns, and destroyed the lives of our people.

He is at this time transporting large armies of foreign mercenaries to complete the works of death, desolation and tyranny, already begun with circumstances of cruelty and perfidy scarcely paralleled in the most barbarous ages, and totally unworthy the head of a civilised nation.

The above charges mentioned only two subjects that would later be addressed in the Bill of Rights—the Third Amendment's proscription on quartering troops and the Sixth and Seventh Amendments' guarantees of trial by jury. Although the Crown had violated most or all of the rights that would later be articulated in the Bill of Rights, the Declaration did not make specific reference to the rights to freedom of religion, speech, and press; to keep and bear arms; and against unreasonable search and seizure.[2] Instead of accusing the Crown of violation of the right to petition, the Declaration complained that the petitions had not been granted: "In every stage of these oppressions we have petitioned for redress in the most humble terms: our repeated petitions have been answered only by repeated injury." In any event, the Declaration did not purport to detail every injury but dwelt on political and military transgressions being committed so as to justify the independence of the colonies.

As the Declaration concluded: "A prince, whose character is thus marked by every act which may define a tyrant, is unfit to be the ruler of a free people." It therefore declared "in the name, and by the authority of the good people of these colonies," that "these united colonies are, and of right ought to be free and independent states; that they are absolved from all allegiance to the British Crown, and that all political connection between them and the state of Great Britain, is and ought to be totally dissolved . . . ."

This right to overthrow the established government that had become tyrannical was not the right of an individual acting alone. The right was asserted by a legislative body representing the people of the several colonies, which assumed all the powers of independent states. Underlying this political theory was the notion that individuals had a right to keep and bear arms, and that these arms could rightly be used to throw off despotism when the decision to do so attained widespread recognition as legitimate. Force of arms was the only method available to achieve independence, and that is why the Declaration closed with the dauntless words: "with a firm reliance on the protection of Divine Providence, we mutually pledge to each other our lives, our fortunes and our sacred honour."

Thomas Jefferson, penman of the Declaration of Independence, wrote that it was based in part on "the elementary books of public right, as Aristotle, Cicero, Locke, Sidney & c."[3] An armed populace was the cornerstone of the ideal polity in the thought of these classical philosophers. Aristotle denounced a social order where "the farmers have no arms . . . mak[ing] them virtually the servants of those who do possess arms."[4] Cicero wrote that "a man who has used arms in self-defense is not regarded as having carried them with a homicidal aim."[5] According to John Locke, the people have not "disarmed themselves, and armed [a legislator], to make prey of them when he pleases."[6] In a popular government, argued Algernon Sidney, "every man is armed and disciplined."[7]

When independence was declared, great festivities took place throughout the states. Related symbolic expression included the firing of thirteen musket shots, representing the thirteen states, and the desecration of pictures of George III and other symbols of the British rule.[8] Images of the king were stomped, burned, and shot.

The great promise of the Declaration of Independence, with its fine philosophical phraseology and the euphoria it entailed, would soon give way to suffering, defeat, and the occasional victory. In addition to the war being waged between combatants, the British continued to confiscate arms, particularly from those considered disloyal. The pro-British New York Governor William Tryon decreed on December 2, 1776, as to such persons, "That all offensive arms, indiscriminately, be forthwith collected, in each manor, township and precinct, as soon as possible, to deliver them up at head-quarters, to the Commander-in-chief of the King's troops." Such former patriots must then serve the Crown: "That those who have been active in the rebellion, if fit to bear arms, forthwith to wait on the Gen'l, and enlist in the regular service for the term of the present war; if not fit to bear arms, to send one of their sons to enlist in their stead; if no sons, then to perform some unasked signal service, that may merit the protection of Gov't."[9]

With General Washington's army withdrawing through New Jersey, Thomas Paine wrote *The American Crisis* on a drumhead by campfire. When the pamphlet appeared under Paine's pseudonym "Common Sense" on December 23, 1776, despair filled the ranks.[10] Paine began with these immortal words:

> These are the times that try men's souls. The summer soldier and the sunshine patriot will, in this crisis, shrink from the service of their country; but he that stands it *now*, deserves the love and thanks of man and woman. Tyranny, like hell, is not easily conquered; yet we have this consolation with us, that the harder the conflict, the more glorious the triumph.[11]

The Americans had not wanted a war, but force must be used to defend against evil. While Paine believed that a strong army was now needed, he praised the contribution to the cause by "the temporary defence of a well-meaning militia," which "set bounds to the progress of the enemy. . . ." "I always considered militia as the best troops in the world for a sudden exertion, but they will not do for a long campaign."[12]

For Paine, the right to defend life and liberty extended both to individuals and to groups. Referring to Parliament's Declaratory Act of 1766, Paine reasoned:

> If a thief breaks into my house, burns and destroys my property, and kills or threatens to kill me, or those that are in it, and to "*bind me in all cases whatsoever*" to his absolute will, am I to suffer it? What signifies it to me, whether he who does it is a king or a common man; my countryman or not my countryman; whether it be done by an individual villain, or an army of them?[13]

Protection of life and liberty, whether from private criminals or governmental aggressors, required that individuals be armed. Well aware of that, the British stepped up their campaign to disarm the Americans, individually and as communities. As Paine wrote:

> Howe's first object is, partly by threats and partly by promises, to terrify or seduce the people to deliver up their arms and receive mercy. The ministry recommended the same plan to Gage, and this is what the Tories call making their peace . . . . Were the back counties to give up their arms, they would fall an easy prey to the Indians, who are all armed: this perhaps is what some Tories would not be sorry for. Were the home counties to deliver up their arms, they

would be exposed to the resentment of the back counties, who would then have it in their power to chastise their defection at pleasure. And were any one state to give up its arms, *that* state must be garrisoned by all Howe's army of Britons and Hessians to preserve it from the anger of the rest.[14]

Just three days after the appearance of *Crisis*, the morning after Christmas, Washington surprised and routed the Hessians at Trenton. Paine was emboldened in the subsequent issues of *Crisis* issued in the coming weeks. He took note of the frequently repeated British order that "all inhabitants who shall be found with arms, not having an officer with them, shall be immediately taken and hung up."[15] Addressing British Commander-in-Chief Howe, Paine asserted that even if the American soldiers all went home, "You would be afraid to send your troops in parties over the continent, either to disarm or prevent us from assembling, least they should not return."[16] Not surprisingly, Paine recalled General Gage's letter "in which he informs his masters, 'That though their idea of his disarming certain counties was a right one, yet it required him to be master of the country, in order to enable him to execute it.'"[17]

The American Revolution was hardly exempt from the basic phenomenon of war: Enemy forces seek to destroy the lives, liberties, and properties of their opponents. Supporters of independence sought to protect themselves with arms by disarming, neutralizing, incapacitating, capturing, or killing supporters of the Crown. The patriots were particularly concerned with confiscating the firearms and estates of Tories as well as suppressing Tory publications and associations. After all, the Tories and their British allies were meting out the same punishments to the patriots and indeed had initiated the aggression years before.

That the patriots attempted to disarm some of their enemies—a more humane practice than just killing them—no more denigrated their belief in the right to keep and bear arms than their repression of the Tory press and organizations impeached their values of freedom of the press and of association. The following describes some of the patriots' activities regarding the disarming of persons deemed to be disaffected to the cause of American independence, particularly as exemplified in New York. While illuminating the limits of rights in wartime, this analysis shows that limits can be counterproductive in same instances and that measures may be taken when war ends to prevent future abuses.

On September 16, 1775, the Committee of Safety of the New York Provincial Congress ordered the seizure of arms from "any person who has not signed the general association in this Colony"—who would have included not only Tories, but also persons who wished to avoid joining either side. Such impressed arms were to be appraised and were promised to be returned (or the value thereof paid) at the end of the conflict. Under the direction of the county committees, the local militias would enforce the seizures.[18]

Such orders to disarm "the disaffected" were regularly published in the press before and after this specific order,[19] including in some cases the reasons for disarming specific persons. For instance, three witnesses testified that one Amos Knapp cursed the Provincial Congress and threatened to join the king's standard. "The Committee have ordered to disarm the said Amos Knapp immediately, and he is hereby held up to public view as an avowed enemy to his country."[20] These proceedings were not trials in which one could protest his innocence, but were bills of attainder—legislative trials without any ability of the condemned persons to rebut the charges.

After a futile attempt to execute the September 16 directive, Major William Williams reported that his efforts in the towns of Jamaica and Hempstead were ineffectual, in that "the people conceal all their arms that are of any value; many declare they know nothing about the Congress, nor do they care any thing for the orders of the Congress, and say that they would sooner lose their lives than give up their arms; and that they would blow any man's brains out that should attempt to take them from them."[21]

The problem was exemplified in a letter from the Westchester Committee, which convicted one Godfrey Hains "of denying the authority, and speaking contemptuously of" the patriotic authorities. "He was ordered to be disarmed, and upon examining him respecting his arms and ammunition, he confessed that he has a gun, pistol, sword, powder and ball, but refused informing the committee where they are; and as Hains is a single man, the committee think it highly improbable that his arms can be found."[22]

Such policies may have been counterproductive, in that those targeted for being disarmed—whether Tories or uncommitted persons—resented and resisted the orders, without which some may have been won over to the cause of independence. Agnes Hunt wrote:

> The Tory farmers might have come to acquiesce in time to the new regime had
> they been left unmolested, or at least would hardly have felt the impulse to

organise an active resistance, but this proposal to take away their arms because they would not join a rebel faction against their lawful King, touched them too nearly for indifference and made the new government a synonym for irresponsible tyranny. Many of the loyalist inhabitants either hid their arms, or boldly declared they knew nothing of the Congress or its orders, and stood ready to fight and die before yielding their weapons. Those that submitted cherished a hatred for the Revolution, and large number of the indifference passed definite opposition.[23]

The members of the Provincial Congress temporarily saw the light, and on October 24 disapproved the resolution of the Committee of Safety "relating to the impressing of arms."[24] But the patriots continued to detain known or suspected Tories, and rumors that the disarming of a broader group would recommence may have actually prompted some not ready to commit perceived treason to arm themselves for defense. The Declaration of the Inhabitants of Queens County, New York, of December 6, 1775, protested:

> Reports have been circulated, and messages delivered to us, importing that we are to be disarmed, and some of our principal people taken in custody . . . . We call upon every man who values himself upon the inheritance of an Englishman, to say what he would do in such a case. Would he suffer himself to be disarmed, and tamely confess himself an abject slave? Certainly no. . . . Impelled by the most powerful arguments of self-defence, we have at last been driven to procure a supply of those means for protecting ourselves, of which we have been, till now, almost totally destitute . . . .[25]

Whatever the lack of success at seizing arms, the Provincial Congress decided on and published the names of hundreds of persons in Queens County deemed to be disaffected or delinquent.[26] While such proceedings were perhaps necessary considering the wartime circumstances, the Provincial Congress acted as judge, jury, and executioner in condemning suspects who never appeared before it to contest such findings. Such bills of attainder, so contemptible in peacetime, were just another weapon in the necessarily unfair and unjust institution of war.

The same debate was simmering in the Continental Congress. George Washington noted that "I did not think myself Authorised to seize upon any Arms the property of private Person; but if they can be collected and the owners satisfied for them, it would be of very essential service."[27] However, on January 3, 1776, the committee on New York reported that the majority of inhabitants of Queen's County, "being incapable of resolving to live and die freemen, . . . have deserted the American cause, by refusing to send Deputies, as usual, to the Convention of that Colony . . . ."[28] It resolved that Minutemen from New Jersey and Connecticut march to Queen's County and "disarm every person in the said County; who voted against sending Deputies to the said Convention, and cause them to deliver up their arms and ammunition on oath, and that they take and confine in safe custody, till further orders, all such as refuse compliance."[29]

The patriotic forces swept through Queen's County, forcing the listed persons to swear that their "fire-arms, side-arms, powder and lead," which were "delivered up" to or "taken from us," were all that they possessed, and that they had not hidden any arms. The signatories were required to characterize themselves as among those "who are disaffected to the opposition now making in America against ministerial tyranny."[30] Such confessed attestations were bound to be falsely sworn.

Lists were made of the owner's name, type of weapon seized, and appraised value. Three examples out of many included Charles Nicolls, who had two guns and a silver hilted sword; Samuel Skinner, who had a small blunderbuss and a pair of pocket pistols; and Benjamin Huggit, who had a rifle gun and a cartridge box.[31] The listings are revealing of the types of arms possessed by the colonists at that time. It is unfortunate that no comparable listing apparently survives of the names, types of arms, and values thereof for the arms of Boston's inhabitants seized by General Gage in 1775.

While disarming, detaining, and/or killing enemies have always been the hallmarks of war, some in the Continental Congress suggested pushing beyond what was considered civilized warfare. A committee appointed to confer with General Lee respecting the defense of New York issued a report dated March 14, 1776, advocating the seizure not only of the arms but also of the *children* of Tories and of all other families in the vicinity:

> I wou'd therefore humbly propose that the Inhabitants of Statten Island shou'd without loss of time be disarm'd and their arms delivered to some Regiment already raised but unfurnished with muskets. I do not imagine that the disarming the Tories will incapacitate them from acting against us, as they can easily

be supplied by the Ships. I shou'd therefore think it prudent to secure their Children as Hostages if a measure of this kind (hard as it may appear) is not adopted, the Childrens Children of America may rue the fatal omission.[32]

Fortunately, the Continental Congress did not endorse the kidnapping of children, but it did on the same date recommend that the various patriotic organizations and committees

immediately to cause all persons to be disarmed within their respective colonies, who are notoriously disaffected to the cause of America, or who have not associated, and shall refuse to associate, to defend, by arms, these United Colonies, against the hostile attempts of the British fleets and armies; and to apply the arms taken from such persons in each respective colony, in the first place to the arming the continental troops as are raised by the colony for its own defence, and the residue to be applied to the arming the associators . . . .[33]

These were desperate times—disarming the "notoriously disaffected" was only one form of fighting the enemy, who were also liable to lose life, liberty, or property. Repression against those who had "not associated" with the patriots, however, was problematic. This was an attempt to force neutral people to side with the patriots, who were regarded as traitors by the established authorities. It may have been that the arms obtained did not compensate for the hostility generated within the farming communities that only wanted to be left alone.[34]

The British and their Tory allies repressed the patriotic press, and those dedicated to American independence replied in kind, probably also netting those who eschewed conflict of any kind. In April 1776, for instance, one Samuel Loudon identified persons who burned his pamphlets and then published *Reflections on the Crime of Pamphlet Burning*, stating: "The freedom of the press is now insulted and infringed by some zealous advocates for liberty. A few more nocturnal assaults upon printers may totally destroy it, and America in consequence may fall a sacrifice to a more fatal despotism than that with which we are threatened."[35]

Indeed, thought crimes were the order of the day. New York's "An Act more effectually to punish adherence to the King" (1781) punished any person who "by preaching, teaching, speaking, writing, or printing, declare, or maintain, that the King of Great-Britain hath, or of Right ought to have, any

Authority or Dominion, in or over this State, or the Inhabitants thereof," or who communicated similar thoughts. The crime was a felony punishable by death, which could be avoided by three years of impressment on an American ship of war.[36]

Proceedings typically involved a trial by a committee of safety, which decided the policy, determined who was in violation without any notice or opportunity for hearing by the accused, and condemned the accused as a traitor, whose firearms, real estate, and other property could be seized and forfeited. Often, the targeted person's violation was merely that he had not taken a test oath or had not affirmatively advocated independence.[37]

The Founders would later adopt a Constitution and Bill of Rights that rose above their own as well as their enemies' violations of rights. Bills of attainder would be absolutely prohibited. The fact that members of that generation seized arms from perceived traitors no more denigrates what would become the Second Amendment than the facts that they tarred and feathered Royalist henchmen or that they suppressed the pro-Crown press indicates that they really did not believe in due process or a free press. Having been denied such rights during peacetime and willing to wage war to regain them, the patriots found themselves in a life-or-death struggle.

Another significant feature of this struggle was the cat-and-mouse game of the Americans attempting by any means to obtain arms and ammunition and of the British attempting to seize them.[38] Gage wrote to Dartmouth in the fall of 1775:

> Governor Bruere has sent Intelligence of Vessels from the Continent going to Bermuda, and carrying away a Quantity of Powder from the Magazine, which some of the Islanders had assissted in forceing in the Night.

> We hear that the Colonies have fitted out several armed Vessels and sent them to Europe and the West-Indies in Search of Ammunition, and there is Advice that a Privateer from South Carolina has plundered an Ordnance Ship off the Barr of St Augustine, where She was bound with Military Stores.[39]

A typical issue of the *Virginia Gazette* in 1776 noted: "They write from St. Maloes, that the Commander in Chief of the maritime department there had ordered four American vessels laden with muskets, pistols, swords, bayonets, & c. to reland their cargoes and proceed home in ballast." The seizure of American arms on a vessel at St. John's, Antiqua, was reported.[40] When the British fleet descended on Martha's Vineyard in 1778, its commanders demanded "all the arms, ammunition, and accouterments on the island."[41] Pistols, muskets, and blunderbusses were common arms that were eagerly sought after and continued to be sold on the civilian market.[42]

By 1777, confident of a British military victory, Colonial Undersecretary William Knox circulated to members of the ministry a comprehensive policy entitled "What Is Fit to Be Done with America?" Besides a state church, unlimited tax power, a standing army, and a governing aristocracy, the plan anticipated: "The Militia Laws should be repealed and none suffered to be re-enacted, & the Arms of all the People should be taken away, . . . nor should any Foundery or manufactuary of Arms, Gunpowder, or Warlike Stores, be ever suffered in America, nor should any Gunpowder, Lead, Arms or Ordnance be imported into it without Licence . . . ."[43]

But it was too late for that, and a populace composed of partisans, militias, independent companies, and the Continental army (with help from the French) would win the American Revolution.[44] Don Higginbotham wrote about the American militia: "Seldom has an armed force done so much with so little—providing a vast reservoir of manpower for a multiplicity of military needs, fighting (often unaided by Continentals) in the great majority of the 1,331 land engagements of the war."[45]

Not unexpectedly, there were episodes in the Revolutionary War when the militia proved unreliable. The military history of the war and the issue of the efficiency of the militia compared with the Continental Army are beyond the scope of this study.[46] In paying tribute to "a well regulated militia" in state declarations and in the Second Amendment, the Founders would seek to promote "the security of a free State," not just military efficiency.

Henry Lee, lieutenant colonel commandant of the partisan legion, a relative of Algernon Sidney and father of Robert E. Lee, provided an example of such perceptions in his *Memoirs of the War*. The Americans were inferior in arms "imputable to our poverty"[47] and to British repression, and were "a corps of peasants . . . defectively armed with fowling pieces, and muskets without bayonets."[48] But "the American war presents example of first-rate courage occasionally exhibited by corps of militia, and often with the highest success."[49] Such was the effectiveness of "armed citizens vying with our best soldiers"[50] that "our upper militia were never alarmed in meeting with equal numbers of British infantry,"[51] and it was "chiefly undisciplined militia" that forced the surrender of Burgoyne's veterans in 1777.[52]

Consistent with the above, Thomas Jefferson attributed American successes in part to their superior marksmanship. He sent to Giovanni Fabbroni a list of the number of enemy casualties beginning with Lexington in April 1775 through November 1777, explaining he could not enclose comparable data on the Americans but that:

> . . . [I]t has been about one half the number lost by them, in some instances more, but in others less. This difference is ascribed to our superiority in taking aim when we fire; every soldier in our army having been intimate with his gun from his infancy.[53]

The War for Independence might be considered as a people's war in which the armed populace defeated the world's greatest empire. In theory and in practice, the American Revolution had both as an objective and as an indispensable means the right to keep, bear, and use arms to check governmental oppression.

But only feeble efforts were made to adopt, and even feebler efforts made to give life to, a federal authority over what the Declaration of Independence declared to be "free and independent states." The formal structure approved as the Articles of Confederation essentially provided that the Continental Congress could impose requirements on the states but allowed no mechanism to enforce its will.

The Continental Congress agreed to the Articles of Confederation in 1777, but they were not operable until 1781. A look at the Articles is useful as background to what would become the federal Constitution.

The Articles began with a version of the future Constitution's Tenth Amendment: "Each state retains its sovereignty, freedom, and independence, and every power, jurisdiction, and right, which is not by this Confederation expressly delegated to the United States, in Congress assembled."[54]

The Articles had no bill of rights, and none was appropriate in that the Congress had authority only over the states and not individuals. The states regulated individual conduct, and hence recognition of the rights of persons was a matter for the states.

However, the Articles did declare a broad concept of rights throughout the states: "The better to secure and perpetuate mutual friendship and intercourse among the people of the different States in this Union, the free inhabitants of each of these States, paupers, vagabonds, and fugitives from justice excepted, shall be entitled to all privileges and immunities of free citizens in the several States . . . ."[55] These privileges and immunities were not specified, but they were limited to "free citizens."

The above was in part a guarantee against discriminatory action imposed by states on residents of other states. No other reference to individual rights was made, not surprisingly in that the Congress had few powers. Free speech was declared only for members of Congress: "Freedom of speech and debate in Congress shall not be impeached or questioned in any court or place out of Congress . . . ."[56]

States were prohibited from keeping vessels of war or any body of forces in peacetime without the consent of Congress. However, "every State shall always keep up a well regulated and disciplined militia, sufficiently armed and accoutered, and shall provide and constantly have ready for use, in public stores, a due number of field pieces and tents, and a proper quantity of arms, ammunition and camp equipage."[57] While each state required militiamen generally to provide their own arms, this provision for arms in public stores would have made arms available to those who could not afford or otherwise obtain them.

In the raising of armed forces, Congress made the decisions, and the states were responsible to carry them out. As to land forces raised by a state "for the common defence," officers of or under the rank of colonel were appointed by the state.[58] A similar provision would find its way into the Constitution's militia clause, which reserved the appointment of officers to the states.

However, the Congress appointed the officers (except regimental officers) of the land forces in the service of the United States.[59] Congress also had power to designate the number of land forces, and to requisition each state for its quota, in proportion to the state's number of white inhabitants. The state legislature would then appoint regimental officers, and "raise the men and cloath, arm and equip them in a soldier like manner," at the expense of the United States.[60]

The nature of the militia in the above system was clarified in the report of a committee to the Continental Congress dated October 23, 1783. It averred:

[I]n considering the means of national defence, Congress ought not to overlook that of a well regulated militia; that as the keeping up such a militia and proper arsenals and magazines by each State is made a part of the Confederation, the attention of Congress to this object becomes a constitutional duty; that as great advantages would result from uniformity in this article in every State, and from the militia establishment being as similar as the nature of the case will admit to that of the Continental forces, it will be proper for Congress to adopt and recommend a plan for this purpose.[61]

The militia consisted of "all the free male inhabitants in each state from 20 to fifty," divided between the two classifications of married and unmarried men, except those exempt under state law. "Those who are willing to be at the expence of equipping themselves for Dragoon service to be permitted to enter into that corps, the residue to be formed into Infantry . . . ." All were to provide their own arms:

Each officer of the Dragoons to provide himself with a horse, saddle &c. pistols and sabre, and each non-commissioned officer and private with the preceding articles and these in addition, a carbine and cartouch box, with twelve rounds of powder and ball for his carbine, and six for each pistol.

Each officer of the Infantry to have a sword, and each non-commissioned officer and private, a musket, bayonet and cartouch box, with twelve rounds of powder and ball.[62]

"These united colonies are, and of right ought to be free and independent states," proclaimed the Declaration of Independence. And independent states they became, each deciding her own constitution and bill of rights, or declining to adopt either or both. The next two chapters tell the story of how, at the state level, constitutions were framed and the great rights of mankind proclaimed or otherwise recognized, particularly the right to keep and bear arms.

## CHAPTER 6

# "That the People Have a Right"

THE REVOLUTION EVOLVED from a defensive war in 1775 to a war for independence in 1776. Once the complete break with Great Britain was decided, the states began to hold conventions and to adopt forms of government. Some framed constitutions with declarations of rights, others wrote constitutions that contained no bills of rights, and still others simply continued to operate under their colonial charters and adopted neither a constitution nor a declaration of rights. Regardless of whether rights were formalized in written instruments, supporters of the Revolution shared some fundamental conceptions of basic rights.[1] These generally included freedom of the press, the right to keep and bear arms and other familiar liberties.

The following traces the actions of the states that adopted constitutions during 1776. Those states were, in chronological order, South Carolina, Virginia, New Jersey, Pennsylvania, Delaware, Maryland, and North Carolina. The next chapter details actions by the other states that took place during 1777 through 1784.

## SOUTH CAROLINA

South Carolina was the first of the colonies to adopt a constitution. On February 11, 1776, the Provincial Congress elected an eleven-man committee to prepare a form of government.[2] In early March, committee member Charles Cotesworth Pinckney delivered a report on the proposed constitution.[3] Deliberations ensued, and on March 26 the assembly adopted a constitution for the state of South Carolina.

The right to have arms and to use them defensively was expressed in the Constitution's preamble as follows:

> Hostilities having been commenced in the Massachusetts Bay, by the troops under command of General Gage, whereby a number of peaceable, helpless, and unarmed people were wantonly robbed and murdered, and there being just reason to apprehend that like hostilities would be committed in all the other colonies, the colonists were therefore driven to the necessity of taking up arms, to repel force by force, and to defend themselves and their properties against lawless invasions and depredations.[4]

Although the Constitution contained no bill of rights, no precedent existed yet in any of the newly-independent states for such a declaration. Pinckney would later explain that "we had no bill of rights inserted in our Constitution; for, as we might perhaps have omitted the enumeration of some of our rights, it might hereafter be said we had delegated to the general government a power to take away such of our rights as we had not enumerated . . . ."[5]

When the Provincial Congress adopted the Constitution, it also elected its president, William Henry Drayton, as the chief justice of the Supreme Court. Drayton was also a member of the Continental Congress. His son wrote: "Mr. Drayton always had about his person, a dirk and a pair of pocket pistols; for the defense of his life."[6]

Chief Justice Drayton soon delivered the first charge to the grand jury of Charleston District. In the course of this patriotic oration he warned that the King of England "will effectually disarm the Colony."[7] Drayton accused George III of "the violation of the fundamental laws" in the same manner as James II had done.[8] The grand jurors were then reminded of the charges

against James in the English Bill of Declaration of 1689, including: "By causing several good subjects, being Protestants, to be disarmed, at the same time
when Papists were both armed and employed contrary to law."[9]

Indeed, the English Declaration of Rights, which "declares the Rights
of the Citizens," remained in effect in South Carolina.[10] Under the category
"Subjects Arms" the following appeared: "The Subjects which are Protestants
may have arms for their Defence suitable to their Conditions, and as allowed
by Law."[11]

The American Revolution in South Carolina would be waged more by
armed partisans than by a regular army.[12] John Drayton wrote that "a spirit
of independence, which their fathers had brought with them from England,
gave to the inhabitants of those Colonies a knowledge of arms, and a spirit
of intolerant of oppression."[13] On the eve of the Revolution a South Carolina
writer urged: "The inhabitants of this colony . . . ought therefore never to be
without the most ample supply of arms and ammunition . . . ."[14]

The South Carolina Provincial Congress had declared in 1775 "that solely
for the Preservation and Defense of our Lives, Liberties, and Properties, we have
been impelled to associate, to take up Arms."[15] It required "that every person
liable to bear arms, shall appear completely armed, once in every fortnight"
for militia exercises.[16] The Congress also adopted measures to encourage a
"regiment of Rangers . . . composed of *expert* Rifle-men . . . ; each man, at his
own expense to be constantly provided with a good horse, rifle, shot-pouch
and powder-horn, together with a tomahawk or hatchet."[17]

Slaves were generally deprived of rights. South Carolina laws enacted in
the 1740s and reenacted in 1783 included prohibitions on slaves being taught
to write,[18] to assemble, and to travel,[19] and "to carry or make use of fire-arms,
or any offensive weapons whatsoever," unless "in the presence of some white
person" or with a license from the master.[20] A slave could shoot birds on the
plantation without a license, "lodging the same gun at night within the dwelling-house of his master, mistress or white overseer."[21]

Militiamen were subjected to patrol duty to guard against a slave insurrection.[22] Patrols were required to apprehend slaves outside their plantation
without permission and had "power to search and examine all negro-houses
for offensive weapons and ammunition."[23]

While slaves had few rights, citizens had many, even though not formalized in the constitution.

As will be seen, a formal statement of rights would be seen as necessary elsewhere. Virginia, the second state to adopt a constitution in 1776, became the first to adopt a declaration of rights.

## VIRGINIA

Virginia was the first of all the colonies to adopt a bill of rights, which became the prototype for those of other colonies. The Virginia Declaration of Rights, adopted in convention on June 12, 1776, included the following interconnected propositions:

> I. That all Men are by Nature equally free and independent, and have certain inherent Rights . . . ; namely, the Enjoyment of Life and Liberty, with the Means of . . . pursuing and obtaining . . . Safety.
>
> II. That all Power is vested in, and consequently derived from, the People . . . .
>
> XIII. That a well regulated Militia, composed of the Body of the People, trained to Arms, is the proper, natural, and safe Defence of a free State; that standing Armies, in Time of Peace, should be avoided, as dangerous to Liberty.

The author of the Declaration was George Mason, who had employed similar phraseology during the previous two years in his writings on the Fairfax Independent Militia Company, which Mason and George Washington organized as a defense force against the Royal militia. "Threat'ned with the Destruction of our Civil-rights, & Liberty," wrote Mason in 1774, the members of this company of volunteers, who elected their own officers, pledged that "we will, each of us, constantly keep by us" a firelock, six pounds of gunpowder, and twenty pounds of lead.[24]

In early 1775, Mason drafted a Fairfax County Militia Plan "For Embodying the People." It reiterated that "a well regulated Militia, composed of the Gentlemen, Freeholders, and other Freemen" was necessary to protect "our antient Laws & Liberty" from the standing army. "And we do each of us, for ourselves respectively, promise and engage to keep a good Fire-lock in proper Order, & to furnish Ourselves as soon as possible with, & always keep by us, one Pound of Gunpowder, four Pounds of Lead, one Dozen Gun Flints, & a pair of Bullet-Moulds, with a Cartouch Box, or powder-horn, and Bag for Balls."[25]

Mason provided a philosophical basis for the above in his Remarks on Annual Elections for the Fairfax Independent Company, asserting as fundamental that "all men are by nature born equally free and independent." Government is the source of "the most arbitrary and despotic powers this day upon earth," and liberty is secured only by "frequently appealing to the body of the people."[26] The Roman experience proved that mercenaries destroy freedom, while the people must be introduced to "the use of arms and discipline" in order to "act in defence of their invaded liberty."[27]

This background clarifies the meaning of the Declaration of Rights adopted a year later. Every freeman would have the means of obtaining "safety," "all power" would remain in "the people," and "a free State" would be defended where the citizens kept and trained with "arms" and associated themselves into "militia."[28]

Probably because its principles were taken for granted, the Declaration of Rights occasioned virtually no public debate. The chief exception was the free exercise of religion clause, which sparked some newspaper controversy.[29] A free press was included in the Declaration, but speech and assembly were not explicitly mentioned. Arms bearing was not characterized as a "right," but that was perhaps considered unnecessary in a society where every man was required to arm himself and was even encouraged to learn to make his own gunpowder. For instance, "A friend to the American cause" detailed the formula so that "every man, after he is furnished with the ingredients [saltpeter and sulphur], may make, or cause to be made, a pound and a half of good gunpowder," in one day.[30]

Having adopted the Declaration of Rights, the 1776 convention proceeded to consider various proposals for a constitution. Thomas Jefferson, who was in Philadelphia at the time, prepared a draft constitution for Virginia that consisted of three parts. The first part contained the grievances and charges against George III that the Continental Congress would adopt less than a month later on July 4, in the Declaration of Independence. Next followed a proposed political system that would have altered the existing aristocratic structure. A third portion included a bill of rights that stated: "All persons shall have full & free liberty of religious opinion . . . . No freeman shall ever be debarred the use of arms . . . . There shall be no standing army but in time of . . . actual war. Printing presses shall be free, except . . . where by commission of private injury they shall give cause of private action."[31]

Jefferson's proposals contain matters that thirteen years later would find expression in the First and Second Amendments—the freedoms of religion, arms, and the press. In a second draft, Jefferson added a prohibition on the holding of newcomers to the state in slavery and a tentative bracketed item to the arms guarantee: "No freeman shall be debarred the use of arms [within his own lands or tenements]."[32] Jefferson used brackets to indicate that the contents thereof were optional or open to question.[33] The reference to use of arms on one's own lands and tenements may have been a rebuke to English game laws, which prohibited commoners from hunting on their own land. It also would have allowed legislation to establish a deer hunting season and thus to prevent taking of deer when off of one's own property, which Jefferson proposed to the Virginia assembly not long after.[34] A third draft of the constitution listed the above and other matters under the title "Rights Private and Public."[35]

Jefferson, who was only 33 years old at the time, was himself one of the freemen at large who exercised the right of the "use of arms." When Thomas was 10 years old, his father Colonel Peter Jefferson gave him a gun and sent him into the forest to promote self-reliance.[36] By the time his father died when the lad was only 14, "he had already taught him to sit his horse, fire his gun, boldly stem the Rivanna when the swollen river was 'Rolling red from brae to brae,' and press his way with unflagging foot through the rocky summits of the contiguous hills in pursuit of deer and wild turkeys."[37]

On August 20, 1768, just days before the Redcoats landed to disarm the pesky Bostonians, the 25-year-old Jefferson recorded his entry in a target match in which he "won shooting 1/6,"—that is, a shilling sixpence.[38] He made numerous references throughout his life to the acquisition, repair, and use of firearms.[39] Probably many of the other delegates in the 1776 Virginia convention shared similar backgrounds and experiences.

On June 29, 1776, the Virginia convention adopted a constitution. The preface incorporated Jefferson's strictures against George III, while the text was based on proposals submitted by George Mason and others.[40] The Declaration of Rights written by George Mason having already been adopted, Jefferson's draft bill of rights was not used.

But Jefferson's proposal that "no freeman shall ever be debarred the use of arms" was fundamental to the worldview of the American patriots. Jefferson kept a *Commonplace Book* during the years 1774–1776, which has been called "the source-book and repertory of Jefferson's ideas on government."[41]

Perhaps the most significant figures detailed by Jefferson in the *Commonplace Book* were the penal reformers Montesquieu, Beccaria, and Eden. Besides reading Montesquieu's vindication of the right of armed self-defense and his denunciation of Venice's death penalty for bearing firearms,[42] Jefferson copied this passage: "In republics, it would be extremely dangerous to make the profession of arms a particular state, distinct from that of civil functions . . . . In republics a person takes up arms only with a view to defend his country and its laws; it is because he is a citizen he makes himself for a while a soldier."[43]

Writing "False idee di utilità ("false ideas of utility") in the margin, Jefferson copied in Italian into his *Commonplace Book* the following passage from Beccaria:

> False is the idea of utility that sacrifices a thousand real advantages for one imaginary or trifling inconvenience; that would take fire from men because it burns, and water because one may drown in it; that has no remedy for evils, except destruction. The laws that forbid the carrying of arms are laws of such a nature. They disarm those only who are neither inclined nor determined to commit crimes. Can it be supposed that those who have the courage to violate the most sacred laws of humanity, the most important of the code, will respect the less important and arbitrary ones, which can be violated with ease and impunity, and which, if strictly obeyed, would put an end to personal liberty—so dear to men, so dear to the enlightened legislator—and subject innocent persons to all the vexations that the guilty alone ought to suffer? Such laws make things worse for the assaulted and better for the assailants; they serve rather to encourage than to prevent homicides, for an unarmed man may be attacked with greater confidence than an armed man. They ought to be designated as laws not preventive but fearful of crimes, produced by the tumultuous impression of a few isolated facts, and not by thoughtful consideration of the inconveniences and advantages of a universal decree.[44]

Jefferson read similar sentiments in William Eden, who combined observations of Montesquieu and Beccaria as follows: "It is a Law at Venice, that those, who carry fire-arms about their persons, shall suffer death. This law is founded in apparent utility; nevertheless it is contrary to the nature of things, to make the bare possession of the means of mischief equally penal with the most criminal use of those means."[45] By contrast, under English law "homicide is justifiable . . . in the case of any woman, who kills a ravisher in defence of her chastity; or of any traveller, who, in the immediate defence of his property, shoots a highwayman."[46] Further, homicide is excusable "by self-defence."[47]

The sources Jefferson consulted in preparation of his *Commonplace Book* reveal the premises for his proposal that "no freeman shall ever be debarred the use of arms." The armed citizen would protect himself and the community from both the private criminal and tyrannical government. Both of these concepts would be formalized by the next state to adopt a declaration of rights, Pennsylvania.

Jefferson's proposal included no militia clause, but in 1777 he introduced a bill for regulating and disciplining the militia. Enacted that same year, it provided that the militia would consist of all free males, hired servants and apprentices, between the ages of 16 and 50 years.[48] Every private was required to equip himself "with a rifle and tomahawk, or common firelock and bayonet," and to "constantly keep one pound of powder and four pounds of ball." If any "be so poor that he cannot purchase such arms, the said court shall cause them to be procured at the expence of the public."[49] Jefferson's militia bill deleted the restriction in a previous act that "free mulattoes, negroes, and Indians" shall "appear without arms" at muster.[50]

## NEW JERSEY

On July 2, 1776, the New Jersey Provincial Congress, assembled as a convention, adopted a constitution. It contained no bill of rights, although it did provide that "no Protestant inhabitant of this Colony shall be denied the employment of any civil right, merely on account of his religious principles."[51] The common law of England, and the statute law that had been in effect in the colony, to the extent not "repugnant to the rights and privileges contained in this Charter," was declared to remain in force, together with trial by jury.[52]

The New Jersey Constitution was framed by a committee of ten chaired by Jacob Green, a Presbyterian minister.[53] At most five days passed between its drafting and final adoption by the state Congress.[54] The chief draftsman appears to have been Jonathan D. Sergeant, a young attorney who was a friend of John Adams and an advocate of independence.[55]

Why was no bill of rights included in New Jersey's first Constitution? First, it was believed that the common law protected fundamental rights.[56] The right to petition and the right of Protestants to have arms were both recognized as common law and in the English Declaration of Rights of 1689.[57] Second, the British fleet was anchored off the coast of the colony, and there was no time for theoretical discussions.[58] Judge William Griffith wrote two decades later that "public sentiment in New Jersey in 1776 dwelt with slight regard upon the *forms* of constitution. Engaged in a desperate conflict for freedom itself, it was thought of more consequence to exert courage in repelling foreign tyranny, than to sit canvassing the comparative merits of *theories*, which were to secure internal liberty, not yet won from our oppressors."[59]

The conventions of the states that adopted the most elaborate declarations of rights—Virginia and Pennsylvania—were not under military threat as they deliberated. When it adopted its Constitution, the New Jersey Congress was mostly concerned with organizing the militia for immediate defense and sending Tories to jail.[60] In the fall of 1776, Governor William Livingston recommended to the Council and Assembly of New Jersey "some further regulations respecting the better ordering the Militia,"[61] and the assembly agreed with "the necessity of a well regulated militia for the defence of a free State."[62] Indeed, the year before, the people of New Jersey had responded to Lexington and Concord by arming and associating, and the first Provincial Congress created a militia system in May 1775.[63]

Just across the river, in late summer 1776, New York City fell to the British. A proclamation was issued to Suffolk County directing that "every man in arms lay them down forthwith, and surrender themselves, on pain of being treated as Rebels."[64] Compliance was thought to be incomplete, for three months later, the Newark-based *New York Gazette* published the following directive by New York's Royal Governor William Tryon addressed "to the inhabitants of Suffolk county": "That all offensive arms, indiscriminately, be forthwith collected, in each respective manor, township, and precinct, as soon as possible, to deliver them up at headquarters, to the Commander in Chief of the King's troops."[65]

The war would soon spill over into New Jersey, where patriot leaders counted on the armed populace to respond. General George Washington addressed the county militia of New Jersey in 1777 as follows: "I therefore call upon you, by all you hold dear, to rise up as one Man, and rid your Country of its cruel invaders. . . . [T]his can be done by a general appearance of all its Freemen armed and ready to give them opposition . . . . I am convinced every Man who can bear a Musket, will take it up."[66]

Typical of the epoch was New Jersey's 1781 act for the regulating, training, and arraying of the militia, and for providing more effectually for the defense and security of the state.[67] The militia included "all effective Men between the Ages of sixteen and fifty Years."[68] "Every person enrolled as aforesaid, shall constantly keep himself furnished with a good Musket . . . [or] a good Rifle-Gun,"[69] while each horseman "shall at all Time keep himself provided with a good Horse, a Saddle properly furnished with a Pair of Pistols and Holsters."[70] To say the least, in New Jersey the right and duty to keep and bear arms was recognized as a fact and as a dire necessity.

## PENNSYLVANIA

Pennsylvania was the first state to adopt a formal guarantee of the right of the people to bear arms.[71] That state's constitutional convention, presided over by Benjamin Franklin, met from July 15 through September 28, 1776, a longer period than most state conventions.[72] The Virginia Declaration of Rights had been published in Philadelphia the month before the convention began.[73] A majority in the convention were "Associators," members of armed organizations.[74]

Initially, eleven delegates were appointed to the Declaration of Rights Committee.[75] The session on July 25 approved the Declaration of Independence and appointed James Cannon and Colonel Timothy Matlack to the committee for drafting a frame of government.[76] Interestingly, after the Continental Congress adopted the Declaration of Independence, it gave the job of hand lettering the document to Matlack. Cannon and Matlack had been elected to the Pennsylvania convention by ultra radicals with the backing of the militia, which originated in extralegal associations of armed men.[77]

Cannon, a militia leader and the state's leading patriot writer next to Thomas Paine, was chief author of the Declaration of Rights, adopted some three weeks later.[78] Cannon was apparently assisted by Judge George Bryan and Colonel Matlack. A contemporary wrote that the Pennsylvania Constitution "was understood to have been principally the work of Mr. George Bryan, in conjunction with Mr. Cannon, a schoolmaster."[79] John Adams asserted that the Pennsylvania "Bill of Rights is taken almost verbatim from that of Virginia . . . . It was by Mr. Mason, as that of Pennsylvania was by Timothy Matlack, James Cannon and Thomas Young and Thomas Paine."[80]

George Bryan, later a justice of the Pennsylvania Supreme Court, was the most influential member of the convention.[81] Professor James Cannon of the College of Philadelphia contributed most of the phraseology of the document.[82] Cannon, along with Dr. Thomas Young, and Thomas Paine, were leaders of the radical Whig Society.[83] Thomas Paine was not actually in Philadelphia during the convention, but he wrote in the *Pennsylvania Magazine* the same month the convention began its deliberations:

> The supposed quietude of a good man allures the ruffian; while on the other hand, arms like laws discourage and keep the invader and the plunderer in awe, and preserve order in the world as well as property. The balance of power is the scale of peace. The same balance would be preserved were all the world destitute of arms, for all would be alike; but since some *will not*, others *dare not* lay them aside . . . . Horrid mischief would ensue were one half the world deprived of the use of them; . . . the weak will become a prey to the strong.[84]

Paine had established his reputation in early 1776 with the publication in Philadelphia of *Common Sense*, in which he depicted "taking up arms"[85] as both necessary and realistic: "Our small arms [are] equal to any in the world . . . Saltpeter and gunpowder we are every day producing."[86] His Epistle to Quakers published in the appendix of the third edition of *Common Sense* addressed a pro-Tory double standard: "As if all sin was reduced to, and comprehended in, *the act of bearing arms*, and that by the *people only*." Not condemning the invading soldiers was illogical, "*for they likewise bear ARMS*."[87]

Judge Bryan sought "to identify himself with the people, in opposition to those, who were termed the *well born*."[88] Cannon had a "scholastic predilection for the antique in liberty."[89] Matlack, an Associator, when once asked by a Quaker why he wore a sword, replied: "That is to defend my property and my liberty."[90]

It is not surprising that these patriots would frame the Declaration of Rights with the provision: "That the people have a right to bear arms for the defence of themselves, and the state; and as standing armies in the time of peace, are dangerous to liberty, they ought not to be kept up; and that the military should be kept under strict subordination to, and governed by the civil power."[91] While the declaration of a right to bear arms to defend the state against the established Royal government was more radical, the Framers did not overlook the less disputed right to bear arms for self-defense.

Recognition of the people's right to bear arms "for the defence of themselves" meant that individuals were entitled to carry arms for personal protection. Use of the terms "the people" and "themselves" did not mean that arms could be borne only in groups organized by the state and only to defend the people in some collective sense. Bearing arms to defend "the state" meant defense of the Commonwealth and its people as a whole. If "themselves" also meant the collective body and not individuals, it would be redundant to "the state."[92]

The term "bear arms" was not limited to bearing arms in a military force. Bearing arms for self-defense is "a right" of "the people," while bearing arms in a military unit is either voluntary or compulsory but is not considered "a right." Bearing arms was not limited to the militia, and indeed, the militia was not mentioned in the Declaration of Rights, but was the subject of another article of the Constitution. Declaring in the same sentence that standing armies may be dangerous to liberty and that the military must be subordinate to the civil power did not negate that "the people have a right to bear arms for the defence of themselves . . . ."

The declaration of a right to bear arms to defend self and state appears not to have been disputed in the convention or in the press. While some parts of the declaration were highly controversial, no objections were voiced in the newspapers from the time the declaration was first published.[93] By contrast, freedom of religion sparked controversy. When Benjamin Franklin revised the Declaration of Rights, he suggested no change in the right to bear arms clause yet unsuccessfully opposed the profession of faith required for assemblymen.[94] Newspaper attacks on the religious guarantees and certain other matters were extreme and persistent, but bearing arms was not questioned.[95]

One writer saw the Declaration of Rights as "equal to any thing of the kind now extant in the various governments that we know in the world."[96] "The Magna Carta or the Great Charter of Britain, and the Bill of Rights exhibited at the Revolution, are not touched, nor allowed to be touched, by their Parliaments, and we at this time blame them, and bear arms against them, because they have deprived us, and still attempt to deprive us, of the privileges of that Constitution."[97] "Casa" wrote: "The Bill of Rights should always include the natural rights of every freeman, and the essential principals of free government . . . . This bill should be unalterable. The least violation of any part of it, whether by legislature—the courts of law—or the people, should always be punished as high treason against the state."[98]

The article in the Constitution on the militia provided in part: "The free-men of this commonwealth and their sons shall be trained and armed for its defence, under such regulations, restrictions and exceptions as the general assembly shall by law direct."[99] This met with some sarcasm in satire on the Constitution which stated:

> In section the *fifth*—the freemen shall be *trained and armed* for their defence, and the militia shall elect their officers, & c. Oh, how I am transported at the velocity of the mental operations of these geniuses! They ought not to be compared to any thing but *leaden* bullets flying from the muzzles of rifles, hot, heavy, rapid, and yet twisting to their marks.[100]

It is worth recalling that, years before, Benjamin Franklin had devised a plan "for organizing men willing to bear arms into voluntary militia associations."[101] Its object was "our mutual Defence and Security, and for the Security of our Wives, Children and Estates, and the Preservations of the Person and Estates of others, our Neighbours and Fellow Subjects." Its members, who would elect their officers, would "provide ourselves with a good Firelock, Cartouch Box, and at least twelve Charges of Powder and Ball, . . . to be kept always in our respective Dwellings, in Readiness, and good Order."[102] Franklin explained, "The general Word *Firelock* is used (rather than *Musket*, which is the Name of a particular kind of Gun) most People having a Firelock of some kind or other already in their Hands."[103] This confirms the widespread ownership of arms.

Providently, another section of the Constitution provided: "The inhabitants of this state shall have liberty to fowl and hunt in seasonable times on the lands they hold, and on all other lands not inclosed."[104] This provision was criticized in the most comprehensive attack on the new constitution, adopted by an assembly of dissidents, which devoted most of its attention to issues such as "the Christian religion is not treated with proper respect."[105] A minor objection was "that several regulations improper to betaken notice of therein, are mentioned in the said Constitution . . . . Fishing, fowling, and hunting."[106]

Much more was at stake than the right to hunt, "Remarks on the Resolves" replied. Under English law, game belongs to the king, who grants rights to lords of manors. From this privilege stemmed deprivation of the right to keep and carry guns:

In order to prevent poachers, as they are called, from invading this aristocratical prerogative, the possession of hunting dogs, snares, nets, and other engines by unprivileged persons, has been forbidden, and, under pretence of the last words, guns have been seized. And though this was not legal, as guns are not engines appropriated to kill game, yet if a witness can be found to attest before a Justice that a gun has been thus used, the penalty is five pounds, or three months imprisonment fall on the accused.

The prosecutors are generally fox-hunters, and if the Justices are such, alas, the culprit has no chance of escaping punishment though the evidence be slender! Thus penal laws, and trial without juries, are multiplied on a trivial subject, and the freeholders of moderate estates deprived of a natural right. Nor is this all; the body of the people kept from the use of guns are utterly ignorant of the arms of modern war, and the kingdom effectually disarmed, except of the standing force . . . . Is any thing like this desired in Pennsylvania?[107]

The above remarks combine apparent knowledge about how England's game laws were actually enforced with the observations of Sir William Blackstone, who wrote that "a reason oftener meant, than avowed, by the makers of forest or game laws" was "for preventing of popular insurrections and resistance to the government, by disarming the bulk of the people."[108] European feudalism was founded on conquest, and the rulers wanted to keep the subjects "in as low a condition as possible, and especially to prohibit them the use of arms. Nothing could do this more effectually than a prohibition of hunting and sporting . . . ."[109] Blackstone proceeded to detail the property qualifications and penalties set forth in the game laws that were alluded to by the above writer.

Thomas Paine had lambasted gun seizures under English game law based on lack of sufficient wealth in a poem published in 1775 in *Pennsylvania Magazine*. Based on a true story about three judges who hung a farmer's dog, the poem referred to the requirement that one must have an annual income of at least one hundred pounds to hunt:

Each knew by instinct when and where
A farmer caught or killed a hare;
Could tell if any man had got
On hundred pounds per ann. or not;

Or what was greater could divine

If it was only ninety-nine.

For when the hundred wanted one,

They took away the owner's gun.[110]

While modeled on the Virginia Declaration, the Pennsylvania Declaration of Rights made significant improvements. The rights of assembly and petition, and an unprecedented recognition of religious liberty, were included only in the latter.[111] Although Virginia recognized that a free state requires "a well regulated Militia, composed of the Body of the People, trained to Arms,"[112] Pennsylvania more explicitly provided "that the people have a right to bear arms for the defence of themselves, and the state."[113] As the chief authority on the first Pennsylvania constitution concludes, "the *Declaration of Rights* was the true expression of the ideals of the American Colonists, and the guarantees contained therein were the product of long and severe experience."[114]

Years later, Thomas Paine would write of Pennsylvania's 1776 Declaration: "By this mutual compact, the citizens of a republic put it out of their power, that is, they renounce, as detestable, the power of exercising, at any future time any species of despotism over each other . . . ." Paine proceeded to quote the Declaration in full.[115]

The same provincial conference that called for the constitutional convention also resolved that a militia be raised, and "that each Private procure his own Musket or Rifle."[116] Similarly, the first General Assembly to meet after adoption of the Constitution declared that it is the duty of all freemen to be at all times prepared to resist the enemy.[117] Another militia act stated: "A well regulated militia is the only safe and constitutional method of defending a free state, as the necessity of keeping up a standing army, especially in times of peace, is thereby superceded."[118]

Legislation that predated the Revolution and remained on the books for decades thereafter imposed a fine on any person or persons, "who shall fire any gun or other fire arms . . . within the city of Philadelphia."[119] Any person who "wantonly, and without reasonable occasion, discharge and fire off any hand-gun, pistol or other firearms" in inhabited areas on New Years' night was subject to fine.[120] A hunting regulation punished any person who "shall presume to carry any gun, or hunt" on the land of others without permission, or who "shall presume to fire a gun on or near any of the king's highways."[121]

These were the only firearms regulations in Pennsylvania, and they were not perceived as violating the right to bear arms.


DELAWARE

Before 1776, Delaware was part of Pennsylvania. Although most of its people supported independence from Pennsylvania, they were divided on the question of independence from Britain. In the Continental Congress, two of Delaware's delegates—Thomas McKean and Caesar Rodney—voted for independence[122] while George Read voted against it.[123]

The split vote over independence foretold political divisions in Delaware for the following two decades. McKean and Rodney would lead the Whigs, otherwise known as the Country or Democratic Party. The Tories, the Court or Aristocratic Party, would be led by Read and John Dickinson, who had voted against independence while representing Pennsylvania. In their first test of strength, the election of a convention of delegates to frame a state constitution, the Tories predominated.[124]

The constitutional convention began on August 27, 1776, with George Read presiding. On September 2, Read and nine other delegates were appointed to "be a Committee to prepare a Declaration of Rights and Fundamental Rules of this State."[125] Three days later, the committee reported having made progress.[126]

Thomas McKean was then appointed to the committee.[127] McKean was a follower of Judge George Bryan,[128] the most influential member of the Pennsylvania convention, which had recently adopted a declaration of rights.[129]

One source claims that McKean authored the Delaware constitution.[130] However, the Pennsylvania Declaration of Rights (and later the rest of the Pennsylvania Constitution) had been published in August in Pennsylvania newspapers,[131] which circulated in Delaware. A declaration of rights had been reported, but not adopted, in the Maryland convention by late August.[132] By September 11, the Delaware Declaration of Rights was debated paragraph-by-paragraph, amended, and adopted.[133] George Read, convention president and chairman of the committee, wrote Caesar Rodney that the Declaration "is made out of the Pennsylvania and Maryland Draughts."[134]

As adopted, the Delaware Declaration provided for an armed populace as follows: "That a well regulated Militia is the proper, natural and safe Defence of a free Government."[135] Similar language appeared in the Maryland[136] and Virginia Declarations,[137] but not that of Pennsylvania. Such language also appeared in Delaware on the eve of the Revolution, such as the New Castle County committee resolution that "a well regulated Militia, composed of the gentlemen, freeholders, and other freemen, is the natural strength and stable security of a free Government."[138] It added that each militia company would choose its own officers, and "each man be provided with a well fixed Firelock." Both Delaware and Pennsylvania Declarations also included provisions that standing armies are dangerous to liberty, and that the military should be kept subordinate to the civil power.[139]

Unlike Pennsylvania, Delaware did not specifically declare that the people may bear arms for defense of self and state.[140] However, much of the Delaware convention concerned the arming of the people and the encouragement of independent militia companies. Just after the Declaration was approved, Thomas McKean was appointed to a committee to evaluate a gunsmith's proposals for erecting a gunlock manufactory in the state.[141]

Not all rights were taken for granted. The Declaration of Rights failed explicitly to protect freedom of speech. Only "Persons professing the Christian Religion ought forever to enjoy equal Rights and Privileges in this State."[142] A critic commented that "there are some good things in the Delaware constitution, which are evidently borrowed from the Pennsylvanian, but mangled like a school-boy's abridgement of a Spectator's paper. Some of their bill of rights, explained by tories, might prevent all American defence."[143]

Like the other colonies, Delaware traditionally recognized keeping and bearing arms as both a right and a duty. Pre-Revolutionary militia acts required each male to "provide himself" with a firearm and "to keep such Arms and Ammunition by him."[144] "Being persuaded that a well regulated militia is the most effectual Guard and Security to every Country," the colonial assembly provided "that the Inhabitants may be armed, trained and disciplined in the Art of War . . . to defend themselves, their Lives and Properties."[145]

For security against pirates, "all the Inhabitants and Freemen" of the seaport of Lewes were obliged to meet armed on the sound of the alarm.[146] The only traditional restriction on possession of firearms in Delaware was "that no bought Servant, or Negro or Mulatto slave, shall, upon any Pretence whatever, be allowed to bear Arms, or to be mustered in any of the Companies of the Militia within this Government."[147]

During the Revolution Whigs and Tories disarmed each other whenever possible, which was not surprising given that they were frequently trying to kill each other. The delegates at the 1776 constitutional convention considered a petition of persons who apologized for their involvement in a recent insurrection. Since they promised to conduct themselves peaceably, the convention resolved "that they be again restored to the Favour of their Country, and that their Arms be redelivered to them."[148] As for the people at large, the convention resolved that militia members were required to provide their own arms.[149]

MARYLAND

On June 27, 1776, the militia of Anne Arundel County adopted resolves directed to their delegates in the upcoming Maryland constitutional convention.[150] Proposing a constitution for Maryland, the resolves sought guarantees for jury trial and habeas corpus.[151] Declaring against standing armies, it added: "That a well regulated militia be established in this province, as being the best security for the preservation of the lives, liberties and properties of the people."[152] Militiamen should choose their own officers, and firearms would be provided to men who could not afford them.[153]

The above resulted from the participation in the election of all taxpayers who bore arms.[154] Contrary to the usual property qualifications, Rezin Hammond told protesters in Anne Arundel County "that every man that bore arms in defence of his country had a right to vote, and if they were allowed no vote they had no right to bear arms."[155] Election officials reciting property qualifications were interrupted with shouts of "let every free man vote that carries arms."[156]

The Maryland constitutional convention began its deliberations in mid-August 1776. The militia resolves were repeated as instructions to the delegates from Anne Arundel County.[157] While the Whig-dominated convention would reject the democratic Constitution proposed in the resolves,[158] both Whigs and Democrats were in accord with a militia composed of the whole people. The Democrats were inspired by Dr. Richard Price, the English philosopher, Thomas Paine, and the radicals of the Pennsylvania constitutional convention, which was proceeding at the same time.[159] John Adams and Charles Carroll of Carrollton inspired the Whigs.[160]

The committee appointed to draft a declaration of rights and constitution included Matthew Tilghman, Charles Carroll of Carrollton, Thomas

Johnson, George Plater, William Paca, Samuel Chase, Robert Goldsborough, Robert T. Hooe, and, until he lost his convention seat, Charles Carrollton the Barrister. Each of the committee members were Whigs, assuring defeat for the Democratic faction.[161]

A Declaration of Rights was soon reported, but not debated for some time. At the end of September, the draft Declaration and Constitution were ordered to be printed for the people to consider.[162] There were constant interruptions to convention business, so that by mid-October John Parnham moved "that this Convention will enter on no new business (except from evident necessity) until they have finished the consideration of the declaration of rights and form of government."[163] The convention proceeded to do so, but after "the bill of rights formerly printed . . . has been materially altered by a committee of the whole house," the convention rejected a motion by William Fitzhugh that it be printed before further consideration for the people at large to read.[164]

Little else is known about the drafting of the Declaration of Rights. It was reported, considered, slightly amended, and adopted by November 3.[165] The rights it recognized were limited. Freedom of speech was guaranteed only in the legislature.[166] The clause "all persons, professing the Christian religion, are equally entitled to protection in their religious liberty," limited freedom of religion to Catholics and Protestants.[167]

The right to bear arms was not explicitly mentioned, but Maryland's patriots well knew about and had doubtlessly agreed with Boston's 1768 resolution that all householders should keep arms, based on the English Declaration of Rights provision that "Protestants may have Arms for their Defence."[168] They could only have read with dismay reports from Boston at that time "that the Inhabitants of this Province are to be disarmed"[169] and the more recent 1775 report anticipating a proclamation that all Americans would be required to turn in their arms by a certain date.[170] The Association of the Freemen of Maryland found Gage's actions in Boston "sufficient causes to arm a free people in defence of their liberty" and directed that "the minute men exercise with their own firelocks."[171]

Maryland's 1776 Declaration of Rights did include the following: "That a well regulated militia is the proper and natural defence of a free government."[172] It also contained a provision rejecting standing armies.[173]

The above was a shortened version of a resolution passed in late 1774 by the deputies appointed by the counties of Maryland as follows:

That a well regulated militia, composed of the gentlemen, freeholders, and other freemen, is the natural strength and only stable security of a free government . . . ; will . . . render it unnecessary to keep any standing army (ever dangerous to liberty) in this province; and therefore it is recommended . . . that each man be provided with a good firelock . . . and be in readiness to act on any emergency.[174]

Not only was keeping and bearing arms a civic duty, but there were no legal restrictions on firearm possession. The only exception was a 1715 enactment providing "that no negro or other slave within this province shall be permitted to carry any gun, or any other offensive weapon, from off their master's land, without license from their said master," which was punishable by whipping.[175] At any rate, Maryland was among those states with minimal bills of rights.

### NORTH CAROLINA

The delegates at the North Carolina constitutional convention that met in November and December 1776, had been instructed by their constituents to adopt a declaration of rights. The inhabitants of Mecklenberg directed "that you shall endeavour that the form of Government shall set forth a bill of rights containing the rights of the people and of individuals which shall never be infringed in any future time by the law-making power or other derived powers in the State."[176] The delegates were urged to acknowledge certain maxims, including that "the principal supreme power is possessed by the people at large, the derived and inferior power by the servants which they employ."[177]

The North Carolina convention had two guides for an arms guarantee. Virginia rested a free state on "the body of the people, trained to arms,"[178] while Pennsylvania declared "that the people have a right to bear arms for the defence of themselves, and the state."[179] The committee appointed to frame a bill of rights and constitution included convention President Richard Caswell and Joseph Hewes.[180] These leaders had a year earlier, as members of the Continental Congress, sent a message to the committees of safety asserting: "It is the Right of every English Subject to be prepared with Weapons for his Defence." They urged "the necessity of arming and instructing yourselves, to be in Readiness to defend yourselves against any Violence that may be exerted against your Persons and Properties."[181]

The committee reported the Bill of Rights a month later. It was debated, paragraph by paragraph, for three days, and then adopted.[182] Willie Jones appears to have been its draftsman, and Richard Caswell its inspiration. In a convention decades later, one delegate relied on the tradition that Caswell "dictated the principles, if not the terms" of the Constitution.[183] Another delegate averred: "The existing Constitution is thought to have been as much or more the work (the 32nd section [a religious test oath] excepted) of Willie Jones, than any other one individual, yet under that very charter was he [as a deist] proscribed by the bigotry of the framer of the 32nd section." Jones was "the Champion of the Whigs in the Convention of 1776."[184]

Little debate appears to have been raised by proposals to declare such rights as bearing arms and free assembly. The free exercise of religion was another matter. Delegate Samuel Johnston described a proposal requiring each member of the legislature to take a test oath swearing "that he believed in the holy Trinity and that the Scripture of the Old Testament was written by divine inspiration. This was carried after a very warm debate and has blown up such a flame that every thing is in danger of being thrown into confusion."[185] But a watered down sectarian test oath was finally adopted as Article 32.

As adopted, the Declaration of Rights asserted the following guarantees recognizing two rights of "the people":

> XVII. That the People have a right to bear Arms for the Defence of the State; and as standing Armies in Time of Peace are dangerous to Liberty, they ought not to be kept up . . . .
>
> XVIII. That the People have a Right to assemble together.[186]

It was "the People" who had "a right" to bear arms and to assemble. The militia was not mentioned. Having assembled in arms against the Royal forces since the days of the colonial Regulators, North Carolinians now engaged in armed revolt found these propositions unquestionable. "The right of every *English* Subject to be prepared with Weapons for this Defence"[187] was radically expanded to include explicit recognition of arms bearing "for the Defence of the State" and against the Royal government.

To be sure, the guarantee did not explicitly recognize the people's right to bear arms "for defence of themselves" as did that of Pennsylvania. Yet the right remained in "the People," and "the Defence of the State" presumably included local defense such as in the hue and cry as well as defense from invaders.

The Constitution did include a provision declaring a collective right: "The Property of the Soil in a free Government being one of the essential Rights of the collective Body of the People, it is necessary . . . that the Limits of the State should be ascertained with Precision."[188] By contrast, arms bearing and assembly were rights of "the People."

Of course, North Carolina did impose the duty of militia service. The Provincial Congress had resolved in April 1776 "that each Militia Soldier shall be furnished with a good Gun, Bayonet, Cartouch Box, Shot Bay and Powder Horn, a Cutlass or Tomahawk; and where any person shall appear to the Field Officers not possessed of sufficient Property to afford such Arms and Accoutrements, the same shall be provided at Public Expense."[189]

Similarly, a 1787 North Carolina enactment declared "that all Freemen and indentured Servants within this State, from 15 to 50 years of age, shall compose the militia thereof."[190] Privates furnished their own muskets and rifles, while horsemen had pistols.[191] Remaining on the books was legislation requiring every man to pursue felons and follow the hue and cry.[192]

No laws in North Carolina during and after this period prohibited possession of guns and pistols by freemen.[193] However, a mid-eighteenth-century enactment remained on the books providing that "no slave shall go armed with Gun, Sword, Club, or other Weapon," unless he had a certificate to carry a gun to hunt, issued with the owner's permission.[194] Having arms was manifestly an attribute of free citizenship.

The year 1776 was rich in the making of constitutions and bills of rights. Virginia and Pennsylvania particularly stand out as contributing to these novel attributes of republicanism. Other states would follow this example between 1777 and 1784.

## CHAPTER 7

# "A Musket to Defend These Rights"

I N  A M E R I C A , declared Dr. Richard Price in 1779, "every inhabitant has in his house (as a part of his furniture) a book on law and government, to enable him to understand his civil rights; a musket to enable him to defend these rights; and a Bible to enable him to understand and practice his religion."[1] These words captured the spirit in every one of the newly independent states, regardless of the extent to which rights were formally articulated in a constitution.

Following the constitution making by seven states in 1776, five states adopted constitutions (three with bills of rights) in the period 1777 through 1784, and two states simply continued to operate under their colonial charters. British war measures often left the constitutional conventions with little leisure to declare abstract rights. Further, the philosophical view would be expressed that a free people had little use of a written list of rights, the existence of which would be misconstrued by future despots to deny any rights not mentioned.

This chapter concerns the states that approved their first constitutions after 1776 or did not adopt any constitution during the Revolution at all, including Georgia, New York, Vermont, Massachusetts, New Hampshire, Connecticut, and Rhode Island. Particular regard will be paid to conceptions of the right to keep and bear arms.

## GEORGIA

At the coming of the American Revolution, Georgia had the smallest population of all the colonies.[2] Even though the agricultural colony produced no declarations of rights like those of Virginia or North Carolina, its settlers took for granted such rights as keeping and bearing arms. When the colonies to the north began to resist British tyranny, a writer from Georgia praised the model of the Fairfax County Independent Militia Company and implored that "the English troops in our front, and our governors forbid giving assent to militia laws, make it high time that we enter into *associations* for learning the use of arms, and to choose officers . . . ."[3]

As of April 1776, Georgia was governed by temporary Rules and Regulations that reflected the Whig doctrine that governmental power originated with the people.[4] When a convention assembled early the next year to frame a permanent constitution, it was led by radical Whigs,[5] whose political creed emphasized the role of the armed citizen in a republic.

Convention records reflect that on January 24, 1777, a committee of seven was elected to draft a constitution.[6] Its chairman and perhaps most active member was Button Gwinnett,[7] president of Georgia under the old Rules and Regulations. Five days later, Gwinnett reported a proposed constitution to the convention, which amended and then unanimously adopted it on February 5.[8]

The preamble recited that British tyranny "has obliged the Americans, as freemen, to oppose such oppressive measures, and to assert the rights and privileges they are entitled to, by the laws of nature and reason."[9] The text contained no bill of rights, although it declared against excessive fines and bail and guaranteed habeas corpus, free press, and jury trial.[10] The rights to free speech, assembly, and bearing arms were not specifically recognized but were assumed as fundamental by the Whigs who wrote the Constitution. Arms bearing was more than a right, it was mandatory: "Every County in this State that has, or hereafter may have, two hundred and fifty men upwards, liable to bear arms, shall be formed into a battalion."[11]

The Whigs were split between the Radical, Popular, or Country Party and the Conservative, City, or Merchant Party.[12] The former, led by Button Gwinnett, favored civilian control over the military while the latter, led by Brigadier General Lachlan McIntosh, believed Georgia's new Constitution to be too democratic.[13] Gwinnett and McIntosh clashed over leadership of an expedition against St. Augustine, Florida. When the legislature approved Gwinnett's conduct, the two faced each other in a duel. Both were wounded, and Gwinnett died in three days.[14]

The British held most of the settled areas of Georgia from 1778 through the end of the Revolution. Patriot guerrilla bands composed of self-armed and independent citizens harassed the invaders without end. British expeditions burned homes and destroyed property as they marched, sparing only those who surrendered their arms on demand.[15]

Georgia's delegates at the Continental Congress in 1778 sought to deny citizenship rights to those who refused to pick up the gun in defense of the Revolution. Article IV of the Articles of Confederation excepted paupers, vagabonds, and fugitives from the guarantee that "the free inhabitants of each of those states . . . shall be entitled to all privileges and immunities of free citizens in the several states." Georgia proposed that "all persons who refuse to bear Arms in defence of the State to which they belong," and persons convicted of treason, should also be excepted from the privileges and immunities of free citizens.[16] Congress declined to add the provision.

Under the laws in effect in Georgia in that epoch, bearing arms was required. Conflicts with Native Americans prompted a 1770 enactment that "every male white inhabitant of this province, (the inhabitants of the sea port towns only excepted who shall not be obliged to carry any other than side arms) who is or shall be liable to bear arms in the militia . . . and resorting . . . to any church . . . shall carry with him a gun, or a pair of pistols."[17] Each man was required to "take the said gun or pistols with him to the pew or seat," and these arms were to "be fit for immediate use and service."[18]

Pre-Revolutionary legislation also required that every white man liable to patrol duty "shall provide for himself, and keep always in readiness, and carry with him on patrol service a good gun or pistol."[19] The patrols "shall have full power to search and examine all negro houses for offensive weapons and ammunition."[20] It was unlawful "for any slave, unless in the presence of some white person, to carry and make use of fire arms," unless the slave had a written license from his master to hunt, albeit "lodging the same gun at night within the dwelling house of his master, mistress or white overseer."[21] No license was required for a slave to use a gun to kill birds and beasts of prey on the plantation.[22] Any person finding a slave off the plantation without permission, "if he be armed with such offensive weapons aforesaid, him or them to disarm, take up, and whip."[23]

Having arms was the right and duty of the free man, while deprivation of arms was the mark of the slave. Georgia recognized the rights of her citizens, but was far from ready to extend these rights to African Americans.

## NEW YORK

New York would not adopt a constitution until 1777, and it would have no bill of rights, but New York patriots shared similar concepts of rights as elsewhere. In revolutionary New York, keeping and bearing arms was an unquestioned fact. This reality is exemplified by newspapers of New York City in 1776, before its occupation that fall by the British under General Howe.

Detailed instructions for the home manufacture of gunpowder and advertisements for sword canes were published in the *New York Packet*'s first issue for 1776.[24] That summer, the New York convention passed a resolution supporting the private manufacture of gunpowder, which that body called "the Means of Defence and Self-preservation."[25] Until the city was occupied by the British, the following advertisements regularly appeared: "Those Gentlemen who are forming themselves into Companies in Defence of their Liberties; and others who are not provided with SWORDS may be suited therewith by applying to Charles Oliver Bruff."[26] Various sword designs inscribed with one's favorite patriot slogan could be had.

Discussion ensued in the press about how the armed people could defeat standing armies. "An English American" proposed: "For our security against the introduction of British troops to enslave us in times of tranquility, when we had forgot the use of arms, a perpetual standing militia bill should form part of the compact, by which means the people of the colonies would keep up their martial spirit, and always be prepared against the attack of arbitrary power."[27] The writer proposed that the king could retain a limited force to prevent sudden invasion. "Whoever asserts that 10 or 12,000 soldiers would be sufficient to control the militia of this Continent, consisting of 500,000 brave men, pays but a despicable compliment to the spirit and ability of Americans."[28]

"An Independent Whig" rejected the idea of an armed elite in place of a general militia composed of the whole people: "The Praetorian guards at Rome, were . . . not a larger body, if so large; yet they kept the whole world in slavery for many years, raised any one to be Emperor whom they pleased, and cut him off if he happened to disoblige them . . . . A standing army have great power to do mischief, and enslave countries, because they are already raised."[29] Ineffective at resisting invasion, "the soldiers are the dregs of every nation."[30] "They ought not to be named with the Provincials and Militia, who are freemen, sons of liberty, property, and bravery." A militia trained to be expert at arms would defeat any invader.[31]

Such subversive talk ended in September 1776 with the British conquest of New York City, and instead city newspapers included a Proclamation of General Howe at the top of page one of every issue that decried that "several Bodies of armed Men . . . do still continue their Opposition to the Establishment of legal Government and Peace."[32] The occupation lasted through November 1783, months after the surrender at Yorktown.

Due to the British onslaught, the provincial convention of New York was one of the most erratic of all the newly independent states. Its place of assembly was repeatedly pushed around the state by British troop movements.[33] In his biography of Gouverneur Morris, Theodore Roosevelt noted that "the members were obliged to go armed, so as to protect themselves from stray marauding parties."[34]

The convention began its deliberations on August 1, 1776, and unanimously resolved that a committee draft a plan for a new form of government. The committee would "report at the same time a bill of rights; ascertaining and declaring the essential rights and privileges of the good people of this State, as the foundation for such form of government."[35] Thirteen members were elected to this committee, several of whom would be major figures in the debates over the federal Constitution a dozen years later.[36] The committee was ordered to report a constitution and bill of rights on August 26, but the journal includes no mention of the subject on that day. For the next six months, the convention functioned mainly as a committee of safety whose members were dispersed throughout the state. Some fought the invaders while others procured arms and ammunition.[37]

At the end of March 1777, a draft of the Constitution in John Jay's hand-writing was reported from committee. Jay played the leading role in framing the instrument, with Gouverneur Morris and Robert R. Livingston as his chief advisors.[38] Contrary to the charge resolved by the convention, the committee reported no bill of rights. Yet no record exists of any objection by the convention members, even those of radical persuasions.[39]

To be sure, the text of the Constitution guaranteed jury trial where already practiced, as well as religious toleration. Yet a proposal for complete freedom of religion was staunchly opposed and led to the longest debate of the session. Jay's biographer notes:

> The power of the Church of Rome he knew and feared; he urged, accord-ingly, amendment after amendment to except Roman Catholics till they should abjure the authority of the pope to absolve citizens from their allegiance and to grant spiritual absolution. The result of his objections was the adoption of a proviso "that the liberty of conscience hereby granted shall not be so con-strued as to excuse acts of licentiousness or justify practices inconsistent with the safety of the State."[40]

There appears to have been little controversy over other provisions of the Constitution, or its lack of a bill of rights. The convention journal reflects that on April 20, 1777, the Constitution "was agreed to by every member present, except Colo. Peter R. Livingston, who desired that his dissent thereto be en-tered on the minutes."[41]

New York's Constitution of 1777—which took nine months to frame— included no specific declarations about rights such as a free press and bearing arms, but the latter was declared to be a civic obligation:

> [I]t is the duty of every man who enjoys the protection of society to be prepared and willing to defend it; this convention therefore . . . doth ordain, determine, and declare that the militia of this State, at all times hereafter, as well in peace as in war, shall be armed and disciplined, and in readiness for service. That all such of the inhabitants of this State being of the people called Quakers as, from scruples of conscience, may be adverse to the bearing of arms, be therefrom excused by the legislature; and do pay to the State such sums of money, in lieu

of their personal service, as the same may, in the judgment of the legislature, be worth.[42]

A decade later, New Yorkers who had no bill of rights in their own Constitution were demanding one for the proposed federal Constitution. Writing under the pseudonym "Sydney," Abraham Yates, Jr., who had been chairman of the committee that drafted New York's 1777 Constitution, explained why it had no bill of rights:

> While the constitution of this state was in agitation, there appeared doubts upon the propriety of the measure, from the peculiar situation in which the country then was; our connection with Britain dissolved, and her government formally renounced—no substitute devised—all the powers of government avowedly temporary, and solely calculated for defence. . . . Those in opposition admitted, that in established governments, which had an implied constitution, a declaration of rights might be necessary to prevent the usurpation of ambitious men, but that . . . our situation resembled a people in a state of nature, . . . and as such the constitution to be formed would operate as a bill of rights.
>
> These and the like considerations operated to induce the convention of New York to dismiss the idea of a bill of rights.[43]

Whatever effects the lack of a written bill of rights may have had on other rights, bearing arms was encouraged rather than suppressed. As chief justice of the New York Supreme Court, John Jay wrote in 1778 that criminals "multiply exceedingly. Robberies become frequent."[44] Reflecting the traditional hue and cry, New York law required "that all men generally be ready, and armed and accoutered, . . . and at the cry of the country, to pursue and arrest felons."[45]

A statute passed in early 1787 declared "that no authority shall, on any pretence whatsoever, be exercised over the citizens of this state, but such as is or shall be derived from and granted by the people of this state."[46] Containing provisions for the rights of petition and speech, and against excessive bail and the quartering of soldiers, the act declared: "that no citizen of this state shall be constrained to arm himself, or to go out of this state" unless approved by the legislature.[47] New York would soon insist on a federal declaration of these principles, but that story will be told later in this work.

## VERMONT

Keeping and bearing arms was not only an abstract right, but also a constant practice of Vermont's founding fathers. Led by Ethan and Ira Allen, the Green Mountain Boys sought independence first from New York and later from Great Britain. In his detailed accounts of their exploits, Ira Allen vividly exposited the role of firearms in the hands of the people for purposes of defending the person and the incipient state as well as for hunting and target shooting.[48]

Before the Revolution, the Allens were in constant conflict with New York's royal governor and British troops over the Vermonters' land claims. In one incident, they set out to purchase land. Lodging with a Quaker, Ira Allen recalled: "We took our pistols out of our holsters and carried them in with us. He looked at the pistols saying 'What doth thee do with those things?' He was answered 'Nothing amongst our friends,' but we were Green Mountain boys, and meant to protect our persons and property . . . ."[49]

Throughout 1776, conventions and committees met in Vermont to plan resistance to the British and to secure land titles against New York's claims. Petitioning the Continental Congress, Vermonters argued that they had the same right of independence from New York as America had from Britain.[50]

A committee including Ira Allen and six others at a September 1776 convention reported objectives for Vermont, including: "To regulate the Militia; To furnish troops according to our ability, for the defence of the Liberties of the United States of America."[51] The convention resolved "that each non-commissioned officer and soldier immediately furnish himself with a good gun with a Bayonet, sword or tomahawk."[52]

Town representatives decided in January 1777 that Vermont should be a free and independent state. The convention declared that the rights of Vermont inhabitants included the privileges and immunities of the free citizens of the other states and that "such privileges and immunities shall be regulated in a bill of rights, and by a form of government," to be established at the next session of the convention.[53]

The constitutional convention, which met July 2–8, 1777, was predisposed toward the example set by Pennsylvania.[54] The address "To the Inhabitants of Vermont" by Dr. Thomas Young of Philadelphia urged the Pennsylvania Constitution "as a model, which, with a very little alternation, will, in my opinion, come as near perfection as anything yet concocted by mankind."[55]

Among the provisions included in the Declaration of Rights adopted by the Vermont convention taken verbatim from that of Pennsylvania was the following: "That the people have a right to bear arms for the defence of themselves and the State; and, as standing armies, in the time of peace, are dangerous to liberty, they ought not to be kept up . . . ."[56] Vermont also copied Pennsylvania in declaring "that the inhabitants of this State, shall have liberty to hunt and fowl, in seasonable times, on the lands they hold, and on other lands (not enclosed)."[57]

The Declaration included a separate provision relating to militia service. Since every person had "a right to be protected in the enjoyment of life, liberty and property," each must "yield his personal service, when necessary," except that "any man who is conscientiously scrupulous of bearing arms" would not "be justly compelled thereto" if he paid an equivalent.[58] The difference between being "compelled" to bear arms and having the "right" to bear arms was clear.

The only laws on the books in this epoch concerning firearms was an act "Regulating the Militia." It required that all males aged 16 to 50 "shall bear arms, and duly attend all musters," and that "every listed soldier and other householder, shall always be provided with, and have in constant readiness, a well fixed firelock . . . : or other good fire-arms."[59] Another act reiterated that every male shall "provide himself, at his own expense, with a good musket or firelock,"[60] and that horsemen "shall always be provided with . . . holsters with bear-skin caps, a case of good pistols, a sword or cutlass."[61]

In 1787, Vermont adopted a new constitution that became binding just before the federal constitutional convention met in Philadelphia. It reenacted the guarantee "that the people have a right to bear arms for the defence of themselves and the State . . . ."[62] Although Vermont functioned as a state, it was not officially admitted by Congress into the Union until February 18, 1791.


MASSACHUSETTS

Following rejection in 1778 by the Massachusetts populace of a constitution with no bill of rights, a convention met the following year to frame a more acceptable constitution. The resultant Constitution of 1780 included a Declaration of Rights which began:

I. All men are born free and equal, and have certain natural, essential, and unalienable rights; among which may be reckoned the right of enjoying and defending their lives and liberties; that of acquiring, possessing, and protecting property; in fine, that of seeking and obtaining their safety and happiness.[63]

The Declaration included the following further guarantee which was the first time a state bill of rights recognized the right to "keep" arms:

XVII. The people have a right to keep and bear arms for the common defence. And as, in time of peace armies are dangerous to liberty, they ought not to be maintained without the consent of the legislature; and the military power shall always be held in an exact subordination to the civil authority, and be governed by it.[64]

The subcommittee charged with drafting what would become the Constitution of 1780 included James Bowdoin, Samuel Adams, and John Adams.[65] While John Adams alone drafted the Constitution and Declaration of Rights, presumably the three discussed the general concept and drafts. Bowdoin had been a patriot leader in the 1768 crises and chaired the Boston town committee that protested the Boston Massacre.[66] Sam Adams, of course, was a leading defender of the right to have arms.

John Adams needed little prompting to add "to keep and" to the phrase "bear arms." Besides the experience of the Minute Man grabbing his musket from the mantle, keeping arms in the home for security was well recognized. In a 1774 court case, Adams wrote that "an Englishman's dwelling House is his Castle," and that every person "shall enjoy in his own dwelling House as compleat a security, safety and Peace and Tranquility as if it was . . . defended with a Garrison and Artillery."[67] Adams exercised the right personally—when he sailed to France in 1778, he took along a pocket pistol.[68]

Appealing to "the Laws of Self Preservation," Samuel Adams had urged patriots "to provide themselves without Delay with Arms" for defense against despotism, and elsewhere remarked that "we may all be soon under the necessity of keeping Shooting Irons."[69]

As noted, the Declaration provided that "the people have a right" to arms. That phrase appeared in the following further provision:

XIX. The people have a right, in an orderly and peaceable manner, to assemble to consult upon the common good; give instructions to their representatives, and to request of the legislative body, by the way of addresses, petitions, or remonstrances, redress of the wrongs done them, and of the grievances they suffer.[70]

As drafted by Adams and reported by the committee, the phrase that "the people have a right" further appeared as follows:

> The people have a right to the freedom of speaking, writing, and publishing their sentiments. The liberty of the press, therefore, ought not to be restrained.[71]

As finally adopted, that language was changed to the following: "The liberty of the press is essential to the security of freedom in a State; it ought not, therefore, to be restrained in this commonwealth."[72] Nonetheless, it is clear that the phrase "the people have a right" meant that individuals composing the populace at large had a liberty to do something without permission of the state, whether it was possessing arms, petitioning, or publishing. It would not make sense to say that "the people have a right" to do something only if the state authorizes it.

The reservation of the "right" to "the people" clarified that keeping and bearing arms was a civil liberty, not a state military power. Contrasting language was employed to refer to duties of citizens, such as militia service. Thus, the Declaration provided that each individual in society had a right to be protected. "He is obliged, consequently, . . . to give his personal service, or an equivalent, when necessary . . . ."[73]

The right to bear arms was declared to be "for the common defence," similar to the right to assemble being "to consult upon the common good." Neither phrase negated that each activity was a right of the people, not a decision of the government. Further, the arms that a person would bear for the common defense were the same personal arms that such person would "keep."[74] These arms were available for other lawful purposes.

The American patriots saw themselves as bearing arms for the common defense against the lawless government of the Crown. To bear arms for the common defense included not only defense against foreign invasion but also institutions such as the hue and cry in which citizens defended themselves from and pursued felons. Yet the clause would give rise to controversy for not explicitly recognizing self-defense.

The section providing for the right to have arms also had a second sentence declaring that "in time of peace armies are dangerous to liberty." As drafted by Adams and reported by the committee, it used the term "standing armies."[75] The minutes reflect that this was the only change to that section: "The Convention went into the consideration of the 18th article, (the subject military power), and after considerable debate, and expunging the word 'standing' before the word 'armies,' accepted the same."[76] All armies, not just standing armies, were dangerous to liberty.

The proposed frame of government was subjected to critical scrutiny at town meetings throughout Massachusetts. At least two towns objected to the Declaration's arms guarantee as too narrow. The town of Northhampton resolved:

> We also judge that the people's right to keep and bear arms, declared in the seventeenth article of the same declaration is not expressed with that ample and manly openness and latitude which the importance of the right merits; and therefore propose that it should run in this or some like manner, to wit, The people have a right to keep and bear arms as well for their own as the common defence. Which mode of expression we are of opinion would harmonise much better with the first article than the form of expression used in the said seventeenth article.[77]

Similarly, the town of Williamsburg wanted a more explicit guarantee of the right to have arms for self-protection, proposing that the section be amended to read: "that the people have a right to keep and to bear Arms for their Own and the Common defence." The following explanation was presented:

> Voted Nemine Contradic. Our reasons gentleman for making the Addition Are these. 1st that we esteem it an essential privilege to keep Arms in Our houses for Our Own Defence and while we Continue honest and Lawful subjects of Government we Ought Never to be deprived of them.
>
> Reas. 2 That the legislature in some future period may confine all the fire Arms to some publick Magazine and thereby deprive the people of the benefit of the use of them.[78]

The above arguably glossed over the fact that the Declaration guaranteed the right "to keep" not just to "bear" arms. If "the people" could "keep" their firearms in the home, the arms would be available—as expressed in Article

I—for "defending their lives and liberties; . . . and protecting property."[79] John Adams himself upheld the right of "arms in the hands of citizens, to be used at individual discretion, . . . in private self-defence . . . ."[80]

A review of the Boston *Independent Chronicle* for 1780 reveals no controversy over the arms or press guarantees but bitter dispute on freedom of religion.[81] That paper's only references to firearms just before adoption of the Constitution was an advertisement for "100 Pair Horseman's Pistols, neatly mounted with Steel."[82]

The Declaration's strictures against armies won praise from Abbé de Mably in a 1785 pamphlet addressed to John Adams. Mably noted: "You must expect that your people, of whom the laws have so clearly established the sovereignty, may prove difficult to manage, because they will perceive of their power. Armed in the defence of their country, they will become jealous of their dignity."[83]

In the two decades that followed the adoption of the Declaration of Rights in 1780, no laws were passed to prohibit the possession of firearms for lawful purposes. Shays' Rebellion in September 1786 led to two arms-related acts. The first provided that if twelve or more persons "armed with clubs, or other weapons" gathered, a justice of the peace could order them to disperse and could "require the aid of a sufficient number of persons in arms" to help.[84] The second act declared:

> Whereas in a free government, where the people have a right to bear arms for the common defence, and the military power is held in subordination to the civil authority, it is necessary for the safety of the State that the virtuous citizens thereof should hold themselves in readiness, and when called upon, should exert their efforts to support the civil government, and oppose the attempts of factious and wicked men who may wish to subvert the laws and Constitution of Their country.[85]

In newspaper commentary in 1786–87, an adherent to making Maine a separate state from Massachusetts reflected on the guarantee of the right to arms. One "Scribble Scrabble" opined that it "does not prohibit the people, or take from them, the right originally in them of using arms for other purposes than common defence. Who will say that if an honest farmer were to discharge his musket, ten times a day, at pigeons or other game, he thereby becomes an enemy to the constitution?"[86] Averring that "the constitution does not directly say the people have a right to keep & bear arms for squibing at pigeons and other game," the writer stated that "the legislature have a power to control it in all cases, except the one mentioned in the bill of rights . . . ." Absent regulation, "the people have the full uncontrolled use of arms . . . ."

While the legislature could regulate the use of arms for purposes other than the common defense, the right to keep arms appeared more absolute. As "Senex" wrote in response: "The idea that Great Britain meant to take away their arms, was fresh in the minds of the people; therefore in forming a new government, they wisely guarded against it."[87]

"Scribble Scrabble" wrote further that rights such as voting are not natural rights but are conferred by law. "How different is the case of keeping and bearing arms. This is a right almost coeval with man."[88] Since the time of Adam, who "had a right, in Paradise, to have grasped a club and smashed the old Serpent," all men have had "a right to keep and bear arms for their common defence, to kill game, fowl, &c." He continued: "The Bill of Rights secures to the people the use of arms in common defence; so that, if it be an alienable right, one use of arms is secured to the people against any law of the legislature." And unless the legislature acted, "whatever right people had to use arms in a state of nature, they retain at the present time . . . ."

While the use of arms for purposes other than the common defense could be regulated, the possession of arms was constitutionally protected. Among the rights of "every subject," according to a 1793 summary, was "that he may keep arms . . . ."[89] As the Supreme Judicial Court of Massachusetts would state, the guarantee protects "the right to keep fire arms," but does "not protect him who uses them for annoyance or destruction."[90]

### NEW HAMPSHIRE

New Hampshire was the eighth of the independent states to adopt a bill of rights, but it did not do so until 1784, three years after the British surrendered at Yorktown. New Hampshire's brief constitution of 1776 complained that the British were "depriving us of our national and constitutional rights and privileges."[91] A constitution proposed and rejected by the town meetings in 1779 included a short declaration of rights that stated: "We the people of this State, are entitled to life, liberty, and property; and all other immunities and privileges which we heretofore enjoyed."[92]

Several drafts of constitutions were developed in a series of conventions and town meetings between 1781 and 1783. A convention address to the people held that "the strength and safety of this State will greatly depend on the keeping up a well regulated militia"[93] and that "the bill of Rights . . . is the foundation on which the whole political fabric is reared."[94] One of the convention leaders was John Sullivan, then attorney general and soon to be president of the state.[95]

Also a militia chief, on December 14–15, 1774, Sullivan had led New Hampshire citizens to break open His Majesty's Castle William and Mary at Portsmouth Harbor, seizing one hundred barrels of gunpowder and sixty stand of small arms.[96]

Sullivan now joined with his compatriots in drafting a constitution. Ratified by the towns and made effective in 1784, its Bill of Rights included the following interrelated articles:

> II. All men have certain natural, essential, and inherent rights; among which are—the enjoying and defending life and liberty—acquiring, possessing and protecting property—and in a word, of seeking and obtaining happiness . . . .
>
> X. The doctrine of non-resistance against arbitrary power, and oppression, is absurd, slavish, and destructive of the good and happiness of mankind . . . .
>
> XXIV. A well regulated militia is the proper, natural, and sure defence of a state.
>
> XXV. Standing armies are dangerous to liberty, and ought not to be raised or kept up without the consent of the legislature.

The right of each individual of "defending life and liberty," the right to resist oppression, and the preference of a militia over a standing army all embodied a right that was not explicitly articulated but was inherent in those concepts: the right to keep and bear arms.

The Constitution also proclaimed the right to be protected and the duty of each "to contribute his share in the expense of such protection, and to yield his personal service when necessary."[97] Even so, the right of a pacifist *not* to bear arms was recognized too: "No person who is conscientiously scrupulous about the lawfulness of bearing arms, shall be compelled thereto, provided he will pay an equivalent."[98] To be sure, the Bill of Rights had limits. The Protestant religion was state supported, and only Christians "shall be equally under the protection of the law."[99] Freedom of speech was recognized only in the legislature.[100]

The Act for the Establishment and Regulation of the Militia of 1786 provided that "the training band . . . shall consist of all the able-bodied male persons within the state, from sixteen years old to forty,"[101] and that all exempt males "shall constitute an alarm list . . . and shall, in all respects, be equipped with arms and accoutrements, as is by this act directed for those of the training band."[102] The act required that all persons "both in the alarm list and training band, shall be provided, and have constantly in readiness, a good musket, and a bayonet fitted thereto" with ammunition and supplies.[103] Persons unable to furnish themselves with arms would be issued arms by the towns.[104] Once every six months, the commanding officer of each alarm company would "call his company together, and examine their arms and accoutrements," and punish any deficiency of arms.[105]

The Perpetual Laws of the State of New Hampshire, the statutes enacted from 1776 to 1788, contain no restriction on the right to keep and bear arms. However, a 1786 act found that "the keeping of large quantities of gun-powder in private houses in Portsmouth . . . Would greatly endanger the lives and properties of the inhabitants thereof, in case of fire; which danger might be prevented, by obliging the owners of such powder, to deposit the same in the magazine provided by said town for that purpose."[106] The act provided that if a person "shall keep in any dwelling-house, store or other building . . . more than ten pounds of gun-powder," the powder would be forfeited. There would be chosen annually by the voters "a keeper of said magazine, all the powder so deposited, and to account therefore."[107]

The purpose of the law was not to control the populace but to prevent urban fires caused by large quantities of black powder, a volatile substance. The owners of the powder were protected by being able to elect the keeper of the magazine and to retrieve their powder on request. As they proved in 1774, the citizens of Portsmouth knew how to withdraw their deposits if the keepers were reluctant.

While the New Hampshire bill of rights did not explicitly recognize the right to bear arms, when the federal Constitution was proposed three years later, that state's convention demanded recognition that "Congress shall never disarm any citizen, unless such as are or have been in actual rebellion."[108] As elsewhere, rights may not have been listed in a state declaration, but recognition was demanded in a federal bill of rights.

CONNECTICUT

"The Provinces of [Connecticut and Rhode Island]," complained William Knox in 1763, who would later become the British undersecretary of state, "are modeled upon the Ideas of corporate Towns; they . . . enact what Laws they please with[out] any Check or Controul, nor has the Crown any Hold, or scarcely any knowledge of them."[109] After independence was declared, these two colonies saw no need to adopt formal constitutions, much less bills of rights. Connecticut's charter of 1662, which originated in town meetings, was reaffirmed by the General Assembly in October 1776 and remained operative until the adoption of a constitution and bill of rights in 1818.[110]

All males aged 16 through 50 were required to bear arms under the old militia law still in force in 1775.[111] When Gage disarmed Boston, Connecticut passed legislation to encourage the manufacture of firearms and gunpowder and established regulations for Minutemen.[112] The Revolutionary press, led by the Hartford *Courant* and the New Haven *Post Boy*, called for the people to take arms and spread the alarm.

As reflected in Connecticut's 1784 code, citizens were required to come armed to the watch and ward[113] and to pursue felons in the hue and cry.[114] The Militia Act declared that "the Defence and Security of all free States depends (under God) upon the Exertions of a well regulated and Disciplined Militia."[115] All males aged 16 through 45 were in the militia. Both militia infantrymen "and Householders under fifty-five Years of Age, shall, at all times be furnished at their own Expense, with a well fixed Musket," and horsemen with "a Case of good Pistols, a Sword or Cutlass."[116] The commander reviewed the required arms annually, including those of "Householders and others by Law obliged to keep Arms."[117]

That same year, Dr. Richard Price published his *Observations on the Importance of the American Revolution*. The British philosopher, whose works sold widely in England and America, was well familiar with the theory of rights underlying the above laws. Price stated:

> God forbid, that standing armies should ever find an establishment in America. . . . No wise people will trust their defence out of their own hands, or con-

sent to hold their rights at the mercy of armed *slaves*. Free states ought to be bodies of armed *citizens*, and always ready to turn out, when properly called upon, to execute the laws, to quell riots, and to keep the peace. Such . . . are the citizens of America.[118]

Price, who had been awarded the LL.B. from Yale College, referred to "Connecticut, and some others of the American provinces; where the inhabitants consist . . . of an independent and hardy Yeomanry, all nearly on a level—trained to arms,—instructed in their rights."[119] Price contrasted Britain, "consisting as it does of unarmed inhabitants," with the American states, which all had "a well-trained militia."[120]

Minister and politician Timothy Dwight, a chaplain in the Connecticut Continental Brigade during the Revolution and later president of Yale College, would write: "The people of New-England have always had, and have by law always been required to have, arms in their hands. Every man is, or ought to be, in the possession of a musket." Yet he did not know of "a single instance, in which arms have been the instruments of carrying on a private quarrel."[121]

## RHODE ISLAND

Two years of Revolutionary War only confirmed the assessment of colonial Undersecretary William Knox about two of the colonies that would adopt no new constitution during the Revolution. In 1777 he observed: "That the Constitutions under which the Charter Colonies have been settled are ill adapted to excite in the Inhabitants a Love of Monarchy, and the British Government, & a desire to continue connected with Great Britain, need not be proved. Rhode Island & Connecticut are simple Republics."[122] Knox's proposal that "the Arms of all the People should be taken away"[123] was particularly unrealistic in Rhode Island, a proven gateway for smuggling arms.

Just before Lexington and Concord, the *Newport Mercury* urged the readers to arm themselves, for every patriot "will prepare himself to defend (Life, Liberty or Property) against every Invader."[124] In the following months, the *Mercury* reprinted various attacks on Gage for disarming the people of Boston.

In 1775, the people of Rhode Island were generally armed and organized into groups from plain mobs to independent militias.[125] The town of Providence implored nearby inhabitants to "hold yourself in readiness" and bring all weapons "you have by you" when the alarm sounds.[126] This was possible because of the traditional public policy of the colony. The Militia Act, reenacted several times during 1718–1798, provided that every citizen aged 18 through 44 must "provide himself with a good musket or firelock."[127] The horseman was to furnish himself with a pair of pistols and a saber.[128]

The public laws as printed in 1798 began with the colonial charter, which was reenacted "to secure them in the exercise of all their civil and religious rights."[129] Of all the laws passed in that century and still on the books, none restricted the right to keep and bear arms. Even a broad prohibition on any Native American or slave from doing such things as going abroad after 9:00 p.m., or selling alcohol to them, did not mention arms.[130] The offensive use of arms was restricted beyond the usual crimes of robbery and murder. Dueling was prohibited.[131] The sheriff was authorized to disperse twelve or more persons if they were "armed with clubs or other weapons" or thirty or more persons if they were riotously assembled. The sheriff could "require the aid of a sufficient number of persons in arms."[132]

Rhode Island continued to rely on its colonial charter in the Revolution and until adoption of its first constitution in 1842. But lack of a constitution and bill of rights of its own did not dissuade Rhode Island from rejecting the federal Constitution until after the Bill of Rights had been proposed.

## ON THE EVE OF THE FEDERAL CONVENTION

Additional developments took place on the eve of the 1787 federal convention at Philadelphia that illuminate the nature of the right to keep and bear arms. In the Virginia General Assembly, a Committee of Revisors had for several years been drafting restatements of statutory law for the Commonwealth. Thomas Jefferson played the leading role, with George Wythe and Edmund Pendleton also participating. One of the committee's products, the Bill for Preservation of Deer, illustrates the common linguistic usage of the term to "bear arms."[133]

The bill was presented to the whole House in 1785 by James Madison, who would later become draftsman of the Second Amendment. The bill provided for deer hunting seasons outside one's enclosed land and punished violations as follows:

> Whosoever shall offend against this act, shall forfeit and pay, for every deer by
> him unlawfully killed, twenty shillings, one half thereof to the use of the com-

monwealth, and the other half to the informer; and moreover, shall be bound to their good behaviour; and, if within twelve months after the date of the recognisance *he shall bear a gun out of his inclosed ground, unless whilst performing military duty*, shall be deemed a breach of the recognisance, and be good cause to bind him anew, and *every such bearing of a gun* shall be a breach of the new recognisance and cause to bind him again.[134]

The bill followed legislation earlier in the century that sought to halt the alarming depopulation of deer. While it deleted as a penalty the "twenty lashes, on his or their back, well laid on" of the colonial act,[135] the bill imposed a monetary fine and placed the violator on his good behavior. A violator who, within a year, "shall bear a gun out of his inclosed ground, unless whilst performing military duty," would be deemed as having breached his recognizance. A "recognisance" is an obligation one acknowledges before a court or magistrate of doing or not doing some act.[136] Breach of the recognizance in this case would have required going before a magistrate, being admonished not to hunt deer unlawfully, and binding oneself to future good behavior.

Two aspects of the bill offer insights into the perceived nature of the right to bear arms. First, the bill would have prohibited the bearing only of "a gun," not of "arms" in general.[137] In the linguistic usage of the time, "guns" were distinguishable from "pistols."[138] Given its purpose to protect deer, the bill would not have prohibited violators from bearing pistols, which were unsuitable for hunting deer but which could be lawfully carried for self-defense. Even so, the House was apparently unwilling to restrict the places where game violators bore their guns, and no further legislative action was taken after the bill was read twice.[139]

Second, the bill would have put a game violator on his good behavior not to "bear a gun out of his inclosed ground, unless whilst performing military duty," and bind him to his good behavior anew for "every such bearing of a gun." To Jefferson, Madison, and their contemporaries, to "bear" a firearm meant broadly to carry it in one's hands or on one's person, as for instance a deer hunter would do. The term "bear arms" was not restricted to militia service in that the bill specifically addressed the "bearing of a gun" by "any person" when *not* "performing military duty."[140]

Another 1785 Virginia bill, which was enacted, sheds insight on the meaning of the right to "keep" arms. Both well before and after this period, Virginia law provided that "no negro or mulatto shall keep or carry any gun, powder, shot, club, or other weapon whatever," except that "every free negro or mulatto, being a housekeeper" may "keep one gun, powder and shot," and "a bond or free negro" may "keep and use" a gun by license at frontier plantations.[141] The 1785 enactment stated: "No slave shall keep any arms whatever or pass unless with written orders from his master or employer, or in his company with arms from one place to another."[142] Jefferson penned an outline of the new law that included the words: "no slave to be witness[,] . . . not to keep arms[,] not to pass with arms."[143]

Under Virginia law, the citizen had a right to keep arms, the slave did not. To "keep arms" was an activity engaged in by individuals at large and had no restrictive military connotation. As the above game bill illuminates, to "bear arms" referred to the carrying of arms by any person, whether a hunter or a person on military duty.

Thus was the status quo when the delegates to the federal constitutional convention assembled at Philadelphia. The mixed state approaches—some having, others eschewing, a declaration of rights—would be reflected as the incipient question loomed: Should the federal Constitution have a bill of rights?

# The Constitution and Compromise

## CHAPTER 8

# A Constitution with No Bill of Rights?

T H E   C O N V E N T I O N of delegates that met on May 25 through September 17, 1787, at Philadelphia were determined to go far beyond the Articles of Confederation in formulating a constitution that would consolidate federal power.[1] But the Articles and initially the Constitution would have one thing in common: lack of a bill of rights.

The reason was fundamental—as the federalists would argue, the Constitution delegated no powers that would authorize the new government to violate rights as they were traditionally understood. The antifederalists would respond that the Articles operated only on the states, but the proposed Constitution would operate on individuals, thereby requiring personal rights to be protected. But these arguments would be articulated in the future. At the Philadelphia convention itself, there was hardly any mention of a declaration of rights.

There was, however, considerable debate on the concept of the militia, given that it was part of the structure of government, which was all the proposed Constitution purported to be. The militia was initially contemplated in relation to governmental forms that would not ultimately be adopted. For instance, George Mason of Virginia envisioned that the office of president should consist of three persons rather than just one. A single leader had the advantages of unity and secrecy, yet monarchies had been defeated when they invaded republics. Republics without a single leader but with an armed populace had advantages too: "Every Husbandman will be quickly converted into a Soldier, when he knows & feels that he is to fight not in defence of the Rights of a particular Family, or a Prince; but for his own. . . . It is this which preserves the Freedom and Independence of the Swiss Cantons, in the midst of the most powerful Nations." That also was the secret to the success of the Americans in the Revolution, Mason asserted.[2]

While it is unclear when Mason may have broached the above, the issue of the militia was squarely raised in reaction to a proposal that the national legislature be empowered to negate state laws. Elbridge Gerry of Massachusetts observed on June 8: "that the proposed negative would extend to the regulations of the militia—a matter on which the existence of the state might depend. The national legislature, with such a power, may enslave the states."[3] The topic was dropped after the negative power was rejected.

George Mason, on August 18, proposed "a power to regulate the militia."[4] Reliance on the militia for the public defense would preclude a peacetime standing army. "Thirteen states will never concur in any one system, if the disciplining of the militia be left in their hands."[5] By regulating or standardizing the militia, the general government would assist the states in preserving their powers.

Mason proposed a power "to make laws for the regulation and discipline of the militia of the several states, reserving to the states the appointment of officers."[6] "He considered uniformity as necessary in the regulation of the militia, throughout the Union."[7] Oliver Ellsworth of Connecticut proposed that "the militia should have the same arms and exercise, and be under rules established by the general government when in actual service of the United States; and when states neglect to provide regulations for militia, it should be regulated and established by the legislature of the United States."[8] He explained: "The whole authority over the militia ought by no means to be taken away from the states, whose consequence would pine away to nothing after such a sacrifice of power."[9]

John Dickinson of Delaware supported both Mason and Ellsworth. A most important matter was "that of the sword. His opinion was, that the states never would, nor ought to, give up all authority over the militia."[10] He proposed that the federal power extend to only part of the militia at any one time, "which, by rotation, would discipline the whole militia."[11] Mason then incorporated this idea of "a select militia" into his proposal.[12] That term had a less innocent meaning in the mind of Ellsworth, who "considered the idea of a select militia as impracticable; and if it were not, it would be followed by a ruinous declension of the great body of the militia. The states would never submit to the same militia laws."[13]

Mason's proposal of a select militia was curious, for, as events would prove, he and others who would become antifederalists held that institution to be just a little less evil than a standing army. He may well have considered a select militia as the lesser of the two evils.

Roger Sherman of Connecticut opined that "the states might want their militia for defence against invasions and insurrections, and for enforcing obedience to their laws."[14] Mason agreed, adding to his motion an exception that the general power would not extend to "such part of the militia as might be required by the states for their own use."[15] Mason's proposals were then referred to committee.

When reported back to the convention, the militia clause provided that Congress may "make laws for organising, arming, and disciplining the militia, and for governing such parts of them as may be employed in the service of the United States, reserving to the states, respectively, the appointment of the officers, and authority of training the militia according to the discipline prescribed . . . ."[16] On August 23, the following debate ensued:

> MR. SHERMAN moved to strike out the last member, "and authority of training," &c. He thought it unnecessary. The states will have this authority, if not given up. . . .
>
> MR. [Rufus] KING [of Massachusetts], by way of explanation, said, that by *organising*, the committee meant, proportioning the officers and men—by *arming*, specifying the kind, size, and calibre of arms—and by *disciplining*, prescribing the manual exercise, evolutions, &c.
>
> MR. SHERMAN withdrew his motion.

> MR. GERRY This power in the United States, as explained, is making the states drill-sergeants. He had as lief let the citizens of Massachusetts be disarmed, as to take the command from the states, and subject them to the general legislature. It would be regarded as a system of despotism.

Mr. [James] Madison [of Virginia] observed, the "*arming*," as explained, did not extend to furnishing arms; nor the term "*disciplining*," to penalties, and courts martial for enforcing them.

Mr. King added to his former explanation, that *arming* meant not only to provide for uniformity of arms, but included the authority to regulate the modes of furnishing, either by the militia themselves, the state governments, or the national treasury; that *laws* for disciplining must involve penalties, and everything necessary for enforcing penalties.[17]

Thus, the power over the militia was intended to establish standards for exercises and for arms. While King's final statement allowed for the furnishing of arms by the militia themselves or by the state or federal governments, the practice in every state was for each individual to furnish his own arms, a policy which the federal Militia Act of 1792 would adopt. The objective was to provide discipline for the self-armed populace, not to arm or disarm select groups.

The provision would be adopted substantially as proposed. The convention rejected a more comprehensive substitute for the second clause to the effect that Congress would "establish a uniformity of arms, exercise, and organisation for the militia . . . ."[18] Geopolitical considerations were at stake:

Mr. [Jonathan] Dayton [of New Jersey] was against so absolute a uniformity. In some states there ought to be a greater proportion of cavalry than in others. In some places, rifles would be more proper; in others, muskets, &c.[19]

Cavalry, of course, were armed with pistol and sword, and perhaps carbine. Rifles were long-range weapons used by frontiersmen and backwoodsmen in the South, while muskets were medium-range arms favored in New England.[20] Uniform bore sizes among militiamen in a given locale would allow interchangeable ammunition, but differing terrain and habits of the people precluded uniform types of arms.

In response to Madison's comment that the states were neglecting the militia, Luther Martin of Maryland replied that "the states would never give up the power over the militia; and that, if they were to do so, the militia would be less attended to by the general than by the state governments."[21] After Gerry warned that granting Congress powers inconsistent with the existence of the states would lead to civil war, Madison rejoined that "as the greatest danger to liberty is from large standing armies, it is best to prevent them by an effectual provision for a good militia."[22] The militia clause would protect the power of the states to maintain militias and to retain their sovereignty by precluding a need for standing armies.

As finally drafted, the federal power over the militia and the division of this power with the states would be inserted with the other congressional powers in Article I, Section 8, delegating power to Congress as follows:

> To provide for calling forth the Militia to execute the Laws of the Union, suppress Insurrections and repel Invasions;

> To provide for organising, arming, and disciplining, the Militia, and for governing such Part of them as may be employed in the Service of the United States, reserving to the States respectively, the Appointment of the Officers, and the Authority of training the Militia according to the discipline prescribed by Congress . . . ."[23]

Congress also had power "To declare War" and "To raise and support Armies, but no Appropriation of Money to that Use shall be for a longer Term than two Years . . . ."[24] Further, "the President shall be Commander in Chief of the Army and Navy of the United States, and of the Militia of the several States, when called into the actual Service of the United States . . . ."[25] Finally, "No State shall, without the Consent of Congress, . . . keep Troops, or Ships of War in time of Peace, . . . or engage in War, unless actually invaded, or in such imminent Danger as will not admit of delay."[26]

The division between the federal government and the states regarding war, standing armies, and militia was thus well drawn. Nothing in the Bill of Rights that would be adopted later, including the Second Amendment, would change the above provisions.

On September 14, Mason moved to insert before the militia clause the preamble "and that the liberties of the people may be better secured against the danger of standing armies in time of peace."[27] Draftsman of the Virginia Declaration of Rights of 1776, Mason was the leading author of such declaratory clauses. Madison supported the motion, reasoning that "as armies in time of peace are allowed, on all hands, to be an evil, it is well to discountenance them by the Constitution . . . ."[28] Gouverneur Morris opposed it, "as setting a dishonourable mark of distinction on the military class of citizens."[29] The convention did not favor abstract principles of political philosophy, and the proposal failed.

As finally drafted, the Constitution did mention a few rights. Similar to the Articles, it declared: "The Citizens of each State shall be entitled to all Privileges and Immunities of Citizens in the several States."[30] Both Congress and the states were forbidden to pass any bill of attainder,[31] and "the Trial of all Crimes . . . shall be by Jury . . . ."[32] But the proposal contained no formal bill of rights.

Indeed, the desirability of a declaration of rights was only barely mentioned. On September 12, with the convention virtually over, George Mason "wished the plan had been prefaced with a bill of rights . . . . It would give great quiet to the people, and, with the aid of the state declarations, a bill might be prepared in a few hours."[33] Roger Sherman thought the state declarations sufficed and that Congress could be trusted.[34] Mason pointed out that "the laws of the United States are to be paramount to state bills of rights."[35] The convention narrowly killed the motion for a committee to prepare a bill of rights.[36]

Attempts to declare various rights also failed. Charles Pinckney of South Carolina and Elbridge Gerry offered a declaration "that the liberty of the press should be inviolably observed."[37] Again, Roger Sherman preempted that proposal with the remark, "It is unnecessary. The power of Congress does not extend to the press."[38] This opinion held sway, and the convention proposed the Constitution without a bill of rights.

Benjamin Franklin, for one, was under no illusions. On the last day of the convention, he stated that "this is likely to be well administered for a course of years, and can only end in despotism, as other forms have done before it . . . ."[39] In a few minutes, the Constitution was signed by all of the delegates present, except for three who believed the convention had exceeded its authority— Mason, Gerry, and Edmund Randolph of Virginia. As the last members were signing, Franklin looked at the painting of a rising sun behind the president's chair and observed to those sitting around him: "I have often and often, in the course of the session, and the vicissitudes of my hopes and fears as to its issue, looked at that behind the president, without being able to tell whether it was rising or setting; but now, at length, I have the happiness to know that it is a rising, not a setting sun."[40]

George Mason was not so sure and was already drafting objections to the Constitution. He sent copies to Virginia's political leaders, including to George Washington on October 7, and before long the objections were widely published in the newspapers. Mason's tract began: "There is no Declaration of

Rights; and the laws of the general Government being paramount to the Laws & Constitutions of the several States, the Declarations of Rights in the separate States are no Security."[41]

Pointing to Congress' power to pass all laws that were "necessary and proper" to implement its enumerated powers, Mason argued that the federal legislature could "constitute new Crimes, inflict unusual & severe Punishments, and extend their power as far as they shall think proper; so that the State Legislatures have no Security for the Powers now presumed to remain to them; or the People for their Rights."[42] Mason's word choice was elementary: The federal and state legislatures had "powers" while the people had "rights" that were not secured by a positive declaration.

Two days before the Philadelphia convention ended, delegate Thomas Fitzsimons of Pennsylvania asked Noah Webster to write in support of the proposed Constitution.[43] Webster, who had penned political essays since the Revolution, lived in Philadelphia while the convention met, conversing with Franklin, Washington, Madison, and other delegates.[44] Webster responded on October 10 with *An Examination of the Leading Principles of the Federal Constitution*, the first pro-Constitution pamphlet.[45] He explained why the armed populace would remain sovereign under a constitution with an army but no bill of rights:

> Another source of power in government is a military force. But this, to be efficient, must be superior to any force that exists among the people, or which they can command; for otherwise this force would be annihilated, on the first exercise of acts of oppression. Before a standing army can rule, the people must be disarmed; as they are in almost every kingdom in Europe. The supreme power in America cannot enforce unjust laws by the sword; because the whole body of the people are armed, and constitute a force superior to any band of regular troops that can be, on any pretence, raised in the United States. A military force, at the command of Congress, can execute no laws, but such as the people perceive to be just and constitutional; for they will possess the power, and jealousy will instantly inspire the inclination, to resist the execution of a law which appears to them unjust and oppressive.[46]

Hamilton and Madison would later repeat the above argument in *The Federalist Papers*.[47] Like those writers, Webster contended that rights to arms and speech need not be spelled out. If a bill of rights was necessary, he sarcastically wrote in the *American Magazine*, then it should include a provision "that Congress shall never restrain any inhabitant of America from eating and drinking, at seasonable times, or prevent his lying on his right side, in a long winter's night, or even on his back when he is fatigued by lying on his right."[48]

Tench Coxe, another rising federalist star, wrote a series called "An American Citizen," which has been characterized as the first major defense of the Constitution.[49] In Number IV of the series, printed as a broadside on October 21 with reprints of other federalist essays,[50] Coxe wrote that, should tyranny threaten, the "friends to liberty . . . using those arms which Providence has put into their hands, will make a solemn appeal to 'the power above.'"[51] He added: "The militia, who are in fact the effective part of the people at large, will render many troops quite unnecessary. They will form a powerful check upon the regular troops, and will generally be sufficient to over-awe them . . . ."[52]

Coxe sent copies to Madison, noting that the essay was written at the request of James Wilson, Dr. Benjamin Rush, and others "to shew the general advantages & obviate some of the Objections to the System." Coxe hoped that Madison and Hamilton "may make any use of them, which you think will serve the cause."[53] Madison responded that Hamilton "will make the best use of them," adding that the essay "is a valuable continuation, and I shall be equally desirous of seeing it in the Virginia Gazettes; and indeed in those of every State."[54]

Already antifederalists were criticizing the lack of a bill of rights. Samuel Bryan, writing as "Centinel I" in the October 5 issue of the *Independent Gazetteer*, declared it "worthy of remark, that there is no declaration of personal rights premised in most free constitutions . . . ."[55] Noting rights guaranteed in the Pennsylvania constitution, he asked "how long those rights will appertain to you, you yourselves are called upon to say, whether your *houses* shall continue to be your *castles* . . . ."[56]

However, James Wilson—the first delegate to the Philadelphia convention to deliver a public speech defending the proposed Constitution—both defended a standing army and denied the need for a bill of rights in that speech.[57] In response, "A Democratic Federalist," writing in the October 17 issue of the *Pennsylvania Herald*, called a bill of rights necessary to secure "our natural rights."[58] He characterized the standing army as "that great support of tyrants," recalled the militias' exploits at Lexington and Bunker Hill and against Burgoyne, and asked, "is not a well regulated militia sufficient for every purpose of internal defence?" As to Wilson's argument that no nation in the world lacked a standing army, he adduced:

> the example of Switzerland, which, like us, is a *republic*, whose *thirteen* cantons, like our thirteen States, are under a *federal government*, and which besides is surrounded by the most powerful nations in Europe, all jealous of its liberty and prosperity: And yet that nation has preserved its freedom for many ages, with the sole help of a militia, and has never been known to have a standing army, except when in actual war.—Why should we not follow so glorious an example, and are we less able to defend our liberty without an army, than that brave but small nation, which with its militia alone has hitherto defied all Europe?[59]

The most comprehensive defense of the Constitution was, of course, *The Federalist Papers*, penned by James Madison, Alexander Hamilton, and John Jay under the pen name "Publius" and addressed to the "People of the State of New-York." Some seventy-six of the essays were published in New York newspapers between October 27, 1787, and April 2, 1788, and then John and Archibald M'Lean reprinted them in two volumes, the first on March 22 and the second (which included eight new essays) on May 28.[60]

Five of the essays are pertinent here. *The Federalist* No. 28, written by Hamilton and first published in the New York *Independent Journal* on December 26, 1787, addressed head-on the antifederalist argument that a federal tyranny could result:

> If the representatives of the people betray their constituents, there is then no resource left but in the exertion of that original right of self-defence which is paramount to all positive forms of government, and which against the usurpations of the national rulers, may be exerted with infinitely better prospect of success than against those of the rulers of an individual state. . . .

> The obstacles to usurpation and the facilities of resistance increase with the increased extent of the state, provided the citizens understand their rights and are disposed to defend them.[61]

Whatever the validity of the first above argument, the second argument—that usurpation will be minimized if "the citizens understand their rights"—implied that a bill of rights could promote this understanding, but

*The Federalist* authors remained impervious to that suggestion. Whether the citizens "are disposed to defend" their rights would have depended in part on whether they were armed.

More explicit was *The Federalist* No. 29, also penned by Hamilton and published in the *Independent Journal* on January 9, 1788—just after the issue of the right to bear arms was raised in the "Dissent of the Minority" in Pennsylvania (discussed in the next chapter). It began by analyzing Congress' power over the militia as follows:

> The power of regulating the militia, and of commanding its services in times of insurrection and invasion are natural incidents to the duties of superintending the common defence, and of watching over the internal peace of the Confederacy.
>
> It requires no skill in the science of war to discern that uniformity in the organization and discipline of the militia would be attended with the most beneficial effects, whenever they were called into service for the public defence. . . . This desirable uniformity can only be accomplished by confiding the regulation of the militia to the direction of the national authority.[62]

This uniformity was particularly necessary in regard to arms—muskets of different bore sizes required different sizes of balls. This "well regulated militia" was provided for in the Federal-State division of duties set forth in Article I, Section 8 of the Constitution, which Hamilton proceeded to quote. He continued:

> If a well regulated militia be the most natural defence of a free country, it ought certainly to be under the regulation and at the disposal of that body which is constituted the guardian of the national security. If standing armies are dangerous to liberty, an efficacious power over the militia, in the body to whose care the protection of the State is committed, ought, as far as possible, to take away the inducement and the pretext to such unfriendly institutions.[63]

The above usage presaged the Second Amendment's declaration that a well regulated militia is necessary to the security of "a free State"—that term meant "a free country," not a state government. The availability of the militia, Hamilton continued, would minimize the need for a standing army. However, opponents of the Constitution objected that "there is nowhere any provision in the proposed Constitution for calling out the posse comitatus, to assist the magistrate in the execution of his duty," which would instead be carried out with military force. (The *posse comitatus*, or power of the county, included all males aged 15 or over, who the sheriff could call out to assist him to keep the peace and pursue felons.[64]) Yet the power of Congress to pass all laws necessary and proper to fulfill its substantive powers "would include that of requiring the assistance of the citizens to the officers who may be intrusted with the execution of those laws."[65] Indeed, the militia power assumed the role of the armed citizen.

The Constitution's detractors also argued that the militia would become dangerous to liberty, because "select corps may be formed, composed of the young and ardent, who may be rendered subservient to the views of arbitrary power."[66] Hamilton responded that the most that could be realistically expected was that the people be armed, not that they be subject to strict military discipline:

> The project of disciplining all the militia of the United States is as futile as it would be injurious, if it were capable of being carried into execution. . . . To oblige the great body of yeomanry and of the other classes of citizens to be under arms for the purpose of going through military exercises and evolutions, as often as might be necessary to acquire the degree of perfection which would entitle them to the character of a well regulated militia, would be a real grievance to the people, and a serious public inconvenience and loss. . . . Little more can reasonably be aimed at with respect to the people at large than to have them properly armed and equipped . . . .
>
> . . . This will not only lessen the call for military establishments, but if circumstances should at any time oblige the government to form an army of any magnitude that army can never be formidable to the liberties of the people while there is a large body of citizens, little if at all inferior to them in discipline and the use of arms, who stand ready to defend their rights and those of their fellow citizens.[67]

The above distinguishes "the people at large" who would be "properly armed" from "a well regulated militia." It refers to "a large body of citizens" hardly inferior to soldiers in the use of arms, "who stand ready to defend their rights." In short, the right of the people to keep and bear arms—especially military arms—was a fact, not a matter for paper guarantees.

In *The Federalist* No. 45, published in the January 26 *Independent Journal*, Madison emphasized the limited powers delegated to the federal government:

"The powers delegated by the proposed Constitution to the federal government are few and defined." These powers "will be exercised principally on external objects, as war, peace, negotiation, and foreign commerce," while "the powers reserved to the several States will extend to all the objects which, in the ordinary course of affairs, concern the lives, liberties, and properties of the people . . . ."[68] As will be seen, the federalists would depict as a blatant falsehood the antifederalist suggestion that the federal government had any power over such rights as a free press and keeping and bearing arms.

From the perspective of what became the Second Amendment, the most important essay was *The Federalist* No. 46, written by Madison and first published in the *New York Packet* on January 29, 1788. It clearly distinguished between the people and the two governments: "The Federal and State governments are in fact but different agents and trustees of the people, constituted with different powers, and designed for different purposes." Further, "the ultimate authority . . . resides in the people alone," not in "the different governments."[69] As for the argument that the federal government would raise a standing army to oppress the people, Madison replied:

> To these would be opposed a militia amounting to near half a million of citizens with arms in their hands, officered by men chosen from among themselves, fighting for their common liberties, and united and conducted by governments possessing their affections and confidence. It may well be doubted, whether a militia thus circumstanced could ever be conquered by such a proportion of regular troops. Those who are best acquainted with the last successful resistance of this country against the British arms, will be most inclined to deny the possibility of it. Besides the advantage of being armed, which the Americans possess over the people of almost every other nation, the existence of subordinate governments, to which the people are attached, and by which the militia officers are appointed, forms a barrier against the enterprises of ambition, more insurmountable than any which a simple government of any form can admit of. Notwithstanding the military establishments in the several kingdoms of Europe, which are carried as far as the public resources will bear, the governments are afraid to trust the people with arms.[70]

A militia of "half a million of citizens with arms in their hands" would have been virtually all able-bodied male citizens out of the American population of three million. The "citizens" constituted the militia, and they had "arms in their hands." The success of this armed citizenry had been demonstrated in the American Revolution. Unlike other peoples, the Americans were armed, and the resistance of the state governments would bar a federal tyranny. By contrast, the European monarchies were "afraid to trust the people with arms." In short, the keeping and bearing of arms by the citizens would preserve the republic and protect liberty.

The authors of *The Federalist Papers* contended that an armed populace and state resistance, not paper guarantees, would prevent federal usurpation based on military force. But they seriously underestimated the groundswell of public support for a bill of rights, including guarantees such as arms bearing and free speech that would help protect other rights. "Publius" failed to mention the agitation for a bill of rights in the essays originally published in the newspapers and tardily mentioned the issue in the second to the last chapter of the second volume of *The Federalist Papers* as printed in book form, which was released on May 28, 1788. Authored by Hamilton, *The Federalist* No. 84 began with the condescending title "Certain General and Miscellaneous Objections to the Constitution Considered and Answered."[71]

Hamilton began by noting that several state constitutions, including New York's, contained no bill of rights. Ironically, the Constitution's opponents in New York professed high regard for the state Constitution, but "are among the most intemperate partisans of a bill of rights." Moreover, like that of New York, the federal Constitution included various guarantees in its text, such as trial by jury in criminal cases and the writ of habeas corpus.[72]

More importantly, bills of rights are for monarchies, not republics: "bills of rights are, in their origin, stipulations between kings and their subjects, abridgements of prerogative in favour of privilege, reservations of rights not surrendered to the prince." Magna Carta, the Petition of Right, and the Declaration of Rights of 1689 were familiar examples. Such instruments "have no application to constitutions professedly founded upon the power of the people," and indeed here "the people surrender nothing; and as they retain every thing they have no need of particular reservations."[73]

To be sure, the Constitution delegated no explicit power to Congress to regulate the press or the keeping and bearing of arms. Indeed, unable to anticipate developments in later epochs, Hamilton wrote that the federal Constitution "is merely intended to regulate the general political interests of the nation, than to a constitution which has the regulation of every species of personal and private concerns." He asserted that the Constitution's preamble—declaring that "we the people" adopt the Constitution "to secure the blessings of liberty to ourselves and our posterity"—"is a better recognition of popular rights, than volumes of those aphorisms which make the principal figure in several of our State bills of rights, and which would sound much better in a treatise of ethics than in a constitution of government."[74] In fact, the preamble has never been interpreted by the courts as having any legal effect, and instead of "volumes of aphorisms" adopted by the people, judges would later pick and choose what would or would not be a "right."

To supporters of a bill of rights, Hamilton's arguments just begged the question, for the actual extent of the powers of the proposed government were in great dispute, and a declaration of reservations would alleviate their apprehensions. Such sarcastic references to the state bills of rights must have only hardened the Constitution's opponents in their opposition. But Hamilton's following warning contained great foresight, which would actually come true:

> I go further, and affirm that bills of rights, in the sense and to the extent in which they are contended for, are not only unnecessary in the proposed Constitution, but would even be dangerous. They would contain various exceptions to powers not granted; and, on this very account, would afford a colourable pretext to claim more than were granted. For why declare that things shall not be done which there is no power to do?[75]

In short, no matter how a bill of rights might be written, those wishing to diminish the rights declared would manipulate the wording of the provisions to do so. For example, Hamilton queried: "What signifies a declaration, that 'the liberty of the press shall be inviolably preserved'? What is the liberty of the press? Who can give it any definition which would not leave the utmost latitude for evasion?" This could be said about what became the First and the Second Amendments. Yet it was not inevitable that clearly written guideposts would always fail. As Hamilton further noted, security for rights would not depend on "fine declarations" but "must altogether depend on public opinion, and on the general spirit of the people and of the government."[76] Yet these "fine declarations" would influence and be a reminder to the people and the government alike.

Stating the case against ratification of the Constitution without a bill of rights were the "Letters from the Federal Farmer," which were first published in October and November of 1787 and were reprinted in pamphlet form throughout the states. From the beginning, they were attributed to Richard Henry Lee of Virginia, although his authorship was never proven, and the consensus today is that the author was Melancton Smith of New York. Edward Carrington of Virginia wrote to Thomas Jefferson that "these Letters are the best of anything that has been written" against the Constitution.[77]

What was it about the "rights" in a bill of rights that was considered so indispensable? In his second "Letter," dated October 9, the "Federal Farmer" declared: "There are certain unalienable and fundamental rights, which in forming the social compact, ought to be explicitly ascertained and fixed—a free and enlightened people, in forming this compact, will not resign all their rights to those who govern, and they will fix limits to their legislators and rulers, which will soon be plainly seen by those who are governed, as well as by those who govern . . . ." Contrary to the Constitution's proponents, "I still believe a complete federal bill of rights to be very practicable."[78]

The federalists contended that the armed populace precluded any federal oppression and rendered a bill of rights unnecessary. In response, the "Letter" dated October 10 predicted the early employment of a standing army and oppressive taxation. The "Federal Farmer" contended:

It is true, the yeomanry of the country possess the lands, the weight of property, possess arms, and are too strong a body of men to be openly offended—and, therefore, it is urged, they will take care of themselves, that men who shall govern will not dare pay any disrespect to their opinions. It is easily perceived, that if they have not their proper negative upon passing laws in congress, or on the passage of laws relative to taxes and armies, they may in twenty or thirty years be by means imperceptible to them, totally deprived of that boasted weight and strength: This may be done in a great measure by congress; if disposed to do it, by modeling the militia. Should one fifth or one eighth part of the men capable of bearing arms, be made a select militia, as has been proposed, and those the young and ardent part of the community, possessed of but little or no property, and all the others put upon a plan that will render them of no importance, the former will answer all the purposes of an army, while the latter will be defenseless. . . . I see no provision made for calling out the *posse comitatus* for executing the laws of the union, but provision is made for congress to call forth the militia for the execution of them—and the militia in general, or any select part of it, may be called out under military officers, instead of the sheriff to enforce an execution of federal laws, in the first instance, and thereby introduce an entire military execution of the laws.[79]

The "Letter" dated October 12 returned to the theme of a bill of rights. In the state constitutions, "certain rights have been reserved to the people," and state legislatures may "make no laws infringing upon them." These rights "are established as fundamental." The federal Constitution itself, by prohibiting a bill of attainder or ex post facto law, establishes "a partial bill of rights," principles on which the federal government "can never infringe." "This bill of rights ought to be carried further, and some other principles established, as a part of this compact between the people of the United States and their federal rulers." It would include "essential rights, which we have justly understood to be the rights of freemen. . . ."[80]

A second series of "Letters from the Federal Farmer to the Republican" were advertised in New York newspapers beginning on May 2, 1788, but each essay was datelined months earlier. It was distributed throughout the states by, most prominently, John Lamb of the New York Federal Republican Committee.[81]

"Letter VI," dated December 25, 1787, noted: "Of rights, some are natural and unalienable, of which even the people cannot deprive individuals: Some are constitutional or fundamental: these cannot be altered or abolished by the ordinary laws; but the people, by express acts, may alter or abolish them." The former, unchangeable rights were substantive in nature, while the latter were procedural rights, such as jury trial and the writ of habeas corpus.[82] Turning to matters of governmental structure, the Federal Farmer depicted the militia clause as follows: "Each state must appoint regimental officers, and keep up a well regulated militia."[83]

"Letter XVI," dated January 20, 1788, noted that it was easier to enumerate the federal powers "than to enumerate particularly the individual rights to be reserved," but "still there are infinite advantages in particularly enumerating many of the most essential rights reserved in all cases; and as to the less important ones, we may declare in general terms, that all not expressly surrendered are reserved."[84] Since the proposed Constitution enumerated some rights and not others, the people "ought to go through enumerating, and establish particularly all the rights of individuals, which can by any possibility come into question in making and executing federal laws."[85] Some of the "fundamental rights" mentioned by the Federal Farmer were the rights of free press, petition, and religion; the rights to speedy trial, trial by jury, confrontation of accusers and against self-incrimination; the right against unreasonable search and seizure; and the right to refuse quartering of soldiers.[86]

In "Letter XVIII," dated January 25, 1788, the Federal Farmer explained the nature of the militia and of the right to keep and bear arms. The militia included the people at large, not some elite force:

> A militia, when properly formed, are in fact the people themselves, and render regular troops in a great measure unnecessary. . . . [T]he constitution ought to secure a genuine [militia] and guard against a select militia, by providing that the militia shall always be kept well organised, armed, and disciplined, and include . . . all men capable of bearing arms; and that all regulations tending to render this general militia useless and defenceless, by establishing select corps of militia, or distinct bodies of military men, not having permanent interests and attachments in the community to be avoided.[87]

The Federal Farmer feared that Congress, through its power over the militia, would establish a "select militia" apart from the people that would be used as an instrument of domination by the federal government. He refuted the argument that it is impractical to view the militia as the whole body of the people, and that reliance must be placed on a select corps, in these terms:

> But, say gentlemen, the general militia are for the most part employed at home in their private concerns, cannot well be called out, or be depended upon; that we must have a select militia; that is, as I understand it, particular corps or bodies of young men, and of men who have but little to do at home, particularly armed and disciplined in some measure, at the public expense, and always ready to take the field. These corps, not much unlike regular troops, will ever produce an inattention to the general militia; and the consequence has ever been, and always must be, that the substantial men, having families and property, will generally be without arms, without knowing the use of them, and defenceless; whereas, *to preserve liberty, it is essential that the whole body of the people always possess arms, and be taught alike, especially when young, how to use them*; nor does it follow from this, that all promiscuously must go into actual service on every occasion. The mind that aims at a select militia, must be influenced by a truly anti-republican principle; and when we see many men disposed to

practice upon it, whenever they can prevail, no wonder true republicans are for carefully guarding against it.[88]

While federalists and antifederalists differed on the need for a paper declaration, and to some extent on the army-militia question, no one disputed the Farmer's above remark that "it is essential that the whole body of the people always possess arms" and should know "how to use them." Individual firearm ownership, whether as a right or a simple fact, simply was not questioned.

Meanwhile, as the ratification struggle ensued, prominent authors recalled philosophical influences and pre-Revolutionary experiences that defined the right to have arms as the mark of a free person. Beginning some six months before the Philadelphia convention started and ending the next year, John Adams published his treatise *Defence of the Constitutions of Government of the United States of America*, which became well known in the states and in Europe. While Benjamin Rush doubted that it had been read by convention delegates,[89] the three-volume work was referred to in the postconvention newspaper debates.[90]

In the first volume, Adams had occasion to contrast Europe's monarchies with the cantons of the Swiss Confederation, which he divided into "democratical" and "aristocratical." Regardless of which category Adams placed a particular canton, he noted two institutions of direct democracy: the rights to bear arms and to vote on laws. In the Canton of Glaris, for instance, "the sovereign is the whole country, and the sovereignty resides in the general assembly, where each male of fifteen, with his sword at his side, has his seat and vote." Further, "this assembly, which is annually held in an open plain, ratifies the laws, lays taxes, enters into alliance, declares war, and make peace."[91] While more aristocratical, Berne had a democratic military system:

> There is no standing army, but every male of sixteen is enrolled in the militia, and obligated to provide himself an uniform, a musket, powder and ball; and no peasant is allowed to marry, without producing his arms and uniform. The arms are inspected every year, and the men exercised.[92]

Adams approvingly quoted Marchamont Nedham's dictum that "the people be continually trained up in the exercise of arms, and the militia lodged only in the people's hands," or as Aristotle put it, "to place the use of and exercise of arms in the people, because the commonwealth is theirs who hold the arms . . . ."[93] Adams noted that the continental European states achieved absolutism by following the Caesarian precedent of erecting "praetorian bands, instead of a public militia."[94] The aristocratic Adams recognized the individual right to use arms for personal protection, but looked askance at the kind of armed protest recently exemplified in Shays' Rebellion:

> To suppose arms in the hands of citizens, to be used at individual discretion, except in private self-defence, or by partial orders of towns, counties, or districts of a state, is to demolish every constitution, and lay the laws prostrate, so that liberty can be enjoyed by no man—it is a dissolution of the government. The fundamental law of the militia is, that it be created, directed and commanded by the laws, and ever for the support of the laws.[95]

For the more radical Thomas Jefferson, individual discretion was acceptable in the use of arms not simply for private but for public defense as well. Writing from Paris on November 13, 1787, to William Stephens Smith, Jefferson noted that he had just received a copy of the Constitution, and "there are very good articles in it & very bad." He opined that the recent troubles (Shays' Rebellion) hardly spelled anarchy and were localized in Massachusetts. Jefferson continued:

> God forbid we should ever be twenty years without such a rebellion. . . . And what country can preserve its liberties, if its rulers are not warned from time to time, that this people preserve the spirit of resistance? Let them take arms. . . . The tree of liberty must be refreshed from time to time, with the blood of patriots and tyrants. . . . Our Convention has been too much impressed by the insurrection of Massachusetts . . . . [96]

Jefferson had served as U.S. minister to France since 1785, and a short digression on that remarkable American is warranted here. Jefferson wrote from Paris on August 19, 1785, to his 15-year-old nephew Peter Carr, advising him on advancement in mind, body, and soul. After recommending the Greek and Roman classics in the original languages, Jefferson noted that "a strong body makes a strong mind," and advised two hours of exercise each day: "As to the species of exercise of exercise, I advise the gun. While this gives a moderate exercise to the body, it gives boldness, enterprise, and independence to the mind. . . . Let your gun therefore be the constant companion of your walks."

Do not take a book, he continued, but relax the mind, look at the surrounding objects, and walk far. Meanwhile, Jefferson noted a number of books in various languages he was sending to his nephew, in "care of Mr. Madison."[97]

While in Europe, Jefferson collected not only books but also firearms. His journal reflects a shopping spree in London in March 1786 in which he "p[ai]d . . . for p[ai]r. pocket pistols, £ 1-18 [one pound 18 shillings]," "powder flask 4/.," and "pr. Pistols silvermounted £ 1-18."[98] One set of the pairs, which are screw-barrel, boxlock flintlock pocket pistols, is preserved today at Monticello.[99] And in July 1787, while his brethren in Philadelphia were drafting the Constitution, Jefferson was back in Paris where he bought "a double barrel gun [for] 60f. [francs]."[100]

In February 1787, Jefferson published from abroad his *Notes on the State of Virginia*. He listed the number of militiamen by county in Virginia, ending with the figure for the "Whole Militia of the State 49,971."[101] Jefferson noted:

> Every able-bodied freeman, between the ages of 16 and 50, is enrolled in the militia. . . . The law requires every militia-man to provide himself with arms usual in the regular service. But this injunction was always indifferently complied with, and the arms they had have been so frequently called for to arm the regulars, that in the lower parts of the country they are entirely disarmed. In the middle country a fourth or fifth part of them may have such firelocks as they had provided to destroy the noxious animals which infest their farms; and on the western side of the Blue ridge they are generally armed with rifles.[102]

Jefferson would remain minister to France through the constitutional ratification period, returning in 1789 to accept appointment by President George Washington as secretary of state. Washington was also a lifelong collector of fine firearms who carried pistols for self-defense and hunted with scatterguns (shotguns).[103]

Back to 1787, as federalist and antifederalist pens clashed, the state ratifying conventions began to meet to consider the Constitution. Six of the smaller states would quickly ratify without proposing a declaration of rights. But in the larger and more influential states, the issue of whether to include a bill of rights would lead to deep chasms and, eventually, to a resounding demand that personal rights be declared after ratification of the Constitution.

## CHAPTER 9

# The "Dissent of the Minority"

I APPROVE of most of the powers proposed to be given," wrote Revolutionary War officer George Turner from Philadelphia to Winthrop Sargent of Boston on November 6, 1787. "But, as a friend to the natural rights of man, I must hold up my hand against others. There are certain great and unalienable rights . . . that should have been secured by a declaration or bill of rights."[1]

The Constitution proposed by the Philadelphia convention would be considered for ratification by each of the states. Several of the smaller states ratified the document without demanding a bill of rights, but among the larger states a declaration of rights would be demanded initially by vocal dissenters and later by majorities of the state conventions. The right to keep and bear arms would be prominent in those demands.

### DELAWARE

The Constitution raised little controversy in Delaware, both Whigs and Tories there favoring the new system.[2] It ratified the Constitution on December 7, 1787, the first state to do so.

## PENNSYLVANIA

The Pennsylvania convention ratified the Constitution five days later, but only after a substantial confrontation. The convention was divided between federalists, who argued that a free people needed no bill of rights, and anti-federalists, who feared that without a bill of rights, the people could be disarmed and have other rights violated. The antifederalists also sought changes to the federal-state structure, including an amendment to recognize the state power to maintain militias.

Few of the debates were recorded, except for the lengthy speeches of James Wilson, a leading delegate to the Philadelphia convention which drafted the Constitution. Speeches of the antifederalists were primarily not transcribed or published.

Yet Wilson clearly articulated two points critical to this study: first, that a bill of individual rights was unnecessary in a free state, and second, that a militia composed of the armed populace would minimize the need for a standing army.[3]

In a speech on October 28, Wilson responded to the request for an explanation of why the Philadelphia convention drafted the proposed Constitution without a bill of rights. He could not speak for every delegate to the convention, but offered:

> Such an idea never entered the mind of many of them. I do not recollect to have heard the subject mentioned till within about three days of the time of our rising. . . . A proposition to adopt a measure that would have supposed that we were throwing into the general government every power not expressly reserved by the people, would have been spurned at, in that house, with the greatest indignation. . . . If we attempt an enumeration, every thing that is not enumerated is presumed to be given.[4]

In hindsight, it is difficult to contest Wilson's premise that "an imperfect enumeration" would lead to interpretations that restrict rights. Still, imperfectly worded guarantees would be better than no guarantees at all. At least the antifederalists so thought.

While the speeches of the antifederalists were poorly recorded and were not published, Wilson's own notes included the following outline of remarks of John Smilie on November 30. Noting that he would be offering a bill of rights, Smilie argued:

> Bill of rights necessary as the instrument of *original compact* and to mention the rights reserved. . . . There must be a people before there is a king; and the people, in the first instance, have inherent and inalienable rights. We ought to know what rights we *surrender,* and what we *retain.*[5]

Against this sketch of the antifederalist argument for a declaration of rights, Wilson's entire rebuttal of December 4 was recorded. Wilson stated that he had spoken in the meantime with a delegate to the Philadelphia convention who had taken full notes, and that person verified that no motion had been made in the convention to include a bill of rights. He rejected the premise that "not only all the powers which are given, but also that all those which are reserved, should be enumerated," observing that the great political treaties do not contain "a complete enumeration of rights appertaining to the people as men and as citizens." Here, "there can be no necessity for a bill of rights, for . . . the people never part with their power. Enumerate all the rights of men!"[6] The task was impossible.

In a speech on December 6, Smilie objected to the power of Congress to keep a standing army, averring: "The Last resource of a free people is taken away; for Congress are to have the command of the militia." The state governors would become the "drill sergeants" of Congress, and further:

> Congress may give us a select militia which will, in fact, be a standing army—or Congress, afraid of a general militia, may say there shall be no militia at all.
>
> When a select militia is formed; the people in general may be disarmed.[7]

While the above is only a sketch of the speech recorded by Wilson, it is clear that Smilie feared that Congress may abolish the "general militia" composed of the people at large. A select militia qua standing army would create the potential to disarm "the people in general."

Wilson responded on December 11, noting that Smilie represented a minority in the convention and taking affront to their claims: "If the minority are contending for the rights of mankind, the majority must be contending for the doctrines of tyranny and slavery. . . . Who are the majority in this assembly?—Are they not the people?"[8]

Wilson further argued that Congress' power to arm the militia would promote standardization, not disarmament. Congress could prescribe common sizes of barrels for firearms required to be possessed by the populace so that ammunition would be interchangeable:

> I believe any gentleman, who possesses military experience, will inform you that men without a uniformity of arms, accoutrements, and discipline, are no more than a mob in a camp; that, in the field, instead of assisting, they interfere with one another. If a soldier drops his musket, and his companion, unfurnished with one, takes it up, it is of no service, because his cartridges do not fit it. By means of this system, a uniformity of arms and discipline will prevail throughout the United States.[9]

Wilson suggested that the proposed militia system would largely supersede any need for a standing army, and indeed: "The militia formed under this system, and trained by the several states, will be such a bulwark of internal strength, as to prevent the attacks of foreign enemies. I have been told that, about the year 1744, an attack was intended by France upon Massachusetts Bay, but was given up on reading the militia law of the province." The European powers would be even more deterred by the body of militia under uniform regulations.[10]

While the lion's share of preserved speeches are those of Wilson, also intact are some of Thomas McKean. As usual, the speechmaker is a federalist refuting an antifederalist whose remarks were not recorded or published. McKean quoted an objection to Congress' power to call out the militia, for it "may call them from one end of the continent to the other, and wantonly harass them; besides, they may coerce men to act in the militia whose consciences are against bearing arms in any case." McKean responded that, while Congress would have power to organize, arm, and discipline the militia, "every thing else is left to the state governments; they are to officer and train them." And while Congress could call out the militia to execute the laws, suppress insurrections, and repel invasions, "can it be supposed they would call them, in such case, from Georgia to New Hampshire? Common sense must oppose the idea."[11]

McKean also responded to the argument that "there is no bill or declaration of rights in this Constitution." Such was not "deemed essential to liberty" except in Great Britain and six of the American states—not a very power-ful argument—but in any event, McKean argued, "it is unnecessary; for the powers of Congress, being derived from the people in the mode pointed out by this Constitution, and being therein enumerated and positively granted, can be no other than what this positive grant conveys."[12]

On December 12, Robert Whitehill proposed that a bill of rights be ad-opted and moved to adjourn the convention for its consideration by the people at large.[13] James Wilson opposed the motion, and John Smilie spoke in favor.[14] The federalists mustered 46 nays against the motion to the antifederalists' 23 yeas, and then voted to ratify the Constitution by a like number for and against.[15]

The antifederalists then published the Dissent of the Minority, demanding the same bill of rights Whitehill proposed above and summarizing the reasons for amendments. Samuel Bryan, author of the newspaper series "Centinel," claimed years later to have authored the document. First appearing on De-cember 18, the Dissent was circulated throughout the country.[16]

The bill of rights proposed in the convention and then published in the Dissent began by declaring the rights of conscience and freedom of religion, and then proceeded to declare certain procedural rights: trial by jury, and against self-incrimination, cruel and unusual punishments, and warrantless searches.[17] It then declared two rights beginning with the clause that "the people have a right" as follows:

> 6. That the people have a right to the freedom of speech, of writing, and of publishing their sentiments, therefore, the freedom of the press shall not be restrained by any law of the United States.

> 7. That the people have a right to bear arms for the defence of themselves and their own state, or the United States, or for the purpose of killing game; and no law shall be passed for disarming the people or any of them, unless for crimes committed, or real danger of public injury from individuals; and as standing armies in the time of peace are dangerous to liberty, they ought not to be kept up; and that the military shall be kept under strict subordination to and be governed by the civil powers.[18]

As to the arms guarantee, the above tracked the language of the Pennsyl-vania Declaration of Rights of 1776 in guaranteeing the right to bear arms for self-defense and defense of the state.[19] Similar to what would become the federal First Amendment, which begins "Congress shall make no law," the above proposed that a free press "shall not be restrained by any [federal] law" and that "no law shall be passed for disarming the people" as a whole "or any of them"—except that criminals or other dangerous persons could be disarmed. Bearing arms to hunt was not out of place in a bill of rights, in that British authorities had been notorious for disarming the people under the guise of game laws.[20]

The above clarifies that the term "bear arms" is not linguistically restricted to matters of the militia or the national defense. Bearing arms for self-defense and hunting were proper purposes. Mention of standing armies and the subordination of the military to the civil power in the same article did not detract from the individual character of the right guaranteed.

Basic elements of what became the First and Second Amendments may be found in the above proposals. The amendments would be more concise and would exclude the embellishments, but they would still protect the rights to free speech and press and to bear arms.[21]

Reflecting the 1776 Pennsylvania guarantee of the right to hunt,[22] the next provision of the proposed bill of rights averred:

> The inhabitants of the several states shall have liberty to fowl and hunt in seasonable times, on the lands they hold, and on all other lands in the United States not enclosed, and in like manner to fish in all navigable waters, and others not private property, without being restrained therein by any laws to be passed by the legislature of the United States.[23]

The influence of the 1776 Pennsylvania Declaration was no accident. Dissident leaders John Smilie and William Findlay were vigorous followers of Justice George Bryan, leader of the 1776 convention.[24] Justice Bryan now played a key role in agitating for amendments to the proposed federal Constitution, and as noted, his son Samuel claimed to have authored the Dissent.[25]

Commentary included with the Dissent of the Minority emphasized the necessity for "a bill of rights ascertaining and fundamentally establishing those unalienable and personal rights of men, without the full, free, and secure enjoyment of which there can be no liberty. . . ."[26] A free press and bearing arms were of that nature.

In separate articles, the Dissent sought amendments to the state-federal structure. One of these articles sought to protect the "power" of the "state"—not the "right of the people"—to maintain the militia:

That the power of organising, arming, and disciplining the militia (the manner of disciplining the militia to be prescribed by Congress) remain with the individual states, and that Congress shall not have authority to call or march any of the militia out of their own state, without the consent of such state, and for such length of time only as such state shall agree.[27]

Like other federal powers, Congress' power over the militia implicated not only the powers reserved to the states, but also personal liberties. The commentary to the Dissent explained:

The absolute unqualified command that Congress have over the militia may be made instrumental to the destruction of all liberty, both public and private; whether of a personal, civil, or religious nature.

First, the personal liberty of every man probably from sixteen to sixty years of age may be destroyed by the power Congress have in organizing and governing of the militia. As militia they may be subjected to fines to any amount, levied in a military manner; they may be subjected to corporal punishments of the most disgraceful and humiliating kind, and to death itself, by the sentence of a court martial. . . .

Secondly, the rights of conscience may be violated, as there is no exemption of those persons who are conscientiously scrupulous of bearing arms. These compose a respectable proportion of the community in the state. . . .

Thirdly, the absolute command of Congress over the militia may be destructive of public liberty; for under the guidance of an arbitrary government, they may be made the unwilling instruments of tyranny. The militia of Pennsylvania may be marched to New England or Virginia to quell an insurrection occasioned by the most galling oppression, and aided by the standing army, they will no doubt be successful in subduing their liberty and independency . . . .[28]

The above proposals by the minority of the Pennsylvania convention constituted the first demand by any part of a ratifying convention for a declaration of individual rights, such as a free press and bearing arms. They were losers in the debate only temporarily, for a federal bill of rights with such liberties would ultimately be adopted. They ultimately lost only regarding their demand for a detailed declaration of reserved state powers, including state militia powers.

Pennsylvania antifederalists continued to agitate for amendments. One concisely expressed their attitude toward gunpowder and lead as follows: "the sons of freedom . . . may know the despots have not altogether monopolised these *necessary articles*."[29]

James Madison sent a copy of *The Federalist* No. 46, which argued that Americans had "the advantage of being armed" over monarchies "afraid to trust the people with arms," to Tench Coxe, who found them "very valuable papers" and used the ideas in his own writings.[30] Coxe responded to the Dissent of the Minority under the pen name "A Pennsylvanian" in "To the Citizens of the United States, III," published in the *Pennsylvania Gazette*, February 20, 1788. He wrote as follows:

> The power of the sword, say the minority of Pennsylvania, is in the hands of Congress. My friends and countrymen, it is not so, for the powers of the sword are in the hands of the yeomanry of america from sixteen to sixty. The militia of these free commonwealths, entitled and accustomed to their arms, when compared with any possible army, must be tremendous and irresistible. Who are the militia? are they not ourselves. Is it feared, then, that we shall turn our arms each man against his own bosom. Congress have no power to disarm the militia. Their swords, and every other terrible implement of the soldier, are the birth-right of an American. . . . [T]he unlimited power of the sword is not in the hands of either the federal or state governments, but, where I trust in God it will ever remain, in the hands of the people.[31]

The contrast could not be starker between the federal and state governments and "the people," consisting of each individual "American" in possession of his militia arms. The above respective essays by Madison and Coxe illustrate the cross-fertilization of federalist arguments as applied to the right to keep and bear arms.

"A Farmer," responding to another Coxe critique of the Minority, wrote in the Philadelphia *Freeman's Journal*: "It is only free republics that can completely and safely form a federal republic: I say free republics, for there are republics who are not free, such as Venice, where a citizen carrying arms is punished with instant death . . . ."[32] Venice's law imposing capital punishment for bearing arms was well known from Montesquieu.[33]

In a different twist to the same theme, a writer in the *Pennsylvania Gazette* criticized "the loyalists in the beginning of the late war, who objected to *associating*, *arming* and *fighting*, in defence of our liberties, because these measures were not *constitutional*. A free people should always be left . . . with every possible power to promote their own happiness."[34]

In *The Government of Nature Delineated*, published in late April 1788, one "Aristocrotis" warned that a standing army and the select or active militia under federal control would "quell insurrections that may arise in any parts of the empire on account of pretensions to support liberty, redress grievances, and the like."[35] "The second class or inactive militia, comprehends all the rest of the peasants; viz., the farmers, mechanics, labourers, & c. which good policy will prompt government to disarm. It would be dangerous to trust such a rabble as this with arms in their hands."[36]

Such antifederalist agitation continued as other state conventions met in the coming months. Refusing to concede defeat, dissident Pennsylvanians gathered at the Harrisburg convention which, on September 3, 1788, reiterated the call for amendments. Instead of a declaration of specific rights, the convention would have incorporated all of the rights declared in the state bills of rights: "that every reserve of the rights of individuals, made by the several constitutions of the states in the Union, to the citizens and inhabitants of each state respectively, shall remain inviolate, except so far as they are expressly and manifestly yielded or narrowed by the national Constitution."[37] In a separate series of amendments on the structure of government, the following (which originated in the Virginia convention) was proposed: "That each state, respectively, shall have power to provide for organising, arming, and disciplining the militia thereof, whensoever Congress shall omit or neglect to provide for the same."[38] Thus, individual rights were sharply contrasted from state powers, a linguistic usage that would prevail in the ratification struggle.

## NEW JERSEY

The third state to ratify the Constitution was New Jersey, which did so on December 18, 1787, with minimal debate. New Jersey had no bill of rights in its own constitution and did not demand one for the federal Constitution.[39]

George Mason's objections to the Constitution began with the observation that "there is no Declaration of Rights,"[40] but the day after that state ratified, the *New Jersey Journal* published a reply arguing that rights must not be restricted by putting them in a written straightjacket:

> The people, or the sovereign power, cannot be affected by any such declaration of rights, they being the source of all power in the government; whatever they have not given away still remains inherent in them . . . . In England the king claims the sovereignty and supports an interest in opposition to the people. It becomes, therefore, both their interest and their duty, at every proper opportunity, to obtain a declaration and acknowledgment of those rights they should hold against their sovereign. But in America . . . the people hold all power, not by them expressly delegated to individuals, for the good of the whole.[41]

### GEORGIA

The date set for the opening of the Georgia convention to consider ratification of the federal Constitution passed without a quorum being reached. A newspaper explained: "Our lower country members are tardy, and our upper ones are generally engaged in defending their families and property on the frontiers."[42] When the convention met and adopted the federal Constitution unanimously on January 2, 1788, without proposing a bill of rights, there was obviously one right the delegates would have deemed basic. A settler's family without firearms in a war with Native Americans would have been deemed a massacre waiting to happen. The state's seizure of tribal lands had recently provoked the killings of settlers.

The federalist argument that the Constitution needed no bill of rights was at home in Georgia, whose state constitution contained no enumeration of rights. In response to the proposal that the federal Constitution declare a free press and jury trial inviolate, one Georgian replied: "What control had the federal government upon sacred palladium of national freedom? . . . The very declaration would have been deemed nugatory, and an implication that some degree of power was given. In short, everything that is not reserved is given."[43]

## CONNECTICUT

Connecticut ratified next, on January 9, 1788, without suggesting any amendments. One writer argued that "the populace will lose no power, nor any right or privilege which they have ever have ever held sacred and dear."[44] As for the claim that Congress could turn the militia into a select force resembling a standing army, it was argued: "The militia comprehends all the male inhabitants from sixteen to sixty years of age. . . . Against whom will they turn their swords? Against themselves!—to execute laws which are unconstitutional, unreasonable, and oppressive upon themselves!"[45]

Another contended that a declaration was unnecessary because the Congress would have no power over rights. *"There is no declaration of any kind to preserve the liberty of the press, etc.* Nor is liberty of conscience, or of matrimony, or of burial of the dead; it is enough that Congress have no power to prohibit either."[46] Later, when the governor of North Carolina sent Connecticut Governor Samuel Huntington a proposed bill of rights including guarantees for the press and arms, the latter responded:

> A Bill of Rights in former times hath been judged necessary, but in this enlightened age, when it seems a self evident truth . . . that all right and authority in Government is derived from the People, and may be resumed whenever the safety or happiness of the People renders it necessary; is it necessary, or expedient, for them to form a Bill of Rights which seems at least to call in question a truth of such importance and which ought ever to be held indisputable?[47]

## MASSACHUSETTS

The demand for a bill of rights reached a high pitch in Massachusetts before the ink on the proposed Constitution had time to dry. A "ships' news" satire published in the Boston *Independent Chronicle* on October 25, 1787, reported on a list of packages found aboard the new ship *Federal Constitution,* when it was searched for possible contraband. "One folio volume, marked, *no bill of rights,*" was opened and found to contain "a *blank volume.*"[48] A chest contained "*thirteen stands of arms,*" about which the officers of the ship argued that "it was absolutely necessary to carry arms for fear of pirates, & c. and . . . their arms were all stamped with peace, that they were never to be used but in case of hostile attack, that it was in the law of nature to every man to defend himself, and unlawful for any man to deprive him of those weapons of self defence." Another trunk contained "the habeas corpus act."[49] Poking fun at incipient proposals for a bill of rights was fair game.

Stringent opposition to a constitution with no bill of rights existed in Massachusetts. Federalist leader Theodore Sedgwick wrote to Henry Van Schaack on November 28 about an opponent who

> is making every possible exertion & by the meanest and basest arts stimulating pub[l]ick passions. He says that it will be a government for great men & law[y]erss. That the people will be disarmed. That a standing army will be immediately formed &ca. &ca. &ca. With these suggestions & insinuations he goes from house to house.—For God sake come down—I think at present that the friends of the Government are gaining ground but appearances may be deceitful. . . .[50]

Antifederalist John DeWitt published a series in Boston that articulated the position against the Constitution and in favor of a bill of rights. In an essay against standing armies appearing in the *American Herald* on December 3, he stated: "It is asserted by the most respectable writers upon government, that a well regulated militia, composed of the yeomanry of the country, have ever been considered as the bulwark of a free people."[51] In a revised version published a few weeks later, he added: "Tyrants have never placed any confidence on a militia composed of freemen."[52] DeWitt predicted that Congress "at their pleasure may arm or disarm all or any part of the freemen of the United States, so that when their army is sufficiently numerous, they may put it out of the power of the freemen militia of America to assert and defend their liberties . . . ."[53]

This was only one of countless salvos against standing armies. Typical is the letter from "Candidus I"—believed by federalists to be a "tool" of Samuel Adams—published in the December 6 *Independent Chronicle* complaining "that a bill of rights is wanted" and warning of Congress' powers to raise armies and to tax.[54] By contrast, "Cassius VI" wrote in the Christmas Day issue of the *Massachusetts Gazette*: "Consider that those immortal characters, who first planned the event of the revolution, and with arms in their hands stepped forth in the glorious cause of human nature, have now devised a plan for supporting your freedom, and increasing your strength, your power and happiness."[55]

The Massachusetts ratifying convention met from January 9 through February 7. Early on, William Symmes came out swinging, warning that the revenue power of Congress "is a power, sir, to burden us with a standing army of ravenous collectors . . . when the Congress shall become tyrannical, these vultures, their servants, will be the tyrants of the village, by whose presence, all freedom of speech and action, will be taken away."[56] He predicted, "who shall dare to gainsay the proceedings of this body, when according to the course of nature it shall be too firmly fixed in the saddle to be overthrown by any thing but a general insurrection?"[57] (Symmes would later vote to ratify the Constitution.)

The first reference in debate to a lack of a bill of rights consisted in an explanation by Colonel Joseph Bradley Varnum that Congress had only express powers, and thus no bill of rights was necessary.[58] General Samuel Thompson was not impressed: "But where is the bill of rights which shall check the power of this Congress; which shall say, Thus far shall ye come, and no farther. The safety of the people depends on a bill of rights." Not surprisingly, among his other objections to the Constitution was the following: "The great Mr. Pitt says, standing armies are dangerous—keep your militia in order . . . ."[59] Another version of this speech had Thompson arguing that "standing armies are a curse—take care of the militia, they are virtuous men . . . ."[60]

James Bowdoin, a radical during the Revolution who as governor in 1786 had suppressed Shays' Rebellion, shot back: "With the rights of particular states, or private citizens, not being the object or subject of the Constitution, they are only incidentally mentioned." The former "would require a volume to describe," and the latter would be improper to list.[61]

Theophilus Parsons, who wanted no bill of rights either, asked: "Is there a single natural right we enjoy, uncontrolled by our own legislature that Congress can infringe? Not one."[62] He also posed jury nullification as a method of preventing oppression:

> But, sir, the people themselves have it in their power effectually to resist usurpation, without being driven to an appeal to arms. An act of usurpation is not obligatory; it is not law; and any man may be justified in his resistance. Let

him be considered as a criminal by the general government, yet only his own fellow-citizens can convict him; they are his jury, and if they pronounce him innocent, not all the powers of Congress can hurt him . . . .[63]

Theodore Sedgwick queried whether "an army could be raised for the purpose of enslaving themselves and their brethren? Or, if raised, whether they could subdue a nation of freemen, who know how to prize liberty; and who have arms in their hands?"[64] Similarly, outside the convention hall "The Yeomanry of Massachusetts" argued in the *Massachusetts Gazette* that should those who come to power attempt "to deprive the people of their liberties," then "the people may, and will rise to arms and prevent it . . . ."[65]

Meanwhile, Governor John Hancock proposed amendments to the Constitution, although none concerned substantive rights. Its first article was the declaration "that all powers not expressly delegated to Congress, are reserved to the several States, to be by them exercised."[66] Various structural amendments, along with the right to trial by jury in civil cases, followed. The convention would ultimately recommend passage of these amendments.

Anxious to open the door to guarantees of substantive rights, Samuel Adams suggested that conditional amendments now would be better than relying on uncertain amendments in the future and moved the passage of the Hancock proposals.[67] Adams called Hancock's above first article as "a summary of a bill of rights."[68] But Adams was only getting warmed up for his declaration of individual rights.

Samuel Nasson then picked up the gauntlet, making "a short apostrophe to Liberty. . . . I cannot, sir, see this brightest of jewels tarnished—a jewel worth ten thousand worlds; and shall we part with it so soon?"[69] Among other defects, "let us consider the Constitution without a bill of rights. When I give up any of my natural rights, it is for the security of the rest; but here is not one right secured, although many are neglected."[70]

Nasson recalled the Boston Massacre, warning that standing armies "are too frequently used for no other purpose than dragooning the people into slavery . . . ." He continued:

What occasion have we for standing armies? We fear no foe. If one should come upon us, we have a militia, which is our bulwark. Let Lexington witness that we have the means of defence among ourselves. If, during the last winter, there was not much alacrity shown by the militia in turning out, we must consider that they were going to fight their countrymen.[71]

The militia had indeed been reluctant to suppress Shays' Rebellion, for "against deluded, infatuated men they did not wish to exert their valour or their strength." Had the British invaded, it would have been a different story.[72]

On February 5, Dr. John Taylor ridiculed the suggestion "that, had the Constitution been so predicated as to require a bill of rights to be annexed to it, it would have been the work of a year, and could not be contained but in volumes." To the contrary, "any gentleman in that Convention could form one in a few hours . . . ."[73]

Theophilus Parsons argued the impracticability of "a bill, in a national constitution, for securing individual rights," noting that "no power was given to Congress to infringe on any one of the natural rights of the people by this Constitution; and, should they attempt it without constitutional authority, the act would be a nullity, and could not be enforced."[74]

At that point Gilbert Dench moved that the convention adjourn to a future date to give the delegates an opportunity to confer with their constituents. The motion lost by a vote of 329 to 115.[75]

In addition to a bill to secure individual rights, amendments to the structure of government were sought. On the same day as the above debate, an address to the convention by "Agrippa XVI" published in the *Massachusetts Gazette* proposed the structural amendments that "Each state shall have the command of its own militia," and that "No continental army shall come within the limits of any state, other than garrison to guard the publick stores, without the consent of such states in time of peace."[76]

The next day—February 6—Samuel Adams moved to add to the above first article of John Hancock's proposed amendments the following substantive rights:

> And that the said Constitution be never construed to authorise Congress, to infringe the just liberty of the press, or the rights of conscience; or to prevent the people of the United States, who are peaceable citizens, from keeping their own arms; or to raise standing armies, unless when necessary for the defence of the United States, or of some one or more of them; or to prevent the people from petitioning in a peaceable and orderly manner, the federal legislature, for a redress of grievances; or to subject the people to unreasonable searches & seizures of their persons, papers, or possessions.[77]

Adams' proposals would find expression in the First, Second, and Fourth Amendments to the federal Constitution. Adams had been a prolific proponent in the pre-Revolutionary era of individual rights in general and the right to keep and bear arms in particular. The above declaration stressed the "keeping" of arms, a favorite theme of Bostonians who experienced the most dramatic arms seizures by the British before the Revolution. However, the right to keep arms extended only to "peaceable citizens," not to criminals. Adams proposed only a bill of personal rights, and—other than the restriction on standing armies— did not propose structural amendments, such as clarifying state powers over the militia. The mention of standing armies in the same sentence as the right to keep arms did not detract from the individual character of that right.

A contemporary account described the fate of Adams' proposals as follows: "The Hon. Mr. Adams, introduced some amendments, to be added to those reported by the Committee—but they not meeting the approbation of those gentlemen whose minds they were intended to ease, after they were debated a considerable time, the Hon. Gentleman withdrew them."[78]

Adams' motion agitated the federalists, who wanted the unconditional ratification of the Constitution with no bill of rights. Federalist and Congregational Pastor Jeremy Belknap wrote in his diary:

> S Adams offered some additional amendments to secure (the) Rights of Consc[ience]—Liberty of [the] Press—Right to keep Arms—Protection of Persons & Property from Seizure &c—wh[ich] gave an alarm to both Parties—the Antifeds supposed [that] so great a Politician would not offer these amendments unless he tho't there was danger on these Points—[the] Feds were afraid [that] new Converts would desert—A[dams] perceived [the] mischief & withdrew his Proposal—another renewed it—but it was voted out & A[dams] himself was obliged to vote agt it.[79]

Four days later, Belknap wrote to Ebenezer Hazard—who, as postmaster general, had been accused by antifederalists of interrupting their mail—with a further partisan description of Adams' motion:

> S Adams had almost overset the apple-cart by intruding an amendment of his own fabrication on ye morng of the day of ratification—it was to this purpose "That Congress should not infringe the Rights of Conscience, the Liberty of the Press, the right of peaceable citizens to bear arms, nor suffer unwarrantable seizure of persons, papers nor property &c" Feds & Antis were alarmed—the former because they saw the fatal Tendencey of creating such apprehensions as

immediately appeared in the latter, Some of whom said that such a Man as Mr. A would not have guarded against these Evils if he had not seen a foundation for them in ye Constitution—When A perceived the mischief he had made he withdrew his motion, but some of the anti leaders revived it—& he was obliged finally to *vote against it*—it was thrown out by a very general Vote, but it is apprehended this manoeuvre lost the Constitution several Votes—Some suspect his *Intention* was to overset the whole, but "Charity hopeth all things" & I am seriously of the mind that it rather proceeded from a vanity of increasing his *own* popularity as Hancock had his by the midwifing the other amendments into ye World—Had it not been for this step the whole exertion had been in vain; *A* has made himself unpopular.[80]

Belknap's paraphrasing of the proposals is revealing. Adams proposed that the Constitution could not be "construed to authorise Congress . . . to prevent the people of the United States, who are peaceable citizens, from keeping their own arms." Belknap summarized this to read: "That Congress should not infringe . . . the right of peaceable citizens to bear arms . . . ." What became the Second Amendment would also use the term "infringe" and would refer to the right to "bear arms" as well as to keep them. This exemplifies the conceptual similarity between the two renditions.

The ad hominem character of Belknap's above account is evident. Allegedly out of vanity, Adams sought a bill of rights. Belknap's following further description indicates that Adams' proposals enjoyed considerable support—by obstructionists, of course—but that the federalists were able to use procedural tactics to cause the vote on the Constitution to be taken when they were sure of victory:

> Some of the Delegates from Maine were converted, but I believe not a greater Proportion of them than of the other Counties—there were near 100 in all—Some of ye most virulent Opposers were Mainites viz Nason, Wedgery & Saml Thompson. . . .

> The Antis would have had the Question called much sooner but the fed's protracted the debates on paragraphs till they were *sure* of a Majority . . . .[81]

The vote on ratification of the Constitution without amendments was close—187 in favor and 168 opposed.[82] The resolution of ratification recommended passage of Hancock's proposed amendments,[83] but they included no substantive rights. It bears emphasis that the federalists were not opposed to the personal rights declared in Samuel Adams' draft—to the contrary, they argued that Congress had no power over such subjects.

Firearms ownership at that time was taken for granted. When the convention ratified the Constitution, the mass celebrations in Boston included the following:

> In a cart, drawn by five horses, the British flag was displayed, and insulted by numbers placed in the cart, armed with muskets, who repeatedly discharged the contents of them through the tattered remnant, in contempt of that faithless nation, whose exertions have been unremitted since the peace, to cramp our commerce and obstruct all our nautical proceedings.[84]

One man objected not on the basis that the firing was unsafe, but to the content of the speech: "the Bostonians have acted very imprudently in Carrying the King of Englands Coulors in a Cart pulld with five Horses, armed with muskets and fireing through the same with Great Indecent Speches about England and &c."[85]

The gun firing must have been widespread. Jeremy Belknap wrote in his diary: "Then for 2 or 3 Days ye Town was over head & Ears in joy—Bells—Drums—Guns—Procession &c."[86] Belknap then returned to the subject of proposals for a bill of rights, which he saw as a conspiracy between antifederalists of different states:

> It was matter of speculation how Mr. Adams came to propose such amendments—many suspicions were formed & some thos't he meant to overthrow ye Constitution.—Certainly it was ye worst blow which had been given to it—In a Week or two afterward came along a protest of ye Pennsylva minority—in wh[ich] these very things are objected to ye Constitution wh[ich] he proposed to guard against by his motion—
>
> It is sd. ye Copies of these Protests were purposely *detained* on ye Road—but it is supposed A[dams] had a Copy in a Letter before ye Convention was dissolved—
>
> An attempt was made by the antifeds in Pennsylva to thow an Odium on ye Post officers for detaing these & other papers.—but in fact the Office has nothing to do with them.[87]

The bill of rights proposed by the Pennsylvania Dissent of Minority had been circulated in Boston when the Massachusetts convention met. The antifederalists accused postal authorities of interfering with their mailings. In the above passage, Belknap sought to disprove these allegations based on the avowal that Adams had received communications from the Pennsylvania minority. Whatever the true facts, it was hardly a secret that antifederalists—like federalists—worked together on a nationwide basis. As Belknap continued:

> A in ye Course of debate in Conventn. sd but little—what he sd was *rather in favour of* the Constituon—when it came to ye last pinch his introduced Amendments had well-nigh *overset it.*

> When he perceived ye uneasiness in ye minds of both parties—he withdrew his Motion—one of the antifeds revived it—Adams he *Opposed it*—Sd he shd vote agt it & actually did so—but it is tho't his Manoe[u]vre lost sevl Votes for ye Constn.—it is sd CJ was with him 3 Evengs previous—pwersuadg him *not to make ye Motion but could not prevail.*[88]

The above private musings of Jeremy Belknap are significant because virtually no other records exist with such details about the attempt in the Massachusetts convention to require a federal bill of rights. Even after the Constitution was ratified and James Madison introduced the Bill of Rights in the Congress, the stubborn Belknap continued to attack Adams and to oppose a bill of rights.[89] Others viewed Madison's proposals as having vindicated Adams' role the previous year. A writer explained in the Boston *Independent Chronicle*:

> It may well be remembered, that the following "amendments" to the new constitution of these United States, were introduced to the convention of this commonwealth by its present Lieutenant-Governour, that venerable patriot SAMUEL ADAMS.—It was his misfortune to have been misconceived, and the proposition was accordingly withdrawn—le[a]st the business of the convention (the session of which was then drawing to a period) might be unexpectedly protracted. His enemies triumphed exceedingly, and asserted to represent his proposal as not only an artful attempt to prevent the constitution being adopted in this state but as an unnecessary and improper alteration of a system, which did not admit of improvements. To the honour of this gentleman's penetration, and of his just way of thinking on this important subject, every one of the intended alterations but one [i.e., proscription of standing armies] have been already reported by the committee of the House of Representatives, and most probably will be adopted by the federal legislature. In justice therefore for that long tried Republican, and his numerous friends, you gentlemen, are requested

to republish his intended alterations, in the same paper, that exhibits to the public, the amendments which the committee have adopted, in order that they may be compared together.[90]

The writer proceeded to quote Adams' proposals that Congress could not prevent a free press, the keeping of arms by peaceable citizens, or petitioning for redress of grievances, nor could it conduct unreasonable searches and seizures. Adams' proposals would come to life after all.


## MARYLAND

Luther Martin's "Letter on the Constitution," which was delivered to the Maryland legislature in early 1788, became a major antifederalist tract. Martin had served in the constitutional convention in Philadelphia. Among his many objections was that the proposed government was given power "to increase and keep up a standing army as numerous as it would wish, and, by placing the militia under its power, enable it to leave the militia totally unorganised, undisciplined, and even to disarm them."[91] This was contrary to the principle that the armed citizenry should be able to check oppression: "By the principles of the American revolution, arbitrary power may, and ought to, be resisted even by arms, if necessary."[92]

Records on the Maryland constitutional convention are sparse, partly because the Constitution's supporters knew they had a majority and refused to debate. Opponents were allowed to speak, but members of the majority simply remained mum. The majority then voted to ratify the Constitution on April 28, 1788, without proposing any amendments.[93]

After doing so, a committee was appointed to consider possible amendments. Three of the committee members had been members of the committee that had drafted the Maryland Declaration of Rights of 1776,[94] but they were apparently now in the minority. While the 1788 committee would not recommend a bill of rights, it drafted several amendments concerning the structure of government, the first of which was "that Congress shall exercise no power but what it expressly delegated by this Constitution."[95]

The committee also proposed that the militia shall not be subject to martial law in peacetime, "for all other provisions in favour of the rights of men would be vain and nugatory, if the power of subjecting all men, able to bear arms, to martial law at any moment should remain vested in Congress."[96] However, the committee rejected proposals against standing armies and a national religion.[97] Despite the above tentative proposals, the committee ultimately determined not to report any proposed amendments at all.[98]

### SOUTH CAROLINA

South Carolina was the next state to ratify—it did so on May 23. While records of the South Carolina convention are meager, records exist of the debates of the legislative session in mid-January, which considered whether to call a convention. The antifederalist case was made by James Lincoln as follows:

> What is liberty? The power of governing yourselves. If you adopt this Constitution, have you this power? No: you give it into the hands of a set of men who live one thousand miles distant from you.[99]

Among other defects, Lincoln asked: "Why was not this Constitution ushered in with the bill of rights? . . . Perhaps this same President and Senate would, by and by, declare them. He much feared they would."[100]

The objection was met by Charles Cotesworth Pinckney, a leading player in framing the South Carolina Constitution of 1776 as well as a prominent delegate to the Philadelphia convention of 1787. The Constitution lacked a bill of rights, "for, as we might perhaps have omitted the enumeration of some of our rights, it might hereafter be said we had delegated to the general government a power to take away such of our rights as we had not enumerated; but by delegating express powers, we certainly reserve to ourselves every power and right not mentioned in the Constitution."[101] Lack of a bill of rights did not imply that a free press and bearing arms were not protected rights.

But Pinckney also gave another, sinister reason why no bill of rights was inserted: "Such bills generally begin with declaring that all men are by nature born free. Now, we should make that declaration with a very bad grace, when a large part of our property consists in men who are actually born slaves."[102]

The South Carolina legislature voted to call a constitutional convention on May 12. Only a few of the speeches are extant. Charles Pinckney, who had also been a delegate to the Philadelphia convention, averred that among the major European states, only Great Britain "confirms to its citizens their civil liberties, or provides for the security of private rights," although it violated religious liberty. "The rest of Europe affords a melancholy picture of the depravity of human nature, and of the total subversion of those rights . . . ."[103] But the "sense of liberty, and of the rights of mankind," was spreading to Europe, and thus "let it be our prayer that the effects of the revolution may never cease to operate until they have unshackled all the nations that have firmness to resist the fetters of despotism."[104]

The antifederalists also laid claim to the Revolutionary heritage. Patrick Dollard stated about his constituents:

> In the late bloody contest, they bore a conspicuous part, when they fought, bled, and conquered, in defence of their civil rights and privileges, which they expected to transmit untainted to their posterity. They are nearly all, to a man, opposed to this new Constitution, because, they say they have omitted to insert a bill of rights therein, ascertaining and fundamentally establishing, the unalienable rights of men, without a full, free, and secure enjoyment of which there can be no liberty . . . .[105]

Dollard denounced the despotic principle of "non-resistance," predicted that the people would not accept the new government "unless compelled by force of arms, which this new Constitution plainly threatens; and then, they say, your standing army, like Turkish janizaries enforcing despotic laws, must ram it down their throats with the points of bayonets."[106]

Inflammatory rhetoric aside, the call for a bill of rights fell on deaf ears, and two-thirds of the delegates voted to ratify the Constitution without proposing amendments.[107] But the supporters of a bill of rights would soon get the last word.

Thus far, federalists successfully led the respective conventions to ratify the Constitution without any formal demand for amendments. That would now end. Henceforth, the antifederalists would persuade convention majorities to propose both bills of rights and structural amendments.

### NEW HAMPSHIRE

New Hampshire would distinguish itself in the process of constitutional ratification in a twofold sense. First, it was the ninth state to ratify the Constitution, thereby making the Constitution effective. Second, it was the first state formally to demand a bill of rights.

The first session of the New Hampshire convention contained an antifederalist majority, and the federalists maneuvered an adjournment so the convention would not reject the Constitution.[108] At the second session of the convention, on June 21, 1788, a committee of fifteen was appointed to consider amendments. The eight federalists on this committee were led by convention president John Sullivan; the seven antifederalists were led by Joshua Atherton.[109]

The proposed amendments were apparently already drafted, because they were reported back to the convention the same day. The amendments began: "That it be explicitly declared that all powers not expressly and particularly delegated by the aforesaid Constitution are reserved to the several states, to be by them exercised."[110] There followed some recommended changes to the structure of the government and then three individual rights:

> 10th. That no standing army shall be kept up in time of peace, unless with the consent of three fourths of the members of each branch of Congress; nor shall soldiers in a time of peace, be quartered upon private houses without the consent of the owners.
>
> 11th. Congress shall make no laws touching religion or to infringe the rights of conscience.
>
> 12th. Congress shall never disarm any citizen, unless such as are or have been in actual rebellion.[111]

Freedom of religion and conscience, possession of arms, and no non-consensual peacetime quartering of soldiers in private houses would be reflected in the First, Second, and Third Amendments. The prohibitions on Congress would be absolute—"Congress shall make no laws" touching religion or conscience and "shall never disarm any citizen."

The qualification that "actual" insurgents could be disarmed was proposed with recent events in mind. In September 1786, during agitation for abolition of debts and after passage of an act allowing former Tories to return to their estates, two hundred "rioters" with fifty muskets demonstrated at the General Court in Exeter, New Hampshire. Two thousand militiamen turned out to disperse them.[112] Shays' Rebellion followed immediately in Massachusetts.

The proposal that Congress could not disarm "any citizen" except those in rebellion made clear that the right to keep and bear arms was not limited to the able-bodied male population that constituted the militia.[113]

Having reached an agreement over amendments, one critical difference remained. Antifederalist leader Atherton moved that the convention ratify the Constitution subject to the condition that it not be operable in New Hampshire without ratification of the amendments.[114] The federalists moved unconditionally to ratify the Constitution and to recommend the amendments to Congress.[115] The convention then voted 57 to 47 to ratify.[116] New Hampshire's ratification made the Constitution effective.

The arms guarantees proposed by New Hampshire and the Pennsylvania minority were discussed in a broader critique of proposals by state conventions. Entitled "Remarks on the Amendments to the Federal Constitutions," the Reverend Nicholas Collin of Philadelphia, writing under the pen name "A Foreign Spectator" (from Sweden), opposed any amendment. If the Constitution contained "a scrupulous enumeration of all the rights of the states and individuals, it would make a larger volume than the Bible . . . ."[117] Further, an army was no danger "especially when I am well armed myself." "While the people have property, arms in their hands, and only a spark of noble spirit, the most corrupt Congress must be mad to form any project of tyranny."[118]

Collin further held that "a good militia is the natural, easy, powerful and honorable defence of a country."[119] Identifying "a citizen, as a militia man," he referred to "that noble art, by which you can defend your life, liberty and property; your parents, wife and children!"[120]

Collin then considered "those amendments which particularly concern several personal rights and liberties."[121] Attacking a proposal that the privilege of habeas corpus should not be suspended for more than six months, he supported his position by referring to two of the proposed arms guarantees:

> What is said on this matter, is a sufficient reply to the 12th amend. of the New-Hampshire convention, *that congress shall never disarm any citizen, unless such as are or have been in actual rebellion.* If, by the acknowledged necessity of suspending the privilege of *habeas corpus,* a suspected person may be secured, he may much more be disarmed. In such unhappy times it may be very expedient to disarm those, who cannot conveniently be guarded, or whose conduct has been less obnoxious. Indeed to prevent by such a gentle measure, crimes and misery, is at once justice to the nation, and mercy to deluded wretches, who may otherwise, by the instigation of a dark and bloody ringleader, commit many horrid murders, for which they must suffer digan punishments.

The minority of Pennsylvania seems to have been desirous of limiting the federal power in these cases; but their conviction of its necessity appears by those very parts of the 3rd and 7th amendments framed in this view, to wit, *that no man be deprived of his liberty except by the law of the land, or the judgment of his peers—and that no law shall be passed for disarming the people, or any of them, unless for crimes committed, or real danger of public injury from individuals.* The occasional suspension of the above privilege [of habeas corpus] becomes pro tempore the law of the land, and by virtue of it dangerous persons are secured. Insurrections against the federal government are undoubtedly real dangers of public injury, not only from individuals, but great bodies; consequently the laws of the union should be competent for the disarming of both.[122]

This is the only discussion in the ratification period of the limited power of Congress to disarm any person or group under the two proposed amendments. Since persons involved in an insurrection could be arrested, Collin reasoned, they could certainly also be disarmed. There is no hint in Collin's discussion that Congress could pass any law restricting firearms ownership by law-abiding citizens. However, he did oppose amendments to the Constitution, including guarantees of a free press and jury trial, prohibitions on general warrants and cruel and unusual punishment, and all other proposals.[123]

In 1789, the federalists won the congressional elections in New Hampshire, in part by championing adoption of a federal bill of rights that had been demanded by several states. Antifederalist Joshua Atherton wrote: "To carry on the farce the Federalists have taken the liberty to step onto the ground of their opponents, and, clothing themselves with their armour, talk high of amendments . . . . New York, Virginia, and other states having gone so fully into the detail of amendments, the strokes of abler hands ha[ve] rendered the lines of my feeble pen unnecessary."[124] This suggests that Atherton may have authored the Bill of Rights proposals adopted by the New Hampshire convention.

Insistence on a bill of rights—which mustered the votes only of minorities in the Pennsylvania and Massachusetts conventions—finally commanded a majority in the New Hampshire convention. Momentum in favor of a declaration of individual liberties now escalated, as all eyes focused on Virginia.

## CHAPTER 10

# Virginia Tips the Scales

I N  A N  E S S A Y  "To the Citizens of Virginia," Alexander White replied to the Pennsylvania Dissent of Minority. White was running in the election for delegates to the Virginia ratifying convention, and would be elected.[1] He depicted the objections of the Pennsylvania minority as bordering on the dishonest:

> There are other things so clearly out of the power of Congress, that the bare recital of them is sufficient, I mean the "rights of conscience, or religious liberty—the rights of bearing arms for defence, or for killing game—the liberty of fowling, hunting and fishing. . . ." These things seem to have been inserted among their objections, merely to induce the ignorant to believe that Congress would have a power over such objects and to infer from their being refused a place in the Constitution, their intention to exercise that power to the oppression of the people.[2]

White then repeated the federalist dogma that a bill of rights would be dangerous, because it would suggest that Congress had power over any subject not explicitly guaranteed: "But if they had been admitted as reservations out of the powers granted to Congress, it would have opened a large field indeed for legal construction: I know not an object of legislation which by a parity of reason, might not be fairly determined within the jurisdiction of Congress."[3]

Nonetheless, White recognized that abuse of a right could be penalized: "The freedom of speech and of the press, are likewise out of the jurisdiction of Congress.—But, if by an abuse of that freedom I attempt to excite sedition in the Commonwealth, I may be punished . . . ."[4] Similarly, Congress had no power over bearing arms for defense or hunting but could punish armed sedition.

But supporters of a bill of rights could hardly be regarded as crackpots. Thomas Jefferson wrote to James Madison from Paris on December 20, 1787, approving of some parts of the Constitution but adding what he disliked: "First the omission of a bill of rights providing clearly & without the aid of sophisms for freedom of religion, freedom of the press, protection against standing armies . . . . A bill of rights is what the people are entitled to against every government on earth, general or particular, & what no just government should refuse, or rest on inference."[5]

Many others were beating the same drum. Joseph Spencer sent Madison a copy of John Leland's "Objections to the Constitution," which began: "There is no Bill Rights, whenever a Number of men enter into a State of Society, a Number of individual Rights must be given up to Society, but there should always be a memorial of those not surrendered . . . ."[6] Madison would meet with Leland and win him over to the federalist cause.[7]

The Virginia convention was preceded by a great deal of debate in the public forum. "A Native of Virginia" asked in an April 2, 1788, publication: "What is a Bill of Rights? A declaration insisted on by a free people, and recognised by their rulers, that certain principles shall be the invariable rules of their administration . . . ."[8]

"Cassius II" in the April 9 *Virginia Independent Chronicle* replied to a published letter from Richard Henry Lee to Edmund Randolph as follows:

> "There is no restraint," you say, "in form of a bill of rights to secure (what Doctor Blackstone calls) that residuum of human rights, which is not intended to be given up to society, and, which is, not indeed, necessary to be given up for

any social purpose. The rights of conscience, the freedom of the press, and the trial by jury are at mercy." . . . You certainly, must know, sir, that bills of rights are only necessary in those governments, in which there is a claim of power independent of, and not derived from, the people; such as the divine and hereditary right claimed by Kings.[9]

The Society of Western Gentlemen proposed revisions to the Constitution in the April 30 *Virginia Independent Chronicle*. In addition to a free press, it would have declared: "The people have a right to keep and bear arms, for the national defence; standing armies in time of peace are dangerous to liberty, therefore the military shall be subordinate to the civil power." A separate provision would have made bearing arms a duty: "The community have a right to require of every individual his personal services when necessary for the common defence . . . ."[10]

James Monroe, in "Some Observations on the Constitution," wrote on May 25 that "fundamental principles form a check, even when the spirit of the times hath changed, indeed they retard and controul it." Examples included trial by jury and freedom of conscience and the press. He added concerning the militia:

Let them regulate the disciplining and training of the militia—the calling them forth and commanding them in service; for the militia of a country, is its only safe and proper defence. . . . [T]he greater the authority of Congress over the respectable body of men, in whose hands every thing would be safe, the less necessity there would be to have recourse to that bane of all societies, the destroyer of the rights of men, a standing army.[11]

George Mason wrote to Thomas Jefferson on May 26, complaining about the "Compromise between the Eastern, & the two Southern States, to permit the latter to continue the Importation of Slaves for twenty odd Years; a more favourite Object with them, than the Liberty and Happiness of the People." He continued:

There are many other things very objectionable in the proposed new Constitution; particularly the almost unlimited Authority over the Militia of the several States; whereby, under Colour of regulating, they may disarm or render useless the Militia, the more easily to govern by a standing Army; or they may harass the Militia, by such rigid Regulations, and intolerable Burdens, as to make the People themselves desire its Abolition.[12]

Richard Henry Lee wrote to Edmund Pendleton the same day of the need for a declaration "to regulate the discretion of Rulers in a legal way, restraining the progress of Ambition & Avarice within just bounds.[13]

Lee's antifederalist colleagues in Virginia, Patrick Henry and George Mason, would effectively argue the above positions in that state's ratifying convention. The result would be an irresistible push for what became the Second Amendment and the rest of the Bill of Rights. They would not ultimately succeed, however, in adopting any structural changes, such as on state-federal powers over the militia.

The Virginia ratifying convention met from June 2 through June 26, 1788. On June 5, Edmund Pendleton, president of the convention and opponent of a bill of rights, weakly argued that abuse of power could be remedied by recalling the delegated powers in a convention.[14] Patrick Henry shot back that the power to resist oppression rests upon the right to possess arms:

> Guard with jealous attention the public liberty. Suspect every one who approaches that jewel. Unfortunately, nothing will preserve it but downright force. Whenever you give up that force, you are ruined.[15]

Henry sneered, "O sir, we should have fine times, indeed, if, to punish tyrants, it were only sufficient to assemble the people! Your arms, wherewith you could defend yourselves, are gone . . . . Did you ever read of any revolution in a nation . . . inflicted by those who had no power at all?"[16]

Since the Constitution had not been tested by experience, Henry's arguments cannot be considered mere exaggerations. He queried, "of what service would militia be to you, when, most probably, you will not have a single musket in the state? for, as arms are to be provided by Congress, they may or may not furnish them."[17] Quoting the militia clause of the Constitution, Henry continued: "By this, sir, you see that their control over our last and best defence is unlimited. If they neglect or refuse to discipline or arm our militia, they will be useless: the states can do neither—this power being exclusively given to Congress."[18]

The next day, June 6, Edmund Randolph—who had joined Mason and Gerry in refusing to sign the proposed Constitution as delegates at the Philadelphia convention but who now had switched sides—made the following comments about defense:

The other States have upwards of 330,000 men capable of bearing arms: This
will be a good army, or they can very easily raise a good army out of so great
a number. Our militia mounts to 50,000; even stretching it to the improbable
amount (urged by some) of 60,000. . . . I will pay the last tribute of gratitude to
the militia of my country: They performed some of the most gallant feats during the last war, and acted as nobly as men enured to other avocations could be
expected to do: But, Sir, it is dangerous to look to them as our sole protectors.[19]

James Madison also responded that the militia provision was "an additional
security to our liberty, without diminishing the power of states in any considerable degree. . . . Congress ought to have the power to establish a uniform
discipline throughout the states, and to provide for the execution of the laws,
suppress insurrections, and repeal invasions: these are the only cases wherein
they can interfere with the militia . . . ."[20]

In response to a suggestion that the militia would be made into an instrument of tyranny, on June 7 Frances Corbin asked: "Are we not militia? Shall
we fight against ourselves?"[21]

But Patrick Henry relentlessly returned to the theme of a declaration of
rights. On the same day, he noted "certain political maxims, which no free
people ought ever to abandon":

We have one, Sir, *That all men are by nature free and independent, and have
certain inherent rights, of which, when they enter into society, they cannot by any
compact deprive or divest their posterity.* We have a set of maxims of the same
spirit, which must be beloved by every friend to liberty, to virtue, to mankind.
Our Bill of Rights contains those admirable maxims.[22]

Henry wished not to leave rights such as jury trial and a free press to chance,
which the doctrine of implied rights entailed: "If they can use implication *for*
us, they can also use implications *against* us. We are *giving* power, they are
*getting* power, judge then, on which side the implication will be used."[23] A bill
of rights was conceived when the Revolution began precisely to exclude construction and implication.[24]

Before the convention began, George Mason working with the Virginia
antifederalists had already drafted a declaration of rights, which the convention would later adopt nearly verbatim. On June 9, just after the convention
opened, Patrick Henry wrote to John Lamb, chairman of the Federal Repub-

lican Committee of New York, that "Colo. George Mason has agreed to act as Chairman of our republican Society" and that they were sending a copy of "the Bill of Rights & of the particular Amendments we intend to propose in our Convention."[25] Mason wrote Lamb on the same date, enclosing a copy of the proposals.

The proposals were divided into two parts. The first was "a Declaration or Bill of Rights, asserting and securing from Encroachment, the Essential and unalienable Rights of the People."[26] It was an expanded version of the Virginia Declaration of Rights of 1776, which Mason also penned. It contained three successive provisions beginning with identical terms: first, "That the People have a Right peaceably to assemble . . ."; second, "That the People have a Right to Freedom of Speech . . ."; and third, "That the People have a Right to keep and to bear Arms; that a well regulated Militia, composed of the Body of the People, trained to arms, is the proper, natural, and safe Defence of a free State . . . ."[27]

According to one source, there is a draft in Mason's handwriting with the terminology: "That the people have a Right to mass & to bear arms . . . ."[28] It is uncertain whether this was a correct transcription. If correct, perhaps a right to "mass" with arms and bear them recalled the Revolutionary days when the armed multitudes would descend upon British colonial officials. This term would be dropped for the more conservative term "keep," which connotes the quiet possession of arms in the home.

The second part of the proposals consisted of amendments to the structure of the proposed government. It began: "That each State in the Union shall retain its Sovereignty, Freedom and Independence, and every Power, Jurisdiction and Right which is not by this Constitution expressly delegated to the Congress of the United States."[29] Among other provisions, it proposed that two-thirds of both houses of Congress would be necessary to keep up a standing army.[30] It did not mention the militia. These issues would be revisited throughout the debates and particularly at the conclusion of the convention.

In convention debate on June 9, Patrick Henry objected to the power of Congress to erect forts and magazines in each state,[31] arguing:

Are we at last brought to such an humiliating and debasing degradation, that we cannot be trusted with arms for our own defence? Where is the difference between having our arms in our own possession and under our own direction, and having them under the management of Congress. If our defence be the *real* object of having those arms, in whose hands can they be trusted with more propriety, or equal safety to us, as in our own hands?[32]

Similarly, Henry reiterated objections to the clause providing that Congress would arm and discipline the militia, reserving to the states the appointment of officers. If Congress failed to discipline the militia, would the states be precluded from doing so? The states could act only through "the doctrine of constructive implied powers." Henry added: "If by implication the States may discipline them, by implication also, Congress may officer them . . . ." The quandary was not just logical but was practical: "We have not one fourth of the arms that would be sufficient to defend ourselves. The power of arming the militia, and the means of purchasing arms, are taken from the states by the paramount power of Congress. If Congress will not arm them, they will not be armed at all." Henry concluded: "Congress by the power of taxation—by that of raising an army, and by their controul over the militia, have the sword in one hand, and the purse in the other. Shall we be safe without either?"[33] Henry also asserted of the states that "you are not to have the right of having arms in your own defence . . . ."[34]

In response to Patrick Henry's argument "that militia alone ought to be depended upon for the defence of every free country," Henry Lee—lieutenant colonel commandant of the American partisan legion in the Revolution[35]— averred: "I have seen them [the militia] perform feats that would do honour to the first veterans, and submitting to what would daunt German soldiers." However, "the militia cannot always be relied upon." Moreover, Congress' power was not exclusive: "The states are, by no part of the plan before you, precluded from arming and disciplining the militia, should Congress neglect it."[36]

Edmund Randolph returned to the theme of the danger of a bill of rights in a limited government, noting that Virginia's declaration was not part of its constitution, leaving a question about which was paramount. The same dispute would arise with a federal bill of rights: "Some [judges] will say, the bill of rights is paramount:—Others will say, that the Constitution being subsequent in point of time, must be paramount."[37]

Similarly, George Nicholas averred: "It is a principle universally agreed upon, that all powers not given, are retained." He would depend on the legislature to protect rights as done in England:

They have no express security for the liberty of the press. They have a reliance on Parliament of its protection and security. In the time of King William, there passed an act for licencing the press. That was repealed. The people have depended on their representatives. They will not consent to an act to infringe it . . . .[38]

Edmund Randolph, in debate on June 10, denied that the federal power was exclusive of the states. "Should Congress neglect to arm or discipline the militia, the states are fully possessed of the power of doing it; for they are restrained from it by no part of the Constitution."[39] A penman "Denatus" published an address to the convention the next day advocating academies for citizens to learn military arts and militia exercises. After training, they would "return home, prepare our arms for a moments warning, and each man fall to his occupation as before."[40]

But under the Constitution, argued George Mason on June 14, the militia would be destroyed "by rendering them useless—by disarming them. Under various pretences, Congress may neglect to provide for arming and disciplining the militia; and the state governments cannot do it, for Congress has an exclusive right to arm them . . . ."[41] A standing army would be supreme: "When, against a regular and disciplined army, yeomanry are the only defence,—yeomanry, unskillful and unarmed,—what chance is there for preserving freedom?"[42] Mason recalled:

Forty years ago, when the resolution of enslaving America was formed in Great Britain, the British Parliament was advised by an artful man [Sir William Keith], who was governor of Pennsylvania, to disarm the people; that it was the best and most effectual way to enslave them; but that they should not do it openly, but weaken them, and let them sink gradually, by totally disusing and neglecting the militia. [Here Mr. Mason quoted sundry passages to this effect.] This was a most iniquitous project. Why should we not provide against the danger of having our militia, our real and natural strength, destroyed? The general government ought, at the same time, to have some such power. But we need not give them power to abolish our militia. If they neglect to arm them, and prescribe proper discipline, they will be of no use. . . . I wish that, in case the general government should neglect to arm and discipline the militia, there should be an express declaration that the state governments might arm and discipline them.[43]

Mason undoubtedly quoted from Sir William Keith's *Collection of Papers and Other Tracts* published in London in 1740. Colonial Pennsylvania Governor Keith violated every tenet of the Whig-republican philosophy that so influenced the Americans with the following words:

> A Militia in an arbitrary and tyrannical Government may possibly be of some Service to the governing Power; but we learn from Experience, that in a free Country it is of little use. The People in the Plantations are so few in Proportion to the Lands they Possess, that Servants being scarce, and Slaves so exceedingly dear, the men are generally under a Necessity to work hard themselves, in order to provide the common Necessaries of Life for their Families; so that they cannot spare a Day's Time without great Loss to their Interest; wherefore a Militia there would become more burdensome to the poor People, than it can be in any Part of *Europe*. Besides, it may be question'd how far it would be consistent with good Policy, to accustom all the able Men in the Colonies to be well exercised in Arms; it seems at present to be more advisable, to keep up a small regular Force in each Province, which on Occasion might be readily augmented; so that in Case of a War, or Rebellion, the whole of the regular Troops on the Continent, might without Loss of Time be united or distributed at Pleasure . . . .[44]

Keith's fear of "accustom[ing] all the able Men in the Colonies to be well exercised in Arms" was directly related to his fear of "rebellion." He was the apologist of colonial imperialism par excellence, holding that "Every Act of a dependant Provincial Government therefore ought to terminate in the Advantage of the Mother State"[45] and that none of the colonies "can with any Reason or good Sense pretend to claim an absolute legislative Power within themselves . . . ."[46]

In a 1767 publication Keith advocated resort to the stamp tax in order to support a "Body of Regular Troops" under the control of the Crown and independent of the colonial governors.[47] As if this addition of insult to injury was not enough, he referred to the "loose, disorderly, and insignificant Militia."[48]

James Madison countered Mason's arguments and quotations from Keith with the assertion that the federal and state governments were "coequal sovereignties," adding: "I cannot conceive that this Constitution, by giving the general government the power of the arming the militia, takes it away from the state governments. The power is concurrent, not exclusive."[49]

Patrick Henry retorted in a single argument asserting both the individual right to have arms and the state power to encourage a militia consisting of the armed populace:

> May we not discipline and arm them, as well as Congress, if the power be concurrent? So that our militia shall have two sets of arms, double sets of regimentals, & c.; and thus, at a very great cost, we shall be doubly armed. *The great object is, that every man be armed.* But can the people afford to pay for double sets of arms, & c.? *Every one who is able may have a gun.* But we have learned, by experience, that, necessary as it is to have arms, and though our Assembly has, by a succession of laws for many years, endeavoured to have the militia completely armed, it is still far from being the case. When this power is given up to Congress without limitation or bounds, how will your militia be armed? You trust to chance; for sure I am that nation which shall trust its liberties in other hands cannot long exist. If gentlemen are serious when they suppose a concurrent power, where can be the impolicy to amend it? Or, in other words, to say that Congress shall not arm or discipline them, till the states shall have refused or neglected to do it?[50]

Henry thus recognized that the objective "that every man be armed" presupposed the right to have arms, in that "every one who is able may have a gun." However, state legislation had not achieved a "militia completely armed," a situation which would be exacerbated if the federal government required different arms, given that the people could not afford two sets.

Again the federalists countered, with George Nicholas articulating more precisely why the militia power was not exclusive:

> But it is said, the militia are to be disarmed. Will they be worse armed than they are now? Still, as my honourable friend said, the states would have power to arm them. The power of arming them is concurrent between the general and state governments; for the power of arming them rested in the state governments before; and although the power be given to the general government, yet it is not given exclusively. . . . It is, therefore, not an absurdity to say, that Virginia may arm the militia, should Congress neglect to arm them after Congress had armed them, when it would be unnecessary . . . .[51]

In debate on June 16, William Grayson reasserted the exclusive-power interpretation, warning that the militia "might be armed in one part of the Union, and totally neglected in another." He pointed out that England had an excellent militia law for itself, entailing "thirty thousand select militia," but neglected the militia of Scotland and Ireland.[52]

John Marshall explained why powers not exclusively delegated are retained, as was illustrated by the provision that "no state shall engage in war" unless invaded.[53] He worried that some states would regulate their militias but others would neglect them, averring: "If Congress neglect our militia we can arm them ourselves. Cannot Virginia import arms? Cannot she put them into hands of her militia-men?" Nothing in the Constitution divested the states of their preexisting militia power.[54]

George Mason returned to the issue of "Who are the militia? They consist of now of the whole people, except a few public officers. . . . If that paper on the table gets no alteration, the militia of the future day may not consist of all classes, high and low, and rich and poor . . . ."[55] The republican militia was the armed populace at large, not a select militia or standing army.

In response, George Nicholas detected a contradiction in the antifederalists, in that Grayson objected because there would be no select militia, while Mason objected that there would be. Grayson had referred to Britain's select militia, which was "more thoroughly exercised than the militia at large," but Mason worried about "the exemption of the highest classes of the people from militia services . . . ."[56] Grayson agreed that "a well-regulated militia ought to be the defence of this country."[57]

In the last word on the state militia power, Edmund Pendleton noted that "though Congress *may* provide for arming them, . . . there is nothing to preclude [the states] from arming and disciplining them, should Congress neglect to do it."[58] Regarding Congress' power to protect the states from domestic violence,[59] he added: "The state is in full possession of the power of using its own militia to protect itself against domestic violence; and the power in the general government cannot be exercised, or interposed, without the application of the state itself."[60]

On June 23, the clause-by-clause debates over the Constitution ended. In a letter to his brother Ambrose, James Madison anticipated that advocacy of previous amendments would be countered by "a conciliatory declaration of certain fundamental principles in favour of liberty, in a form not affecting the validity & plenitude of the ratification . . . . The final question is likely to be decided by a very small majority."[61]

On the 24th, George Wythe proposed that the Committee of the Whole
ratify the Constitution and then recommend any amendments thought necessary to the Congress when it assembled.[62] The resolution of ratification declared
that "the powers granted under the proposed Constitution are the gift of the
people, and every power not granted thereby remains with them, and at their
will,—no right, therefore, of any denomination, can be cancelled, abridged,
restrained, or modified" by any branch of government, except where the power
is granted. It added that "among other essential rights, liberty of conscience
and of the press" could not be abridged.[63]

Patrick Henry objected that it was premature to consider ratification without amendments.[64] "I feel myself distressed, because the necessity of securing
our *personal rights* seems not to have pervaded the minds of men . . . ." Lack
of a prohibition on general warrants meant that "every thing the most sacred
may be searched and ransacked by the strong hand of power." Regarding
standing armies, "In our bill of rights of Virginia, they are said to be dangerous to liberty, and it tells you that the proper defence of a free state consists in
militia . . . ." Referring to Wythe's mention only of conscience, the press, and
"other" essential rights, Henry asked whether "these three rights, and these
only, are valuable?"[65]

Henry implored that the convention "stipulate that there are rights which
no man under heaven can take from you" and proposed a resolution to refer
a declaration of rights and certain amendments to the other states prior to
ratification. The recommendations were nearly the same as the convention
would adopt.[66]

Henry characterized the declaration of rights as containing "those fundamental unalienable privileges, which I conceive to be essential to liberty and
happiness."[67] He reiterated about the Wythe resolution's mention of two specific rights and the undefined "other essential rights—What are they?—The
world will say, that you intended to give them up."[68]

Governor Randolph opposed Henry's proposed declaration on the basis
that "the rights intended to be thereby secured were either provided for in the
Constitution itself, or could not be infringed by the general government, as
being unwarranted by any of the powers which were delegated therein . . . ."[69]
It is a pity that the stenographer did not record Randolph's specific remarks
about the declaration, particularly the proposal "That the people have a right
to keep and bear arms . . . ."[70]

Randolph's comments about the amendments to the federal-state balance in the structure of government, however, were recorded. One provision guaranteed that each state had power to provide for organizing, arming, and disciplining its own militia if Congress neglected to do so.[71] Randolph found it unnecessary, as "the same powers rest in the states by the Constitution."[72]

John Dawson insisted on amendments before ratification, including a declaration protecting freedom of the press and other "liberties of the people."[73]

James Madison saw only chaos brewing if each state proposed amendments before ratification. Those supporting amendments "have brought no less than forty amendments, a bill of rights which contains twenty amendments, and twenty other alterations, some of which are improper and inadmissible. Will not every state think herself equally entitled to propose as many amendments?"[74] He then fell back on the dogma that an enumeration of rights would imply that omitted rights were given up.[75]

Patrick Henry shot back, "I will not insist on any [amendment] that does not stand on the broad basis of human rights. He says there are forty. I say there is but one half the number, for the bill of rights is but one amendment." The legendary orator launched a series of dramatic remarks:

> I see the awful immensity of the dangers with which it is pregnant. I see it. I feel it. I see beings of a higher order anxious concerning our decision. . . . All nations are interested in the determination. We have it in our power to secure the happiness of one half of the human race. Its adoption may involve the misery of the other hemisphere.

Underscoring Henry's dramatization, the stenographer wrote: "Here a violent storm arose, which put the house in such disorder, that Mr. Henry was obliged to conclude."[76]

Madison closed the day's debate by insisting that a declaration of rights was unnecessary in that "the general government had no power but what was given it," and dangerous, "because an enumeration which is not complete is not safe." But he softened the argument by declaring that he would not oppose amendments that were "without danger."[77]

The next day, June 25, George Nicholas opened the proceedings by declaring that the friends of the Constitution wished for no further debate—the Constitution should be ratified and the convention should recommend amendments to be taken up later according to the procedures in the Constitution. He then moved that the question be taken on the Wythe resolution. John Tyler moved that the amendments and bill of rights proposed by Patrick Henry also be considered.[78]

Benjamin Harrison urged amendments previous to ratification. While some states had ratified unconditionally,

> New Hampshire does not approve of the Constitution as it stands. . . . In Massachusetts, we are told that there was a decided majority in their Convention who opposed the Constitution as it stood, and were in favour of previous amendments, but were afterwards, by the address and artifice of the federalists, prevailed upon to ratify it. . . . New York, we have every reason to believe, will reject the Constitution, unless amendments be obtained. . . . Virginia is divided . . . . North Carolina is decidedly against it.[79]

James Madison reiterated his personal commitment to work for amendments after ratification and his prediction that they would be adopted. Delaying ratification would also delay the amendatory process.[80] James Monroe rejoined that amendments would never be adopted after ratification: "An alteration will be a diminution of their power, and there will be great exertions made to prevent it. I have no dread that they will immediately infringe the dearest rights of the people, but that the operation of the government will be oppressive in process of time."[81] More speeches followed on the dreadful consequences of either previous or subsequent amendments.

One of the final speeches, and the final word on the right to have arms, was by Zachariah Johnson, who observed that the new Constitution could never result in religious persecution or other oppression. He added: "The people are not to be disarmed of their weapons. They are left in full possession of them."[82] He not only found amendments prior to ratification to be improper, but objected that the proposed bill of rights deleted key portions of the Virginia declaration of rights—the admonition of "frequent recurrence to fundamental principles" and the affirmation that "all men are by nature equally free and independent."[83]

Patrick Henry made a final plea for his proposals. He noted that the federalists would not admit the necessity of certain structural amendments, including a prohibition on direct taxation and the militia article, on which he noted: "With respect to your militia, we only request that, if Congress should refuse to find arms for them, this country may lay out their own money to purchase them." He noted the inconsistency of promising subsequent amendments and objecting to the substance of proposed amendments.[84]

The resolution of the Committee of the Whole originally reported by Wythe was at this point taken up.[85] A substitute was then proposed that, prior to ratification, there should be referred to the other states a declaration of rights asserting "the great principles of civil and religious liberty, and the unalienable rights of the people," together with amendments to objectionable portions of the Constitution.[86]

The substitute was defeated by a vote of 88 to 80. Then the convention voted 89 to 79 to ratify the Constitution.[87] The resolution declared that "the powers granted under the Constitution, being derived from the people of the United States, [may] be resumed by them whensoever the same shall be perverted to their injury or oppression"; "that every power, not granted thereby, remains with them"; and that "no right, of any denomination, can be cancelled, abridged, restrained, or modified," by the federal government except where a power is given to do so. Finally, "among other essential rights, the liberty of conscience and of the press" could not be abridged.[88]

A committee was appointed to prepare and report amendments deemed necessary. It included both federalist and antifederalist luminaries—Wythe, Henry, Randolph, Mason, Nicholas, Grayson, Madison, John Marshall, Monroe, and others.[89]

On June 27, George Wythe reported that the committee recommended certain amendments to be taken up by the new Congress at its opening session. It first proposed a bill of rights "asserting, and securing from encroachment, the essential and unalienable rights of the people," including a number of declaratory clauses gleaned from the Virginia Declaration of Rights. The first section declared "certain natural rights, . . . among which are the enjoyment of life and liberty, with the means of acquiring, possessing, and protecting property, and pursuing and obtaining happiness and safety." The next two proclaimed that "all power is naturally invested in, and consequently derived from, the people," and that "the doctrine of non-resistance against arbitrary power and oppression is absurd, slavish, and destructive to the good and happiness of mankind."[90]

After provisions on the political rights of citizens and procedural rights of the accused, the declaration included three successive sections all beginning with the clause "that the people have a right":

15th. That the people have a right peaceably to assemble together to consult for the common good, or to instruct their representatives; and that every freeman has a right to petition or apply to the legislature for redress of grievances.

16th. That the people have a right to freedom of speech, and of writing and publishing their sentiments; that the freedom of the press is one of the greatest bulwarks of liberty, and ought not to be violated.

17th. That the people have a right to keep and bear arms; that a well regulated militia, composed of the body of the people, trained to arms, is the proper, natural, and safe defence of a free state; that standing armies, in time of peace, are dangerous to liberty, and therefore ought to be avoided, as far as the circumstances and protection of the community will admit; and that, in all cases, the military should be under strict subordination to, and governed by, the civil power.[91]

While rooted in the Virginia Declaration of Rights, each of the above "the people have a right" clauses was new. The Virginia Declaration did not mention the right to assemble and to petition at all; it protected a free press but neglected free speech; and it included the above militia language but not the right to keep and bear arms. Also new was the allowance that standing armies should be avoided only "as far as" possible.

The author apparent was George Mason, who simply added these new clauses to the Declaration's language he had drafted in 1776.[92] As noted, Mason, Henry, and Grayson had sent copies of a declaration with essentially the same language to New York antifederalists at the beginning of the Virginia convention.[93]

There then followed three successive sections regarding matters military or religious or both—a prohibition on quartering soldiers in houses without consent; a provision that "any person religiously scrupulous of bearing arms ought to be exempted, upon payment of an equivalent to employ another to bear arms in his stead"; and a declaration that religion is a matter for reason and not force, and therefore all men have a right to the "free exercise of religion," and that no religious sect "ought to be favoured or established, by law, in preference to others."[94]

The genesis of what became the First, Second, and Third Amendments is readily apparent in the above provisions.

Following the bill of rights, the committee recommended an entirely different set of articles under the title "Amendments to the Constitution." These structural changes clarified or modified the federal-state balance. The first section would mirror what became the Tenth Amendment: "That each state in the Union shall respectively retain every power, jurisdiction, and right, which is not by this Constitution delegated to the Congress of the United States, or to the departments of the federal government."[95] That did not specify what those powers were, but succeeding provisions did.

The structural amendments included three sections regarding military matters. No standing army could be kept up in time of peace without consent of two-thirds of the Congress. No soldier could be enlisted for more than four years except during war. Finally, the militia was addressed as follows:

> 11th. That each state respectively shall have the power to provide for organis-
> ing, arming, and disciplining its own militia, whensoever Congress shall omit
> or neglect to provide for the same. That the militia shall not be subject to mar-
> tial law, except when in actual service, in time of war, invasion, or rebellion;
> and when not in the actual service of the United States, shall be subject only to
> such fines, penalties, and punishments, as shall be directed or inflicted by the
> laws of its own state.[96]

This clarification of the state power over the militia would be considered and rejected by the first federal Congress.[97] However, some of the second sentence would find its way into the Fifth Amendment, which requires indictment by grand jury for serious crimes except for army and militia personnel in actual service in war.

The above language reserving state militia powers had not been included in the amendments the Virginia antifederalists sent to their New York counterparts on June 9.[98] The militia proposal, along with the standing army provision, was included in a later draft entitled "Amendments Proposed to the New Constitution of Government in Addition to the Declaration of Rights." Moreover, William Grayson drafted amendments that were never introduced to the convention and that included the proposal that "The several States shall not be restrained from providing Arms for their own Militia."[99]

The fundamental difference between the Bill of Rights as a declaration of individual liberties and the structural amendments as a division of federal-state powers could not have been clearer. The Bill of Rights declared "that the people have a right"—"peaceably to assemble," "to freedom of speech, and of writing and publishing their sentiments," and "to keep and bear arms." Under the structural amendments, each state shall "retain every power" not delegated to Congress and specifically "the power to provide for organising, arming, and disciplining its own militia," if Congress neglected to do so.

The resolution of adoption of the above enjoined Virginia's representatives in Congress to secure ratification of the Bill of Rights and amendments. A federalist motion to strike a provision on direct taxation failed. The convention then voted in favor of the proposals.[100]

Virginia had taken the decisive step—this large and influential state ratified the Constitution but was committed to use her great influence to demand a bill of rights. The remaining states, both large (New York and North Carolina) and small (Rhode Island and the future state of Vermont), would ratify the Constitution and follow Virginia in insisting that individual rights be declared.

## CHAPTER II

# "A Majority That Is Irresistible"

T HE GROUNDSWELL for a bill of rights became over-
whelming with Virginia's ratification of the Constitution.
The remainder of the states would hammer nails in the coffin. New York,
another influential and populous state, would ratify and demand a declaration of rights a month after Virginia. North Carolina delayed ratification of
the Constitution until after the first federal Congress met and proposed the
Bill of Rights. Rhode Island and Vermont would not ratify the Constitution
until it appeared that the ratification of the Bill of Rights by the states was a
foregone conclusion.

## NEW YORK

The New York convention was preceded by serious antifederalist agitation.
Significantly, the *New York Journal* published calls for what became both
clauses of the Second Amendment: the militia clause and the right-to-have-
arms clause.

As for the militia clause, "Brutus" (thought by some scholars to be Robert
Yates) wrote in the *Journal* on November 1, 1787: "In the bills of rights of the

states it is declared, that a well regulated militia is the proper and natural defence of a free government . . . ." Standing armies were also denounced. "The same security is as necessary in this constitution, and much more so . . . ."[1]

Regarding the arms guarantee, "Common Sense" noted in the April 21, 1788, *Journal* "that the chief power will be in the Congress, and that what is to be left of our government, will be a mere shadow is plain, because a citizen may be deprived of the privilege of keeping arms for his own defence, he may have his property taken without a trial by jury . . . . These things are entirely contrary to our constitution . . . ."[2] Appearing originally in a North Carolina newspaper, this article may have been distributed by antifederalists elsewhere for reprinting.

The New York federalists were led by John Jay and Alexander Hamilton, who had argued in *The Federalist* No. 29 that military establishments would not be a danger where "a large body of citizens, little if at all inferior to them in discipline and the use of arms," were ready to defend their rights.[3] The antifederalists included John DeWitt, who had warned that Congress "at their pleasure may arm or disarm all or any part of the freeman of the United States."[4]

George Mason and his Virginia colleagues sent a draft declaration of rights and amendments to the New York antifederalists. Newspaper editor Eleazer Oswald carried and delivered this correspondence to John Lamb, chairman of the Federal Republican Committee. New York Governor George Clinton, who would become president of the New York convention, gave copies to a Special Committee of Correspondence.[5]

Robert Yates, chairman of the Special Committee, wrote to Mason on June 21, thanking him for the proposed amendments and enclosing a draft agreed to by many of the New York convention delegates.[6] While this draft has not been located, the New York convention would adopt much of the Virginia language but added its own distinct proposals as well.

The New York ratification convention met on June 17 through July 26, 1788. The recorded debates were not kept well as were those of Virginia, and in the final days—when a bill of rights was being debated—virtually nothing other than bare minutes were taken down. In the recorded debates, the federalists gave long speeches on the urgency of saving the states from foreign powers and of promoting commerce. Antifederalists spoke at length on the basis of representation in Congress and in favor of an amendment against direct taxation.

In the opening debate in the convention, Chancellor Robert R. Livingston gave a glowing speech with varied arguments for the Constitution, just brushing on "the necessity of adding to the powers of Congress, that of regulating the militia . . . ."[7]

Leading the antifederalists was John Lansing, Jr., who had been a delegate at the federal convention but who, with his colleague Robert Yates, opposed a strong national government and withdrew from the convention more than two months before it finished.[8] Delivering the second speech of the New York convention, Lansing declared "the almost unanimous opinion" of his constituents in support of amendments, which "will have a tendency to lessen the danger of invasion of civil liberty by the general government."[9]

Among others, John Williams foresaw that the new system would lead to the destruction of the states:

> And what restraint have they against tyranny in their head? Do they rely on any thing but arms, the ultima ratio? . . . Are they [the states] not deprived of the command of the purse and the sword of their citizens? Is not the power, both over taxation and the militia, wrested from their hands by this Constitution, and bestowed upon the general government?[10]

Chancellor Robert R. Livingston rejoined: "What, then, is taken away? Have not the states the right of raising money, and regulating the militia?"[11] He and his federalist colleagues depicted the antifederalists as alarmists.

On July 1, Thomas Tredwell delivered the last lengthy speech of the convention that was recorded, and it was the foremost demand for a bill of rights. Tredwell averred: "The first and grand leading, or rather misleading, principle in this debate, and on which the advocates for this system of unrestricted powers must chiefly depend for its support, is that, in forming a constitution, whatever powers are not expressly granted or given the government, are reserved to the people . . . ."[12]

This was demonstrated by the enumeration of certain rights in the Constitution—restrictions on suspension of the writ of habeas corpus and on passage of any bill of attainder or title of nobility. "Are there any clauses in the Constitution extending the powers of the general government to these objects?" In response to the suggestion that these were inserted for greater caution, Tredwell argued, why had not "a greater caution" been used to secure other rights, such as a free press, trial by jury, and religious liberties? It was to be wished "that these and other invaluable rights of freemen had been as cautiously secured as some of the paltry local interests of some of the individual states."[13] The latter included items such as the importation of slaves until 1808, which was "repugnant to every principle of humanity."[14] Tredwell implored:

> In this Constitution, sir, we have departed widely from the principles and po-litical faith of '76, when the spirit of liberty ran high, and danger put a curb on ambition. Here we find no security for the rights of individuals, no security for the existence of our state governments; here is no bill of rights, no proper re-striction of power; our lives, our property, and our consciences, are left wholly at the mercy of the legislature . . . .[15]

Tredwell also spoke on the structure of the government, asking at one point: "What sovereignty, what power is left to it, when the control of every source of revenue, and the total command of the militia, are given to the gen-eral government? That power which can command both the property and the persons of the community, is the sovereign, and the sole sovereign."[16]

Tredwell minced no words: "we may now give away, by a vote, what it may cost the dying groans of thousands to recover; that we may now sur-render, with a little ink, what it may cost seas of blood to regain; the dag-ger of Ambition is now pointed at the fair bosom of Liberty, and, to deepen and complete the tragedy, we, her sons, are called upon to give the fatal thrust."[17] As he had noted earlier, in opposition to the tyranny of Philip in the Netherlands, "the people took up arms in their own defence," defeat-ing "all the armies of that haughty monarch." The same might be necessary in America, as historically a great cause of human misery was the abuse of power by government.[18]

Following this speech, motions were made to restrict the powers of Con-gress. John Lansing moved to require a two-thirds vote of Congress to raise a standing army in time of peace. He also moved to amend Congress' power over the militia as follows:

> *Provided,* That the militia of any state shall not be marched out of such state without the consent of the executive thereof, nor be continued in service out of the state, without the consent of the legislature thereof, for a longer term than six weeks; and provided, that the power to organise, arm, and discipline the

militia, shall not be construed to extend further than to prescribe the mode of arming and disciplining the same.[19]

Melancton Smith, another prominent antifederalist, then moved to amend the clause granting Congress power to make all laws necessary and proper to implement its other powers with the following: "*Provided*, That no power shall be exercised by Congress, but such as is expressly given by this Constitution; and all others, not expressly given, shall be reserved to the respective states, to be by them exercised."[20] Thus, state powers—including the power to maintain the militia—were considered as amendments to the provisions regarding congressional powers.

Other amendments were offered as the convention hurried to complete debate on the remainder of the Constitution. Then, on July 7, John Lansing "read, and presented to the committee, a *bill of rights* to be prefixed to the Constitution."[21] Unfortunately, by now the convention reporter was no longer recording any speeches at all but was taking down only the barest of minutes, so no debate on the proposed bill of rights was recorded. The minutes reflect that on July 10, Lansing "submitted a plan of amendments, on a new arrangement, and with material alterations. They are divided into three—1st, explanatory; 2d, conditional; 3d, recommendatory."[22]

Debate continued for several more days—again, none of it recorded—until on July 19, Lansing "moved to postpone the several propositions before the house, in order to take into consideration a draft of a conditional ratification, with a *bill of rights* prefixed, and amendments subjoined. Debates arose on the motion, and it was carried. The committee then proceeded to consider separately the amendments proposed in this plan of ratification."[23] Finally, on July 26, the convention ratified the Constitution as well as a recommendation to the other states that amendments, including a bill of rights, promptly be considered.[24]

The form of ratification began with a declaration of a number of propositions that constituted a bill of rights. It clearly differentiated the people from the government, whether federal or state:

> That all power is originally vested in, and consequently derived from, the people, and that government is instituted by them for their common interest, protection, and security.

That the enjoyment of life, liberty, and the pursuit of happiness, are essential rights, which every government ought to respect and preserve.

That the powers of government may be reassumed by the people whensoever it shall become necessary to their happiness; that every power, jurisdiction, and right, which is not by the said Constitution clearly delegated to the Congress of the United States, or the departments of the government thereof, remains to the people of the several states, or to their respective state governments, to whom they may have granted the same . . . .[25]

Having distinguished above between "the people of the several states" and "their respective state governments," the declaration next set forth the following, which refer to rights of "the people":

That the people have an equal, natural, and unalienable right freely and peaceably to exercise their religion, according to the dictates of conscience; and that no religious sect or society ought to be favored or established by law in preference to others.

That the people have a right to keep and bear arms; that a well regulated militia, including the body of the people *capable of bearing arms*, is the proper, natural, and safe defence of a free state.[26]

Thus, "the people" had a right to religious freedom and to have arms. Regarding the latter, New York followed Virginia in beginning with the declaration "that the people have a right to keep and bear arms," and then including a separate clause declaring the militia to be necessary for a free state. While Virginia referred to the militia as "composed of the body of the people, trained to arms,"[27] New York characterized the militia as "including the body of the people *capable of bearing arms*."[28]

Next were three military-related provisions that implicated individual rights. The first declared: "That the militia should not be subject to marital law, except in time of war, rebellion or insurrection." The other two proclaimed that standing armies are dangerous to liberty, and that soldiers should not be quartered in houses.[29]

Several procedural guarantees for persons accused of crime followed, including that of indictment by grand jury, "except in the government of the land and naval forces, and of the militia when in actual service." The following provision included a declaration about the political benefit of a right, similar to the above militia clause following the right-to-bear-arms clause: "That the trial by jury . . . is one of the greatest securities to the rights of a free people, and ought to remain inviolate."[30]

Rights of "the people" were no different than those of the "person," and in the following both terms are used separately without any difference in meaning: "That the people have a right peaceably to assemble together to consult for their common good, or to instruct their representatives, and that every person has a right to petition or apply to the legislature for redress of grievances."[31]

The New York convention ratified the Constitution "declaring that the rights aforesaid cannot be abridged or violated" and with confidence that the proposed amendments would be promptly considered.[32]

The convention then added more conditions to the ratification, including that until a convention was convened for proposing amendments to the Constitution, "the militia of this State will not be continued in service out of this State for a longer term than six weeks, without the consent of the Legislature thereof."[33]

The convention adopted a separate resolution urging their representatives in Congress to approve a list of amendments concerning the structure of the federal government and the federal-state relation.[34] No standing army could be raised, and war could not be declared, without the consent of two-thirds of Congress.[35] While not including the same proposal as Virginia for a state militia power, the convention proposed its above ban on compulsion of militia service outside a state for over six weeks without consent of the state legislature.[36]

The tables were now turned. In the first state ratifications, the federalists had rammed through the Constitution without allowing so much as a suggestion that a bill of rights should be adopted. This was not without strong opposition in the populous states of Pennsylvania and Massachusetts, where significant bills of rights were proposed. New Hampshire bucked the trend with its recommendatory amendments, and by now the influential states of Virginia and New York based their ratifications on the propositions that individuals have basic rights. The individual right to keep and bear arms figured prominently in the demands for a bill of rights in each of these five states.[37]

## NORTH CAROLINA

Well before that state's convention met, one "Common Sense" warned in "To the People of North Carolina," published in the *Wilmington Centinel*, that under the proposed Constitution, "a citizen may be deprived of the privilege of keeping arms for his own defence, he may have his property taken without a trial by jury, he may be ordered to march with the rest of the militia to New Hampshire, or any where else . . . . These things are entirely contrary to our constitution . . . ."[38] The guarantee of the North Carolina Constitution that "the People have a right to bear Arms for the Defence of the State"[39] was understood as protecting the right of "a citizen"—a person, not a collective—"of keeping arms for *his own* defence."

A chief objection to the Constitution in North Carolina was exemplified in a federalist's account of a sermon that mentioned the proposed federal capital: "'This, my friends,' said the preacher, 'will be walled in or fortified. Here an army of 50,000, or perhaps 100,000 will be finally embodied, and will sally forth and enslave the people, who will be gradually disarmed.' This absurd assumption set our blood in fermentation strongly excited already in party feeling."[40]

While the federalists thought it ludicrous that the federal government would disarm the people, the antifederalists were the majority in the North Carolina ratification convention, and they were leaving nothing to chance. The convention met between July 21 and August 4, 1788, and refused to ratify the Constitution until after Congress proposed the Bill of Rights. Willie Jones, the draftsman of North Carolina's Declaration of Rights of 1776, would lead the antifederalist majority in the convention.[41]

In the opening days, most of the debate centered on the individual clauses of the proposed Constitution in which hot topics like direct taxes received great attention. To be sure, David Caldwell opined that "Unalienable rights ought not to be given up, if not necessary."[42] And Governor Samuel Johnston noted, "The British Parliament can do every thing they please. Their bill of rights is only an act of Parliament, which may be, at any time, altered or modified, without a violation of the constitution."[43]

The usual controversy over the militia arose. Mr. Maclaine asked, "Will the militia be called out by the general government to enslave the people—to enslave their friends, their families, themselves? The idea of the militia being made use of, as an instrument to destroy our liberties, is almost too absurd to merit a refutation."[44]

Midway through the convention, a great debate ensued over a bill of rights— not about what specific guarantees it should contain, but about whether it was necessary and the general nature of the guarantees it would contain. Samuel Spencer started the debate as follows:

> There is no declaration of rights, to secure to every member of the society those unalienable rights which ought not to be given up to any government. . . . There ought to be a bill of rights, in order that those in power may not step over the boundary between the powers of government and the rights of the people, which they may do when there is nothing to prevent them. They may do so without a bill of rights; notice will not be readily taken of the encroachments of rulers, and they may go a great length before the people are alarmed.[45]

In short, as Spencer concluded, a bill of rights was necessary "to secure those unalienable rights, which are called by some respectable writers the residuum of human rights, which are never to be given up."[46]

Maclaine replied that "the powers of Congress are expressly defined," which was superior to a bill of rights.[47] Governor Johnston added that "it would have been the highest absurdity to undertake to define what rights the people of the United States were entitled to; for that would be as much as to say they were entitled to nothing else." Eyes would roll today at his further assertion that "the rights of the people . . . cannot be affected by the federal courts."[48]

But it was James Iredell who became the leading federalist advocate. England had no written constitution, and such bills of rights as originated there were wrested from monarchs. Under the proposed federal Constitution, "no power can be exercised but what is expressly given."[49] Iredell's explanation was classic:

> A bill of rights, as I conceive, would not only be incongruous, but dangerous. No man, let his ingenuity be what it will, could enumerate all the individual rights not relinquished by this Constitution. Suppose, therefore, an enumeration of a great many, but an omission of some, and that, long after all traces of our present disputes were at an end, any of the omitted rights should be in-

vaded, and the invasion be complained of; what would be the plausible answer of the government to such a complaint? Would they not naturally say, ". . . So long as the rights enumerated in the bill of rights remain unviolated, you have no reason to complain. This is not one of them."[50]

The following year, Iredell would go on to become a Justice of the U.S. Supreme Court. It is worth noting as an aside that, as a young lawyer in 1771, Iredell wrote the following in a letter to his mother, capturing the sentiments of his generation about a right that went unquestioned:

> Be not afraid of the Pistols you have sent me. They may be necessary Implements of self Defence, tho' I dare say I shall never have Occasion to use them . . . . It is a Satisfaction to have the means of Security at hand if we are in no danger, as I never expect to be. Confide in my prudence and self regard for a proper use of them, and you need have no Apprehension.[51]

Samuel Spencer was not persuaded by Iredell's above assurances in the convention. The applicability of federal law to individuals, and its implementation by federal officers and courts, required a declaration "for securing the rights of individuals. . . . There are certain human rights that ought not to be given up . . . ."[52]

Maclaine replied that "if there be certain rights which never can, nor ought to, be given up, these rights cannot be said to be given away, merely because we have omitted to say that we have not given them up. . . . If we have this inherent, this unalienable, this indefeasible title to those rights, if they are not given up, are they not retained?"[53] All of those "ifs" could not have raised the comfort level of the bill of rights proponents—Maclaine did not even concede that such rights existed.

Iredell was more charitable. He granted the existence of unalienable rights but reiterated that Congress had no authority to legislate in any manner to violate them:

> Those rights which are unalienable are not alienated. They still remain with the great body of the people. . . . But when it is evident that the exercise of any power not given up would be a usurpation, it would be not only useless, but dangerous, to enumerate a number of rights which are not intended to be given up; because it would be implying . . . that every right not included in the exception might be

impaired by the government without usurpation; and it would be impossible to enumerate every one.[54]

Bloodworth was not persuaded. "Without the most express restrictions, Congress may trample on your rights. . . . Rulers are always disposed to abuse them."[55]

Samuel Spencer added that "we could not guard with too much care those essential rights and liberties which ought never to be given up. . . . When there is no rule but a vague doctrine, they might make great strides, and get possession of so much power that a general insurrection of the people would be necessary to bring an alteration about."[56] That would be precluded with a declaration "securing every unalienable right."[57]

By now the ultimate question—whether to adopt the Constitution—loomed. Bloodworth opposed adoption until amendments were adopted.[58] Governor Johnston moved that the amendments be proposed after ratification and that the Constitution be ratified now. William Lenoir contended that the Constitution "endangers our liberties," whereas it should "secure those rights which ought never to be infringed."[59] Lenoir saw grave peril in the powers of Congress:

> We find no provision against infringement on the rights of conscience. . . . They have also an exclusive legislation in their ten miles square, to which may be added their power over the militia, who may be carried thither and kept there for life. . . . They can disarm the militia. If they were armed, they would be a resource against great oppressions. . . . If the laws of the Union were oppressive, they could not carry them into effect, if the people were possessed of proper means of defence.[60]

Richard D. Spaight retorted that ten states had already ratified, and only by ratifying now could North Carolina have had any influence on what amendments were adopted.[61] As for the "ten miles square" capital, he demanded: "Is there the least colour or pretext for saying that the militia will be carried and kept there for life?" A claim that dissidents would be taken to the capital and tried without a jury was "an astonishing misrepresentation!"[62]

Charles M'Dowall took a more moderate course: "I am for the strongest federal government. A bill of rights ought to have been inserted, to ascertain our most valuable and unalienable rights."[63] Willie Jones announced his intent to introduce amendments to be adopted prior to ratification.[64]

James Iredell took the floor, refuting claims that the new government could criminalize free speech on the basis that the Constitution delegated power to Congress "to define and punish piracies and felonies committed on the high seas, and offences against the law of nations. They have no power to define any other crime whatever."[65] While Iredell was a poor prophet regarding the powers that Congress would later claim, this was the federalist position—Congress could not violate rights such as a free press and keeping arms because it had no power to pass criminal laws over those (or virtually any other) subject.

Yet Iredell was conciliatory as to the eventual adoption of a bill of rights: "The first session of Congress will probably be the most important of any for many years. . . . [N]or do I doubt that every amendment, not of a local nature, nor injuring essentially the material power of the Constitution, but principally calculated to guard against misconstruction the real liberties of the people, will be readily obtained."[66]

The next day, the motion of Willie Jones was taken up. "I am very sensible that there is a great majority against the Constitution," he averred.[67] They had every right to refuse to ratify the Constitution and would thereby achieve their goal of amendments:

> I have, in my proposition, adopted, word for word, the Virginia amendments, with one or two additional ones. . . . There is no doubt we shall obtain our amendments, and come into the Union when we please. Massachusetts, New Hampshire, and other states, have proposed amendments. New York will do also, if she ratifies.[68]

Iredell urged that Virginia's example of ratification previous to amendments be followed and predicted the adoption of worthy amendments "such as tend to secure more effectually the liberties of the people against an abuse of the powers granted."[69]

William R. Davie "hoped they would not take up the whole collectively, but that the proposed amendments would be considered one by one." However, the great majority voted to adopt the resolution as it stood.[70]

On the next day, August 1, 1788, James Iredell conceded that "all debate is now at an end. It is useless to contend any longer against a majority that is irresistible."[71] The resolution then adopted by the whole house required that, prior to North Carolina's ratification, there be laid before Congress or a convention of states a declaration of rights "securing from encroachment the great principles of civil and religious liberty, and the unalienable rights of the people," together with amendments to "the most ambiguous and exceptionable parts" of the Constitution.[72]

The resolution included a "Declaration of Rights" and a separate document entitled "Amendments to the Constitution" with structural changes. The Declaration was copied virtually word-for-word from Virginia's recommendations. The first three sections declared the natural rights to life and liberty, including the means of "protecting property" and obtaining "safety"; that "all power" is invested in "the people"; and that "the doctrine of non-resistance against arbitrary power" is absurd.[73]

The Declaration included three successive sections all beginning with the same clause: "That the people have a right peaceably to assemble together . . ." (§ 15); "That the people have a right to freedom of speech" (§ 16); and finally Section 17:

> That the people have a right to keep and bear arms; that a well regulated militia, composed of the body of the people, trained to arms, is the proper, natural, and safe defence of a free state; that standing armies, in time of peace, are dangerous to liberty, and therefore ought to be avoided, as far as the circumstances and protection of the community will admit; and that, in all cases, the military should be under strict subordination to, and governed by, the civil power.[74]

Three more sections followed on military and religious matters: Soldiers may not be quartered in houses; "any person religiously scrupulous of bearing arms" may be exempt; and religion may be freely exercised.[75] The above six provisions would be distilled into what became the First, Second, and Third Amendments to the Constitution.

The separate "amendments" dealt exclusively with the powers of the state and federal governments. Again mirroring the Virginia proposals, it began with a Tenth Amendment-type declaration "that each state in the Union shall respectively retain every power" not delegated to the federal government.[76] The succeeding structural amendments included three concerning military matters: No standing army in peacetime without consent of two-thirds of the Congress; no enlistments for more than four years except during war; and finally:

> That each state respectively shall have the power to provide for organising, arming, and disciplining its own militia, whensoever Congress shall omit or

neglect to provide for the same; that the militia shall not be subject to martial law, except when in actual service in time of war, invasion, or rebellion; and when not in the actual service of the United States, shall be subject only to such fines, penalties, and punishments, as shall be directed or inflicted by the laws of its own state.[77]

The North Carolina convention went beyond that of Virginia and added several more structural amendments. For instance, Congress "shall not introduce foreign troops into the United States" without a two-thirds vote.[78]

James Iredell made one last attempt to turn the tide. He proposed that the Constitution be adopted prior to amendments, but that a few of the structural amendments—not including the declaration of rights—be recommended for adoption at a later date. The amendments he recommended included, among others, the above quasi-Tenth Amendment provision and the proposal that "Each state respectively shall have the power to provide for organising, arming, and disciplining, its own militia, whensoever Congress shall omit or neglect to provide for the same." The convention rejected Iredell's motion by a vote of 84 to 184.[79]

The next day, August 2, the convention had but formally to adopt the resolution of refusing to ratify the Constitution before amendments were proposed, and the vote was the reverse of the above vote.[80]

The great state conventions of 1788 were finished. James Madison now expressed positive support for a bill of rights—a complete break from the previous spring when Hamilton, in *The Federalist* No. 84, characterized a bill of rights as "dangerous."[81] Madison sent a pamphlet with proposed amendments to Thomas Jefferson on October 17, explaining:

> Not a few, particularly in Virginia have contended for the proposed alterations from the most honourable & patriotic motives; and that among the advocates for the Constitution, there are some who wish for further guards to public liberty & individual rights. As far as these may consist of a constitutional declaration of the most essential rights, it is probable they will be added . . . . My own opinion has always been in favour of a bill of rights; provided it be so framed as not to imply powers not meant to be included in the enumeration.[82]

Madison also wrote to Edmund Pendleton, just three days later, noting the dangers of a new constitutional convention, which antifederalists were advocating. The alternative was that Congress would propose a bill of rights: "In the mean time the other mode of amendments may be employed to quiet the fears of many by supplying those further guards for private rights which can do no harm to the system in the judgments even of its most partial friends . . . ."[83] The references in these letters to "individual rights" and "private rights" were hardly accidental—Madison opposed amendments that would have changed the distribution of federal-state powers.

How Madison came to propose the Bill of Rights in Congress the following year is the subject of the next chapter. By coincidence, the same day Madison would do so—June 10, 1789—William R. Davie wrote him a letter noting: "Our Convention meet again in November, with powers to adopt the Constitution and any Amendments that may be proposed; this renders it extremely important that the Amendments, if any, should be proposed before that time."[84] Madison and his colleagues did just that, and North Carolina adopted the Constitution on November 21, 1789, several weeks after Congress passed the Bill of Rights and proposed it to the states.[85]

"To Keep and Bear Their Private Arms"

## CHAPTER 12

# Mr. Madison's Amendments

## MADISON'S PROPOSED AMENDMENTS

In the first federal elections under the new Constitution, James Madison ran for a seat in the House of Representatives against James Monroe, who supported the antifederalist cause. Departing from previous federalist positions, Madison championed a bill of rights and won the election.[1] In what is thought to be a speech he drafted to deliver to the House had he won the election, Monroe advocated a declaration of rights, stating:

> The following appears to be the most important objects of such an instrument. It should more especially comprise a doctrine in favour of the equality of human rights; of the liberty of conscience in matters of religious faith, of speech and of the press; of the trial by jury of the vicinage in civil and criminal cases; of the benefit of the writ of habeas corpus; of the right to keep and bear arms . . . . If these rights are well defined, and secured against encroachment, it is impossible that government should ever degenerate into tyranny.[2]

As fate would have it, Madison would write a similar speech. The Virginian had a compilation of proposed amendments from around the country, including those from the state conventions.[3] In his notes for a speech introducing what became the Bill of Rights, Madison noted three kinds of objections to the Constitution: "the theory of its structure," the "substance of its powers," and "omission of guards in favor of rights & liberties." The last objection was the "most urged & easiest obviated." He continued: "Read the amendments— They relate 1st to private rights."[4] Madison observed a "fallacy on both sides— espec[ially] as to English Decl[aratio]n. of Rights—1. mere act of parliament. 2. no freedom of press—Conscience . . . attainders—arms to protest[an]ts."[5]

Madison thus saw the rights he would propose, such as freedom of the press and keeping and bearing arms, as not involving the structure or powers of government but as involving private rights. The "fallacy" of the English Declaration was that it was a mere legislative act that Parliament could repeal; by contrast, the American bill of rights would be part of the Constitution and not subject to repeal by Congress. Moreover, the English Declaration either omitted or unreasonably limited fundamental rights. Freedom of the press and religion were not recognized at all, and bills of attainder were not prohibited. The right to keep and bear arms was limited to Protestants, further limited by class, and limited yet more by the legislature: "That the Subjects which are Protestants, may have Arms for their Defence suitable to their Condition, and as are allowed by Law."[6]

On June 8, 1789, in the House of Representatives, Madison proposed his long-awaited bill of rights. Madison's draft contained both philosophical declarations and substantive restrictions. First, the Constitution would contain a new preamble declaring fundamental principles: "all power is originally vested in, and consequently derived from the people"; "government is instituted . . . for the benefit of the people"; and "the people have an indubitable, unalienable, and indefeasible right to reform or change their government . . . ."[7] Having the ultimate power, it went without saying that the people had the right to be armed.

Madison then proposed that the text of the Constitution be amended to limit the powers of Congress. Civil rights could not be abridged on account of religious belief, no national religion could be established, and the rights of conscience could not be "in any manner, or on any pretext infringed."[8] "The people shall not be deprived or abridged of their right to speak," and a free press, "as one of the great bulwarks of liberty," would be inviolable.[9] "The people shall not be restrained from peaceably assembling and consulting for their common good," and petitioning the legislature for redress of grievances.[10] The next guarantee referred to the same entity with rights—"the people"—and interposed a philosophical declaration between two restrictions: "The right of the people to keep and bear arms shall not be infringed; a well armed, and well regulated militia being the best security of a free country: but no person religiously scrupulous of bearing arms shall be compelled to render military service in person."[11]

This provision began with a substantive guarantee in the nature of a command that the right to keep and bear arms shall not be infringed. While the Virginia, New York, and North Carolina proposals stated simply "that people have a right to keep and bear arms," Madison inserted the stronger guard that this right "shall not be infringed."

Madison's proposal next made the philosophical declaration that a well-armed and regulated militia is "the best security of a free country." While the state conventions had used the term "free state," this reverted to the language of *The Federalist* No. 29, in which Hamilton stated that "a well-regulated militia [is] the most natural defence of a free country . . . ."[12] Whichever way worded, this declaration did not limit the substantive right but gave the chief political reason for guaranteeing the right against governmental infringement. Keeping and bearing arms would be protected for all lawful purposes, but mention of self-defense, hunting, shooting at the mark (target shooting), and other purposes had no place in a federal Constitution that delegated no power to regulate these activities. Since Congress could raise and support armies, the superiority of the militia in securing a "free" country must be declared. Moreover, conscientious objectors should not be forced to bear arms in military service.

Other than the above substantive guarantees, most of the remainder of Madison's resolutions related to procedural guarantees are about double jeopardy, search and seizure, and other criminal matters. A longer version of what became the Ninth Amendment concluded the limitations on the power of Congress:

> The exceptions here or elsewhere in the constitution, made in favour of particular rights, shall not be so construed as to diminish the just importance of other rights retained by the people; or as to enlarge the powers delegated by the constitution; but either as actual limitations of such powers, or as inserted merely for greater caution.[13]

Of significance is where in the Constitution Madison would have inserted the substantive rights that became the First, Second, Third, Fourth, Eighth, and Ninth Amendments and portions of the Fifth and Sixth Amendments. These provisions would have been in Article I, Section 9, which exclusively provides for limits on federal power. The guarantees would specifically be placed between clause 3, which prohibits suspension of the privilege of the writ of habeas corpus, and clause 4, which prohibits passage of any bill or attainder or ex post facto law. Both the new and old provisions protected individual rights and did not concern the powers of the states vis-à-vis the federal government.

To the existing prohibitions on state action in Article I, Section 10, Madison would have added that no state shall "violate" the equal rights of conscience or a free press, or deprive the accused of jury trial.[14] To the provisions on the judiciary in Article II, Section 2, would have been added other parts of what became the Fifth and Sixth Amendments, together with the Seventh—in common law suits, "the trial by jury as one of the best securities to the rights of the people, ought to remain inviolate."[15]

Toward the end of the Constitution (in a new Article VII), Madison would have inserted a version of what became the Tenth Amendment, absent recognition of power in "the people": "The powers not delegated by this constitution, nor prohibited by it to the states, are reserved to the states respectively."[16] A provision on the separation of powers would also have been added there.

Throughout, Madison utilized consistent word choice: the federal and state governments have "powers," while only "the people" as individuals have "rights," albeit the people also have "powers."[17] At no point did Madison suggest that any of the Bill of Rights provisions were intended to protect state powers from federal intrusion, that "the people" really meant the state governments, that a state government had "rights" instead of "powers," or that the term "infringe" applied to anything other than governmental violation of individual rights.

In his speech introducing the proposals, Madison acknowledged that a great number of people were dissatisfied with the Constitution and that he and his colleagues should "conform to their wishes, and expressly declare the great rights of mankind secured under this constitution."[18] He noted that "the first of these amendments relates to what may be called a bill of rights."[19] Madison conceptualized the different sources of the rights sought to be guaranteed as follows:

The people of many States have thought it necessary to raise barriers against power in all forms and departments of Government, and I am inclined to believe, if once bills of rights are established in all the States, as well as the federal constitution, we shall find that although some of them are rather unimportant yet, upon the whole, they will have a salutary tendency. . . .

In some instances they assert those rights which are exercised by the people in forming and establishing a plan of Government. In other instances, they specify those rights which are retained when particular powers are given up to be exercised by the Legislature. In other instances, they specify those positive rights, which may seem to result from the nature of the compact. Trial by jury cannot be considered as a natural right, but a right resulting from a social compact which regulates the action of the community, but is as essential to secure the liberty of the people as any one of the pre-existent rights of nature. In other instances, they lay down dogmatic maxims with respect to the construction of the Government; declaring that the legislative, executive, and judicial branches shall be kept separate and distinct. . . .

But whatever may be the form which the several States have adopted in making declarations in favour of particular rights, the great object in view is to limit and qualify the powers of Government, by excepting out of the grant of power those cases in which the Government ought not to act, or to act only in a particular mode.[20]

According to the above analysis, the press, religion, arms, and similar substantive guarantees are "rights which are retained" and among "the pre-existent rights of nature." These are the areas in which the Government "ought not to act." Jury trial and other procedural rights arise from the social compact. They specify that the government must "act only in a particular mode."

The Bill of Rights was conceived to deny exercise of power whether by direct infringement or indirectly through exercise of a delegated power. Those federalists who still opposed a bill of rights pointed only to the lack of an explicit power over any of the proposed guarantees. Congressman James Jackson of Georgia argued: "The gentleman endeavours to secure the liberty of the press; pray how is this in danger? There is no power given Congress to regulate this subject as they can commerce, or peace, or war."[21] Madison had already responded to this argument using search and seizure as an example:

The general government has a right to pass all laws which shall be necessary to collect its revenue; the means for enforcing the collection are within the direction of the legislature: may not general warrants be considered necessary for the purpose, as well as for some purposes which it was supposed at the framing of their constitutions the state governments had in view? If there was reason for restraining the state governments from exercising this power, there is like reason for restraining the federal government.[22]

In other words, Congress has no delegated power to abridge freedom of the press or to infringe on the right to keep and bear arms. But under the "necessary and proper" clause, it might seek to exercise a delegated power—such as collecting revenue—by issuance of general warrants. What became the Fourth Amendment would guard against such unreasonable search and seizure. Similarly, the exercise of the tax or commerce powers could not violate freedom of the press or the right to have arms.

Although he followed the recommendations of several state conventions that a declaration of rights be adopted, Madison did not offer extensive amendments concerning the structure of government. One such amendment was conspicuously absent—the proposal by the Virginia, North Carolina, and Harrisburg conventions, "That each state respectively shall have the power to provide for organising, arming, and disciplining its own militia, whensoever Congress shall omit or neglect to provide for the same."[23]

Some die-hard federalists continued to scorn declarations of rights. Representative Fisher Ames of Massachusetts privately quipped:

> Mr. Madison has introduced his long expected amendments. . . . He has hunted up all the grievances and complaints of newspapers, all the articles of conventions, and the small talk of their debates. It contains a bill of rights, the right of enjoying property, of changing the government at pleasure, freedom of the press, of conscience . . . . Oh! I had forgot, the right of the people to bear arms.[24]

Ames wrote under the above paragraph: "Risum teneatis amici [Could you forbear the laughter of a friend?]." He then continued that the Amendments "may do good towards quieting men who attend to sounds only, and may get the mover some popularity – which he wishes."

Ames wrote to another correspondent: "The rights of conscience, of bearing arms, of changing the government, are declared to be inherent in the people. Freedom of the press, too."[25]

Others were pleased with the proposals for individual rights but were disappointed that structural changes strengthening state powers were not included. Senator William Grayson of Virginia informed Patrick Henry: "Last Monday a string of amendments were presented to the lower House; these altogether respected personal liberty . . . ."[26] Still others agreed that the amendments should focus on individual rights and not alter the Federal-State balance. After reading the amendments that Madison sent him, Joseph Jones wrote to Madison that "they are calculated to secure the personal rights of the people so far as declarations on paper can effect the purpose, leaving unimpaired the great Powers of the government . . . ."[27]

Ten days after Madison proposed his amendments to the House, Tench Coxe published "Remarks on the First Part of the Amendments to the Federal Constitution," under the pen name "A Pennsylvanian," in the Philadelphia *Federal Gazette*.[28] Probably the most complete exposition of the Bill of Rights to be published during its ratification period, the "Remarks" included the following: "As civil rulers, not having their duty to the people duly before them, may attempt to tyrannize, and as the military forces which must be occasionally raised to defend our country, might pervert their power to the injury of their fellow-citizens, the people are confirmed by the next article in their right to keep and bear their private arms." In short, the proposal was designed to guarantee the right of the people to have "their private arms" in order to prevent tyranny and to overpower an abusive standing army.

Coxe sent a copy of his article to Madison along with a letter of the same date. "It has appeared to me that a few well tempered observations on these propositions might have a good effect . . . . It may perhaps be of use in the present turn of the public opinions in New York state that they should be republished there."[29] Madison replied on the 24th, acknowledging "your favour of the 18th instant. The printed remarks inclosed in it are already I find in the Gazettes here [New York]."[30] The *New York Packet*, for one, had reprinted it the day before.[31] Madison added that ratification of the amendments "will however be greatly favoured by explanatory strictures of a healing tendency, and is therefore already indebted to the co-operation of your pen."[32]

Coxe's defense of the amendments was also prominently reprinted on the front page of the special July 4, 1789, issue of the Boston *Massachusetts Centinel*.[33] A search of the literature reveals no writer who disputed Coxe's analysis that what became the Second Amendment protected the right of the people to keep and bear "their private arms."

The significance of Coxe's interpretation has been challenged on the grounds that it was not published widely enough, that readers were too indifferent to dispute it, that Madison did not specifically approve Coxe's words, and that Madison's placement of the arms-bearing and militia clauses were reversed in the Amendment's final form.[34] Yet such skepticism fails to address why Coxe, a prominent federalist in his own right, got it wrong as well as why Madison in his laudatory letter failed to correct Coxe. The essay was published in at least three prominent newspapers and apparently other "Gazettes." By contrast, no writing from this epoch has been found which states that what became the Second Amendment did not protect a personal right to keep and bear private arms. And readers did indeed respond when they disagreed with Coxe's analyses, as is illustrated below.

The long-running dispute was over whether a bill of rights was even necessary to protect fundamental rights. On that issue, Coxe wrote about what became the Ninth Amendment in his "Remarks on the Second Part of the Amendments" in the June 30 issue of the *Federal Gazette*:

> It has been argued by many against a bill of rights, that the omission of some in making the detail would one day draw into question those that should not be particularised. It is therefore provided, that no inference of that kind shall be made, so as to diminish, much less to alienate an ancient tho' unnoticed right, nor shall either of the branches of the Federal Government argue from such omission any increase or extension of their powers.[35]

"One of the People" replied to Coxe in "On a Bill of Rights," arguing "the very idea of a bill of rights" to be "a dishonourable one to freemen." "What should we think of a gentleman, who upon hiring a waiting-man, should say to him 'my friend, please take notice, before we come together, that I shall always claim the liberty of eating when and what I please, of fishing and hunting upon my own ground, of keeping as many horses and hounds as I can maintain, and of speaking and writing any sentiments upon all subjects.'" The government had no power to interfere with individual liberties without a specific delegation, just as "a master reserves to himself . . . everything else which he has not committed to the care of those servants."[36]

Samuel Nasson, a delegate to the Massachusetts convention who voted against ratification of the Constitution, explained the common understanding of the arms guarantee in letter dated July 9 to Representative George Thatcher, a federalist from that state:

> I find that Amendments are once again on the Carpet. . . . A Bill of Rights well secured that we the people may know how far we may Proceed in Every Department. Then there will be no Dispute Between the people and rulers in that may be secured the right to keep arms for Common and Extraordinary Occasions such as to secure ourselves against the wild Beast and also to amuse us by fowling and for our Defence against a Common Enemy. You know to learn the Use of arms is all that can Save us from a foreign foe that may attempt to subdue us, for if we keep up the Use of arms and become well acquainted with them, we Shall always be able to look them in the face that arise up against us.[37]

The above is the most extraordinary correspondence from a constituent to a congressman on the meaning of what became the Second Amendment. The right to keep arms exists for "common," that is, ordinary occasions and for "extraordinary" occasions, such as hunting beasts and fowl ("fowling") and protection from a common foe. Only a citizenry familiar with the use of arms could prevent the oppression of a standing army, about which Nasson further remarked:

> Only think how fatal they were to the peace of this Country in 1770, what Confusion they Brought on the Fatal 5 of March [the Boston Massacre]. I think the remembrance of that Night is enough to make us Careful how we Introduce them in a free republican Government—I therefore hope they will be Discouraged, for I think the man that Enters as a Soldier in a time of peace only for a living is only a fit tool to enslave his fellows.[38]

Not all constituent mail favored a bill of rights. A week before Madison had introduced the amendments, federalist and Congregational pastor Jeremy Belknap wrote to Senator Paine Wingate of New Hampshire that Samuel Adams, on taking office as lieutenant governor, expressed his "devout & fervent wish" that "the people may enjoy well grounded confidence that their *personal & domestic* rights are *secure*." This is the same Language or nearly the same which he used in the Convention when he moved for an addition to the proposed Amendments—by inserting a clause to provide for the Liberty of the press—the right to keep arms—Protection from seizure of person & property & the *Rights of Conscience*. By which motion he gave an alarm to both sides of the house & had nearly overset the whole business which the Friends of the Constitution had been labouring for several Weeks to obtain. Should a Man tell me that he devoutly wished I might not break into his house & rob his desk—I think I should have a right to suspect that he viewed me in no better light than a Burglar. So if a Man publickly expresses a *devout* wish that the new Government may not rob him of his personal & domestic rights—I think it not uncharitable to conclude that he has a jealousy of its intentions.[39]

Still fuming at Adams' effort to have the Massachusetts convention in 1788 recommend a bill of rights,[40] the pastor clearly did not support the impending federal bill of rights. Yet he correctly characterized bill-of-rights supporters who wished for recognition of the "personal" rights to keep arms, a free press, and against unreasonable searches—they indeed feared the intentions of a government with no restraints.

Writing to Madison from Paris, Thomas Jefferson offered "a word on the declaration of rights you have been so good as to send me. I like it as far as it goes; but I should have been for going further." He suggested a stronger version of "the right to speak to write or *otherwise* to publish any thing but false facts," and made recommendations concerning the rights of the accused and against standing armies.[41] Yet neither here nor in any other writing did Jefferson express any dissatisfaction with the language of what became the Second Amendment. Given his 1776 proposal for Virginia that "no freeman shall ever be debarred the use of arms"[42] and his lifelong enthusiasm for firearm ownership, Jefferson must have perceived that these values were expressed in the guarantee that "the right of the people to keep and bear arms, shall not be infringed."

### ACTION BY THE HOUSE SELECT COMMITTEE

On July 21, 1789, the House appointed a select committee to consider Madison's amendments together with those proposed by various states. The committee included John Vining of Delaware as chairman, Madison, Roger Sherman of

Connecticut, and a member from each of the other states.[43] Sherman formulated his own draft of proposed amendments to the Constitution. Seven of the ten amendments in the Sherman draft declared rights of the people, while three concerned the structure and power of government. Sherman's rights guarantees were far more limited than those of Madison: The draft included no declaration of the rights of the people to keep and bear arms, against unreasonable search and seizure, to counsel and to due process of law, and no mandate on separation of church and state (hardly a surprise from a Connecticut representative).[44]

Among the structural amendments Sherman drafted was a proposal, similar to those of the Virginia, North Carolina, and Harrisburg conventions, that the states retained power over the militia:

> The militia shall be under the government of the laws of the respective states, when not in the actual service of the United States but such rules as may be prescribed by Congress for their uniform organisation and discipline shall be observed in officering and training them; but military service shall not be required of persons religiously scrupulous of bearing arms.[45]

The last phrase concerning conscientious objectors resembled the last clause in Madison's proposal guaranteeing the right of the people to keep and bear arms. Its placement in the Sherman draft with a state militia power was perhaps more logical, because it concerned not a "right" to bear arms but an exemption from being "required" to bear arms in military service.

Although there is no record of the select committee's proceedings, Sherman's restrictive notions of freedom raised eyebrows. Senator Richard Henry Lee wrote to Samuel Adams bemoaning the decline of the libertarian values which were universal in 1774, giving as an example:

> You well know our former respected, republican friend, old Mr. R-g-r-Sh-n [Roger Sherman] of Con[necticut] whose person, manners, and every sentiment appeared formerly to be perfectly republican. This very gentleman, our old republican friend opposed a motion for introducing into a bill of rights, an idea that the Military should be subordinate to the Civil power. His reason as stated was "*that it would make the people insolent!*" This was in a committee of the H. of R. for reporting amendments to the Constitution.[46]

The committee did not adopt the amendment, although subordination of the military to the civil power was already implicit in the Constitution. While Sherman's remark was consistent with his restrictive concept of some rights, it would be a mistake to attribute to him a narrow view of the personal right to have arms. In debates over the militia bill the following year, Sherman "conceived it to be the privilege of every citizen, and one of his most essential rights, to bear arms, and to resist every attack upon his liberty or property, by whomsoever made."[47]

The House select committee disregarded Sherman's draft of amendments and instead amended Madison's proposals, reporting them on July 28. Had the House committee intended to confirm a state militia power, Sherman's proposal or the comparable state proposals would have been appropriate. Instead, the committee reported back a list of individual rights, including the following: "A well regulated militia, composed of the body of the people, being the best security of a free state, the right of the people to keep and bear arms shall not be infringed; but no person religiously scrupulous shall be compelled to bear arms."[48]

The select committee did not change Madison's words that "the right of the people to keep and bear arms shall not be infringed," although it moved the philosophical declaration about a well regulated militia to its position before, rather than after, the substantive guarantee. It also inserted, consistent with the phraseology of the Virginia and North Carolina convention demands, the definition of such a militia as "composed of the body of the people."[49]

The committee also changed Madison's formulation that a well regulated militia is "the best security of a free country" to "the best security of a free state." Retaining the adjective *free* differentiated other uses of *state* throughout the constitutional text to denote the state governments. "A free state" and "a free country" meant, in eighteenth-century usage, a free political society.

The select committee version used the word *infringed* in three other places besides the arms guarantee, including two instances in which Madison's original draft had used the terms "violated" or "inviolate."[50] The equal rights of conscience, and the freedom of speech, press, assembly, and petition could not be "infringed,"[51] and no state could "infringe" conscience, speech, press, or jury trial in criminal cases.[52] The term "infringe" was invariably tied to a "right" of the "people," never a state power.

The reporting of the House committee version was perceived as the triumph of the attempt by Samuel Adams to cause the Massachusetts ratifying convention to demand a declaration of rights, including the right of peaceable citizens to keep their own arms. A writer opined in Boston newspapers:

> It may well be remembered, that the following "amendments" to the new constitution of these United States, were introduced to the convention of this commonwealth by its present Lieutenant-Governour, that venerable patriot SAMUEL ADAMS. . . . To the honour of this gentleman's penetration, and of his just way of thinking on this important subject, every one of the intended alterations but one [i.e., proscription of standing armies] have been already reported by the committee of the House of Representatives, and most probably will be adopted by the federal legislature. In justice therefore for that long tried Republican, and his numerous friends, you gentlemen, are requested to republish his intended alterations, in the same paper, that exhibits to the public, the amendments which the committee have adopted, in order that they may be compared together. . . .

> "And that the said constitution be never construed to authorise Congress to infringe the just liberty of the Press, or the rights of Conscience; or to prevent the people of the United States who are peaceable citizens, from keeping their own arms; . . . or to prevent the people from petitioning in a peaceable and orderly manner, the federal Legislature, and for a redress of grievances; or to subject the people to unreasonable searches and seizures of their persons, papers, or possessions."[53]

Adams had continued actively to promote amendments, but no evidence exists that he read the proposed Bill of Rights in any manner inconsistent with his above proposals. "Should a strong *Federalist* as some call themselves see what has now dropt from my Pen," Adams wrote to Richard Henry Lee on August 24, "he would say that I am an Antifed, an *Amendment Monger* . . . ."[54] Adams had written to Lee that spring that governmental powers "ought to be critically defined and well understood" to prevent "Misconstruction of ambiguous Expressions, and by interested Judges too."[55]

The amendments were viewed as protective of individual rights but as not affecting state powers. On August 9, Representative William L. Smith of South Carolina wrote to fellow federalist Edward Rutledge: "The Committee on amendmts. have reported some, which are thought inoffensive to the federalists & may do some good on the other side . . . . There appears to be a disposition in our house to agree to some, which will more effectually secure private rights, without affecting the structure of the Govt."[56]

## DEBATE IN THE HOUSE

On July 28, Chairman Vining presented the select committee report. The proposed amendments as revised by the select committee were debated in the House committee of the whole from August 13–22. Unfortunately, the recorded debate reflected "the unreliable shorthand reports of one Thomas Lloyd, the incompetent, often inebriated stenographer" assigned to record the proceedings.[57]

As had Madison, the select committee recommended that amendments be inserted into the Constitution's existing text. Roger Sherman immediately objected that "we ought not to interweave our propositions into the work itself, because it will be destructive of the whole fabric." Madison wanted them "interwoven into those parts to which they naturally belong" for ease of understanding.[58] Debate on the question consumed the first day. "The amendments reported are a declaration of rights, the people are secure in them whether we declare them or not," quipped Sherman,[59] who did not want to sully the masterpiece with such unimportant details.

The next day began with the consideration of the amendments from top to bottom. The first proposal was to add to the Constitution's preamble the affirmation that "Government being intended for the benefit of the people." Elbridge Gerry moved to amend it to refer to "Government *of right*," explaining:

> This holds up an idea that all the Governments of the earth are intended for the benefit of the people: . . . I do not believe that one out of fifty is intended for any such purpose. . . . If we contemplate the history of nations, ancient or modern, we shall find they originated either in fraud or force, or both. If this is demonstrable, how can we pretend to say that governments are intended for the benefit of those who are oppressed by them.[60]

While his motion failed, this political realism was shared by many. The very purpose of declaring rights was to check oppressive government. In any event, the above amendment to the preamble carried.[61] The convention on the same day approved two structural amendments—one fixing a formula for the number of representatives in the House and another prohibiting any law varying the compensation of members until after new elections to the House.[62]

Debate over the declaration of rights began on August 15. Just as in the Philadelphia convention of 1787,[63] Roger Sherman continued to object to guarantees because Congress had no power to violate rights. He thought the amendment that "no religion shall be established by law" to be "altogether unnecessary, inasmuch as Congress had no authority whatever delegated to them by the constitution to make religious establishments . . . ."[64]

Once again, Madison responded that delegated powers could not be exercised to infringe on rights, but that explicit guarantees would prevent misconstruction:

> Whether the words are necessary or not, he did not mean to say, but they had been required by some of the state conventions, who seemed to entertain an opinion that under the clause of the constitution, which gave power to Congress to make all laws necessary and proper to carry into execution the constitution, and the laws made under it, enabled them to make such laws of such a nature as might infringe the rights of conscience, and establish a national religion; to prevent these effects he presumed the amendment was intended, and he thought it as well expressed as the nature of the language would admit.[65]

Use of the term "national" provoked Elbridge Gerry to regret the misuse of language entailed by the naming of the two major political parties: "those who were called antifederalists at that time [of the state conventions] complained that they had injustice done them by the title, because they were in favour of a federal government, and the others were in favour of a national one; the federalists were for ratifying the constitution as it stood, and the others not until amendments were made. Their names then ought not to have been distinguished by federalists and antifederalists, but rats and antirats."[66]

Even the "rats" must have chuckled as the House members passed the above provision. Next up was the proposition that free speech and press, and "the right of the people peaceably to assemble" and apply for redress of grievances, "shall not be infringed." Egbert Benson, a New York federalist, characterized such rights as follows: "The committee who framed this report, proceeded on the principle that these rights belonged to the people; they conceived them to be inherent, and all that they meant to provide against, was their being infringed by the government."

Theodore Sedgwick of Massachusetts, who had moved to strike out the reference to assembly—"it is a self-evident unalienable right which the people possess"—thought it unnecessary "to enter these trifles in a declaration of rights, under a government where none of them were intended to be infringed."[67] The year before, in the Massachusetts convention, Sedgwick had discounted any federal oppression—how could a standing army "subdue a nation of freemen, who know how to prize liberty; and who have arms in their hands?"[68]

Madison replied that "if we confine ourselves to an enumeration of simple acknowledged principles, the ratification will meet with but little difficulty." His further comment shed light on the meaning of "infringe": "the liberty of the press is expressly declared to be beyond the reach of this government."[69] The amendment passed as proposed.[70]

The House committee of the whole would consider and approve most of the rest of what became the Bill of Rights on August 17. First up was the following: "A well regulated militia, composed of the body of the people, being the best security of a free state, the right of the people to keep and bear arms shall not be infringed; but no person religiously scrupulous shall be compelled to bear arms." The recorded debates do not include any objection to the self-evident phrase "the right of the people to keep and bear arms," and the nature of the phrase "shall not be infringed" was clear enough in this and the previous contexts where those words appeared.

But the clause providing for an exemption from the militia of conscientious objectors raised a firestorm. Elbridge Gerry clarified that the purpose of the amendment was protection from oppressive government, and thus the government should not be in a position to exclude the people from bearing arms:

> This declaration of rights, I take it, is intended to secure the people against the mal-administration of the government; if we could suppose that, in all cases, the rights of the people would be attended to, the occasion for guards of this kind would be removed. Now, I am apprehensive, sir, that this clause would give an opportunity to the people in power to destroy the constitution itself. They can declare who are those religiously scrupulous, and prevent them from bearing arms.
>
> What, sir, is the use of militia? It is to prevent the establishment of a standing army, the bane of liberty. Now, it must be evident, that, under this provision, together with their other powers, Congress could take such measures with respect to a militia, as to make a standing army necessary. When-

ever Government mean to invade the rights and liberties of the people, they always attempt to destroy the militia, in order to raise an army upon their ruins. This was actually done by Great Britain at the commencement of the late revolution. They used every means in their power to prevent the establishment of an effective militia to the eastward. The assembly of Massachusetts, seeing the rapid progress that administration were making to divest them of their inherent privileges, endeavoured to counteract them by the organisation of the militia; but they were always defeated by the influence of the crown.[71]

Gerry argued that the federal government should have no authority to categorize any individual as unqualified under the amendment to bear arms. "Now, if we give a discretionary power to exclude those from militia duty who have religious scruples, we may as well make no provisions on this head." He therefore moved that the "conscientious objector" clause be limited to actual members of religious sects scrupulous of bearing arms.[72] Keeping and bearing arms was a right of "the people," none of whom should be disarmed under any pretense, such as the government's arbitrary determination that they are religiously scrupulous.

In reply, James Jackson of Georgia "did not expect that all the people of the United States would turn Quakers or Moravians; consequently, one part would have to defend the other in case of invasion." The reference to "all the people" indicated again the centrality of the armed populace for defense. Jackson moved to add to the clause "upon paying an equivalent to be established by law."[73]

Roger Sherman opposed the addition, given that "those who are religiously scrupulous of bearing arms, are equally scrupulous of getting substitutes or paying an equivalent . . . ." He noted that "the states respectively will have the government of the militia, unless when called into actual service"—an obvious reference to the Constitution's existing militia provisions in Article I, Section 8, not to the proposed amendment—and that whole sects should not be excluded, in that some Quakers would turn out and defend their country.[74] A motion to strike out the entire clause about the religiously scrupulous then failed.[75]

Gerry proceeded to object to the wording of the first part of the proposed amendment, the militia clause:

A well regulated militia being the best security of a free state, admitted an idea that a standing army was a secondary one. It ought to read, "a well regulated militia, trained to arms;" in which case it would become the duty of the government to provide this security, and furnish a greater certainty of its being done.[76]

Gerry's words exhibit again the sentiment that security rested on the armed populace as a whole, not on specialized bodies of armed men. But his proposal was not seconded. The keeping and bearing of arms by the citizens at large would promote a sufficiently well regulated militia without an explicit duty of the government to train them to arms.

Antifederalists held that mere recognition of an individual right to have arms was necessary but not sufficient to promote a well regulated militia and discourage a standing army. Aedanus Burke of South Carolina sought to add to the personal arms guarantee the following structural amendment:

> A standing army of regular troops in time of peace is dangerous to public liberty, and such shall not be raised or kept up in time of peace but from necessity, and for the security of the people, nor then without the consent of two-thirds of the members present of both houses; and in all cases the military shall be subordinate to the civil authority.[77]

The motion was defeated,[78] reflecting allowance for a limited army approved by a majority of both houses.

The House went on to approve the proposals against quartering of soldiers in homes; prohibitions on double jeopardy, self-incrimination, cruel and unusual punishment; and guarantees of due process and just compensation. It also confirmed the proposals in favor of "the right of the people" to security from unreasonable search and seizure and that the enumeration of rights did not deny rights "retained by the people."[79] For the time being, all of the above substantive rights were to be inserted in Article I, Section 9, squeezed between other restraints on the power of Congress—the restriction on suspension of the writ of habeas corpus and the prohibitions on bills of attainder and ex post facto laws.

To be inserted among the restrictions on state powers was the proposal that "no state shall infringe the equal rights of conscience, nor the freedom of speech, or of the press, nor of the right of trial by jury in criminal cases." Madison "conceived this to be the most valuable amendment on the whole list; if there was any reason to restrain the government of the United States from infringing upon these essential rights, it was equally necessary that they should be secured against the state governments . . . ." Samuel Livermore of New Hampshire moved to transpose the sentence to read that the listed rights "shall not be infringed by any state." The motion carried and the amendment passed.[80]

While the above would not survive, it specified "essential rights" that "shall not be infringed." The linguistic parallel to the Second Amendment is striking, particularly the usage identifying "rights" as things that may not be "infringed." The term "infringe" just was not used in relation to state powers.

To be sure, the proposed prohibition on state action did not include subjects such as petition, arms, and search and seizure, and it certainly did not include an establishment clause—some states at that time had established religions. Did this mean that Madison deemed the rights to conscience, press, and jury trial to be more important, that these rights were more threatened by the states, or that this limited list was the most likely to be adopted? Whatever Madison's thoughts on the subject, the Congress would reject these restrictions on state action.

The House finished what must have been an incredibly long day by approving amendments to the article on the judiciary providing for certain common-law rules in trials and the right to trial by jury in criminal cases.[81]

The following day saw the approval of two more judiciary provisions: indictment by grand jury except in cases, among others, "in the militia when in actual service in time of war, or public danger," and trial by jury in civil cases. Also approved was the new article declaring that the legislative, executive, and judicial powers would not be intermixed.

Next up was the proposal that "The powers not delegated by the constitution, nor prohibited by it to the states, are reserved to the states respectively." Thomas Tudor Tucker of South Carolina proposed the prefix "all powers being derived from the people," and alteration of the first clause to refer to "the powers not *expressly* delegated." Madison recalled that "expressly" had been defeated in the Virginia convention, and the motion failed.[82]

Gerry then "proposed to add, after the word 'states,' *and people thereof.*" Daniel Carroll of Maryland, who had served at the Philadelphia convention, opposed the addition because "it tended to create a distinction between the people and their legislatures." This addition was defeated—for the moment—and then the reservation of powers clause was approved.[83]

The committee of the whole rose and reported the approved amendments to the House. Representative Frederick A. Muhlenberg of Pennsylvania, the

Speaker of the House, wrote to Benjamin Rush, giving him the inside scoop on the above proceedings:

> But this Day has at length terminated the Subject of Amendments in the Comittee of the whole House, & tomorrow we shall take up the Report & probably agree to the Amendments proposed, & which are nearly the same as the special Comittee of eleven had reported them. I have no Doubt but there will be two thirds as required by the Constitution in our House, but cannot say what Reception they will meet with in the Senate. Mr. Gerry & Mr. Tucker had each of them a long string of Amendts. which were not comprised in the Report of the special Comittee, & which they stiled Amendments proposed by the several States. There was a curious medley of them, and such as even our Minority in Pennsylvania would rather have pronounced dangerous Alterations than Amendments—these they offered in separate Resolution to the House in Order to get them referred to a Comittee of the whole, but both Attempts failed—the previous question having been ruled against Gerrys Motion, & carried, and Mr. Tuckers was negatived by a very large Majority.[84]

Wishing for no further amendments, Speaker Muhlenberg—who had been president in Pennsylvania's ratifying convention in 1787[85]—continued: "I hope it will be satisfactory to our State, and as it takes in the principal Amendments which our Minority had so much at Heart, I hope it may restore Harmony & unanimity amongst our fellow Citizens . . . ."[86] Among the amendments that "our Minority" in the Pennsylvania convention had proposed were that "the people have a right to the freedom of speech, . . . therefore, the freedom of the press shall not be restrained by any law of the United States," and that "the people have a right to bear arms for the defence of themselves and their own state, or the United States," and "no law shall be passed for disarming the people or any of them, unless for crimes committed, or real danger of public injury from individuals . . . ."[87]

On the 19th, Roger Sherman renewed his motion to add the amendments at the end of the Constitution rather than intersperse them throughout. This time the motion was approved by two-thirds of the House.[88] As Madison explained to Alexander White, compromising on this matter of form was necessary to secure the objective of passing the substance of the amendments.[89]

The House would now consider the amendments, albeit in no particular order. On August 20, it debated the exemption of religiously scrupulous persons from being compelled to bear arms. Thomas Scott of Pennsylvania objected that the exemption would mean that "you can never depend on your militia. This will lead to the violation of another article in the constitution, which secures to the people the right of keeping arms, as in this case you must have recourse to a standing army."[90]

"What justice can there be in compelling them to bear arms, when, if they are honest men they would rather die than use them," queried Elias Boudinot of New Jersey. "In forming a militia we ought to calculate for an effectual defence, and not compel characters of this description to bear arms. . . . If we strike out this clause, we shall lead such persons to conclude that we mean to compel them to bear arms." The proposed amendment was finally accepted after the insertion of the words "in person" at the end of the clause.[91] This discussion highlighted the sentiment that not only "bearing," but also merely "keeping" of arms by the people was considered both a right and a duty to prevent standing armies.

Gerry, on the next day, made a last, unsuccessful attempt to insert "expressly" into the clause reserving to the states the powers not delegated to the United States. But then, surprisingly, Roger Sherman moved to add that those powers "are reserved to the states respectively, or to the people." And that motion passed without debate.[92] This reinforced, as the words dictate, that "the states" and "the people" are indeed distinct. Moreover, the clause referred to "powers" not delegated as being "reserved" to the states or to the people, in contrast with the usage discussed above in which "rights" of the people may not be "infringed."

While this provision—which became the Tenth Amendment—concerned Federal-State powers, it was a rule of interpretation and did not structurally alter the balance of those powers. Indeed, the House had now passed a declaration of individual rights gleaned from the recommendations of the state conventions, but had all but ignored the structural amendments proposed by those conventions. Thomas Tudor Tucker sought to raise the latter on August 22 by proposing that Congress may not impose direct taxes unless it first seeks to requisition the amounts from the states and such states do not pay their proportions. Tucker noted that "this proposition was referred to the committee, along with many others in the gross; but the committee of eleven declined reporting upon it."[93] Among those "many others" was the proposal that the states may arm and organize the militia should Congress neglect the same.

But the House members were in no mood to add new amendments, and certainly not structural ones. The proposal on direct taxes did not prevail, and no further amendments were considered.[94] The final amendment proposals were agreed to and sent to the Senate.

The provisions that survived were the most fundamental and least controversial. Madison wrote to Edmund Randolph on August 21:

> For a week past the subject of amendts. has exclusively occupied the H. of Reps. Its progress has been exceedingly wearisome . . . . It has been absolutely necessary in order to effect any thing, to abbreviate debate, and exclude every proposition of a doubtful & unimportant nature. . . . Two or three contentious additions would even now frustrate the whole project.[95]

Those who demanded amendments were essentially happy with the declaration of individual rights but did not get the structural changes they wanted. Patrick Henry "is pleased with some of the proposed amendments; but still asks for the great desideratum, the destruction of direct taxes."[96] Certainly the right to have arms figured into Henry's dictum: "For Rights, without having power and might is but a shadow."[97] For Richard Henry Lee, the amendments were "short of some essentials, as Election interference & Standing Army & C. . . ."[98]

Agitation over amendments raged in the newspapers. The guarantee of an armed populace must have alleviated the following concern: "Power should be widely diffused . . . . The monopoly of power, is the most dangerous of all monopolies."[99] Further, citizens must keep, bear, and exercise in arms to sustain a well regulated militia:

> A late writer . . . on the necessity and importance of maintaining a well regulated militia, makes the following remarks:—A citizen, as a militia man is to perform duties which are different from the usual transactions of civil society. . . . [W]e consider the extreme importance of every military duty in time of war, and the necessity of acquiring an habitual exercise of them in time of peace . . . .[100]

Several of the proposed amendments were subjected to criticism. But what became the Second Amendment was apparently not attacked, aside from one editorial that argued the inefficiency of the militia clause, never questioning the arms guarantee. After quoting the House-approved language, the prominent antifederalist "Centinel" opined on September 9 in the *Independent Gazetteer*:

> It is remarkable that this article only makes the observation, "that a well regulated militia, composed of the body of the people, is the best security of a free state;" it does not ordain, or constitutionally provide for, the establishment of such a one. The absolute command vested by other sections in Congress over the militia, are not in the least abridged by this amendment. The militia may still be subjected to martial law . . . , may still be marched from state to state and made the unwilling instruments of crushing the last efforts of expiring liberty.[101]

"Centinel" was, of course, Samuel Bryan, apparent author of the Pennsylvania Dissent of the Minority,[102] which demanded recognition of the right to bear arms for defense of self, state, and country, and for hunting. By not objecting to lack of a list of purposes in the proposed arms guarantee, such antifederalists must have assumed that exercise of the right to keep and bear arms would extend to all lawful purposes. Had anyone interpreted "the people" in the guarantee to exclude ordinary citizens and to include only government-chosen militiamen, Bryan would have squawked loudly. By the same token, Samuel Adams and the drafters of the New Hampshire proposal did not object to the lack of an explicit exclusion of criminals from the individual right to keep and bear arms, because this too was understood.

Centinel's observations indicate the understanding that the Second Amendment's militia clause merely declared an abstract principle and did not alter the balance of Federal-State powers over the militia set forth in Article I, Section 8, of the Constitution. The clause did not declare, as urged by the Dissent of Minority and the Virginia, North Carolina, and Harrisburg conventions, "That each state respectively shall have the power to provide for organising, arming, and disciplining its own militia, whensoever Congress shall omit or neglect to provide for the same."[103]

However, the fact that Bryan and the other antifederalists never attacked the "right to bear arms" clause demonstrates that it recognized a full and complete guarantee of individual rights to have and use private arms. A storm of protest would have ensued had anyone hinted that the right extended only to persons selected by a governmental unit to serve in a militia.

### ACTION IN THE SENATE

"The lower house sent up amendments which held out a safeguard to personal liberty in great many instances, but this disgusted the Senate," Senator William Grayson of Virginia wrote to Patrick Henry after the House transmitted its amendments to the Senate.[104] Senator William Maclay of Pennsylvania wrote in his diary on August 25 that the amendments "were treated contemptuously by Z [Ralph Izard of South Carolina], [John] Langdon [of New Hampshire] and Mr. [Robert] Morris [of New York]. Z moved they should be postponed to next Session Langdon seconded & Mr. Morris got up and spoke angrily but not well. They however lost their Motion and Monday was assigned."[105]

The twenty-two members of the Senate, which met in secret and did not record debates, began consideration of the amendments on September 2, 1789. In the next two days, it sliced out parts of what became the First Amendment, including the phrase "nor shall the rights of conscience be infringed," but rejected a motion to delete a version of the First Amendment altogether.[106] It then passed a modified amendment protecting speech, press, and petition, and recognized "the right of the people peaceably to assemble and consult for their common good . . . ."[107]

The Senate next considered a motion to add the following to the House version of what would become the Second Amendment:

> That standing armies, in time of peace, being dangerous to liberty, should be avoided, as far as the circumstances and protection of the community will admit; and that in all cases the military should be under strict subordination to, and governed by, the civil power; that no standing army or regular troops shall be raised in time of peace, without the consent of two-thirds of the members present in both Houses; and that no soldier shall be enlisted for any longer term than the continuance of the war.[108]

This failed by a vote of 6 to 9. Those favoring the clauses included Virginia senators Richard Henry Lee and William Grayson, and Senators Pierce Butler (South Carolina), James Gunn (Georgia), John Henry (Maryland), and Paine Wingate (New Hampshire). The majority was inclined to add neither declaratory clauses nor structural changes.

The Senate's dim view of some amendments is reflected in a letter from Theodorick Bland Randolph to St. George Tucker, both antifederalist Virginians and relatives of congressmen. He stated:

> The house of Representatives have been for some time past engaged on the subject of amendments to the constitution, though in my opinion they have not made one single material one. The senate are at present engaged on that subject; Mr. Richd. H. Lee told me that he proposed to strike out the standing army in time of peace but could not carry it. He also says that it has been proposed, and warmly favoured that, liberty of Speech and of the press may be stricken out, as they only tend to promote licentiousness.[109]

The members of the majority who killed the anti-standing-army propositions[110] likely eschewed declarations of abstract political principle as well as opposed the requirement that two-thirds of the Congress must authorize a standing army. However, the Senate went on to pass the individual-rights guarantee proposed by the House but "amended to read as followeth: 'A well regulated militia, being the best security of a free state, the right of the people to keep and bear arms, shall not be infringed.'"[111]

In comparing the House draft with this Senate version, the House redundantly mentioned "the people" twice—once in defining "militia" as the "body of the people," and again as the entity with the right to keep and bear arms. The Senate more succinctly avoided repetition by deleting the well-recognized definition of the militia as "the body of the people."

It is also plausible to interpret the Senate's editing as leaving more discretion to Congress to define and compose the militia. If not defined constitutionally as "the body of the people," the militia could be statutorily defined as something less than that, such as a select militia.[112]

The Senate also deleted the phrase that "no person religiously scrupulous shall be compelled to bear arms"—perhaps because the basic guarantee of the amendment depicted the keeping and bearing of arms as an individual "right" and not as a duty and also to leave the matter of conscientious objection to the legislature. Deletion of the clause also addressed Congressman Gerry's argument in the House that it would allow the federal government to "declare who are those religiously scrupulous, and prevent them from bearing arms."[113]

On September 7, the Senate rejected the proposal that Congress may not impose direct taxes unless particular states failed to pay amounts requisitioned.[114] However, it passed the House version of what became the Tenth Amendment: "The powers not delegated to the United States by the constitution, nor prohibited by it to the states, are reserved to the states respectively, or to the people."[115] Apparently, the House-transmitted version had not included the clause "or to the people," but the Senate version restored it.[116]

The next day, September 8, the Senate rejected a string of amendments declaring the natural rights to life, liberty, and property; that "all power" is vested in "the people"; and that "the doctrine of non-resistance, against arbitrary power and oppression, is absurd, slavish, and destructive of the good and happiness of mankind."[117] Unlike the declaration of specific rights, such as the press and arms, these were perceived perhaps as useless truisms or platitudes.

A number of structural amendments, clarifying or redefining the powers of the government, were proposed and rejected. A renewed proposal to require two-thirds of both houses of Congress to consent to a standing army, and limits on the terms of enlistment of soldiers, failed.[118] The Senate then rejected an explicit reservation of the state power to maintain militias incorporating the language of the Virginia, North Carolina, and Harrisburg conventions:

> That each state, respectively, shall have the power to provide for organising, arming, and disciplining its own militia, whensoever Congress shall omit or neglect to provide for the same; that the militia shall not be subject to martial law, except when in actual service, in time of war, invasion, or rebellion; and when not in the actual service of the United States, shall be subject only to such fines, penalties, and punishments, as shall be directed or inflicted by the laws of its own state.[119]

The above action highlights the clear distinction between the "right" of "the people" to keep and bear arms, and the "power" of the "state" to organize, arm, and discipline its militia. Besides the linguistic differences, the individual right was considered with other personal liberties, and the state power was considered with other governmental powers. The two were completely separate proposals. The Senate passed the individual right to have arms and rejected the state power to maintain militia. By declaring the right of the people to keep and bear arms, Congress did not actually intend to declare the power of states to maintain militias—the very proposal Congress rejected.

John Randolph commented on the Senate rejection of the militia amendment, apparently from information he received from Senator Richard Henry Lee, as follows: "A majority of the Senate were for not allowing the militia arms & if two thirds had agreed it would have been an amendment to the Constitution. They are afraid that the Citizens will stop their full career to Tyranny & Oppression."[120] Yet as the federalists had argued in the Virginia convention, the militia power was concurrent, and thus states had a residual power to provide for arming the militia such as by requiring citizens to arm themselves. Proponents of this amendment wanted an explicit clarification, but were unsuccessful.

On September 9, the Senate returned to the declaration of rights, passing a form of the First Amendment similar to the final version.[121] The Senate then rejected a proposal to add "for the common defence" after "bear arms" in what became the Second Amendment.[122] Had it succeeded, recognition of "the right of the people to keep and bear arms for the common defence" would have protected an individual right to keep arms. But what did it mean to "bear arms for the common defence," and who would decide on exercise of this "right"?

In the Revolution, the patriots asserted a right to bear arms for the common defense against the established government which they deemed as lawless. They, not the lawless government, decided what was the common defense and when to bear arms in what they perceived to be the common defense.

The clause thus might have been interpreted liberally to allow the bearing of arms for lawful purposes, with the greatest protection for the important civic purpose of the common defense. The common defense could include armed defense against foreign aggression, insurrection, domestic tyranny, and criminal violence.

The clause might also have been interpreted strictly as allowing arms to be borne only for "the common defence," and only as defined by the government. But it would be a curious "right" if it could be exercised only by persons selected by the government and only when the government so ordered.

Similarly, the earlier version of the right of the people to assemble "for their common good"[123] could have been interpreted narrowly to limit that right only to the "common good" as defined by government. But a "right" to assemble only with the government's permission would be no right at all.

Rejection of both the "common defence" and "common good" phrases expressed an intent that the people have a right to keep and bear arms, and to assemble, for private as well as public purposes. Moreover, the decision of whether to exercise these rights rests with the people, not the government.

The Senate then made a change in the precatory clause of the Second Amendment. The declaration that a well regulated militia is "*the best* security of a free state" was neutralized or perhaps strengthened to state that a well regulated militia is "*necessary to the* security of a free state."[124] This met Gerry's objection in the House debate that "a well regulated militia being the best security of a free State, admitted that a standing army was a secondary one."[125] The Senate then passed its final version: "A well regulated militia being necessary to the security of a free state, the right of the people to keep and bear arms shall not be infringed."[126]

After completing work on other provisions, the Senate then resolved the passage of the proposed amendments by over the necessary two-thirds vote and transmitted such passage back to the House of Representatives.[127] On September 19 and 21, the House debated and agreed to the Senate amendments. A conference committee—including James Madison, Roger Sherman, and John Vining from the House and Oliver Ellsworth, Charles Carroll, and William Paterson from the Senate—met and resolved final details.[128]

On September 25, 1789, the Senate agreed to the House resolution approving the final version of the amendments and recommended it to the states (including North Carolina and Rhode Island, which had not yet ratified the Constitution) with a preamble initiated in the Senate.[129] It stated: "The conventions of a number of the states having, at the time of their adopting the constitution, expressed a desire, in order to prevent misconstruction or abuse of its powers, that further declaratory and restrictive clauses should be added . . . ."[130] The Second Amendment (the fourth article of the amendments submitted to the states) as it finally passed Congress read: "A well regulated Militia, being necessary to the security of a free State, the right of the people to keep and bear Arms, shall not be infringed."

## CHAPTER 13

# The Bill of Rights in the States

THE ADOPTION of the proposed amendments by the states was by no means a foregone conclusion, and the ratification struggle ensued through 1791.[1] Three positions emerged during the controversy: The proposed amendments were adequate, further guarantees were needed, and freemen had no need of a bill of rights. None of the proponents of these three different positions ever called into question the basic, individual right of keeping and bearing arms. In fact, little dispute erupted about such personal and unalienable rights—the most prominent criticism was that the amendments failed to include provisions limiting federal powers and enhancing state powers.

At the same time that the proposed federal bill of rights was being considered by the states—about which few records remain—some states were revising their own constitutions and bills of rights. These state proceedings shed further light on the perceived nature of the rights guaranteed both at the federal and state levels.

The view that the rights of freemen are too numerous to enumerate was coupled with the argument that the ultimate protection of American liberty would be provided by the armed populace rather than by paper guards. The pro-amendment view held that both the existence of a bill of rights and an armed populace provided complementary safeguards. The following editorial from the *Gazette of the United States* in October 1789 assumes that keeping and bearing arms would contribute to a well regulated militia, and vice versa:

> The right of the people to keep and bear arms has been recognised by the General Government; but the best security of that right after all is, the military spirit, that taste for martial exercises, which has always distinguished the free citizens of these States; From various parts of the Continent the most pleasing accounts are published of reviews and parades in large and small assemblies of the militia. . . . Such men form the best barrier to the Liberties of America.[2]

As to the nature of "rights" that should not be "infringed"—terms that appear only in the Second Amendment—a writer in the *Independent Gazetteer* wrote: "But there are some rights too essential to be delegated—too sacred to be infringed. These each individual reserves to himself; in the free enjoyment of these the whole society engages to protect him . . . . All these essential and sacred rights, it would be difficult if not impossible, to recount, but some, in every social compact, it is proper to enumerate, as specimens of many others . . . ."[3]

The abuses of British rule were still fresh in the minds of Americans, but if anyone needed a reminder, in 1789 Dr. David Ramsay published his acclaimed *History of the American Revolution*. The work featured detailed accounts of the Crown's violations of the colonists' rights, including Gage's disarming of the inhabitants of Boston in 1775.[4]

### STRUGGLE FOR THE BILL OF RIGHTS IN VIRGINIA

Since debates were not recorded, little is known about what was said in the state legislatures that considered the proposed amendments. Action by the Virginia General Assembly, however, was described by correspondents of James Madison. A legislative report there also revealed concerns with the proposed bill of rights.

Hardin Burnley, a member of the Virginia House of Delegates, wrote to Madison on November 5, 1789, that most of the delegates who opposed the adoption of the amendments "are not dissatisfied with the amendments as far as they go" but wanted delay to prompt an amendment on direct taxes.[5] On November 25, House of Delegates member Henry Lee—the Revolutionary war leader who more recently had served in the Virginia ratifying convention—wrote to Madison:

> The assembly . . . are now engaged in consideration of the amendments proposed
> by Congress, to the constitution. Some time ago Mr. Henry made a motion for
> postponing this business to the next session. This gentleman has left us & since
> his departure his motion has been taken up & rejected. It is probable that all
> the amendments will be adopted here. The two last are disapproved of by Mr.
> Randolph & others. The enmity to govt. is I believe as strong as ever in this state.
> Indeed I have no doubt of this fact if the assembly be considered as a just index of
> the feelings of the people. Never adventure direct taxation for years.[6]

The "last two" amendments were numbered the eleventh and twelfth and would become the Ninth and Tenth Amendments, which respectively protected undefined "rights . . . retained by the people" and "powers reserved to the states respectively, or to the people." As noted above, these provisions were opposed by Edmund Randolph, who had refused to sign the Constitution at the end of the 1787 convention in Philadelphia but who supported it at the 1788 Virginia convention. At this point, Randolph was not only a member of the Virginia legislature but two months before had been appointed the first attorney general of the United States by President Washington.[7]

More insight in this debate was set forth in a letter from Hardin Burnley to Madison dated November 28 as follows:

> The fate of the Amendments proposed by Congress to the General Government
> is still in suspence. In a committee of the whole house the fi[r]st ten were ac-
> ceeded to with but little opposition for on a question taken, on each separately,
> there was scarcely a dissenting voice. On the two last a debate of some length
> took place, which ended in rejection. Mr. E. Randolph who advocated all the
> others stood in this contest in the front of opposition. His principal objection
> was pointed against the word retained in the eleventh proposed amendment,
> and his a[r]gument if I understood it was applied in this manner, that as the
> rights declared in the first ten of the proposed amendments were not all that a
> free people would require the exercise of; and that as there was no criterion by
> which it could be determined whether any other particular right was retained

or not, it would be more safe, & more consistent with the spirit of the 1st & 17th amendments proposed by Virginia, that this reservation against constructive power, should operate rather as a provision against extending the powers of Congress by their own authority, than as a protection to rights reducable to no definitive certainty.[8]

The "1st & 17th amendments proposed by Virginia" could be characterized as differently worded versions of the Ninth and Tenth Amendments that the Virginians thought were superior. As noted, the other proposed amendments seem to have aroused little if any controversy.

The committee of the whole approved the amendments on November 30. Hardin Burnley wrote Madison again on December 5, describing the debate after the amendments had been reported by the committee to the House:

> Those which respected the ten first were agreed to with even less opposition than they experienced in the Committee, & that wh. passed on the 11th & 12th was rescinded by a majority of about twelve. The amendments with the resolutions on them are now with the Senate, where from the best information which I have been able to collect there is such a division in opinion as not to furnish a ground for probable conjecture as to their decision. Some of that body I am informed propose rejection in toto, others adoption, & others again wish to postpone a decision on them 'till next Session of assembly. I believe it may be said with certainty that the greater part of those who wish either to postpone or reject, are not dissatisfied with the amendments so far as they have gone, but are apprehensive that the adoption of them at this time will be an obstacle to the chief object of their persuit, the amendment on the subject of direct taxation.[9]

The Virginia Senate would postpone consideration of the proposed amendments until the next session. A majority report dated December 12, 1789, extensively criticized some amendments as too narrow, but no one questioned the right to bear arms provision.[10] While some of the proposals were similar to those proposed by Virginia and other states, others "are not substantially the same, and fall far short of affording the same security to personal rights, or of so effectually guarding against the apprehended mischiefs of the government . . . ."

Most prominent was the First Amendment (which was then the third proposed amendment), which allegedly condensed and weakened four separate articles of the bill of rights Virginia had proposed. The report stated in part:

The 3d amendment, recommended by Congress, does not prohibit the rights of conscience from being violated or infringed; and although it goes to restrain Congress from passing laws establishing any national religion, they might, notwithstanding, levy taxes to any amount, for the support of religion or its preachers; and any particular denomination of christians might be so favoured and supported by the General Government, as to give it a decided advantage over others, and in process of time render it as powerful and dangerous as if it was established as the national religion of the country.

This amendment does not declare and assert the right of the people to speak and publish their sentiments, nor does it secure the liberty of the press. Should these valuable rights be infringed or violated by the arbitrary decisions of Judges, or by any other means than a legislative act directly to that effect, the people would have no avowed principle in the constitution to which they might resort for the security of these rights.[11]

The above predicted that Congress would use taxation and other delegated powers to exercise powers that were otherwise denied, such as supporting an establishment of religion. The criticism of the speech and press guarantees focused on the opening words of the First Amendment—"Congress shall make no law"—which appeared to allow other branches of the government such as the judiciary to violate those rights.

The Virginia Senate report further complained about the deletion of state proposals for "the right of the people to instruct their representatives, and their right to consult with each other for the common good," noting that "these rights are denied by Congress, and they have refused to allow any amendment declaratory of them, as we discover by their Journals; and even the humble privilege of petitioning against oppression is not fully asserted or secured . . . ."[12]

The report also criticized the Sixth Amendment as not sufficiently protecting the right of the accused to be tried by a jury in his own neighborhood. Criminal defendants could be tried in distant parts of a state, "where a person, obnoxious to Congress, might fall an innocent sacrifice to their resentment."[13]

Among the structural amendments proposed by the Virginia ratifying convention was the declaration that "those clauses which declare that Congress shall not exercise certain powers be not interpreted in any manner whatsoever to extend the powers of Congress," but made "exceptions to the specified powers" or were "inserted merely for greater caution."[14] By contrast, the Ninth Amendment—under which the enumeration "of certain rights" may not be construed to deny "others retained by the people"—had not been requested by Virginia or any other state. The report's criticism of that language as ambiguous may still be heard today:

> If it is meant to guard against the extension of the powers of Congress by implication, it is greatly defective . . . ; and as it respects personal rights, might be dangerous, because, should the rights of the people be invaded or called in question, they might be required to shew by the constitution what rights they have retained; and such as could not from that instrument be proved to be retained by them, they might be denied to possess. Of this there is ground to be apprehensive, when Congress are already seen denying certain rights of the people, heretofore deemed clear and unquestionable.[15]

The Virginia Senate report also found vagueness lurking in what became the Tenth Amendment. Virginia had proposed that "each state in the Union shall respectively retain every power" not delegated to the federal government.[16] The Tenth Amendment—which declared that "the powers not delegated to the United States" are "reserved to the states respectively, or to the people"— would have meant the same "were it not for the words 'or to the people.'" Consequently, continued the report:

> It is not declared to be the people of the respective States; but the expression applies to the people generally as citizens of the United States, and leaves it doubtful what powers are reserved to the State Legislatures. Unrestrained by the constitution or these amendments, Congress might, as the supreme rulers of the people, assume those powers which properly belong to the respective States, and thus gradually effect an entire consolidation.[17]

Use of the term "the people" may have been an unclear expression in regard to reserved "powers," a criticism paralleling that of use of "We the People" in the preamble of the Constitution. Is the reference to the people at large or to the people of the states respectively? But the report found no such ambiguity in the phrase "the right of the people" to assemble, bear arms, and against unreasonable search and seizure. Where "rights" are concerned, "the people" unambiguously refers to individuals.

Other than the Tenth Amendment, Congress had not proposed any of the structural amendments affecting the Federal-State balance that Virginia and other states had advocated. One such proposal was the state power "to provide for organising, arming, and disciplining its own militia," if Congress neglected to do so.[18] The Virginia Senate report stated about this deficiency:

> We consider that of the many and important amendments recommended by the Conventions of Virginia and other States, these propositions contained all that Congress are disposed to grant; that all the rest are by them deemed improper, and that these are offered in full satisfaction of the whole . . . . Considering therefore, that they are far short of what the people of Virginia wish, and have asked, and deeming them by no means sufficient to secure the rights of the people, or to render the government safe and desirable, we think our countrymen ought not to be put off with amendments so inadequate.[19]

The Virginia Senate voted to reject what became the First, Sixth, Ninth, and Tenth Amendments, "these to be referred to the consideration of the people," Edward Carrington (a member of the House of Delegates) wrote to Madison on December 20. The House of Delegates insisted on adoption of all of the amendments, a conference committee could not resolve the differences, and "thus the whole amendments have fallen." Carrington concluded: "My information from the various parts of the Country is that the people are at ease on the subject of amendments, expecting nothing but that those sent on would be adopted and that others will be supplied as further deliberation and experience shall discover the want of them."[20]

The Virginia Senate voted to take up the proposed amendments in its next session, which was two years later. The delaying tactic failed to create impetus for more expansively worded individual rights or for clarification or alteration of the state-federal balance, such as regarding the state militia power. The final ratification of the Bill of Rights would be forestalled until Virginia's ratification on December 15, 1791.

In the interim, the commonplace view continued to prevail that ultimately the armed citizenry would prevent tyranny. Representative Theodorick Bland wrote Patrick Henry on March 19, 1790, that "I have founded my hopes to the single object of securing (in terrorem) the great and essential rights of freemen from the encroachments of Power—so far as to authorise resistance when they should be either openly attacked or insidiously undermined."[21]

Some continued to support structural amendments, such as a requirement that two-thirds of Congress authorize a standing army or declare war.[22] But criticism of the Bill of Rights was minimal, and no disapproval existed of the declared right to arms.

That, indeed, is the significance of Virginia's debate on the Bill of Rights for purposes of this study. Some of the proposed amendments were subjected to intense criticism based on their alleged ambiguities or insufficient protection for the particular rights guaranteed. But no vagueness lurked in the phrase "the right of the people to keep and bear arms."

## MASSACHUSETTS FAILS TO RATIFY

The debate over ratification of the Bill of Rights continued throughout 1790. Writers in the *Federal Gazette* parroted that no bill of rights was necessary: "A bill of rights for freemen appears to be a contradiction in terms. . . . [I]n a free country, every right of human nature, which are as numerous as sands upon the sea shore, belong to the quiet, peaceable citizen."[23] Another opined: "The absurdity of attempting by a bill of rights to secure to freemen what they never parted with, must be self-evident."[24]

Probably more indifference than the above die-hard sentiment resulted in the failure of Massachusetts to ratify the Bill of Rights. Governor John Hancock, in a speech to the General Court on January 14, 1790, commented on that body's coming consideration of the proposed amendments, at one point referring to the protections of petit and grand juries in the Fifth and Sixth Amendments. "Some of the others appear to me as very important to that personal security, which is so truly characteristick of a free Government."[25] While he was not more specific, perhaps he had in mind the Second and Fourth Amendments, which promote personal security in different ways. The General Court answered the governor by promising a careful consideration of the amendments, adding that "the whole body of the People should have the fullest confidence, that their rights and liberties are secured to them in the General Government, by the most explicit declarations which have a tendency to give energy to its authority and laws."[26]

The legislative journals reflect that the Senate agreed to all of the Bill of Rights, the House concurred except as to what became the Tenth Amendment, and that the Senate then agreed to the House version but failed to complete action.[27]

The Report of the Committee of the General Court on Further Amendments, issued in early 1790, did not criticize any of the Bill of Rights provisions but recommended twelve structural amendments further defining federal-state powers. It proposed "that Congress shall by law provide for calling forth the posse comitatus for executing the laws of the United States." The posse comitatus consisted of the armed citizens of a community who the sheriff could call out to help keep the peace.[28] The committee also urged an amendment that would have recognized a state power to veto congressional action establishing a "system for forming the militia" or making an "establishment of troops in a time of peace, beyond a limited number."[29]

The General Court referred the report to the next session. However, no action was thereafter taken on the Bill of Rights or other amendments.[30] Massachusetts, along with Connecticut and Georgia, belatedly ratified the Bill of Rights in 1939.

## RHODE ISLAND ENTERS THE UNION

For over a year after the first federal Congress met, Rhode Island remained a sovereign state outside the Union. After refusing to call a convention seven times, in January 1790 the Rhode Island legislature finally voted to have a convention to consider ratification of the federal Constitution. Rhode Island would at last ratify the Constitution on May 29, 1790, and the Bill of Rights on June 15, 1790.

Rhode Island newspapers were more apt to print news of constitutional developments of neighboring states than of the federal government. The *Providence Gazette* printed nothing on the federal Bill of Rights in the above period but did publish a proposed new bill of rights for Pennsylvania that included the following: "That the right of citizens to bear arms in defense of themselves and the State, and to assemble peaceably together . . . shall not be questioned."[31]

The convention finally met in March 1790 to consider ratification. Federalist leader Henry Marchant moved that the amendments be read.[32] A debate ensued on whether, as Madison had originally proposed, states should be "precluded from making any Law respecting Religion or abridging the Rights of Consci[ence]." James Sheldon argued: "If it is right that Congress should not make any Laws respecting it no State ought to have the Right."[33] Marchant thought it was "enough for us to keep it out of the Gen[eral] Gov[ernmen]t."[34]

In the conventions of the other states, the federalists had supported adoption of the Constitution without amendments, but by now their strategy was to support adoption of a bill of rights as an inducement to adoption of the

Constitution. A committee of ten was appointed, including delegates opposed to the Constitution.[35] The idea was to get the antifederalists to support ratification of the Constitution with a bill of rights they would support.[36] The committee reported back, and the minutes reflected with a flourish:

> A Time of Expectation and the House very much crowded—Generals, Colonels, Delegates &c being obliged to Stand. The House now calling—Thus Life Passes and carries along the Tide of Time to land us in Eternity—of what consequence will then be all this Parade?[37]

A bill of rights was read, and its arms guarantee was the New York language verbatim.[38] This provision followed guarantees against cruel and unusual punishment and unreasonable search and seizure, and in favor of the rights to assembly, petition, speech, and the press.[39]

Seeking to stall a vote on the Constitution, antifederalist Job Comstock "moves that before the Bill of (40) Rights be discussed—Moves that the Bill of Rights and Amendment[s] be Referred to the People at large to have the Opinion and Sentim[en]ts thereon . . . ." Marchant countered that "the Bill of Rights being agreed to it appears agreeable to our Minds—that it contains our professed Sentiments and is agreeable to the Constitutions of the United [States]." He moved for a vote on whether the bill of rights would be approved.[40]

Comstock argued that "by adopting this Bill some Rights essential may be omitted," and Elisha Brown moved to refer the issue to the regular town meetings.[41] Marchant urged a convention vote because "we may declare that the People have such and such Rights and that when we adopt the Constitu[tion] it may appear that we claim such and such Rights Similar to what was done by New York and may go on to give instances and the Wishes of the People."[42]

The antifederalists then maneuvered an adjournment without voting on the Constitution.[43] Town meetings proceeded to discuss the Constitution and proposed Bill of Rights. Meanwhile, the U.S. Congress was threatening to boycott any shipping to or from Rhode Island.[44] As reflected in his diary entry for May 18, 1790, Senator William Maclay of Pennsylvania observed:

> That the design of this bill evidently, was to impress the People of Rhode Island, with Terror. It was an Application to their fears, hoping to obtain from them, an Adoption of the Constitution, a thing despaired of, from their free Will

or their Judgment. That it was meant to be Used the same Way That a Robber does a dagger or a Highwayman a pistol & to obtain the end desired by putting the party in fear.[45]

After the town meetings, the delegates reconvened, and the federalists moved to adopt the Constitution with the Bill of Rights already agreed upon. The same committee met and suggested additional amendments.[46] On May 29, the convention voted 34 to 32 to ratify the federal Constitution. The Bill of Rights formed the basis for Rhode Island's ratification, which declared that the following rights "cannot be abridged or violated":

> That there are certain natural rights of which men, when they form a social compact, cannot deprive or divest their posterity,—among which are the enjoyment of life and liberty, with the means of acquiring, possessing, and protecting property, and pursuing and obtaining happiness and safety . . . .[47]

It further declared that "all power is naturally vested in, and consequently derived from, the people," and that "the powers of government may be reassumed by the people whensoever it shall become necessary to their happiness." Following several guarantees, the declaration included the following by now familiar threesome: "That the people have a right peaceably to assemble . . .", "That the people have a right to freedom of speech . . .", and "That the people have a right to keep and bear arms; that a well regulated militia, including the body of the people capable of bearing arms, is the proper, natural, and safe defence of a free state . . . ."[48] The last section also declared against standing armies and against the quartering of soldiers in houses.

A separate body of amendments concerning state powers did not mention the militia.[49] However, it declared against federal conscription: "that no person shall be compelled to military duty otherwise than by voluntary enlistment, except in cases of general invasion . . . ."[50]

The convention also recommended that the state legislature ratify what became the federal Bill of Rights.[51] On June 7, 1790, Rhode Island became the ninth state to ratify the Bill of Rights.

As more states adopted the amendments, the great debate over the rights of man dwindled. But admonitions in support of the militia and against standing armies continued to be expressed. As "A Framer" argued in a plea addressed "To the Yeomanry of Pennsylvania":

Under every government the dernier resort of the people, is an appeal to the sword; whether to defend themselves against the open attacks of a foreign enemy, or to check the insidious encroachments of domestic foes. Whenever a people . . . entrust the defence of their country to a regular, standing army, composed of mercenaries, the power of that country will remain under the direction of the most wealthy citizens. . . . [Y]our liberties will be safe as long as you support a well regulated militia.[52]

## THE PENNSYLVANIA DECLARATION OF RIGHTS
## AND JUSTICE WILSON'S LECTURES

At the same time as the federal Bill of Rights was being considered by the states, some of the state constitutions were also being amended. One of the most significant revisions was that of Pennsylvania in 1790, and it was carried out by the guiding hand of James Wilson. A prominent delegate to the Philadelphia convention, which drafted the federal Constitution, and of the Pennsylvania convention, which adopted it, Wilson was appointed by President Washington as Supreme Court Justice in 1789. The following analyzes the concept of the right to keep and bear arms from the perspectives expressed at the 1790 Pennsylvania constitutional convention, which revised that state's bill of rights, and in more detail by Justice Wilson.

"The whole of that Bill is a declaration of the rights of the people at large or considered as individuals, meant as a barrier against the encroachments of any of the Legislative, Executive or Judiciary Departments . . . . [I]t establishes some rights of the individual as unalienable and which consequently, no majority has a right to deprive them of." Thus wrote Albert Gallatin to Alexander Addison, a candidate for election to the Pennsylvania convention, on October 7, 1789.[53]

The Pennsylvania convention met from November 24, 1789, through September 2, 1790. On December 10, 1789, the convention unanimously resolved that the 1776 Declaration of Rights "requires alterations and amendments, in such manner as the rights of the people, reserved and excepted out of the general powers of government, may be more accurately defined and secured."[54]

A committee of nine was elected to draft proposed changes.[55] Influential members included James Wilson, who also presided over the convention, and

William Findley, who had signed the Dissent of Minority stemming from Pennsylvania's 1788 ratifying convention.

The delegates in the Pennsylvania convention were well aware of the progress of the still-pending federal Bill of Rights. As they knew, Madison's original proposal declared that "the right of the people to keep and bear arms shall not be infringed," followed by a militia clause and then the words that "no person religiously scrupulous of bearing arms shall be compelled to render military service in person."[56] As Tench Coxe explained in Philadelphia's *Federal Gazette* about that proposal, "the people are confirmed by the next article in their right to keep and bear their private arms."[57]

While the clause for religiously scrupulous persons was deleted in the final version, the delegates in the Pennsylvania convention would consider a similar provision. In its first report, submitted on December 23, 1789, the committee charged with recommending amendments proposed:

> XIX. That the right of the citizens to bear arms in defence of themselves and the state, and to assemble peaceably together, and apply in a decent manner, to those invested with the powers of government, for redress of grievances or other proper purposes, shall not be questioned.
>
> XX. That those who conscientiously scruple to bear arms shall not be compelled to do so, but shall pay an equivalent for personal service.[58]

The Declaration containing this proposal, which would be published nationally,[59] was made at a time when only three states had ratified the federal Bill of Rights. Combined into a single sentence, bearing arms, assembly, and petition were rights of every citizen. The term "bear arms" could have a militia connotation, as the exemption for the conscientiously scrupulous indicated, but its primary meaning was in the context of the "right of the citizens" to carry arms "in defense of themselves and the state."

The committee of the whole proceeded to act on each of the draft provisions. On February 4, 1790, the committee voted to separate the right of citizens to assemble and to petition from the arms right, which was combined with the conscientious objector provision. The minutes reflect the following:

> The twentieth section of the said bill of rights being under consideration, it was moved by Mr. Pickering, seconded by Mr. McKean, to amend the same so as to read as follows, viz.

That the right of the citizens to bear arms in defence of themselves and the state shall not be questioned; but those who conscientiously scruple to bear arms shall not be compellable to do so, but shall pay an equivalent for personal service. Which was carried in the affirmative, and the said section, as amended, adopted.[60]

Timothy Pickering and Chief Justice Thomas McKean,[61] both of whom had served in Pennsylvania's federal ratifying convention, followed Madison's example by combining a "right to bear arms" guarantee with a conscientious objector exception. Consideration of those two clauses in the same sentence did not detract from the fact that the right to bear arms extended to "defence of themselves and the state."

The following month, on March 10, 1790, Pennsylvania ratified the federal Bill of Rights. It seems fair to say that the Second Amendment's right to bear arms was considered just as much an individual right as it was in the Pennsylvania Declaration.

Meanwhile, months passed as the Pennsylvania convention dealt with other subjects. In a separate article from the Declaration of Rights, the committee of the whole agreed to a provision that "the freemen of this commonwealth shall be armed and disciplined for its defence."[62] The committee rejected a proposal to change "shall" to "may,"[63] thereby authorizing compulsory self-arming and militia service.

Attempts were made unsuccessfully to alter the conscientious objector clause.[64] A memorial from Quakers protested that the "article materially affects our religious liberties, which proposes that those who conscientiously scruple to bear arms shall pay an equivalent for personal service; such an equivalent it is well known we cannot, consistent with our principles, voluntarily pay."[65] The convention refused to reconsider.[66]

In the final version of the state constitution as adopted on September 2, 1790, the troublesome clause was moved to a more logical place. The declaration of rights provision simply stated: "That the right of the citizens to bear arms in defence of themselves and the state shall not be questioned."[67] The militia clause in the body of the Constitution read: "The freemen of this commonwealth shall be armed and disciplined for its defence: Those who conscientiously scruple to bear arms, shall not be compelled to do so, but shall pay an equivalent for personal service."[68]

As noted, James Wilson played a leading role in drafting the new constitution. He had been an influential delegate to the convention that drafted the federal Constitution and then led the federalists at the Pennsylvania convention that ratified it. In 1789, Wilson was appointed by President George Washington as a justice to the U.S. Supreme Court, and the following year he also became the first law professor at the College of Philadelphia.[69] His lectures there significantly addressed the right to have and use arms for self-defense.

Wilson began with the philosophical premise that protection of life is the first law of nature, and that government may not abrogate that right. He explained:

> The defence of one's self, justly called the primary law of nature, is not, nor can it be abrogated by any regulation of municipal law. This principle of defence is not confined merely to the person; it extends to the liberty and the property of a man: it is not confined merely to his own person; it extends to the persons of all those, to whom he bears a peculiar relation—of his wife, of his parent, of his child, of his master, of his servant: nay, it extends to the person of every one, who is in danger; perhaps, to the liberty of every one, whose liberty is unjustly and forcibly attacked.[70]

Thus, the right of self-defense serves the goals of humanity. For his claim that defense of one's self is the most basic law of nature, Wilson quoted Cicero's oration in defense of Milo. In a passage well familiar to America's Founders, Cicero described as a law of nature:[71]

> [I]f our lives are endangered by plots or violence or armed robbers or enemies, any and every method of protecting ourselves is morally right. When weapons reduce them to silence, the laws no longer expect one to await their pronouncements. For people who decide to wait for these will have to wait for justice, too—and meanwhile they must suffer injustice first.[72]

For the proposition that the natural right to self-defense cannot be abrogated by law, Wilson cited Blackstone.[73] Blackstone asked "what wanton lengths of rapine or cruelty outrages . . . might be carried [out], unless it were permitted a man immediately to oppose one violence with another."[74]

In another lecture, Wilson provided the basis for the proposition: "Homicide is enjoined, when it is necessary for the defence of one's person or house."[75] He explained about the defense of one's person:

[I]t is the great natural law of self preservation, which, as we have seen, cannot be repealed, or superseded, or suspended by any human institution. This
law, however, is expressly recognised in the constitution of Pennsylvania. "The
right of the citizens to bear arms in the defence of themselves shall not be questioned." This is one of our many renewals of the Saxon regulations. "They were
bound," says Mr. Selden, "to keep arms for the preservation of the kingdom,
and of their own persons."[76]

The above referred to Nathaniel Bacon's compilation of works by John
Selden, *An Historical and Political Discourse of the Laws and Government of
England*, which the Crown would ban. Selden, co-author of the Petition of
Right (1628), served in Parliament as an enemy of Royalism, as would Bacon.
The actual quotation Wilson took from the *Discourse* reads as follows:

Probable it is that the Lords might have their Villains to follow them in the Battle, but the strength consisted of the Freemen; and though many were bound by
tenure to follow their Lords to the Wars, and many were Voluntiers, yet it seems
all were bound upon call under peril of Fine, and were bound to keep Arms for
the preservation of the Kingdom, their Lords, and their own persons; and these
they might neither pawn nor sell, but leave them to descend to their Heirs . . . .[77]

The Saxon requirement of keeping arms as a duty had now evolved into
a right in the Pennsylvania Declaration and the Second Amendment. Yet it
had elements of being a right even in prior times. The Discourse noted that
the "ancient custom of maintaining Arms by every Freeman, for the defence
of the Kingdom," was "made uncertain by the avarice of Kings . . . ."[78] Moreover, "the arming of a man's own person" contributed to "the safeguard of the
Rights and Liberties of the People, invaded in those times by . . . expressions
of Prerogative Royal . . . ."[79]

The right to keep arms in the home is fundamental to this tradition. Wilson discussed justifiable homicide when necessary to defend one's home as
follows:

"Every man's house is his castle," says my Lord Coke, in one of his reports,
"and he ought to keep and defend it at his peril; and if any one be robbed in it,
it shall be esteemed his own default and negligence." For this reason, one may
assemble people together in order to protect and defend his house.[80]

Wilson discussed the issue of providing for "the common defence" by reference to the army and militia clauses of the federal Constitution, and Pennsylvania's provision that "the freemen of this commonwealth shall be armed for its defence."[81] He did not mention the "right" to bear arms in this context.

The Pennsylvania Declaration of Rights of 1790 and Justice Wilson's lectures provide insight into the meaning of the Second Amendment. The right to keep and bear arms was a pre-existing "right" of "the people" or "the citizens," not just a militia duty. While the right contributed to a well regulated militia, it also ensured the basis for defense of persons and the home.

## THE DELAWARE CONVENTION OF 1791

Delaware held a constitutional convention beginning in late 1791. The committee to consider alterations of the Constitution, chaired by John Dickinson, included twelve members, five of whom had sat in the constitutional convention of 1776.[82] The committee of the whole determined "that the Declaration of Rights should be amended in such manner, as more particularly to enumerate, and more precisely define, the rights reserved out of the general powers of government."[83] Indeed, the 1776 Declaration was rather scant. Renewed interest may have stemmed from Pennsylvania's 1790 Declaration and the federal Bill of Rights, which Delaware had ratified in early 1790 and which had become effective by Virginia's ratification on December 15, 1791.

Two days after Virginia's action, the select committee in the Delaware convention reported a detailed declaration of rights, which included the following: "The right of the citizens to bear arms in defence of themselves, and the state, shall not be questioned."[84] This language, copied from that of Pennsylvania,[85] was substituted for the now deleted militia clause of the 1776 Declaration.[86]

The convention's consideration and ultimate rejection of this amendment reflected an insecurity stemming from the disarming of Whigs by Tories and vice versa dating to the Revolution. Richard Bassett, a member of the committee and a Tory, complained about firearm seizures and was himself disarmed in 1776[87] but went on to serve in the 1776 convention and the federal constitutional convention of 1787. Two other members, Charles Polk and Rhoads Shankland, allegedly encouraged their followers to carry guns at the Sussex election in 1787.[88]

When the right-to-arms proposal reached the committee of the whole, the delegates could not agree on proposed language to qualify the right. The minutes reflect the following:

The eighteenth Section of the first Article being under Consideration, viz.

18. The Right of *the Citizens to bear Arms* in defence of themselves and the State, shall not be questioned.

It was moved by Mr. Batson, seconded by Mr. Polk, to add to the Section the Words *while acting in strict subordination to the Civil Power:*

*Which passed in the Negative.*

A motion was made by Mr. Ridgely, seconded by Mr. Johns, to strike out the Words, *the Citizen to bear Arms,* and, in Lieu thereof, insert the Words, *bearing Arms by Citizens qualified to vote for Representatives.*

It was then moved by Mr. Johnson, seconded by Mr. Clayton, to postpone the last Motion in order to introduce the following:

That there be added to the Section the Words *unless under such Pretensions, any Person disturb the Peace and Happiness, or Safety of Society.*

On the Question for Postponement,

It was determined in the Affirmative.

A Motion was then made by Mr. Bassett, seconded by Mr. Batson, to strike out the said Section,

Which was determined in the Affirmative; And the Section expunged.[89]

Although the delegates did not fear a guarantee of an individual right to bear arms for self-defense, they were apprehensive about groups of armed citizens taking it upon themselves to act in "defence of the state," such as during elections. The first proposed amendment, that citizens bearing arms must act "in strict subordination to the Civil Power," may have been offered to restrict militia interference at the polls. Interestingly, Charles Polk, who seconded the motion, won both disputed elections in Sussex in 1787. He apparently resented the interference by Whig militiamen at the first election and advised his followers to carry firearms at the second.[90]

The second proposed qualification sought to restrict bearing arms to "Citizens qualified to vote for Representatives." This appears to have been an attempt to extend the policy dating from the Revolution of denying suffrage to Loyalists and disarming them. Loyalists had not been re-enfranchised until

1790,[91] and some Whigs in the convention may have relished an opportunity again to take the vote and the arms away from the perceived traitors. This amendment may have been killed by delegates wishing to bury the hatchet and allow the same rights to all citizens.

The third amended version sought to qualify arms-bearing by persons with the proviso that it not "disturb the Peace and Happiness, or Safety of Society." This again may have been directed against interference by armed bodies with elections or otherwise disturbing the peace.

The delegates being unable to agree on specific language, the whole section was stricken. Those moving to strike were Richard Bassett, whose complaint about firearm seizures during the Revolution is noted above, and Mr. Batson, who had proposed that the right to bear arms be exercised in subordination to the civil power. Nonetheless, the convention members did recognize the right of the citizens to bear arms. Many had served the year before in the legislature that adopted the federal Second Amendment. Their own select committee had recommended the arms guarantee. The delegates apparently preferred to leave the right unenumerated when they could not agree on restrictive language.

In its final version, adopted in mid-1792, the Delaware Declaration of Rights included neither a militia clause nor an arms guarantee. The preference against standing armies, and for subordination of the military to the civil power, remained.[92]

Even though the de facto right of the citizen to bear arms went unquestioned, the noncitizen enjoyed no such right. In a message to the constitutional convention of 1791, Warner Mifflin denounced slavery, proposing constitutional recognition of the right of every human born in Delaware to be free.[93] The select committee recommendation that the Declaration of Rights include the phrase all men "are by Birth free and equal" was deleted on motion of John Dickinson.[94] The only legislative infringement on the individual right to bear arms in Delaware was the following: "That if any Negro or Mulatto slave shall presume to carry any guns, swords, pistols, fowling-pieces, clubs, or other arms and weapons whatsoever, without his master's special licence for the same, he shall be whipt with twenty-one lashes, upon his bare back."[95]

The Militia Act of 1793 provided at "each and every free able bodied white male citizen," aged 18 through 44, must "provide himself with the arms" of either a footman, including a musket or firelock, or a horseman, including a sword and a pair of pistols.[96] While the constitutional convention had failed to agree on specific language for a right to bear arms, doing so remained a legal duty in Delaware.

### THE UNION EXPANDS

Unlike Delaware, Kentucky—admitted as the fifteenth state in the union on February 3, 1791—had no reservations about declaring the right to bear arms. Its Constitution of 1792 included a bill of rights with many of the now-familiar provisions of what it called "the general great and essential principles of liberty and free government," but two guarantees were said to be held by the citizens rather than the people. It declared "that the citizens have a right in a peaceable manner, to assemble together for their common good,"[97] and "that the right of the citizens to bear arms in defence of themselves and the state shall not be questioned."[98] A wholly separate article, not part of the bill of rights, provided: "The free-men of this Commonwealth shall be armed and disciplined for its defence."[99]

Founded on a Constitution tempered with a Bill of Rights, it was now time for the young republic to begin admitting more states, each one reflecting a unique history but all agreeing on certain fundamental principles. Not the least of these principles was the right to keep and bear arms. The great federal purpose of that right was to promote a well regulated militia, and to that subject Congress turned its attention.

# The Great Militia Debate

P RESIDENT GEORGE WASHINGTON admonished members of the House of Representatives in early 1790 that "a free people ought not only to be armed, but disciplined."[1] In the ensuing months, congressional debate on military legislation would shed light on contemporaneous thinking on standing armies, militia, and bearing arms both as a right and a duty. The result would be enactment of the federal Militia Act of 1792, which required every "free able bodied white male citizen" aged 18 through 45 to "provide himself with a good musket or firelock," bayonet, and ammunition.[2]

In early 1790, General Henry Knox, secretary of war, laid before the Congress a detailed militia plan. "An energetic national militia," he declared, "is to be regarded as the capital security of a free Republic; and not a standing army, forming a distinct class in the community."[3] While "all men of the legal military age should be armed" and liable for service,[4] "each individual, at his first joining the annual camps of discipline, will receive complete arms and accoutrements, all of which, previously to his being discharged from the said camps, he must return . . . ."[5]

Knox's plan was not well received. While the Senate met in secret and no debates were officially recorded, Senator William Maclay of Pennsylvania kept a diary in which he recorded that a group met "to discuss Secretary Knox's plan for regulating the militia and that, after voting their disapproval of it, they appointed a committee of seven to draft a memorial to present to the citizens, should Congress take up the plan."[6]

Sharp divisions over a military establishment had been simmering since the previous year, when Alexander Hamilton gave a July 4 speech deriding the militia as "the mimicry of soldiership."[7] Now, with Knox's plan submitted, Representative (and Judge) Aedanus Burke of South Carolina made "a Violent personal Attack on Hamilton . . . which the Men of the blade say must produce a duel."[8]

According to Maclay, supporters of an army accused the Spaniards of having "supplied the Indians with Arms and Ammunition,"[9] but argued that "it was dangerous to put Arms into the hands of the Frontier People for their defence, least they should use them against the United States."[10] Maclay protested these allegations as "subterfuges," writing:

> The Constitution certainly never contemplated a Standing Army in time of peace. A Well regulated Militia to execute the laws of the Union, quell insurrections and repel Invasions, is the very language of the Constitution. General Knox offers a most exceptionable bill for a General Militia law which excites (as it is most probable he expected) a general Opposition. Thus the Business of the Militia stands still, and the military establishment bill which increases the standing Troops One half is pushed with all the Art & address of ministerial Management.[11]

The old pro- versus anti-army factions resurfaced. Senators Oliver Ellsworth of Connecticut and Charles Carroll of Maryland declared that a "Military Establishment meant & could mean nothing short of a Standing Army." But "of all the Flamers none blazed like [Ralph] Izard [of South Carolina]. He wished for a Standing Army of 10,000 men. . . . He was well aswered by [Richard Henry] Lee. But it was in Vain."[12]

Maclay recorded on April 23, 1790: "The Military Establishment bill came up concurr'd to. Strange that not a Pennsylvanian should Object to this bill. As it now stands it flatly contradicts the Constitution of Pennsylvania both old & new."[13] Pennsylvania's 1776 Declaration of Rights stated that "as standing armies in the time of peace are dangerous to liberty, they ought not to be kept up,"[14] but the pending 1790 version declared only that no peacetime standing army be kept up "without the consent of the legislature."[15]

In the future Senator Maclay would continue to believe that Alexander Hamilton's faction was promoting war with Native Americans and foreign powers as a "Pretext for raising an Army meant to awe our Citizens into Submission."[16] But the commonplace fact of the citizenry in arms was exemplified in the July 4, 1790, celebration in New York (held a day late because it fell on a Sunday). When Congress adjourned, Maclay saw that "all the Town was in Arms . . . . the firing of cannon and small arms with beating of Drums kept all in uproar."[17] The senators went to President Washington's home for wine and cakes, and then to a reading of the Declaration of Independence.[18]

Some "Political Maxims" published in July 1790 by the *Independent Gazetteer* asserted: "A Well regulated militia is the best defence to a free people, a standing army in time of peace are not equal to a well regulated militia."[19] "Where a standing army is established, the inclinations of the people are but little regarded."[20]

While Knox's militia proposal continued to languish, on December 14, 1790, Representative Elias Boudinot of New Jersey introduced "A Bill more effectually to provide for the national Defence, by establishing a uniform Militia throughout the United States."[21] The bill's fundamental feature was that every male citizen would arm himself and participate in the militia.[22]

House debate began two days later. Congressman Josiah Parker of Virginia objected that the requirement that "every man in the United States shall 'provide himself' with military accoutrements would be found impracticable, as it must be well known that there are many persons who are so poor that it is impossible they should comply with the law."[23] He proposed that if a militiaman demonstrates to his commanding officer that he is unable to provide the arms required by law, the officer shall furnish the arms at the expense of the United States. John Vining of Delaware moved to add that the arms could be used only on militia duty and that the officer could demand the return of the arms at any time.[24]

Several members doubted that every man should be a member of the active militia, but there was a consensus that every man be armed.[25] "As far as the whole body of the people are necessary to the general defence, they ought to be armed," explained Thomas Fitzsimons of Pennsylvania.[26]

James Jackson of Georgia argued that "the people of America would never consent to be deprived of the privilege of carrying arms. Tho it may prove burdensome to some individuals to be obliged to arm themselves, yet it would not be so considered when the advantages were justly estimated." He noted some positive historical examples:

> The Swiss cantons owed their emancipation to their militia establishment— The English cities rendered themselves formidable to the Barons, by putting arms into the hands of their militia—and when the militia united with the Barons, they extorted *Magna Charta* from King John—In France we recently see the same salutary effects from arming the militia—In England, the militia has of late been neglected—the consequence is a standing army . . . . In a Republic every man ought to be a soldier, and be prepared to resist tyranny and usurpation, as well as invasion, and to prevent the greatest of all evils—a standing army.[27]

Another account of Jackson's speech quoted him as opining "that the people would never be dissatisfied with bearing arms in their own defence; this right, he observed, was one of the dearest to a freeman." He recalled "the history of the emancipation of the Swiss nation from tyrannical oppression" and "the exertions made lately by Ireland to secure that invaluable privilege of bearing arms in their own defence."[28] The latter referred to the fact that, during the American Revolution, Irish Protestants were authorized to arm themselves to defend against a French attack, which made them more powerful later in negotiations with Britian.[29]

Yet another account of Jackson's speech attributed to him the words that "the people of America would be highly displeased at being debarred the privilege of carrying arms." He urged: "'tis our duty to prepare against contingencies, and to provide the means for every man to protect himself as well against tyranny and usurpation, as against assault and invasion."[30]

These three accounts of Jackson's remarks refer to "the people" as having "the privilege of carrying arms," and as having a "right"—"one of the dearest to a freeman"—of "bearing arms in their own defence." They aver that "every man" should be a soldier, and "be prepared to resist" and have "the means . . . to protect himself" against, tyranny, usurpation, assault, and invasion. These comments suggest a broad understanding of the Second Amendment.

The debate turned to whether the federal government could be trusted with the power to provide, and hence not to provide, arms to the militia. Jeremiah Wadsworth of Connecticut opposed "the plan proposed of providing arms for the militia at the expence of the United States, and especially against giving the general government a power of disarming part of the militia, by ordering the arms and accoutrements by them lent, to be returned."[31] Representative Jackson also opposed the proposal:

> by the constitution, the general government was only authorised to fix the manner of providing accoutrements, &c. and not to furnish them; which would be improper, as they would then have the power of disarming the militia. Every man in the country had his gun, and if provision was made to furnish the militia with arms, it would, he conceived, be an unequal provision merely to favour the city residents.[32]

James Madison spoke against the amendment, noting that "if the militia from the different states presented themselves completely equipped for the service of the United States, it would not be asked where they got their arms, which, without impropriety, could be furnished by the states."[33]

Roger Sherman of Connecticut analyzed the militia clause in Article I, Section 8, of the Constitution in the same manner he had heard it explained in the Philadelphia convention of 1787:

> He believed it to have been the intention of the Convention, who put this article into the constitution, that the United States were to be put to no expence about the militia, except when they were called forth into the actual service of the union. . . . That relates to arming and disciplining them, means nothing more than providing, by a general regulation, the nature and uniformity of the arms, which ought to be of one calibre.

> Upon the whole, he thought there were so few free men in the United States incapable of procuring themselves a musquet, bayonet and cartouchbox, as to render any regulation by the general government respecting them improper. If the people were left to themselves, he was pretty certain the necessary warlike implements would be provided without inconvenience or complaint, whereas if they were furnished by Congress, the public arsenals would be speedily drained, & from the careless manner in which many persons are disposed to treat such public property, he apprehended they would be speedily lost or destroyed.[34]

Sherman's recollection about the 1787 convention was accurate. In response to remarks by Sherman himself, Rufus King had explained about the

Constitution's militia clause that "by *organising*, the committee meant, proportioning the officers and men—by *arming*, specifying the kind, size, and calibre of arms—and by *disciplining*, prescribing the manual exercise, evolutions, &c." Madison had added that "the '*arming*' . . . did not extend to furnishing arms."[35]

Back to the 1790 debate, Representative Wadsworth warned that supporters of the federal arming proposal seemed to be suggesting that large segments of the population would be armed by the government, with the attendant dangers:

> At first it appeared to be intended for the benefit of poor men who were unable to spare money enough to purchase a firelock: but the gentleman from Delaware (Mr. Vining) had mentioned apprentices and young men in their non-age: he would be glad to know whether there was a man within these walls, who wished to have so large a proportion of the community armed by the United States, and liable to be disarmed by the government, whenever it should be thought proper.[36]

Masters could be expected to furnish arms to their apprentices. As to other young men, "their parents would rather give them guns of their own, than let them take others from the U.S. which were liable to be taken away at the very moment they were most wanted."

A vote was then taken, and Parker's motion to arm the poor at federal expense failed.

Representative Fitzsimons moved to strike the words "provide himself" and amend the bill to read that every citizen "shall be provided" with arms.[37] Congressman Jackson opposed the amendment:

> He believed most of the citizens of America possessed and used guns. In Georgia and in the back country they were useful to procure food, and were to be met with in every House. He had no doubt but the people would supply themselves fully, without the interference of the Legislature . . . .[38]

Boudinot, Madison, and others also opposed the amendment, objecting that it "would leave it optional with the States, or individuals, whether the militia shall be armed or not."[39] Fitzsimons' motion "was lost by a considerable majority."[40]

Debate ensued about persons who may be exempted from militia exercises. Under the Constitution, Hugh Williamson of North Carolina noted, "Congress are to provide for arming and disciplining the militia; but who are the militia? Such men, he presumed, as are declared so to be by the laws of the particular States, and on this principle he was led to suppose that the militia ought to consist of the whole body of citizens without exception."[41]

Regarding classes to be exempt from militia duty, Madison felt that members of Congress "ought ever to bear a share of the burthens they lay on others, in order that their acts may not slide into an abuse of the power vested in them."[42] Jackson opined that anyone objecting to militia duty should pay an equivalent, for "bearing arms was one of the most important duties we owe to society. One great object men have in view, by forming themselves into a state of civil society, is to protect their persons and property; to afford this protection it is necessary . . . that every one either give his personal assistance, or pay an equivalent for it."[43]

As noted above, Jackson had previously offered remarks emphasizing the individual right of persons to bear arms against tyranny and assault. Roger Sherman now made comments equally significant about the meaning of the Second Amendment as follows:

> [E]very power still remained in the people and the state governments, except what had been given up to the United States by the new constitution. The house was not about to relinquish to the state governments any part of its power; but merely to acknowledge a power, that remained in the state legislatures. He asked, if gentlemen imagined, that the state governments had given out of their hands the command of the militia, or the right of declaring who should bear arms? He conceived it to be the privilege of every citizen, and one of his most essential rights, to bear arms, and to resist every attack upon his liberty or property, by whomsoever made. The particular states, like private citizens, have a right to be armed, and to defend, by force of arms, their rights, when invaded.[44]

This is a significant statement about the right to bear arms as perceived by the Framers. While the states retained the power to declare "who should bear arms" in the militia, one of the "most essential rights" of "every citizen" is to bear arms and to resist attack on his liberty or property from any source.

Like "private citizens," the states too were entitled to be armed and to defend themselves.

Jackson reinforced Sherman's sentiments with his further comment "that every citizen was not only entitled to carry arms, but also is duty bound to perfect himself in the use of them, and thus become capable of defending his country." Moreover, its decentralization meant that "the militia of the United States can never be such an unwieldy machine . . . except they should be all assembled together—a case never likely to happen." There was no valid argument "that the whole body of the people ought not to be armed, and properly trained."[45]

While bearing arms individually was a right and bearing arms in the militia was a duty, the latter may still entail voluntary participation. Fisher Ames of Massachusetts discussed "the several independent companies in Massachusetts, particularly that known by the name of the Ancient and Honourable Artillery . . . . This, with other independent companies, rendered essential services in the time of the insurrection in that state; and they prove, by their example, a stimulus to the militia—they have incurred great expences to equip themselves . . . ."[46] The Ancient and Honorable Artillery Company still exists today.[47]

John Laurance of New York defined the militia as "every man in the states who is capable of performing military duty, though not actually enrolled in any particular body," noting that "when the constitution was framed, some states were as yet unprovided with militia laws." Accordingly, "the militia must mean all persons without exception, who are capable of bearing arms in defence of their country . . . ."[48] He argued that if conscientious objectors were to be exempted, it must be by state law, not the federal enactment—the view that would prevail.[49]

The Militia Act slowly worked its way through both houses of Congress—unfortunately, no Senate debate was recorded—and was signed by President Washington on May 8, 1792.[50] The act began by defining who constituted the militia:

> That each and every free able-bodied white male citizen of the respective states, resident therein, who is or shall be of the age of eighteen years, and under the age of forty-five years (except as is herein after excepted) shall severally and respectively be enrolled in the militia by the captain or commanding officer of

the company, within whose bounds such citizen shall reside, and that within twelve months after the passing of this act.[51]

Only narrow classes were excused from militia duty. Exempted classes included the vice president (but not the president, who was the commander in chief of the militia when federalized), federal judicial and executive officers, members of Congress, customs officers, post officers, and certain classes essential to certain types of water transportation. The states could exempt other classes.[52]

The act provided that each militiaman must provide himself with arms, ammunition, and accouterments as follows:

> That every citizen so enrolled and notified, shall, within six months thereafter, provide himself with a good musket or firelock, a sufficient bayonet and belt, two spare flints, and a knapsack, a pouch with a box therein to contain not less than twenty-four cartridges, suited to the bore of his musket or firelock, each cartridge to contain a proper quantity of powder and ball: or with a good rifle, knapsack, shot-pouch and powder-horn, twenty balls suited to the bore of his rifle and a quarter of a pound of powder; and shall appear, so armed, accoutred and provided, when called out to exercise, or into service . . . .[53]

There is no mistaking the act's above language that "every citizen so enrolled . . . shall . . . provide himself with a good musket or firelock." Over two centuries later, a revisionist history purported to quote the act as having read that "every citizen so enrolled, shall . . . be constantly provided with a good musket or firelock," and then asserted that "Congress took upon itself the responsibility of providing those guns."[54] Neither statement was true.

In his 1828 dictionary, Noah Webster—who had been a leading federalist pamphleteer (see Chapter 8)—defined "musket" as "a species of fire-arms used in war, and fired by means of a lighted match." That ignition system was obsolete, but the phrase "in common speech, is yet applied to fusees or firelocks fired by a spring lock."[55] A "firelock" was defined as "a musket, or other gun, with a lock, which is discharged by striking fire with flint and steel."[56] A "fusee" was "a small neat musket or firelock."[57] The rifle was the most accurate arm, which Webster defined as "a gun about the usual length and size of a musket, the inside of whose barrel is *rifled*, that is, grooved, or formed with spiral channels."[58]

The above provision required about ammunition that only the ball (bullet) fit the arm an individual militiaman possessed. But the act further mandated that "from and after five years from the passing of this act, all muskets for arming the militia as herein required, shall be of bores sufficient for balls of the eighteenth-part of a pound."[59] A common bore for all muskets would make the ammunition interchangeable throughout the militia.

The act provided that "the commissioned officer shall severally be armed with a sword or hanger and espontoon" (a half pike),[60] but that such officers in troops of horse must furnish themselves with the horse—at least fourteen and a half hands high—and "be armed with a sword and pair of pistols, the holsters of which to be covered with bearskin caps." Dragoons must also be armed with a pair of pistols along with a saber.[61]

A militiaman's arms and equipment enjoyed a privileged status as personal property: "every citizen so enrolled, and providing himself with the arms, ammunition and accoutrements required as aforesaid, shall hold the same exempted from all suits, distresses, executions or sales, for debt or for the payment of taxes."[62]

The militia of each state, except when called into federal service, would serve under the commander-in-chief of the state—that is, the governor—who would appoint an adjutant general to see that the state militia was organized and effective. Militiamen, "during the time of their being under arms," were subject to having their arms and equipment inspected to ensure compliance with the requirements, and officers of different corps in the state would report "the actual situation of their arms" and equipment to the adjutant general.[63] Since inspection of arms took place only when the militiaman was on duty and extended only to the required arms, the act was not a precedent for a registration system in which authorities kept records on all arms owned by the citizens.

A unity of purpose and activity existed between the militia system and the keeping and bearing of arms for lawful purposes. New York politician and physician Samuel Latham Mitchill, in an address the year after passage of the Militia Act, noted that the militia "proceeds upon the principle, that they who are able to govern, are also capable of defending themselves. The keeping of arms, is therefore, not only not prohibited, but is positively provided for by law . . . ." "These weapons serve for the defence of the life and property of the individual against the violent or burglarious attacks of thieves, a description of persons happily very small among us." Besides being ready to suppress insurrection and invasion, "the bearer, unfettered by oppressive game and forest laws, and without the restraint of a licence may amuse himself with hunting and fowling when he pleases. These are great privileges, . . . and misery may be expected to follow with hasty strides any attempt to deprive you of them."[64]

The Militia Act remained on the books for over a century. After the Civil War, the term "white" was deleted from the reference to every "free able bodied white male citizen" so as to make the now-freed African Americans liable for militia service.[65] The act itself, with its requirement that every male citizen provide himself with a firearm, was not repealed until 1903.[66] But the new enactment continued to define the militia as "every able-bodied male citizen of the respective States," although it divided it between the "organized militia" (National Guard) and the "Reserve Militia."[67] But that is another story.[68]

## CHAPTER 15

# Old Founders Never Die, They Just Fade Away

H AVING ADOPTED the Constitution and Bill of Rights, the Founding generation proceeded to build the American republic. At different times and for different purposes, those who had been instrumental in bringing on the great experiment in government had occasion to comment on its fundamental principles. The following sets forth some of their later reflections that are pertinent to the Second Amendment.

When Thomas Jefferson was elected as president of the United States in 1801, students from the College of William and Mary celebrated with a glass of wine at the house of their acclaimed professor, Judge St. George Tucker.[1] Tucker was already at work writing what would be the first and foremost treatise on the Constitution and Bill of Rights. Published in 1803, the work included the English jurist Blackstone's *Commentaries* along with Tucker's reflections on the American system.[2]

During the Revolution, Tucker had smuggled in arms from the West Indies at the behest of Governor Patrick Henry, and as a militia colonel he had led campaigns against British forces.[3] After the war, Tucker rode the circuit as a judge and was eventually appointed to the Virginia Supreme Court. In 1813, he was appointed by President James Madison as a federal judge.[4]

Tucker's observations in Blackstone's *Commentaries* highlighted the improvements of the American over the English constitution in the expansion of individual rights. The English Declaration of Rights of 1689, for instance, provided: "That the Subjects which are Protestants, may have Arms for their Defence suitable to their Condition, and as are allowed by Law." To this Tucker posited the Second Amendment: "The right of the people to keep and bear arms shall not be infringed . . . and this without any qualification as to their condition or degree, as is the case in the British government . . . ."[5]

In his constitutional treatise, which appeared as an appendix to the *Commentaries*, Tucker expanded on the differences between the English and American concepts of the right to arms. Quoting the Second Amendment, he wrote:

> This may be considered as the true palladium of liberty . . . . The right of self defence is the first law of nature: in most governments it has been the study of rulers to confine this right within the narrowest limits possible. Wherever standing armies are kept up, and the right of the people to keep and bear arms is, under any colour or pretext whatsoever, prohibited, liberty, if not already annihilated, is on the brink of destruction. In England, the people have been disarmed, generally, under the specious pretext of preserving the game: a never failing lure to bring over the landed aristocracy to support any measure, under that mask, though calculated for very different purposes. True it is, their bill of rights seems at first view to counteract this policy: but the right of bearing arms is confined to protestants, and the words suitable to their condition and degree, have been interpreted to authorise the prohibition of keeping a gun or other engine for the destruction of game, to any farmer, or inferior tradesman, or other person not qualified to kill game. So that not one man in five hundred can keep a gun in his house without being subject to a penalty.[6]

Similar criticisms of the English game laws, which prohibited commoners from hunting, were made by supporters of recognition of the right to bear arms. While such game laws may well have been enforced in a manner to prevent subjects from keeping guns, English judicial precedents actually held that the people at large could keep arms at home and that guns could be seized only when actually being used contrary to the hunting prohibitions.[7] In any event, the above is consistent with the view that the Second Amendment protects the individual right to bear arms and to use them for self-defense—"the first law of nature." A form of infringement of the right was the disarming of civilians under the guise of the game laws. The militia was not mentioned in the above context.

Tucker was an early exponent of the power of the judiciary to declare laws unconstitutional, a doctrine that the Supreme Court under Chief Justice John Marshall would later rule to be the cornerstone of judicial review. Tucker wrote:

> If, for example, a law be passed by congress, prohibiting the free exercise of religion, according to the dictates, or persuasions of a man's own conscience; or abridging the freedom of speech, or of the press; or the right of the people to assemble peaceably, or to keep and bear arms; it would, in any of these cases be the province of the judiciary to pronounce whether any such act were constitutional, or not; and if not, to acquit the accused from any penalty which might be annexed to the breach of such unconstitutional act. . . . The judiciary, therefore, is that department of the government to whom the protection of the rights of the individual is by the constitution especially confided, interposing its shield between him and the sword of usurped authority, the darts of oppression, and the shafts of faction and violence.[8]

The right to have arms, under the above view, was on a par with freedom of religion, speech, and assembly, and abridgment of any of these rights should be declared unconstitutional. The judiciary had a special responsibility to protect these "rights of the individual."

Judicial review was particularly applicable to laws purportedly passed not under an enumerated power, but under the "necessary and proper" clause, and which violated Bill of Rights guarantees. A court may declare a federal criminal law unconstitutional in that circumstance:

> If, for example, congress were to pass a law prohibiting any person from bearing arms, as a means of preventing insurrections, the judicial courts, under the construction of the words necessary and proper, here contended for, would be able to pronounce decidedly upon the constitutionality of these means. But if congress may use any means, which they choose to adopt, the provision in the constitution which secures to the people the right of bearing arms, is a mere nullity; and any man imprisoned for bearing arms under such an act, might

be without relief; because in that case, no court could have any power to pronounce on the necessity or propriety of the means adopted by congress to carry
any specified power into complete effect.[9]

Tucker was even more specific in explaining how the British Parliament
would violate basic rights in the guise of some necessary objective, but that
Congress had no such power. He reiterated that in England the game laws
"have been converted into the means of disarming the body of the people,"
and that "the acts directing the mode of petitioning parliament, and those for
prohibiting riots: and for suppressing assemblies of free-masons, are so many
ways for preventing public meetings of the people to deliberate upon the public, or national concerns." By contrast, Congress had "no power to regulate,
or interfere with the domestic concerns, or police of any state," "nor will the
constitution permit any prohibition of arms to the people; or of peaceable assemblies by them, for the purposes whatsoever, and in any number, whenever
they may see occasion."[10]

Regarding the law of treason in England, Sir Mathew Hale's *Pleas of the
Crown* observed that "the very use of weapons by such an assembly, without
the king's licence, unless in some lawful and special cases, carries a terror with
it, and a presumption of warlike force, &c." Tucker commented that "the bare
circumstance of having arms, therefore, of itself, creates a presumption of warlike force in England, and may be given in evidence there, to prove quo animo
the people are assembled." Tucker asked:

> But ought that circumstance of itself, to create any such presumption in Amer-
> ica, where the right to bear arms is recognised and secured in the constitution
> itself? In many parts of the United States, a man no more thinks, of going out
> of his house on any occasion, without his rifle or musket in his hand, than an
> European fine gentleman without his sword by his side.[11]

Tucker synthesized the Founders' aspirations in favor of a declaration of
rights that was more than a scrap of paper. By contrast, Alexander Hamilton
had never put much stock in a bill of rights. Indeed, some of his controversial
positions suggested lack of concern for individual rights—from his endorse-
ment of monarchy and abolition of the states at the constitutional convention
in 1787[12] and his denunciation of a bill of rights in *The Federalist* No. 84,[13]

to his support as treasury secretary in the Washington administration for a centralized government with few bounds. Yet he never doubted the principles behind the Second Amendment. In a seditious libel prosecution in 1803–1804, Hamilton asserted: "Never can tyranny be introduced into this country by arms . . . . The spirit of the country with arms in their hands, and disciplined as a militia, would render it impossible."[14]

As fate would have it, Hamilton would participate in a practice that involved arms, but that had no continence under the Second Amendment and was denounced by many of the Founders—dueling. On July 11, 1804, his pistol was still pointed upward when it discharged first and prematurely, while the pistol of Aaron Burr—vice president of the United States—found its deadly mark. Popular myth suggested that the virtuous Hamilton intentionally fired high to miss Burr. However, unbeknownst to Burr, Hamilton had chosen pistols with hair triggers that allowed a more accurate shot but that Hamilton pulled too soon—perhaps inadvertently. In an era when the gentlemanly object was to satisfy honor by shooting without hitting either opponent, Hamilton's choice would have been considered by some as cheating.[15]

John Adams described Hamilton as the "most restless, impatient, artful, indefatigable and unprincipled intriguer in the United States."[16] Thomas Jefferson said of Burr, "I never indeed thought him an honest, frank-dealing man, but considered him as a crooked gun, or other perverted machine, whose aim or stroke you could never be sure of."[17]

Tench Coxe had been one of Hamilton's federalist colleagues in the old days of 1787–1788, arguing that a constitution without a bill of rights was fine in that the people were armed and could protect their rights. But with Madison he broke ranks with the die-hard, anti-bill of rights faction and supported the great compromise of adding a declaration of individual liberties. When Madison introduced his bill in Congress, Coxe explained that under what became the Second Amendment, "the people are confirmed . . . in their right to keep and bear their private arms."[18]

Coxe would serve in the Washington, Adams, and Jefferson administrations, but his ultimate loyalty was to the Jeffersonian Republican Party, the purer supporter of individual rights and limited government. As late as 1823, Coxe found himself still writing newspaper articles on the right to keep and bear arms, this time on behalf of the Republican Party against the presidential campaign of John Quincy Adams.[19] Coxe referred to "the right to own and use arms and consequently of self-defence and of the public militia power . . . ."[20]

Decrying the English game laws, which were intended to disarm the populace, Coxe wrote that "his own firearms are the second and better right hand of every freeman . . . ."[21] He made the following perceptive observation that having arms is sometimes a duty, but is ever a right:

> So prudent, faithful and provident have our people and constitutions been, that we find in their precious bills of rights, schedules of duties, reasons of powers, and declarations recognising the right to own, keep and use arms, provisions preventing and forbidding the legislatures to interfere with and to abrogate, that all important right of the citizens.[22]

Coxe sought to show that John Adams and his son John Quincy had monarchial tendencies and supported standing armies. Such exaggerated arguments were made in the heat of a campaign for the election of the president. John Quincy Adams won the race and took office in 1824, a few months after which Coxe died.

John Adams proved his bona fides as a supporter of an armed populace at the same time that Coxe had doubted them. In 1823, William H. Sumner published *The Importance of the Militia to a Free Commonwealth*, which was addressed to and endorsed by Adams. Sumner wrote that the United States would be a target for invasion "if its population, like that of Europe, chiefly consisted of an unarmed peasantry, and its whole reliance was on its regular army, one pitched battle would decide its fate. But a country of well trained militia-men is not conquered when its army is beaten . . . . Here, every house is a castle, and every man is a soldier. Arms are in every hand."[23]

Sumner contended that "it is better that the arms should be kept by the men themselves, at their own dwellings, than in the public arsenals. They thus learn to take care of them, at least; and as opportunities for hunting and practical shooting offer, they improve as marksmen." Given the growth of settlements and clearing of forests, "drilling becomes necessary as a substitute for that habitual exercise of shooting at game, which has obtained for Americans the reputation of being the best riflemen in the world."[24]

"Your manuscript dissertation concerning the militia," wrote John Adams in a postscript to Sumner's pamphlet, "is so conformable to all my opinions con-

cerning it from my cradle, that it seemed to be living my life over again . . . ."
Adams continued:

> The American states have owed their existence to the militia for more than
> two hundred years. Neither schools, nor colleges, nor town meetings have been
> more essential to the formation and character of the nation than the militia .
> . . . Impose its constitution by every prudent means, but never destroy its uni-
> versality. A select militia will soon become a standing army . . . . Whenever the
> militia comes to an end, or is despised or neglected, I shall consider this union
> dissolved, and the liberties of North America lost forever.[25]

Those were strong words for the conservative Adams, but together with
Sumner's reflections they represent the significance of the Second Amendment's
principles over three decades after ratification of the Bill of Rights.

Congregationalist minister Timothy Dwight, who had been a chaplain in
the Continental army during the Revolution and served as president of Yale
College from 1795 to 1817, synthesized American concepts of arms possession
as a right and a duty in his 1821 commentary of American life and institutions as follows:

> In both New-England, and New-York, every man is permitted, and in some,
> if not all the States, is required to possess fire arms. To trust arms in the hands
> of the people at large has, in Europe, been believed . . . to be an experiment,
> fraught only with danger. Here by a long trial it has been proved to be perfectly
> harmless: neither public nor private evils having ever flowed from this source,
> except in instances of too little moment to deserve any serious regard.[26]

Under a just government and with proper education, Dwight continued,
"few men will be disposed to use arms, unless for their amusement, and for
the defence of themselves and their country. The difficulty, here, has been to
persuade the citizens to keep arms; not to prevent them from being employed
for violent purposes."[27]

Thomas Jefferson remains perhaps the most interesting of the Founders as
an owner of firearms and advocate of the Second Amendment. "One loves to
possess arms, though they hope never to have occasion for them," he wrote to
George Washington on June 19, 1796.[28] Washington himself owned perhaps
fifty firearms during his life, and some of his pistols (typically silver mounted),

saddle holsters, and fowlers (shotguns) may be seen today at Mt. Vernon and West Point. His diaries contain numerous entries related to the acquisition of firearms and to "ducking" and other hunting activities.[29]

Not long after the Revolutionary War ended, Washington and his servant Billy were riding on horseback from Mount Vernon to Alexandria. The main road was impassable, so the two had to ride through the farm of a man described as "a desperado who had committed murder." The account goes as follows:

> As was then the custom, the General had holsters, with pistols in them, to his saddle. On returning to Mount Vernon, as General Washington was about to enter on this private road, a stranger on horseback barred the way, and said to him, "You shall not pass this way." "You don't know me," said the General. "Yes, I do," said the ruffian; "you are General Washington, who commanded the army in the Revolution, and if you attempt to pass me I shall shoot you." General Washington called his servant, Billy, to him, and taking out a pistol, examined the priming, and then handed it to Billy, saying, "If this person shoots me, do you shoot him;" and cooly passed on without molestation.[30]

In 1791, the year the Bill of Rights was ratified, Washington obtained a Pennsylvania long rifle.[31] Washington's last will and testament included the following: "To General de la Fayette I give a pair of finely wrought steel pistols, taken from the enemy in the Revolutionary war."[32] Washington died in 1799, and the inventory of his estate lists seven swords and seven guns in the study, "1 pr Steel Pistols" and "3 pr Pistols" in an iron chest, "1 Old Gun" in the storehouse, and one gun at the River Farm.[33]

Patrick Henry died a few months earlier, also in 1799, and the inventory of his estate includes "1 large Gun" and "1 pr. pistols."[34]

Washington, of course, had signed the Militia Act of 1792, which required every male citizen to have a firearm. As president, Jefferson reiterated the value of a militia consisting of armed citizens. "Uncertain as we must ever be of the particular point in our circumference where an enemy may choose to invade us," he stated in his First Annual Message on December 8, 1801, "the only force which can be ready at every point and competent to oppose them, is the body of neighbouring citizens as formed into a militia."[35]

"None but an armed nation can dispense with a standing army," Jefferson wrote in 1803. "To keep ours armed and disciplined is therefore at all times important."[36] And in his Eighth Annual Message, on November 8, 1808, Jefferson exhorted:

> For a people who are free, and who mean to remain so, a well-organised and armed militia is their best security. It is, therefore, incumbent on us, at every meeting, to revise the condition of the militia, and to ask ourselves if it is prepared to repel a powerful enemy at every point of our territories exposed to invasion.[37]

"I learn with great concern that [one] portion of our frontier so interesting, so important, and so exposed, should be so entirely unprovided with common fire-arms," Jefferson wrote to Jacob J. Brown that same year. "I did not suppose any part of the United States so destitute of what is considered as among the first necessaries of a farm-house."[38] That suggests how universal firearm ownership was perceived to be and how surprising it was that a particular frontier community was not well armed.

In retirement at Monticello, Jefferson again had ample time for hunting, and he was a true sportsman. His servant Isaac recalled:

> Mr. Jefferson used to hunt squirrels and partridges; kept five or six guns. Oftentimes carred Isaac wid him. Old Master wouldn't shoot partridges settin'. Said "he wouldn't take advantage of 'em"—would give 'em a chance for thar life. Wouldn't shoot a hare settin', nuther; skeer him up fust.[39]

Jefferson acquired arms in the same manner as he sought learned books and fine wines. His memorandum books kept between 1768 and 1823 show numerous references to the acquisition of pistols, guns, muskets, rifles, fusils, gun locks, and other gun parts; the repair of firearms; and the acquisition of shot, gunpowder, powder flasks, and cartridge boxes.[40] Included were a pair of "Turkish pistols . . . so well made that I never missed a squirrel at 30 yds. with them." He presented them to Payne Todd, Dolley Madison's son, in 1816.[41]

A nation of hunters who kept arms contributed to the militia so necessary to a free state. The forces of a tyrant could never prevail in the United States, Jefferson wrote to A. L. C. Destutt de Tracy in a January 26, 1811, letter. Should such forces conquer one state, there were then sixteen other states spread over a great country, and they would "rise up on every side, ready organised for deliberation by a constitutional legislature, and for action by their governor, constitutionally the commander of the militia of the State, that is to say, of every man in it able to bear arms . . . ." That militia would be organized into regiments and battalions, and would be "always in readiness."[42]

In an 1822 letter, Jefferson wrote to Peter Minor that he was sending him a keepsake, "an article of the tackle of a gunman, offering the convenience of carrying the powder & shot together." "Every American who wishes to protect his farm from the ravages of quadrupeds & his country from those of biped invaders" ought to be a gunman. "I am a great friend to the manly and healthy exercises of the gun."[43]

But it was a letter written toward the end of his life that Jefferson best expressed the interrelated principles of the First and Second Amendments, and the higher law that is the foundation of such rights, in language reminiscent of the Declaration of Independence. In a June 5, 1824, missive to English Whig Major John Cartwright, Jefferson wrote that the American Revolution "presented us an album on which we were free to write what we pleased," excluding royal parchments but appealing "to those of nature" that were "engraved on our hearts." Jefferson continued about some of its "important principles: The constitutions of most of our States assert, that all power is inherent in the people; that they may exercise it by themselves, in all cases to which they think themselves competent, . . . that it is their right and duty to be at all times armed; that they are entitled to freedom of person, freedom of religion, freedom of property, and freedom of the press."[44]

Jefferson continued by denying that "one generation [can] bind another, and all others, in succession forever," for "the Creator has made the earth for the living, not the dead. Rights and powers can only belong to persons . . . ." But he concluded with an absolute: "Nothing then is unchangeable but the inherent and unalienable rights of man."[45] As to the above-referenced people's "right and duty to be at all times armed," this meant that the duty could be changed by the majority but that the right was inherent and unalienable.

Thomas Jefferson and John Adams both died on July 4, 1826, exactly fifty years after the signing of the Declaration of Independence. The Founders' generation had faded, but their principles endured.

No firearms were listed in Jefferson's will or the inventories of his estates.[46] Perhaps he had passed on this part of his legacy to the living before his death.

James Madison held on until 1836. He was the sole survivor of the Virginia convention of 1776 and the Philadelphia convention of 1787.[47] Writing at some point in the period 1831–1836, Madison penned some reflections on the 1829 Virginia constitutional convention. Madison's following words best captured the reasons for the Constitution and Bill of Rights, which he himself had drafted: "A Government resting on a minority, is an aristocracy not a Republic, and could not be safe with a numerical [and] physical force against it, without a standing Army, an enslaved press, and a disarmed populace."[48]

# Conclusion

## CHAPTER 16

# What Does the Second Amendment Say?

"A WELL REGULATED MILITIA, being necessary to the security of a free State," declares the Second Amendment, "the right of the people to keep and bear Arms, shall not be infringed." The previous chapters have concerned the historical context facing the Founding generation, which culminated in the adoption of the amendment as part of the Bill of Rights. With those experiences as a backdrop, the focus of this conclusion is: What does the Second Amendment's text actually say?

### THE RIGHT OF THE PEOPLE

The Second Amendment begins with a clause declaring a political principle about the militia, followed by a clause declaring a substantive right. The substantive guarantee is "the right of the people," which can mean only individual rights, not state powers. The term "the people" is in juxtaposition to the government, federal or state. Only individuals have "rights," while the United States and the states have "powers." Historically, all able-bodied males constituted the "militia," but "the people" is broader than the militia. The phrase "the right of the people" appears in the First Amendment—"Congress shall make no law . . . abridging the freedom of speech, or of the press; or *the right of the people* peaceably to assemble, and to petition the government for a redress of grievances." This is an individual right, even if assembly is regarded as a "collective" activity.[1]

"The people" who assemble and petition consist of individuals, or even a single individual, doing so freely and not under government auspices or compulsion. This has no parallel with the "collective right" view of the Second Amendment which would limit the "right" to bear arms to such persons who are selected and possibly conscripted by government for militia duty.

After the Second Amendment's reference to *"the right of the people* to keep and bear arms," the Fourth Amendment guarantees: *"The right of the people* to be secure in their persons, houses, papers, and effects, against unreasonable searches and seizures, shall not be violated . . . ."

This description of "the people" as having "persons, houses, papers and effects" is instructive. These are the same "persons" whose "papers and effects" include printed matter and arms that they keep in their "houses" and bear or carry outside the home. In light of the Crown's abuses, the Fourth Amendment was intended to play a key role in protection of First and Second Amendment rights.

The Ninth Amendment uses the same phraseology, only in the plural rather than the singular: "The enumeration in the Constitution, of certain *rights,* shall not be construed to deny or disparage others retained by *the people."* All four of these Bill of Rights guarantees protect individuals from government action; none of them delegate or reserve powers to governmental bodies.

The term "the right" also appears in reference to a subclass of private individuals constituting less than "the people" at large. The Sixth Amendment provides that "in all criminal prosecutions, the accused shall enjoy *the right* to a speedy and public trial, by an impartial jury . . . ." The Seventh Amendment states in part: "In suits at common law, where the value in controversy shall exceed twenty dollars, *the right* of trial by jury shall be preserved . . . ." In every instance where it is used, the term "right" is a guarantee to individuals against governmental action.

The original Constitution contained but a single use of the term "right," and it referred not to a preexisting right, but to a statutory right of private persons. Congress has power to secure "to Authors and Inventors the exclusive Right to their respective Writings and Discoveries . . . ."[2] By contrast, the term "power" consistently appears in the text in reference to what the United States or the States may or may not do.

Similarly, the original text of the Constitution contained no reference to "the people" standing alone. There is a single reference to the members of the House of Representatives being "chosen every second Year by the People of the several States," but this is qualified by the additional clause that "the Electors in each State shall have the Qualifications requisite for Electors of the most numerous Branch of the State Legislature." That meant the voters rather than the people at large.[3]

The meaning of the Constitution's terminology may be gleaned in the first comprehensive English dictionary compiled by an American, which was accomplished by none other than the prominent federalist Noah Webster. In his preliminary work *A Compendious Dictionary of the English Language* (1806), Webster defined "people" as "persons in general."[4] Webster's *An American Dictionary of the English Language* (1828) was adopted as the standard by Congress and the American people and became the accepted norm even in England.[5] Webster there defined "the people" as "the commonalty, as distinct from men of rank."[6]

The constitutional text also clearly distinguishes between "the people" and "the militia." The Second Amendment itself refers to "a well regulated militia" as being necessary for a free state's security, while the right to keep and bear arms is guaranteed to "the people," not just to the militia. Nor does the text use "the people" and "the State" synonymously, as the Tenth Amendment attests in referring to powers "reserved to the states respectively, or to the people."

In the constitutional lexicon, only "the people" have "rights," while governments have "powers." Webster defined "right" in pertinent part:

> Just claim; immunity; privilege. All men have a *right* to the secure enjoyment
> of life, personal safety, liberty and property. We deem the *right* of trial by jury
> invaluable, particularly in the case of crimes. *Rights* are natural, civil, political,
> religious, personal, and public.[7]

Although the term "States' rights" came into use in the early republic, the constitutional text eschews that usage. As the above demonstrates, "the people" means individuals, and only individuals have "rights."

The term "the" used twice in the phrase "*the* right of *the* people" is significant. The term "the right" expresses a preexisting right, not a new right invented for the Bill of Rights. To declare that "the right" to do or be free of something shall not be abridged, infringed, or violated presupposes that the right already exists. Further, the term "the right" cannot mean a governmental command, such as that a person is compelled to assemble and to petition or to bear arms.

Similarly, "the people" refers to the populace at large. It does not mean "some of the people appointed by the States," similar to the Militia Clause of the Constitution, which reserves to the states respectively "the Appointment of the Officers." Nor does it mean a specifically identified group of people, such as the people "in the Militia, when in actual service," as in the Fifth Amendment, or "the accused," as in the Sixth Amendment.

It would be rather curious if "the people" means only such persons as the government selects. To suggest that "the right of the people" means only a command issued by a government to persons appointed by the government demeans the very nature of a bill of rights.


### TO KEEP AND BEAR ARMS

The Second Amendment refers to the right to "keep" arms as well as to "bear" arms. Webster defined "keep" in part as:

> 1. To hold; to retain in one's power or possession; not to lose or part with; as, to *keep* a house or a farm . . . .
>
> 2. To have in custody for security or preservation. . . .
>
> 3. To preserve; to retain.[8]

Webster's following further definition seems particularly apropos to the right to keep arms: "To have in the house . . . ."[9]

As is clear, the right to "keep" arms is a liberty an individual would exercise. This is borne out by Samuel Adams' proposal in the Massachusetts convention "that the said Constitution be never construed to authorise Congress . . . to prevent the people of the United States, who are peaceable citizens, from keeping their own arms . . . ."[10]

In addition to the non-peaceable persons referenced above, another class of individuals was in fact deprived of the right to "keep" arms. St. George Tucker, writing in 1796, noted that under a 1748 law, slaves were "prohibited from keeping or carrying any gun, powder, shot, club, or other weapon offensive or defensive . . . ."[11] Having no right to keep arms was the mark of a slave.

Where state-owned arms were stored in a public arsenal, the term "deposit" rather than "keep" was ordinarily used. For instance, a 1789 Georgia act on "Indian Violences" concerned the discharge of troops and "collecting and se-curing the public arms," and provided that on a certain date "the troops shall deposit their arms in the public storehouse."[12]

The term "bear," according to Noah Webster, meant "to carry" or "to wear; to bear as a mark of authority or distinction; as, to *bear* a sword, a badge, a name; to *bear* arms in a coat."[13] Only a civilian would "bear arms in a coat"— ordinary soldiers carried muskets in their hands, while officers with pairs of pistols carried them in holsters.[14]

The phrase "to bear arms in a coat" does not mean to carry a weapon, sug-gests historian Garry Wills, for that reading "does not recognize the term 'coat of arms,' a decidedly military form of heraldry presided over by the College of Arms . . . ."[15] Yet saying "bear arms *in* a coat" would be a strange way of mean-ing "to bear a coat of arms."[16] The College of Arms, the historical agency of the British monarchy that officially approves coats of arms, does not use the Queen's English in this manner.[17]

Consistent with the meaning of "bear arms" as carrying weapons on the person, Webster defined "pistol" as "a small fire-arm, or the smallest fire-arm used . . . . Small pistols are carried in the pocket."[18] An arms historian notes: "Among eighteenth-century civilians who traveled or lived in large cities, pis-tols were common weapons. Usually they were made to fit into pockets, and many of these small arms were also carried by military officers."[19]

Slaves were deprived of the right to bear arms. St. George Tucker wrote about restrictions on slaves: "Let no Negroe or mulattoe be capable . . . of keeping, or bearing arms . . . ."[20]

The term "bear arms" was used to describe an activity that "the people" had a right to do as well as prohibited conduct when engaged in by slaves. Persons in military forces also carried arms, but to "bear arms" meant no more than to carry them and had no exclusive military usage.

It has been argued that "bear arms" is an exclusively military usage, and that "keep" has no independent meaning, for "'keep and bear' appears to have been understood as a unitary phrase, like 'cruel and unusual' or 'necessary and proper.'"[21] Yet all of these words have different meanings. Punishment could be cruel but not unusual, a law could be deemed to be necessary but highly improper, and an arm could be kept in the home without bearing it.

What "arms" could the people keep and bear? According to Webster, "arms" are "weapons of offense, or armor for defense and protection of the body."[22] Citing Blackstone's *Commentaries*, Webster noted: "In *law*, arms are any thing which a man takes in his hand in anger, to strike or assault another."[23]

Even though these definitions of "arms" signify weapons carried by hand, Webster added that "fire arms, are such as may be charged with powder, as cannon, muskets, mortars, & c."[24] However, elsewhere Webster states: "The larger species of guns are called cannon; and the smaller species are called muskets, carbines, fowling pieces, & c. But one species of fire-arms, the pistol, is never called a gun."[25] The Framers certainly had in mind the kinds of arms that General Gage confiscated from Boston's civilians and that militia acts required: muskets, shotguns, pistols, bayonets, and swords.

When the Constitution was being debated, Webster asserted that the people were sufficiently armed to defeat any standing army that could be raised, implying that they had similar arms.[26] However, the words "keep and bear arms" suggest that the right includes such hand-held arms as a person could "bear," such as muskets, fowling pieces, pistols, and swords, and not cannon and heavy ordnance that a person could not carry or wear.


SHALL NOT BE INFRINGED

The Bill of Rights uses several terms to provide that the rights it guarantees shall not be violated by government. The First Amendment prohibits "abridging" freedom of speech and press and "the right of the people" to assemble, the Second Amendment provides that "the right of the people" to arms "shall not be infringed," the Fourth Amendment mandates that "the right of the people" to be secure from unreasonable searches "shall not be violated," and the Ninth

Amendment proscribes the Constitution's enumerated rights from being construed "to deny or disparage" other rights "retained by the people."

The above terms refer to governmental action that violates in some manner individual rights. The Constitution nowhere uses these terms to describe what the federal or state governments may or may not do in relation to each other. As the Tenth Amendment exemplifies, the United States and the states have "powers," not "rights," and these powers may be either "delegated" or "reserved." As will be analyzed below, the Militia Clause in Article I, Section 8 refers to state militia powers as being "reserved." Nowhere does the Constitution provide that the United States shall not "infringe" on a state power.

For the breath of the term "infringe," Noah Webster's definition of that term indicates the following direct and indirect transgressions:

1. To break, as contracts; to violate, either positively by contravention, or negatively by non-fulfillment or neglect of performance. A prince or private person *infringes* an agreement or covenant by neglecting to perform its conditions, as well as by doing what is stipulated not to be done.

2. To break; to violate; to transgress; to neglect to fulfill or obey; as, to *infringe* a law.

3. To destroy or hinder; as, to *infringe* efficacy.[27]

It is noteworthy that the Second Amendment proscribes any infringement, not just "unreasonable" infringement. Some guarantees are more relative than others—for instance, the Fourth Amendment proscribes only "unreasonable" searches and seizures. As has been observed:

The kind of protection that particular rights enshrined in the Bill of Rights receive is not identical. Some are guaranteed in the most absolute imperative terms. The first amendment specifies that Congress *shall* make *no* law "respecting an establishment of religion, . . . or abridging the freedom of speech . . . ." The second amendment prescribes that the right of the people to keep and bear *shall* not be infringed.[28]

The pre-Revolutionary experiences exemplified how the right to keep arms could be infringed: King George's ban on import of arms and ammunition, Redcoats breaking into houses at Lexington and Concord to seize firearms, and Gage's decree ordering all Boston inhabitants to report and surrender their arms. Similarly, the patriots perceived the right to bear arms being infringed when British troops stopped citizens to search their persons and carts and seized any arms found, used entrapment to ferret out persons seeking to obtain arms, and ordered the dispersal of persons engaging in militia exercises. These were rather abrupt and open infringements, but the Founders would also have considered more subtle interferences to be infringements too. Being required to give one's name to an official and obtain permission to publish one's sentiments or to own a firearm would have been considered infringements.

### A WELL REGULATED MILITIA

The substantive guarantee of the Second Amendment is preceded by a purpose clause—"a well regulated militia, being necessary to the security of a free state . . . ." What do these terms mean?

The phrase "well regulated militia" was frequently used by the Founders. The Virginia Declaration of Rights of 1776 referred to "a well regulated Militia, composed of the Body of the People, trained to Arms . . . ."[29]

Webster wrote: "The militia of a country are the able bodied men organized into companies, regiments and brigades, with officers of all grades, and required by law to attend military exercises on certain days only, but at other times left to pursue their usual occupations."[30] "Regulated" means "adjusted by rule, method or forms; put in good order; subjected to rules or restrictions." Examples are "to *regulate* our moral conduct by the laws of God and society; to regulate our manners by the customary forms."[31] Thus, a well regulated militia includes all able-bodied men whose training is regulated by customary rules and methods.

Before and during the Revolution, the patriots could distinguish militiamen from troops by the clothes they wore and the nature of their occupations: Militiamen wore civilian clothes or special uniforms and were gainfully employed, while soldiers wore distinctive uniforms—the British wore Redcoats and the Continentals wore blue—and were engaged in military duties as an occupation. A well regulated militia consisted of civilians, not soldiers.

## BEING NECESSARY TO THE
## SECURITY OF A FREE STATE

At the outset, the clause postulates that a well regulated militia is "necessary" to a free state's security. Webster defined "necessary" in part as "that must be; that cannot be otherwise; indispensably requisite."[32] Constitutionally, then, it cannot be argued that in modern times a well regulated militia is no longer necessary to a free state's security. The Founders pointed to the Crown's neglect of the militia in the pre-Revolutionary years as a subtle manner of disarming the populace and thereby undermining republican institutions.

Webster defined "security" as "protection; effectual defense or safety from danger of any kind . . . ."[33] Under this broad meaning, having a well regulated militia helps to secure a free state from any threat, whether invaders, tyrants, insurgents, or even individual criminals who may be repulsed by individual militiamen who keep their arms at home. That "security" means safety for individuals as well as groups of people is exemplified in the Fourth Amendment's reference to "The right of the people to be *secure* in their persons, houses, papers, and effects, against unreasonable searches and seizures"—which by definition are carried out by government agents. By the same token, the Second Amendment's "security of a free State" includes security from governmental oppression.

The reference to a "free State" means a republican polity and is not restricted to a state government. A "free State" is not some elusive "collective" that is more than the sum of its individual parts. Webster defined "free" in part as follows: "In *government*, not enslaved; not in a state of vassalage or dependence; subject only to fixed laws, made by consent, and to a regular administration of such laws; not subject to the arbitrary will of a sovereign or lord; as a *free* state, nation or people."[34] The term "state" meant in pertinent part:

> A political body, or body politic; the whole body of people united under one government, whatever may be the form of the government . . . .
>
> More usually the word signifies a political body governed by representatives; a commonwealth; as the *States* of Greece; the *States* of America.
>
> In this sense, *state* has sometimes more immediate reference to the government, sometimes to the people or community. Thus when we say, the *state* has made provision for the paupers, the word has reference to the government, or

legislature; but when we say, the *state* is taxed to support paupers, the word refers to the whole people or community.[35]

Thus, "the *States* of America" refers to the political units known as states. "A free state" more broadly encompasses the entire body politic, including "the whole body of people."

While not stated in its text, the First Amendment too has "free state" aims. "The liberty of the press is indeed essential to the nature of a free state," in Blackstone's words.[36] The same could be said for the prohibition on the establishment of a religion—Madison's Memorial and Remonstrance Against Religious Assessments declared that "as faithful members of a free State," they protested the bill providing for teachers of the Christian religion, which would be "a dangerous abuse of power."[37]

Had a "free state" clause appeared in the First Amendment, it would not mean that the freedoms declared therein are no more than powers of the state governments. Consider the clause, "A well educated citizenry, being necessary to the culture of a free state, the right of the people to keep and read books, shall not be infringed." It could not be argued that a government-selected intelligentsia is today's well-educated citizenry and thus that this group is the only entity with the right to keep and read books, and then only when on duty. To the contrary, the right would extend to people who were not "well educated," since they are among "the people." Nor is it tenable to argue that only a government-selected militia have a right to keep and bear arms, and then only when on duty.

Variations of the theme that a well regulated militia is needed to secure a free state were common in the eighteenth century. The Earl of Middlesex wrote in a 1752 tract: "almost every free state affords an instance of a national Militia: For Freedom cannot be maintained without Power; and Men who are not in a Capacity to defend their *Liberties,* will certainly lose them . . . ."[38] The Founders concurred with such sentiments.

## THE PURPOSE CLAUSE DOES NOT
## NEGATE THE RIGHT

Nothing in the structure of the Second Amendment—a purpose clause followed by a substantive right—suggests that the former limits or may extinguish the latter. The declared "right of the people" is open-ended and would include all legitimate purposes, from defense of life to lawful hunting. To be sure, the militia clause declared a significant federal purpose and eschewed politically trivial purposes—the amendment does not begin with a purpose such as "duck hunting being lots of fun." But to the Founders, all lawful activities involving the keeping and bearing of arms—from hunting to militia muster—promoted a well regulated militia. Target shooting for sport made one better able to defend a free state. The militiamen of Lexington and Concord had turned their goose guns on the Redcoats.

It might be suggested that the right to have arms is dependent on a militia being necessary for the security of a free state, but despite what the amendment declares, the militia is obsolete, and today the standing army allegedly protects a free state—*ergo*, no right to arms exists. Rephrasing the amendment as a conditional (hypothetical) syllogism, its first premise would state: If a well regulated militia is necessary to the security of a free state *(p)*, then the right of the people to keep and bear arms shall not be infringed *(q)*; that is, *p* implies *q*. If one then asserts *p* as a second premise, then the conclusion *q* would follow. Logicians speak of this syllogism as being valid by reason of *modus ponens.*[39]

Yet the denial of the antecedent, should it be expressed in the second premise, fails to imply the denial of the consequent in the conclusion; that is, even if a militia is not necessary for the existence of a free state, the people still have the right to keep and bear arms. To say that "not *p*" implies "not *q*" is to commit the logical fallacy of denying the antecedent.[40]

These rules concerning syllogisms derive from classic Aristotelian logic and have not changed since ancient Greece. The Founders were familiar with logic.

While the Second Amendment is the only individual right with a purpose clause, the Patent and Copyright Clause is the only delegation of power to Congress with a purpose clause. It provides: "The Congress shall have Power . . . To promote the Progress of Science and useful Arts, by securing for limited Times to Authors and Inventors the exclusive Right to their respective Writings and Discoveries . . . ."[41] This reads as a delegation of power to Congress to exercise within its discretion, and the prefatory clause about promoting science and the arts does not appear to be a limitation on this power.[42]

The preamble to the Constitution also includes a declaration of purpose:

> We the People of the United States, in Order to form a more perfect Union, establish Justice, insure domestic Tranquility, provide for the common defence, promote the general Welfare, and secure the Blessings of Liberty to ourselves and our Posterity, do ordain and establish this Constitution for the United States of America.

Again, the declared purpose does not limit the active part of the preamble—that the Constitution is ordained and established. Nor could one argue that the Constitution no longer, say, promotes the general welfare, and thus is no longer ordained and established. It goes without saying that the preamble is a general statement of purpose that has no effect on the powers and rights set forth in the constitutional text.

When all is said and done, the militia clause of the Second Amendment is a philosophical admonition that neither delegates, reserves, nor prohibits any specific power to the United States or to the states. As discussed below, the federal-state division of power over the militia is precisely delineated in Article I, Section 8 of the Constitution. But the clause serves as a reminder that a well regulated militia, not a standing army, is required to secure a free state.

## THE MILITIA, WHEN IN ACTUAL SERVICE

The Founders distinguished not only between the people and the militia, but also between both of those entities and "the militia, when in actual service." The Fifth Amendment provides: "No person shall be held to answer for a capital, or otherwise infamous crime, unless on a presentment or indictment of a Grand Jury, except in cases arising in the land or naval forces, or *in the Militia, when in actual service* in time of War or public danger . . . ."

If keeping and bearing arms was a "right" only of "the militia, when in actual service," the Framers certainly would have so stated. It would have been odd, when guaranteeing "the right of the people to keep and bear arms," had the Framers really meant "the right of the militia to keep and bear arms when authorized and activated by the state government."

## POWERS RESERVED TO THE STATES

The Framers distinguished between "the people" and "the states." As provided by the Tenth Amendment: "The powers not delegated to the United States by the Constitution, nor prohibited by it to the states, are reserved to the states respectively, or to the people." For the powers delegated to the United States, one looks to Article I, under which "the Congress shall have power" to do what is enumerated; Article II, which defines "the executive power"; and Article III, which provides that "the judicial power" extends to certain objectives.[43] As the Tenth Amendment makes explicit, all other "powers" are reserved either to the states or to the people. No "rights" are delegated to the United States or reserved to the states. Only "the people"—individuals—have "rights."

But as the Tenth Amendment confirms, "the people" also have "powers." These powers include suffrage, jury duty, militia service, and other institutions in which the people govern, administer justice, keep order, disapprove of and nullify governmental actions, and otherwise participate in political society. As the Revolution proved, the ultimate power of the people that the Second Amendment helps secure is the ability to take arms to resist oppression and overthrow tyranny. In a constitutional republic, actual exercise of this power of the people would be rendered unnecessary.

Consistent with the above usage, Noah Webster defined "power" as follows:

> Command; the right of governing, or actual government; dominion; rule; sway; authority. . . . The *powers* of government are legislative, executive, judicial, and ministerial. . . .
>
> Under this sense may be comprehended civil, political, ecclesiastical, and military *power*.[44]

Finally, the Tenth Amendment clarifies that governmental powers are either "delegated" or "reserved," in contrast with rights of the people, which may not be "infringed" or "violated." The people also have powers that are "reserved."

## MILITIA POWERS DELEGATED TO THE
## UNITED STATES AND RESERVED TO THE STATES

It is striking that the state power to maintain militias vis-à-vis the federal military power was already treated in the text of the Constitution before the Bill of Rights was proposed, and the language of this state power does not contain the individual-rights vocabulary of the Second Amendment. Article I, Section 8, clauses 15 and 16 provide that "Congress shall have power":

> To provide for calling forth the Militia to execute the Laws of the Union, suppress Insurrections and repel Invasions;

> To provide for organising, arming, and disciplining, the Militia, and for governing such Part of them as may be employed in the Service of the United States, reserving to the States respectively, the Appointment of the Officers, and the Authority of training the Militia according to the discipline prescribed by Congress . . . .

Thus, "power" and "authority" (not "right") over the militia are "reserved" (not "shall not be infringed") to "the States respectively" (not "the people"). The division of authority between the United States and the states is clear. Congress has power to provide for calling up the militia to enforce the law, suppress insurrections, and repel invasions, but residual authority over the militia remains in the states when not federalized. As further provided in Article II, Section 2, "The President shall be Commander in Chief of the Army and Navy of the United States, and of the Militia of the several States, when called into the actual Service of the United States . . . ." When not federalized, the state governors are the commanders in chief of the respective militias of the states.

Moreover, the Congress has power to provide for organizing, arming, and disciplining the militia, and governing the federalized militia. But the powers to appoint militia officers and to train the militia—albeit under standards set by Congress—are reserved to the states. All other powers over the militia are reserved to the states.

The language of the residual state power to maintain militias is not the individual-rights vocabulary of the Second Amendment. Under the former, the "Congress shall have power . . . to provide for . . . arming . . . the Militia," "reserving to the States" the powers of appointing officers and training the militia. This sharply contrasts with the latter's reference that "the right of the people to keep and bear arms shall not be infringed."

It goes without saying that Article I, Section 8 of the Constitution had already provided for the existence and armament of the organized militia, and it would have been redundant for the Second Amendment to have done the same. Indeed, the Amendment's Militia Clause has none of the specificity of the militia clauses in Article I and adds nothing particular to them.

Moreover, the militia is the only military force the states may normally maintain. Congress has the exclusive power "to raise and support armies" and "to provide and maintain a navy."[45] But "no state shall, without the consent of Congress, . . . keep troops, or ships of war in time of peace, . . . or engage in war, unless actually invaded, or in such imminent danger as will not admit of delay."[46] Since the states may maintain "militia" but not "troops," those terms must have some objective meaning. That meaning can only be the historical understanding of the Founders that militia are part-time armed civilians, while troops signify full-time standing forces.

Moreover, the contrasting use of the word *keep* is revealing: "no state" shall (without Congress' consent) "keep troops," but "the people" have a right to "keep . . . arms." The Second Amendment does not say that "the power of the states to keep militia is reserved."

### READABLE BY ANY CITIZEN

This exhaustive textual analysis of the Second Amendment would never have been necessary in the nearly first two hundred years of the republic. It was only beginning in the second half of the twentieth century that the Orwellian view gained currency that "the people" means the states or state-conscripted militia, that "right" means governmental power, that "keep" does not mean to possess, that "bear" does not mean carry, that "arms" do not include ordinary handguns and rifles, and that "infringe" does not include prohibition.

But the Founders intended to, and did, word the Second Amendment in an easy to understand manner. Individuals have a right to have arms in their houses and to carry them, and the government may not violate that right. Recognition of the right promotes a militia composed of the body of the people, which is necessary for a free society.

The Bill of Rights was intended to inform the ordinary citizen of his or her rights. Its meaning is not a monopoly of the governmental entities whose powers it was intended to limit. St. George Tucker said it best in his 1803 treatise, the first ever published on the Constitution, as follows:

> A bill of rights may be considered, not only as intended to give law, and assign limits to a government about to be established, but as giving information to the people. By reducing speculative truths to fundamental laws, every man of the meanest capacity and understanding may learn his own rights, and know when they are violated . . . .[47]

By knowing when one's rights are violated, the citizen may signify his or her displeasure through mechanisms such as the ballot box and the jury box, and may resort to speech, the press, assembly, and petition to denounce the evil. As the experiences of the American Revolution proved, the right to keep and bear arms serves as the ultimate check that the Founders hoped would dissuade persons at the helm of state from seeking to establish tyranny. In hindsight, it would be difficult to quarrel with the success of the Founders' vision.

# NOTES

PREFACE

1. *Printz v. United States*, 521 U.S. 898, 939 n.2 (1997) (Thomas, J., concurring), citing in part Joyce Lee Malcolm, *To Keep and Bear Arms: The Origins of an Anglo-American Right* (Cambridge: Harvard University Press, 1994), 162; Stephen P. Halbrook, *That Every Man Be Armed: The Evolution of a Constitutional Right* (Albuquerque: University of New Mexico Press, 1984; reprinted, 1994, 2000 by The Independent Institute, Oakland, Calif.). See also William Van Alstyne, *The Second Amendment and the Personal Right to Arms*, 43 Duke L. J. 1236 (1994); Akhil Reed Amar, *The Bill of Rights and the Fourteenth Amendment*, 101 Yale L. J. 1193 (1992); Robert J. Cottrol & Raymond T. Diamond, *The Second Amendment: Toward an Afro-Americanist Reconsideration*, 80 Geo. L. J. 309 (1991); Sanford Levinson, *The Embarrassing Second Amendment*, 99 Yale L. J. 637 (1989); Don Kates, *Handgun Prohibition and the Original Meaning of the Second Amendment*, 82 Mich. L. Rev. 204 (1983).

2. See, *e.g.*, the scores of articles cited in Lawrence Tribe, *American Constitutional Law* (New York: Foundation Press, 3rd ed., 2000), 897-98 n.211; David B. Kopel, *The Second Amendment in the Nineteenth Century*, BYU L. Rev., No. 4, 1359, 1362-65 (1998). Many more have been published since then.

3. Stephen P. Halbrook, *A Right to Bear Arms: State and Federal Bills of Rights and Constitutional Guarantees* (Westport, Conn.: Greenwood Press, 1989).

4. Stephen P. Halbrook, *Freedmen, the Fourteenth Amendment, and the Right to Bear Arms, 1866–1876* (Westport, Conn.: Praeger Publishers, 1998).

5. To be sure, there are many noteworthy contributions to the subject. See Robert H. Churchill, *Gun Regulation, the Police Power, and the Right to Keep Arms in Early America: The Legal Context of the Second Amendment*, 25 Law & History Rev. 139 (2007) (with critical comments by David Konig, William Merkel, and Saul Cornell); Robert E. Shalhope, *The Armed Citizen in the Early Republic*, 49 Law and Contemp. Probs. 125 (1986); Nelson Lund, *The Second Amendment, Political Liberty, and the Right to Self-Preservation*, 39 Ala. L. Rev. 130 (1987); Lawrence D. Cress, *An Armed Community: The Origin and Meaning of the Right to Bear Arms*, 71 Jour. of American History 22 (1984).

INTRODUCTION

1. *E.g., Forum: Rethinking the Second Amendment,* 25 Law & History Rev., Issue 1 (2007).

2. See, *e.g., Symposium on the Second Amendment: Fresh Looks,* 76 Chi.–Kent L. Rev. 1 (2000), revised and reprinted as Carl Bogus ed., *The Second Amendment in Law and History* (New York: New Press, 2001).

3. Saul Cornell, *A Well Regulated Militia: The Founding Fathers and the Origins of Gun Control in America* (New York: Oxford University Press, 2006); David Konig, *The Second Amendment: A Missing Transatlantic Context for the Historical Meaning of the Right of the People to Keep and Bear Arms,* 22 Law & History Rev. 119 (2004).

4. Compare Michael A. Bellesiles, *Arming America* (New York: Alfred A. Knopf, 2000) (a book that was withdrawn from publication) with Robert H. Churchill, *Gun Ownership in Early America: A Survey of Manuscript Militia Returns,* 60 *William & Mary Quarterly,* 3d ser. (2003), 615.

5. William Blackstone, *Commentaries,* St. George Tucker ed. (Philadelphia: William Young Birch and Abraham Small, 1803), vol. 1, at App. 308.

CHAPTER 1

1. *Boston Gazette,* September 26, 1768, at 3, cols. 1–2. Reprinted in, *e.g., Virginia Gazette,* October 27, 1768, at 2, col. 3; *Maryland Gazette* (Annapolis), October 20, 1768, at 3, col. 1; *Georgia Gazette* (Savannah), November 2, 1768, at 1, col. 1.

2. Sidney Kobre, *The Development of the Colonial Newspaper* (Pittsburgh: The Colonial Press, 1944), 118–20.

3. See Pauline Maier, *From Resistance to Revolution: Colonial Radicals and the Development of American Opposition to Britain, 1765-1776* (New York: W.W. Norton, 1991).

4. Bernhard Knollenberg, *Growth of the American Revolution, 1766–1775* (New York: Free Press, 1975; reprinted, Indianapolis: Liberty Fund, 2003), 81, 401 n.3; John R. Alden, *General Gage in America* (New York: Greenwood Press, 1969), 160.

5. *Boston Post Post-Boy & Advertiser,* September 19, 1768, at 1, col. 1.

6. Richard Frothingham, *Life and Times of Joseph Warren* (Boston: Little, Brown, & Co., 1865), 81; William V. Wells, *The Life and Public Services of Samuel Adams,* 2nd ed. (Boston: Little, Brown, & Co., 1888), 212–13.

7. Mercy Otis Warren, *History of the Rise, Progress, and Termination of the American Revolution* (Boston: Manning & Loring, 1805; reprinted, Indianapolis: Liberty Classics, 1988), vol. 1, at 37.

8. Wells, *The Life and Public Services of Samuel Adams,* 212–13.

9. Frothingham, *Life and Times of Joseph Warren,* 85–86.

10. *Boston Chronicle,* September 19, 1768, at 363, col. 2; *Boston Post Post-Boy & Advertiser,* September 19, 1768, at 1, col. 3; *New York Journal, or General Advertiser,* Supplement, September 24, 1768, at 1, col. 3.

11. *An Act Declaring the Rights and Liberties of the Subject,* 1 W. & M., Sess. 2, cl.2 (1689).

12. The act of May 14, 1645, provided in part:

> That all inhabitants, as well seamen as others, are to have armes in their houses fit for service, with powder, bullets, match, as other souldiers, & the fishermen, shipcarpenters, (the deacons are hereby exempted from watches & wards,) & others, not exempted by lawe, shall watch or provide a sufficient man in their roome, & to traine twice a year, according to the order.

*Records of the Governor and Company of the Massachusetts Bay in New England,* Nathaniel B. Shurtleff ed. (Boston: W. White, 1853–54), vol. 2, at 119.

13. William Gerard Hamilton to Gerard Calcraft, February 1767, Chatham Correspondence, in Frank A. Mumby, *George III and The American Revolution* (London: Constable & Co., 1924), 173.

14. *An Act Declaring the Rights and Liberties of the Subject,* 1 W. & M., Sess. 2, cl.2 (1689).

15. *Boston Post Post-Boy & Advertiser*, September 19, 1768, at 1, col. 1.

16. *Pennsylvania Gazette*, September 29, 1768, at 2, col. 1.

17. Warren, *History of the American Revolution*, vol. 1, at 37.

18. Ibid., vol. 1, at 38.

19. See John Phillip Reid, *Constitutional History of the American Revolution: The Authority of Rights* (Madison: University of Wisconsin Press, 1986); Colin Bonwick, *English Radicals and the American Revolution* (Chapel Hill: University of North Carolina Press, 1977); Joyce Lee Malcolm, *To Keep and Bear Arms: The Origins of an Anglo-American Right* (Cambridge: Harvard University Press, 1994).

20. *Boston Gazette*, September 26, 1768, at 3, cols. 1–2.

21. Knollenberg, *Growth of the American Revolution*, 82–83.

22. *Boston Evening Post*, October 3, 1768, at 3, col. 2.

23. Kobre, *Development of Colonial Newspaper*, 114–15.

24. *Essex Gazette* (Salem), October 4, 1768, at 40, col. 3. This was apparently published first in *Draper's Massachusetts Gazette*, but the issue is missing from the Library of Congress collection.

25. *Boston Gazette*, October 3, 1768, at 2, col. 2.

26. Warren, *History of the American Revolution*, vol. 1, at 32, 350 (text of letter).

27. David Ramsay, *The History of the American Revolution* (Philadelphia: R. Aitken, 1789; reprinted, Indianapolis: Liberty Classics, 1990), vol. 1, at 73.

28. Warren, *History of the American Revolution*, vol. 1, at 34–35.

29. Knollenberg, *Growth of the American Revolution*, 54–57.

30. *The Correspondence of General Thomas Gage with the Secretaries of State, and with the War Office and the Treasury, 1763–1775*, Clarence E. Carter ed. (New Haven, Conn.: Yale University Press, 1931–33), vol. 2, at 68–69.

31. Knollenberg, *Growth of the American Revolution*, 67–68.

32. Warren, *History of the American Revolution*, vol. 1, at 35.

33. Ibid.; see also Ramsay, *History of American Revolution*, vol. 1, at 74.

34. Letter of July 30, 1768, in *Correspondence of General Gage*, vol. 2, at 72–73.

35. Knollenberg, *Growth of the American Revolution*, 57–58.

36. Ibid., 58–61.

37. Gage to Hillsborough, September 7, 1768, in *Correspondence of General Gage*, vol. 1, at 191, and vol. 2, at 69.

38. Gage to Hillsborough, September 10, 1768, in *Correspondence of General Gage*, vol. 1, at 195.

39. Warren, *History of the American Revolution*, vol. 1, at 39.

40. *New York Journal*, October 6, 1768, at 2, col. 1.

41. Ibid.

42. *New York Journal*, November 10, 1768, at 3, col. 1.

43. *New York Journal*, October 27, 1768, at 2, col. 3.

44. Knollenberg, *Growth of the American Revolution*, 83.

45. Ibid. 83, 402 n.14.

46. *Boston Evening Post*, November 21, 1768, at 2, col. 3.

47. *Massachusetts Gazette*, January 26, 1769, at 1, col. 1.

48. *Boston Under Military Rule [1768–1769] as Revealed in a Journal of the Times*, Oliver Morton Dickerson, comp. (Westport, Conn.: Greenwood Publishing Group, 1971), xiii–ix.

49. William Cobett, *The Parliamentary History of England from the Earliest Period to the Year 1803* (London: T. C. Hansard, 1813), vol. 16, at 469.

50. Proceedings of December 15, 1768, in ibid., vol. 16, at 478.

51. *Boston Chronicle*, September 19, 1768, at 363, col. 2; *Boston Post Post-Boy & Advertiser*, September 19, 1768, at 1, col. 1.

52. *Boston Gazette*, January 30, 1769, at 2, col. 1 (signed "Shippen"); *The Writings of Samuel Adams*, Harry Alonzo Cushing ed. (New York: G. P. Putnam's Sons, 1904), vol. 1, at 299. For a similar article, see *New York Journal*, Supplement, April 6, 1769, no. 1363, at 2, col. 1.

53. *New York Journal*, February 2, 1769, at 2, col. 2.

54. *Boston Gazette*, October 17, 1768, at 2, col. 3.

55. *Boston Gazette*, March 6, 1769, at 1, col. 3.

56. *Boston Evening-Post*, October 24, 1768, at 2, cols. 2–3.

57. *Massachusetts Gazette*, August 3, 1769, at 1, col. 1.

58. *Massachusetts Gazette*, June 7, 1769, at 4, col. 1.

59. *Massachusetts Gazette*, February 23, 1769, at 1, col. 1.

60. *Boston Gazette*, February 27, 1769, at 3, col. 1; *Writings of Samuel Adams*, vol. 1, at 317.

61. Ibid., vol. 1, at 317–18. Adams is quoting *verbatim* from Blackstone, *Commentaries*, vol. 1, at 140–41, 143–44.

62. Ibid, vol. 1, at 318.

63. *New York Journal*, March 23, 1769, at 2, col. 3. Similar statements made in Commons debate, which are quoted above, may be found in Cobett, *Parliamentary History of England*, vol. 16, at 469, 478.

64. *New York Journal*, Supplement, April 13, 1769, at 1, col. 3.

65. *Pennsylvania Gazette*, April 20, 1769, at 1, col. 1.

66. *New York Journal*, Supplement, April 6, 1769, Number 1370.

67. Knollenberg, *Growth of the American Revolution*, 83.

68. Ibid., 280–81.

69. John Adams, *Legal Papers* (Cambridge: Belknap Press/Harvard University Press, 1965), vol. 2, at 326.

70. Ibid., vol. 2, at 331.

71. Ibid., quoting William Hawkins, *Pleas of the Crown*, vol. 1, at 71.

72. Knollenberg, *Growth of the American Revolution*, 281.

73. Warren, *History of the American Revolution*, vol. 1, at 41–42.

74. *Massachusetts Gazette*, June 15, 1769, at 1, col. 2; *Pennsylvania Gazette*, June 29, 1769, at 1, col. 1.

75. Warren, *History of the American Revolution*, vol. 1, at 42–44.

76. Ibid., vol. 1, at 49–50.

77. John Clark Ridpath, *James Otis the Pre-Revolutionist* (Indypublish.com 2002), text online at http://www.samizdat.com/warren/jamesotis.html (accessed December 9, 2007).

78. Knollenberg, *Growth of the American Revolution*, 83–86, 282–83.

79. Ibid., 86–87.

80. Warren, *History of the American Revolution*, vol. 1, at 54–55; Knollenberg, *Growth of the American Revolution*, 89.

81. Gage to Hillsborough, April 10, 1770, in *Correspondence of General Gage*, vol. 1, at 251.

82. John Adams, *Legal Papers*, vol. 3, at 242.

83. Ibid., vol. 3, at 149.

84. Ibid., vol. 3, at 274.

85. John Adams, *Legal Papers*, vol. 3, at 149.

86. *Writings of Samuel Adams*, vol. 2, at 119.

87. John Adams, *Legal Papers*, vol. 3, at 248.

88. Ibid., vol. 3, at 285.

89. Knollenberg, *Growth of the American Revolution*, 87–88.

90. John Adams, *Legal Papers*, vol. 1, at 160.

91. Ibid., vol. 1, at 160, n.16.

92. Knollenberg, *Growth of the American Revolution*, xlii–xliv.

93. *New York Journal*, April 8, 1773, at 2, col. 3.

94. See Bernard Bailyn, *The Ordeal of Thomas Hutchinson* (Cambridge: Harvard University Press, 1974).

95. Massachusettensis, "To All Nations of Men," *Massachusetts Spy* (Boston), November 18, 1773, reprinted in Charles S. Hyneman & Donald S. Lutz, *American Political Writing During the Founding Era 1760–1805* (Indianapolis: Liberty Fund, 1983), vol. 1, at 213.

96. Ibid., vol. 1, at 191.

97. Ibid., vol. 1, at 194.

98. Ibid., vol. 1, at 197.

99. Ibid., vol. 1, at 192.

100. Ibid., vol. 1, at 198–99.

101. Ibid., vol. 1, at 199–200.

102. Ibid., vol. 1, at 200.

## CHAPTER 2

1. Letter of December 18, 1773, in John Andrews, *Letters of John Andrews, Esq., of Boston, 1772–1776*, Winthrop Sargent ed. (Cambridge, Mass.: John Wilson & Sons, 1866), 12. All of Andrews' letters in this collection were to William Barrell, a Philadelphia merchant.

2. Letter of December 1, 1773, in ibid., 12.

3. David Ramsay, *The History of the American Revolution* (Philadelphia: R. Aitken, 1789; reprinted, Indianapolis: Liberty Classics, 1990), vol. 1, at 99; Bernhard Knollenberg, *Growth of the American Revolution, 1766–1775* (New York: Free Press, 1975; reprinted, Indianapolis: Liberty Fund, 2003), 136–39.

4. Mercy Otis Warren, *History of the Rise, Progress, and Termination of the American Revolution* (Boston: Manning & Loring, 1805; reprinted, Indianapolis: Liberty Classics, 1988), vol. 1, at 79; Knollenberg, *Growth of the American Revolution*, 200–2.

5. Dartmouth to Gage, April 9, 1774, *The Correspondence of General Thomas Gage with the Secretaries of State, and with the War Office and the Treasury, 1763–1775*, Clarence E. Carter ed. (New Haven, Conn.: Yale University Press, 1931–33), vol. 2, at 158–59.

6. Knollenberg, *Growth of the American Revolution*, 123.

7. Dartmouth to Gage, June 3, 1774, *Correspondence of General Gage*, vol. 2, at 164.

8. *Boston Gazette*, January 24, 1774, at 1, col. 3.

9. John Hancock, *An Oration; Delivered March 5, 1774, at the Request of the Inhabitants of the Town of Boston* (Boston: Edes & Gill, 1774), 14–15.

10. *New York Journal*, March 31, 1774, at 1, col. 3.

11. Albert Matthews, *Notes on the Massachusetts Royal Commissions, 1681–1775* (Cambridge, Mass.: John Wilson & Son, 1913), 86–87.

12. Letter of May 18, 1774, in Andrews, *Letters of John Andrews*, 15.

13. Knollenberg, *Growth of the American Revolution*, 196.

14. Andrews, *Letters of John Andrews*, 19–20.

15. Ibid.

16. Ibid.

17. Robert P. Richmond, *Powder Alarm, 1774* (Princeton, N.J.: Auerbach Publishers, 1971), 42.

18. "At an Assembly of the Inhabitants of Hanover, Lancaster County," June 4, 1774, quoted in Joe D. Huddleston, *Colonial Riflemen in the American Revolution* (York, Pa.: George Shumway, 1978), 15.

19. "From the *South Carolina Gazette*, of August 23, 1774," *Virginia Gazette*, September 27, 1774, at 1, cols. 2–3.

20. *Boston Gazette*, August 29, 1774, Supplement, at 1, col. 1.

21. Gage to Dartmouth, August 27, 1774, in *Correspondence of General Gage*, vol. 1, at 366.

22. Andrews, *Letters of John Andrews*, 34.

23. Albert Matthews, "Documents Relating to the Last Meetings of the Massachusetts Royal Council, 1774–1776," *Transactions of the Colonial Society of Massachusetts* (February 1937), vol. 32, at 460, 475.

24. Ibid., vol. 32, at 475–76.

25. Ibid., vol. 32, at 476.

26. *Boston Gazette*, September 5, 1774, at 3, col. 2.

27. *Massachusetts Spy*, September 8, 1774, at 3, col. 3; also in *Pennsylvania Gazette*, September 14, 1774, at 2, col. 3.

28. Matthews, "Documents Relating to the Council," vol. 3, at 476 *ff.*

29. *Newport Mercury* (Rhode Island), September 19, 1774, at 1, col. 3.

30. Oliver to Dartmouth, December 9, 1774, in Matthews, "Documents Relating to the Council," vol. 3, at 492.

31. Ibid., vol. 3, at 494.

32. A 1792 act, which likely stemmed from colonial legislation, required approval of the fire ward for transportation of gunpowder in the streets of Boston "in any quantity, exceeding twenty five pounds, being the quantity allowed by law to be kept in shops for sale." *Perpetual Laws of the Commonwealth of Massachusetts* (1801), vol. 2, at 144.

33. Marie L. Aheam, *The Rhetoric of War: Training Day, the Militia, and the Military Sermon* (Westport, Conn.: Greenwood Press, 1989), 149–50.

34. David Hackett Fischer, *Paul Revere's Ride* (New York: Oxford University Press, 1994), 11, 23–24.

35. *Pennsylvania Gazette*, September 14, 1774, at 2, col. 3.

36. Brattle to Gage, August 26, 1774, in Peter Force ed., *American Archives* (Washington, D.C. 1837–53), 4th series, vol. 1, at 739.

37. Letter dated September 1, 1774, in Andrews, *Letters of John Andrews*, 38.

38. Knollenberg, *Growth of the American Revolution*, 226, 502, n.10; Fischer, *Paul Revere's Ride*, 44–45.

39. Fischer, *Paul Revere's Ride*, 47.

40. Andrews, *Letters of John Andrews*, 38.

41. Unsigned report datelined Boston, September 5, 1774, in Force ed., *American Archives*, 4th series, vol. 4, at 762.

42. Andrews, *Letters of John Andrews*, 39–40.

43. Ibid., 39.

44. *New York Journal*, September 29, 1774, at 1, cols. 1–2.

45. Fischer, *Paul Revere's Ride*, 50.

46. Diary entry dated September 25, 1774, in Ezra Stiles, *Literary Digest*, F. B. Dexter ed. (New York, 1901), vol. 2, at 479, quoted in Fischer, *Paul Revere's Ride*, 46.

47. Gage to Dartmouth, September 3, 1774, *Correspondence of General Gage*, vol. 1, at 373.

48. September 1, 1774, entry, in Andrews, *Letters of John Andrews*, 37.

49. Ibid., 41–42.

50. "A Letter from Rhode Island, Dated the 5th Instant," *Virginia Gazette*, September 15, 1774, at 3, col. 1.

51. *Virginia Gazette*, September 22, 1774, at 3, col. 1.

52. Ibid.

53. James Duane, Notes of Proceedings, in Edmund C. Burnett ed., *Letters of Members of the Continental Congress* (Washington, D.C.: Carnegie Institution, 1921), vol. 1, at 12.

54. Ibid., vol. 1, at 13.

55. Ibid., vol. 1, at 20.

56. Letter of September 14, 1774, in *The Book of Abigail and John: Selected Letters of the Adams Family, 1762–1784*, L. H. Butterfield *et al.* eds. (Cambridge: Harvard University Press, 1975), 72.

57. Richmond, *Powder Alarm*, 82–83, 86–87.

58. Andrews, *Letters of John Andrews*, 46.

59. Ibid., 46–47.

60. Percy to the Duke of Northumberland (his father), September 12, 1774, in Hugh Percy, *Letters of Hugh Earl Percy from Boston and New York, 1774–1776*, Charles Knowles Bolton ed. (Boston: Charles E. Goodspeed, 1902), 37–38.

61. Ibid., 38.

62. *An Act Declaring the Rights and Liberties of the Subject*, 1 W. & M., Sess. 2, cl. 2, (1689).

63. Gage to Dartmouth, September 12, 1774, *Correspondence of General Gage*, vol. 1, at 374.

64. Andrews, *Letters of John Andrews*, 52.

65. Gage to Dartmouth, September 25, 1774, *Correspondence of General Gage*, vol. 1, at 376–77.

66. Fischer, *Paul Revere's Ride*, 43.

67. Richard Frothingham, *Life and Times of Joseph Warren* (Boston: Little, Brown, & Co., 1865), 452.

68. *Boston Gazette*, September 19, 1774, at 1, col. 2; also in *Pennsylvania Gazette*, Sept. 21, 1774, at 1, cols. 1–2. Reprinted in Force ed., *American Archives*, 4th series, vol. 1, at 902. For a summary of the Resolves, see Knollenberg, *Growth of the American Revolution*, 312–13.

69. *Journals of the Continental Congress* (Washington, D.C.: Library of Congress, 1904), vol. 1, at 39.

70. Gage to Dartmouth, November 2, 1774, *Correspondence of General Gage*, vol. 1, at 382. The letter also appears in William Cobett, *The Parliamentary History of England from the Earliest Period to the Year 1803* (London: T. C. Hansard, 1813), vol. 18, at 105.

71. *Boston Gazette*, September 19, 1774, at 2, col. 1. The grievances are reprinted in Force ed., *American Archives*, 4th series, vol. 1, at 903.

72. Document datelined Boston, September 27, 1774, in Force ed., *American Archives*, 4th series, vol. 1, at 806–07.

73. Letter dated September 29, 1774, to Continental Congress, in Force ed., *American Archives*, 4th series, vol. 1, at 907.

74. Frothingham, *Life and Times of Joseph Warren*, 381.

75. Ibid., 382.

76. Letter dated September 30, 1774, in Andrews, *Letters of John Andrews*, 58.

77. Force ed., *American Archives*, 4th series, vol. 1, at 943–44.

78. Letter dated October 1, 1774, in ibid., vol. 1, at 58–59. The full text of this humorous account is as follows:

> It's common for the Soldiers to fire at a target fix'd in the stream at the bottom of the common. A countryman stood by a few days ago, and laugh'd very heartily at a whole regiment's firing, and not one being able to hit it. The officer observ'd him, and ask'd why he laugh'd? Perhaps you'll be affronted if I tell you, reply'd the countryman. No, he would not, he said. Why then, says he, I laugh to see how awkward they fire. Why, I'll be bound I hit it ten times running. Ah! Will you, reply'd the officer; come try: Soldiers, go and bring five of the best guns, and load 'em for this honest man. Why, you need not bring so many: let me have any one that comes to hand, reply'd the other, but I chuse to load myself. He accordingly loaded, and ask'd the officer where he should fire? He reply'd, to the right--when he pull'd tricker, and drove the ball as near the right as possible. The officer was amaz'd--and said he could not do it again, as that was only by chance. He loaded again. Where shall I fire? To the left—when he perform'd as well as before. Come! once more, says the officer.—He prepar'd the third time.—Where shall I fire naow?—In the Center.—He took aim, and the ball went as exact in the middle as possible. The officers as well as the soldiers star'd, and tho't the Devil was in the man. Why, says the countryman, I'll tell you naow. I have got a boy at home that will toss up an apple and shoot out all the seeds as its coming down.

79. Letter dated October 1, 1775, in Andrews, *Letters of John Andrews*, 59.

80. Gage to Dartmouth, October 3, 1774, *Correspondence of General Gage*, vol. 1, at 378.

81. *Boston Gazette*, October 17, 1774, at 2, cols. 2–3.

82. Ibid., col. 3.

83. Gage to Dartmouth, October 17, 1774, *Correspondence of General Gage*, vol. 1, at 378–79.

84. *Boston Gazette*, October 31, 1774, at 3, col. 1; *New York Journal*, November 10, 1774, at 1, cols. 2–3. Also in Force ed., *American Archives*, 4th series, vol. 1, at 852.

85. *Boston Gazette*, November 14, 1774, at 3, col. 2.

86. Knollenberg, *Growth of the American Revolution*, 219–21.

87. Gage to Dartmouth, November 2, 1774, *Correspondence of General Gage*, vol. 1, at 381.

88. Ibid.

89. Knollenberg, *Growth of the American Revolution*, 214–16.

90. *Boston Gazette*, December 5, 1774, at 4, col. 1.

91. Ibid.

92. Gage to Dartmouth, October 30, 1774, *Correspondence of General Gage*, vol. 1, at 380.

93. Dartmouth to Gage, October 17, 1774, ibid., vol. 2, at 175.

94. Gage to Dartmouth, December 15, 1774, ibid., vol. 1, at 386.

95. Gage to Dartmouth, December 15, 1774, ibid., vol. 1, at 387.

96. Cobett, *Parliamentary History of England*, vol. 18, at 106; Warren, *History of the American Revolution*, vol. 1, at 88.

97. *E.g.*, *Boston Gazette*, April 17, 1775, at 3, col. 2; *Pennsylvania Reporter*, May 1, 1775, at 4, col. 1.

98. Josiah Quincy, Jun'r, *Observations on the Act of Parliament Commonly Called the Boston Port-Bill; with Thoughts on Civil Society and Standing Armies* (Boston: Edes & Gill, 1774); reprinted in Josiah Quincy, *Memoir of the Life of Josiah Quincy Jun.* (Boston: Cummings, Hilliard, & Co., 1825), 413.

99. Ibid., 411.

100. Ibid., 428.

101. Daniel Dulany Jr., *Considerations on the Measures Carrying on with Respect to the British Colonies in North America* (London: R. Baldwin, 1774), 57.

102. Ibid., 117.

103. John Allen, *Oration, Upon the Beauties of Liberty; or the Essential Rights of the Americans* (Wilmington, Del.: James Adams, 1775), x–xi.

104. Dartmouth to Gage, January 27, 1775, *Correspondence of General Gage*, vol. 2, at 183.

105. "Paper delivered to a Committee of the Town of Boston by Gov. Gage, containing proposals for maintaining good order and harmony between the soldiers and town people, November 1774," Manuscript in Gage Collection, William L. Clements Library, University of Michigan.

106. *Massachusetts Gazette*, December 29, 1774, at 2, col. 2.

107. Force ed., *American Archives*, 4th series, vol. 1, at 1062.

108. *Massachusetts Gazette*, January 19, 1775, at 2, col. 2.

109. *Connecticut Courant*, January 16, 1775, at 2, col. 3.

110. G. Allan Yeomans, "Introduction" to Charles Lee, *Strictures on a Pamphlet*, reprinted in G. Jack Gravlee & James R. Irvine eds., *Pamphlets and the American Revolution* (Delmar, N.Y.: Scholars' Facsimiles & Reprints, 1976), iii–iv, vii.

111. Charles Lee, *Strictures on a Pamphlet, Entitled a "Friendly Address to All Reasonable Americans, on the Subject of our Political Confusions."* (Philadelphia: William & Thomas Bradford, 1774), 12. This passage was widely reprinted. *E.g.*, *Essex Gazette*, January 17, 1775, at 4, col. 1.

112. Dartmouth to Gage, October 17, 1774, *Correspondence of General Gage*, vol. 2, at 175–76.

113. "Fusee. A small neat musket or firelock. But we now use *fusil*." Noah Webster, *An American Dictionary of the English Language* (New York: S. Converse, 1828).

114. John Adams, *Novanglus; or, A History of the Dispute with America*, no. III, February 1775, in *The Revolutionary Writings of John Adams*, C. Bradley Thompson ed. (Indianapolis: Liberty Fund, 2000), 172.

115. Ibid., 172–73.

116. Richmond, *Powder Alarm*, 38–39.

117. John Adams, *Novanglus; or, A History of the Dispute with America*, no. III, February 1775, in *Revolutionary Writings of John Adams*, 173.

118. Ibid.

119. *Novanglus*, no. V, February 20, 1775, in *Revolutionary Writings of John Adams*, 186–87.

120. *Novanglus*, no. VI, in *Revolutionary Writings of John Adams*, 204.

121. *Novanglus*, no. VI, in *Revolutionary Writings of John Adams*, 204, quoting Grotius B. I, cl. 3, § I.

122. *Novanglus*, no. VI, in *Revolutionary Writings of John Adams*, 206, quoting Pufendorf's *Law of Nature and Nations,* I. Vii. cl. vii. § 5, 6. Barbeyrac's note on § 6.

123. *Novanglus*, no. VI, in *Revolutionary Writings of John Adams*, 206–07, quoting Sidney, *Discourses Concerning Government.*

124. *Peter Oliver's Origin & Progress of the American Rebellion: A Tory View*, Douglass Adair and John A. Schutz eds. (Stanford, Calif.: Stanford University Press, 1961), 116–17. The manuscript was written in 1781.

125. Frederick MacKenzie, *A British Fusilier in Revolutionary Boston, Being the Diary of Lieutenant Frederick MacKenzie, Adjutant of the Royal Welch Fusiliers, January - April 30, 1775*, Allen French ed. (Freeport, N.Y.: Books for Libraries Press, 1926; reprinted 1969), 31–32.

126. Ibid., 33.

127. Ibid.

128. Bancroft Collection, New York Public Library, in French, *Day of Concord and Lexington*, 57–58. This letter is not in the published *Gage Correspondence*. As "200 rods" (1,100 yards) was far beyond the range of accurate fire for firelocks, Gage may have intended to say "200 yards."

129. MacKenzie, *A British Fusilier in Revolutionary Boston*, 37.

130. Ibid., 38–39.

131. John Rowe, *Letters and Diary of John Rowe, Boston Merchant 1759–1762, 1764–1779* (Boston: W. B. Clarke Co., 1903), 290.

132. *New York Journal,* March 30, 1775, at 2, col. 3. Also in Force ed., *American Archives*, 4th series, vol. 2, at 120. See also Fischer, *Paul Revere's Ride*, 70.

133. *Massachusetts Gazette; and Boston Weekly News-Letter*, March 17, 1775, at 3, col. 1. Also in Force ed., *American Archives*, 4th series, vol. 2, at 94.

134. Ibid.

135. Ibid., col. 2.

136. MacKenzie, *A British Fusilier in Revolutionary Boston*, 39–40.

137. *The Writings of Samuel Adams*, Harry Alonzo Cushing ed. (New York: G. P. Putnam's Sons, 1907), vol. 3, at 200.

138. Ibid., vol. 3, at 207.

139. Ibid., vol. 3, at 208.

140. Gage to Dartmouth, March 28, 1775, *Correspondence of General Gage*, vol. 1, at 394–95. See "Remonstrance Presented by the Selectmen of Billerica," March 16, 1775, in Force ed., *American Archives*, 4th series, vol. 2, at 153.

CHAPTER 3

1. That enactment, 29 Geo. II cl. 16 (1756), provided in part:

> Whereas by an Act of Tonnage and Poundage made in the twelfth Year of the Reign of King Charles the Second, Power is expressly reserved to his Majesty to prohibit, at and for such Times as he should see Cause, the transporting of Gunpowder, or any Sort of Arms or Ammunition, into any Parts out of this Kingdom: And whereas Salt Petre is absolutely necessary to the making of Gunpowder, and the publick Safety may require temporary Restraints upon the Exportation thereof, at critical Conjunctures; Therefore to prevent all Doubts, be it hereby declared and enacted . . . That his Majesty may, by Proclamation or Order in Council, when he shall see Cause, and for such Time as shall by therein expressed, prohibit the exporting, or attempting to export, Salt Petre out of this Kingdom, in such Manner and under such Restraints as he shall think fit.

2. 5 Acts Privy Council 401. The enactment was reprinted in the *Connecticut Courant*, December 19, 1774, at 3, cols. 2–3. The decree was renewed from time to time until 1783. James Truslow Adams, *Revolutionary New England 1691–1776* (Boston: Atlantic Monthly Press, 1923), 412.

3. Bernhard Knollenberg, *Growth of the American Revolution, 1766–1775* (New York: Free Press, 1975; reprinted, Indianapolis: Liberty Fund, 2003), 204–5.

4. Dartmouth to Gage, October 19, 1774, *The Correspondence of General Thomas Gage with the Secretaries of State, and with the War Office and the Treasury, 1763–1775*, Clarence E. Carter ed. (New Haven, Conn.: Yale University Press, 1931–33), vol. 2, at 176.

5. Dartmouth to Gage, October 19, 1774, in ibid., vol. 2, at 176–77.

6. See Ibid., vol. 2, at 177.

7. See Daniel A. Miller, *Sir Joseph Yorke and Anglo-Dutch Relations, 1774–1780* (The Hague: Mouton, 1970).

8. "Extract of a letter from Sir Joseph Yorke to the Earl of Suffolk, dated Hague, August 5th, 1774," Manuscript in Gage Collection, William L. Clements Library, University of Michigan. Actually, Nantucket was attached to the New York colony until 1692, when by act of Parliament it became a part of the Bay Colony of Massachusetts.

9. "Extract of a letter from Sir Joseph Yorke to Earl of Suffolk, dated Hague, August 26th, 1774," Manuscript in Gage Collection, William L. Clements Library, University of Michigan.

10. "Copy of a letter from Earl of Suffolk to the Earl of Dartmouth, dated St. James's the 31st August 1774," Manuscript in Gage Collection, William L. Clements Library, University of Michigan. The earl described a further letter from Yorke as confirming that "North America is largely supplied by the way of St. Eustatia, with what it does not chance to take from England, or to export directly from Holland . . . ." "Copy of a letter from Sir Joseph Yorke to Earl of Suffolk, dated Hague 11 October, 1774," Manuscript in Gage Collection, William L. Clements Library, University of Michigan.

11. "Copy of a letter from Sir Joseph Yorke to Earl of Suffolk, dated Hague 11 October, 1774," Manuscript in Gage Collection, William L. Clements Library, University of Michigan.

12. See William R. Staples, *Documentary History of the Destruction of the Gaspee*, Richard M. Deasy ed. (Providence: Rhode Island Publications Society, 1990).

13. "Copy of a letter from the Earl of Suffolk to the Earl of Dartmouth dated St. James's 15th October, 1774," Manuscript in Gage Collection, William L. Clements Library, University of Michigan.

14. Robert P. Richmond, *Powder Alarm, 1774* (Princeton, N.J.: Auerbach Publishers, 1971), 95.

15. Miller, *Sir Joseph Yorke and Anglo-Dutch Relations*, 39. In one incident, "a vessel loaded with arms, ammunition, etc. for New England, on her departure from Amsterdam, was stopped, and all her cargo seized." *Pennsylvania Reporter*, February 13, 1775, vol. IV, no. 173.

16. Miller, *Sir Joseph Yorke and Anglo-Dutch Relations*, 40–41. "Six large ships sailed lately, three from Holland, and the rest from France, with arms and ammunition and other implements

of war, for our colonies in America, and more preparing for the same place." *Pennsylvania Reporter*, April 24, 1775, at 2, col. 1 (referring to a report from London, February 16, 1775).

17. Richmond, *Powder Alarm*, 96.

18. Gage to Dartmouth, December 15, 1774, *Correspondence of General Gage*, vol. 1, at 386.

19. Gage to Dartmouth, December 15, 1774, ibid., vol. 1, 385–86.

20. *Boston Gazette*, December 12, 1774, at 3, col. 1.

21. James Truslow Adams, *Revolutionary New England 1691–1776* (Boston: Atlantic Monthly Press, 1923), 412; John R. Alden, *General Gage in America* (New York: Greenwood Publishing Group, 1969), 224; David Hackett Fischer, *Paul Revere's Ride* (New York: Oxford University Press, 1994), 56.

22. Wentworth to Gage, December 14, 1774, letter reprinted in William Cobett, *The Parliamentary History of England from the Earliest Period to the Year 1803* (London: T.C. Hansard, 1813), vol. 18, at 145. The letter crossed the ocean again and was reprinted in, *e.g.*, *Virginia Gazette* (Williamsburg), June 8, 1775, at 1, col. 2. "Amicus Patriae" claimed that "they surely meant only to seize the Ammunition belonging to every Town, and private Property, which we have been led to suspect would have been seized upon by Administration, to enforce Obedience to their cruel measures." *New-Hampshire Gazette*, February 24, 1775, at 1, col. 1.

23. Percy to Grey Cooper, after December 13, 1774, in Hugh Percy, *Letters of Hugh Earl Percy from Boston and New York, 1774–1776*, Charles Knowles Bolton ed. (Boston: Charles E. Goodspeed, 1902), 46.

24. Wentworth to Gage, December 16, 1774, letter reprinted in Cobett, *The Parliamentary History of England*, vol. 18, at 147.

25. *New Hampshire Gazette and Historical Chronicle*, January 13, 1775, at 1, col. 1. Reprinted in Peter Force ed., *American Archives*, 4th series, vol. 1, at 1065.

26. *Pennsylvania Gazette*, December 14, 1774, at 2, col. 3.

27. *Pennsylvania Gazette*, December 21, 1774, at 3, cols. 1–2.

28. *Massachusetts Gazette*, December 29, 1774, at 3, col. 1.

29. *Connecticut Courant*, January 9, 1775, at 2, col. 2.

30. *New York Journal; or, the General Advertiser*, January 12, 1775, at 3, col. 1.

31. *New York Journal*, January 5, 1775, at 3, col. 3.

32. *Postscript to the Pennsylvania Packet*, March 1775, vol. IV, no. 177, at 1, col. 2.

33. *Pennsylvania Packet*, January 9, 1775, vol. IV, no. 168.

34. Force ed., *American Archives*, 4th series, vol. 1, at 1066. See also Frank A. Mumby, *George III and The American Revolution* (London: Constable & Co., 1924), 365–66.

35. Cobett, *Parliamentary History of England*, vol. 18, at 512.

36. Force, *American Archives*, 4th series, vol. 1, at 1070.

37. Ibid., vol. 1, at 1070–71.

38. Ibid., vol. 1, at 1071.

39. Ibid.

40. *Pennsylvania Journal*, December 14, 1774, at 1, col. 2.

41. *New York Journal*, January 12, 1775, at 2, col. 1.

42. *Pennsylvania Packet*, January 16, 1775; *Virginia Gazette*, February 4, 1775, at 1, col. 3. Reprinted in Force ed., *American Archives*, 4th series, vol. 1, at 1078.

43. *Pennsylvania Reporter*, March 6, 1775, vol. IV, no. 176.

44. *New York Journal*, February 9, 1775, at 1, col. 2.

45. John Adams, *Novanglus*, no. II, February 6, 1775, in *The Revolutionary Writings of John Adams*, C. Bradley Thompson ed. (Indianapolis: Liberty Fund, 2000), 157.

46. James Burgh, *Political Disquisitions* (London: Edward & Charles Dilly, 1774), vol. 2, at 475–76. The quote appeared, *e.g.*, in the *New York Journal*, February 9, 1775, at 1, col. 3.

47. *Postscript to the Pennsylvania Reporter*, February 4, 1775.

48. Fischer, *Paul Revere's Ride*, 59–63.

49. *Journal of Proceedings of Convention Held at Richmond* (Williamsburg: J. Dixon, 1775), 34. Also in the *Virginia Gazette*, April 1, 1775, at 2, cols. 1–2.

50. *Journal of Proceedings*, 10.

51. Ibid., 11.

52. Ibid., 17.

53. John Andrews, *Letters of John Andrews, Esq., of Boston, 1772–1776*, Winthrop Sargent ed. (Cambridge: John Wilson & Sons, 1866), 88.

54. Frederick MacKenzie, *A British Fusilier in Revolutionary Boston, Being the Diary of Lieutenant Frederick MacKenzie, Adjutant of the Royal Welch Fusiliers, January 5--April 30, 1775*, Allen French ed. (Freeport, N.Y.: Books for Libraries Press, 1926; reprinted 1969), 42.

55. Robert Pierpont was born in London, England, in 1621, and died in Roxbury, Massachusetts, in 1684. See genealogical records at http://users.rcn.com/lmerrell/d0003/g0000216.htm#I0926 (accessed December 10, 2007).

56. Deposition, unsigned, by Robert Pierpont, Boston, March 20, 1775 (in handwriting of William Cooper), in *Papers of Samuel Adams, 1635–1826: Photostats from the Collection in the New York Public Library* (Washington, D. C.: Library of Congress, 1929), vol. 7.

57. Ibid.

58. Ibid.

59. *Connecticut Courant*, April 3, 1775, at 2, col. 2. Also in *New York Journal*, March 30, 1775, at 3, col. 2.

60. *Newport Mercury* (Rhode Island), April 10, 1775, at 2, col. 1.

61. *Postscript to Pennsylvania Reporter*, April 1775, at 4, col. 1.

62. Letter of April 11, 1775, in Andrews, *Letters of John Andrews*, 89.

63. John Drayton, *Memoirs of the American Revolution . . . As Relating to South Carolina* (Charleston, 1821), vol. 1, at 166.

64. *New-Hampshire Gazette*, January 27, 1775, at 1, col. 3.

65. *New York Journal*, April 13, 1775, at 1, col. 3.

66. Ibid., at 3, col. 1. Also in *Pennsylvania Reporter*, April 17, 1775, at 3, col. 2. Reprinted in Force ed., *American Archives*, 4th series, vol. 1, at 1202.

67. Robert A. Gross, *The Minutemen and Their World* (New York: Hill & Wang, 1976), 113.

68. *Pennsylvania Reporter*, April 17, 1775, at 2, col. 3.

69. *New York Journal*, June 15, 1775, at 2, col. 1.

70. Force ed., *American Archives*, 4th series, vol. 2, at 276. Regarding the reference to "British Ships," this included American ships because they were still flying the British flag. Miller, *Sir Joseph Yorke and Anglo-Dutch Relations*, 40.

71. Gage to Pownall, June 3, 1775, *Correspondence of General Gage*, vol. 2, at 681.

72. Miller, *Sir Joseph Yorke and Anglo-Dutch Relations*, 40–41.

73. *Virginia Gazette*, November 24, 1774, at 1, col. 3, and at 2, col. 1.

CHAPTER 4

1. *Essex Gazette*, April 25, 1775, at 3, col. 3.

2. *Pennsylvania Reporter*, May 15, 1775, cols. 2–3.

3. *Pennsylvania Reporter*, May 1, 1775, at 5, col. 1.

4. Pitcairn to Gage, April 26, 1775, in Bernhard Knollenberg, *Growth of the American Revolution, 1766–1775* (New York: Free Press, 1975; reprinted, Indianapolis: Liberty Fund, 2003), 333.

5. Robert A. Gross, *The Minutemen and Their World* (New York: Hill & Wang, 1976), 61, 69–70.

6. *Essex Gazette*, April 25, 1775, at 3, col. 3.

7. Gross, *The Minutemen and Their World*, 69.

8. Richard Frothingham, *Life and Times of Joseph Warren* (Boston: Little, Brown, & Co., 1865), 453.

9. Allen French, *General Gage's Informers* (Ann Arbor: University of Michigan Press, 1932), 9–33.

10. Frothingham, *Life and Times of Joseph Warren*, 454.

11. Knollenberg, *Growth of the American Revolution*, 231–32.

12. David Hackett Fischer, *Paul Revere's Ride* (New York: Oxford University Press, 1994), 103.

13. Ibid., 133–34.

14. Ibid., 126, 169.

15. Andrew Carroll, *Letters of a Nation* (New York: Kodansha International, 1997), 53.

16. Gross, *The Minutemen and Their World*, 130.

17. Ibid., 120–23.

18. Ibid., 131.

19. Frederick MacKenzie, *A British Fusilier in Revolutionary Boston, Being the Diary of Lieutenant Frederick Mackenzie, Adjutant of the Royal Welch Fusiliers, January 5–April 30, 1775*, Allen French ed. (Freeport, N.Y.: Books for Libraries Press, 1926; reprinted 1969), 62. This unnamed officer's account was published with MacKenzie's diary.

20. Ibid., 64.

21. Ibid., 67.

22. "Many experienced hunters carried long-barreled muskets and fowling pieces, and used them with deadly accuracy." Fischer, *Paul Revere's Ride*, 413 n.58.

23. Fischer, *Paul Revere's Ride*, 161.

24. Ibid., 160.

25. Ibid., 286. In 1998, the musket was bound by a trigger lock as required by the Massachusetts Gun Control Act passed that year. This was soon revised to delete the requirement as applied to antique firearms. Mass. Acts 1998, Chapter 180, amended by Acts 1999, Chapter 1, § 4.

26. Percy to General Edward Harvey, April 20, 1775, in Hugh Percy, *Letters of Hugh Earl Percy from Boston and New York, 1774–1776*, Charles Knowles Bolton ed. (Boston: Charles E. Goodspeed, 1902), 52–53.

27. *Peter Oliver's Origin & Progress of the American Rebellion: A Tory View*, Douglass Adair and John A. Schutz eds. (Stanford, Calif.: Stanford University Press, 1961), 118. The book was originally written in 1781.

28. Ibid., 120.

29. M. L. Brown, *Firearms in Colonial America* (Washington, D.C.: Smithsonian Institution, 1980), 298, quoting letter from unknown author in *Wm. & Mary Quarterly*, 3rd series, vol. 10 (1953), at 106.

30. Fischer, *Paul Revere's Ride*, 170.

31. Ibid., 251.

32. Ibid., 289.

33. *Massachusetts Spy* (Worcester), May 3, 1775, at 3, col. 2.

34. *The British in Boston* (Cambridge: Harvard University Press, 1924), 39.

35. MacKenzie, *A British Fusilier in Revolutionary Boston*, 56.

36. Ibid., 57.

37. Ibid., 58.

38. Fischer, *Paul Revere's Ride*, 243–44.

39. *Pennsylvania Reporter*, May 1, 1775, at 3, col. 2.

40. Fischer, *Paul Revere's Ride*, 408.

41. Ibid., 321.

42. DAJA-IO (27–1A), Memorandum for Staff Judge Advocate, U.S. Army Special Forces Command (ABN), Fort Bragg, NC 28307–5215, 24 June 1999, Subject: M24 and SR-25 Sniper Weapons Systems; Legal Review, p. 3, n.3.

43. Gage to Dartmouth, April 22, 1775, in *The Correspondence of General Thomas Gage with the Secretaries of State, and with the War Office and the Treasury, 1763–1775*, Clarence E. Carter ed. (New Haven, Conn.: Yale University Press, 1931–33), vol. 1, at 396.

44. John Rowe, *Letters and Diary of John Rowe, Boston Merchant 1759–1762, 1764–1779* (Boston: W. B. Clarke Co., 1903), 293.

45. Ibid.

46. Attested Copy of Proceedings Between Gage and Selectmen, April 22, 1775, in *Connecticut Courant*, July 17, 1775, at 1, col. 3, and at 4, col. 1.

47. Allen French, *The Day of Lexington and Concord, the Nineteenth of April, 1775* (Boston: Little, Brown, & Co., 1925), 56.

48. Gage to Dartmouth, April 22, 1775, *Correspondence of General Gage*, vol. 1, at 396–97.

49. Attested Copy of Proceedings Between Gage and Selectmen, April 23, 1775, in *Connecticut Courant*, July 17, 1775, at 4, col. 2.

50. Ibid.

51. Ibid., at 4, col. 3 (April 23, 1775).

52. Rowe, *Letters and Diary of John Rowe*, 293.

53. John Andrews, *Letters of John Andrews, Esq., of Boston, 1772–1776*, Winthrop Sargent ed. (Cambridge: John Wilson & Sons, 1866), 92.

54. *The British in Boston*, 38.

55. Letter to a Gentleman in Newport, Rhode-Island, datelined Roxbury, April 28, 1775, in Force ed., *American Archives*, 4th series, vol. 2, at 430.

56. *Connecticut Courant*, May 8, 1775, at 3, col. 1.

57. *Connecticut Journal and New-Haven Post-Boy*, May 19, 1775, at 6, col. 2.

58. Rowe, *Letters and Diary of John Rowe*, 293–94.

59. Richard Frothingham, *History of the Siege of Boston* (Boston: Little, Brown, & Co., 1903), 95.

60. Douglas Southall Freeman, *George Washington: A Biography* (New York: Scribner, 1948–57), vol. 3, at 576.

61. Page Smith, *A New Age Now Begins: A People's History of the American Revolution* (New York: McGraw-Hill, 1976), vol. 1, at 506.

62. Letters to author from Massachusetts Historical Society, November 25, 1988, and William L. Clements Library, University of Michigan, January 30, 1989, which houses the Gage Collection.

63. Frothingham, *History of the Siege of Boston*, 95.

64. Illustration in Stephen P. Halbrook, *A Right to Bear Arms: State and Federal Bills of Rights and Constitutional Guarantees* (Westport, Conn.: Greenwood Press, 1989), 19.

65. Rowe, *Letters and Diary of John Rowe*, 294.

66. David Ramsay, *The History of the American Revolution* (Indianapolis: Liberty Classics, 1990), vol. 1, at xliii.

67. *Papers of James Madison*, Charles F. Hobson *et al.* eds. (Charlottesville: University Press of Virginia, 1981), vol. 13, at 233.

68. Ramsay, *History of the American Revolution*, vol. 1, at 176.

69. *Journals of the Continental Congress, 1774–1779*, Worthington Chauncey Ford ed. (Washington, D.C.: Government Printing Office, 1905), vol. 2, at 151. Also in *Connecticut Courant*, July 17, 1775, at 2, col. 1.

70. Ramsay, *History of the American Revolution*, vol. 1, at 177.

71. *Pennsylvania Reporter*, May 8, 1775, at 3, col. 1.

72. *The Journals of Each Provincial Congress of Massachusetts in 1774 and 1775* (Boston: Dutton & Wentworth, 1838), 167.

73. Ibid., 172–73.

74. Attested Copy of the Proceedings Between Gage and Selectmen, April 30, 1775, in *Connecticut Courant*, July 17, 1775, at 4, col. 3.

75. *Journals of Each Provincial Congress of Massachusetts in 1774 and 1775*, 184.

76. Andrews, *Letters of John Andrews*, 93.

77. *Journals of Each Provincial Congress of Massachusetts in 1774 and 1775*, 213.

78. Gage to Dartmouth, May 13, 1775, *Correspondence of General Gage*, vol. 1, at 397–98.

79. Frothingham, *Life and Times of Joseph Warren*, 483–84.

80. Mercy Otis Warren, *History of the Rise, Progress, and Termination of the American Revolution* (Boston: Manning & Loring, 1805; reprinted, Indianapolis: Liberty Classics, 1988), vol. 1, at 106–7.

81. "Extract of a Letter to a Gentlemen in Philadelphia, dated Boston, May 21, 1775," in Force ed., *American Archives*, 4th series, vol. 2, at 666.

82. *Massachusetts Spy*, May 17, 1775, at 2, col. 1.

83. Ibid., at 3, col. 3.

84. *Pennsylvania Reporter*, May 1, 1775, at 2, col. 3.

85. *Journals of the Provincial Congress, Provincial Convention, Committee of Safety and Council of Safety of the State of New York: 1775–1776–1777* (Albany: Thurlow Weed, 1842), vol. 2, at 10.

86. *Journals of Each Provincial Congress of Massachusetts in 1774 and 1775*, 225; *The Writings of Samuel Adams*, Harry Alonzo Cushing ed. (New York: G. P. Putnam's Sons, 1907), vol. 3, at 213.

87. Gage to Hillsborough, November 10, 1770, in *Correspondence of General Gage*, vol. 1, at 278.

88. Peter Edes, "Diary Kept in Boston Gaol," June 19, 1775, ms., Massachusetts Historical Society, cited in Fischer, *Paul Revere's Ride*, 273, 416 n.44.

89. Dartmouth to Gage, April 15, 1775, *Correspondence of General Gage*, vol. 2, at 191.

90. Gage to Dartmouth, June 12, 1775, ibid., vol. 1, at 404.

91. *Connecticut Journal and New-Haven Post Boy*, June 21, 1775, at 3, cols. 1–2.

92. John R. Alden, *General Gage in America* (New York: Greenwood Publishing Group, 1969), 263–64.

93. *Journals of Each Provincial Congress of Massachusetts in 1774 and 1775*, 330–31.

94. Ibid.

95. *Pennsylvania Evening Post*, June 27, 1775, at 1, cols. 1–2.

96. *Connecticut Courant*, July 17, 1775, at 4, col. 1. Also in *New York Journal or General Advertiser*, July 13, 1775, at 4, col. 1.

97. Frothingham, *History of the Siege of Boston*, 95.

98. Noah Webster, *An American Dictionary of the English Language* (New York: S. Converse, 1828) ("gun").

99. George C. Neumann, *The History of Weapons of the American Revolution* (New York: Bonanza Books, 1967), 14, 22.

100. Ibid., 22, 134–35.

101. Ibid., 36, 38.

102. Ibid., 150–51.

103. Ibid., 216–17.

104. Ibid., 217.

105. See also Harold L. Peterson, *Arms and Armor in Colonial America, 1526–1783* (Mineola, N.Y.: Dover Publications, 2000); M. L. Brown, *Firearms in Colonial America: The Impact on History and Technology, 1492–1792* (Washington, D.C.: Smithsonian Institution Press, 1980).

106. Ramsay, *History of the American Revolution*, vol. 1, at 178.

107. Ibid., vol. 1, at 190.

108. *Letters of Members of the Continental Congress*, Edmund C. Burnett ed. (Washington, D.C.: Carnegie Institution, 1921), vol. 1, at 134.

109. Adams to Warren, June 27, 1775, in ibid., at n.5. Elsewhere, Adams wrote about the riflemen that "they use a peculiar kind of musket, called a rifle. It has a circular . . . grooves within the barrel, and carries a ball with great exactness to great distances. They are the most accurate marksmen in the world." *Familiar Letters of John and His Wife Abigail Adams During the Revolution*, Charles F. Adams ed. (Boston, 1857), 65–66.

110. Letter dated June 16(?), 1775, in *The Book of Abigail and John: Selected Letters of the Adams Family, 1762–1784*, L. H. Butterfield *et al.* eds. (Cambridge: Harvard University Press, 1975), 86.

111. Fischer, *Paul Revere's Ride*, 154–56.

112. Ramsay, *History of the American Revolution*, vol. 1, at 207.

113. Gage to Dartmouth, June 25, 1775, *Correspondence of General Gage*, vol. 1, at 407.

114. *New York Journal*, August 31, 1775, at 1, col. 4. Also in Force ed., *American Archives*, 4th series, vol. 2, at 1027.

115. Madison to Bradford, June 19, 1775, *The Papers of James Madison*, William T. Hutchinson *et al.* eds. (Chicago: University of Chicago Press, 1962), vol. 1, at 153.

116. Joe D. Huddleston, *Colonial Riflemen in the American Revolution* (York, Pa.: George Shumway, 1978), 19.

117. *Virginia Gazette*, July 22, 1775, at 3, col. 2. The article is datelined "Philadelphia, July 11," but the incident appears to have originated "in one of our frontier counties" in Virginia. This version stated in part: "He, with a piece of chalk, drew on a board the figure of a nose of the common size, which he placed at the distance of one hundred and fifty yards, declaring that those who should come nearest the mark should be enlisted, when sixty odd hit the object."

118. Extract of a Letter to a Gentleman in London, Dated Philadelphia, June 20, 1775, in Force ed., *American Archives*, 4th series, vol. 2, at 1033.

119. Ibid., vol. 2, at 1034.

120. *London Chronicle*, August 17, 1775, quoted in Huddleston, *Colonial Riflemen in the American Revolution*, 25.

121. Also entitled "The Twelve United Colonies, by their Delegates in Congress, to the Inhabitants of Great Britain," the item was printed as a Postscript to the *Pennsylvania Packet*, July 17, 1775. *Journals of the Continental Congress, 1774–1779*, vol. 2, at 169.

122. *Connecticut Courant*, June 19, 1775, at 4, col. 2.

123. *Journals of the Continental Congress, 1774–1779*, vol. 2, at 140–57.

124. Ibid., vol. 2, at 151. Also printed throughout the colonies, *e.g.*, *Connecticut Courant*, July 17, 1775, at 2, col. 1.

125. Ibid., vol. 2, at 151.

126. Ibid., vol. 2, at 136–37.

127. Gage to Dartmouth, July 24, 1775, *Correspondence of General Gage*, vol. 1, at 409.

128. Gage to Dartmouth, September 20, 1775, *Correspondence of General Gage*, vol. 1, at 416.

129. The address was not actually entered into the *Journals of the Continental Congress*, but was first published in the *Pennsylvania Packet*, August 7, 1775, and then reprinted. *E.g.*, *Connecticut Courant*, August 21, 1775, at 1, col. 3. See *Journals of the Continental Congress, 1774–1779*, vol. 2, at 112, 116.

130. John Joachim Zubly, *Great Britain's Right to Tax . . . By a Swiss* (Philadelphia: [Henry] Miller, 1775), 13.

131. Ibid.,15.

132. Ibid., 17–18.

133. *Virginia Gazette*, June 24, 1775, at 1, col. 1; *New York Journal*, June 24, 1775, at 1, col. 1; *Maryland Gazette* (Annapolis), July 20, 1775, at 1, col. 2.

134. *Pennsylvania Reporter*, May 1, 1775, at 4, col. 1.

135. *Postscript to the Pennsylvania Packet*, vol. IV, at 1, col. 1.

136. *Pennsylvania Reporter*, May 1, 1775, at 3, col. 1.

137. *New York Journal*, May 4, 1775, at 2, col. 3.

138. *New York Journal*, May 11, 1775, at 1, cols. 2–3.

139. Ira Allen, *Natural and Political History of the State of Vermont* (London: J.W. Myers, 1798), 60.

140. Gage to Dartmouth, May 25, 1775, *Correspondence of General Gage*, vol. 1, at 401.

141. *Virginia Gazette* (Williamsburg), August 5, 1775, at 2, col. 1.

142. *Pennsylvania Reporter*, May 8, 1775, at 4, col. 1.

143. *Virginia Gazette*, April 22, 1775, at 2, col. 3, and at 3, col. 1. Also in *Pennsylvania Reporter*, May 8, 1775, at 4, col. 1.

144. R. D. Meade, *Patrick Henry* (Philadelphia: J.B. Lippincott, 1969), 50–51.

145. Ibid., 53.

146. John Carter Matthews, *Richard Henry Lee* (Williamsburg: Virginia Independence Bicentennial Commission, 1978), 30.

147. *Virginia Gazette*, May 6, 1775, at 3, col. 1.

148. R. D. W. Conner, *History of North Carolina: The Colonial and Revolutionary Periods, 1584–1783* (Chicago: Lewis Publishing Co., 1919), vol. 1, at 360.

149. Ibid., vol. 1, at 362.

150. *North Carolina Gazette* (Newbern), July 7, 1775, at 2, col. 3.

151. Ibid., at 3, col. 1.

152. *Colonial Records of North Carolina*, William L. Saunders ed. (Raleigh: Josephus Daniels, 1890), vol. 10, at 144–45.

153. Ibid., vol. 10, at 150.

154. Ibid., vol. 10, at 162.

155. Ibid., vol. 10, at 314.

156. Ibid., vol. 10, at 446.

157. Ibid., vol. 10, at 447.

158. *North Carolina Gazette,* July 14, 1775, at 1, col. 1.

159. Force ed., *American Archives*, 4th series, vol. 3, at 621.

160. Fischer, *Paul Revere's Ride*, 284.

161. *New York Journal*, November 2, 1775, at 3, col. 3.

162. To Esek Hopkins, Cambridge (no signature), October 21, 1775, in "Revolutionary Correspondence from 1775 to 1782," *Collections of the Rhode Island Historical Society* (Providence: Hammond, Angell, 1867), vol. 6, at 132.

## CHAPTER 5

1. See generally Pauline Maier, *American Scripture: Making the Declaration of Independence* (New York: Alfred A. Knopf, 1997); Morton White, *The Philosophy of the American Revolution* (New York: Oxford University Press, 1978); John Phillip Reid, *Constitutional History of the American Revolution: The Authority of Rights* (Madison: University of Wisconsin Press, 1986).

2. "The Declaration of Independence was emphatically not a bill of rights in the American sense, that is, a statement of fundamental rights that government must honor and protect . . . ." Maier, *American Scripture*, 164. This was in contrast to the Bill of Rights to the Constitution introduced by James Madison in 1789, "protecting several basic civil rights—including freedom of religion, of speech, and of the press, the rights of assembly and of petition, and the right to bear arms . . . ." Ibid., 195.

3. Thomas Jefferson, *The Living Thoughts of Thomas Jefferson*, John Dewey ed. (New York: Longmans, 1963), 42. For a detailed analysis of these and similar sources, see Stephen P. Halbrook, *That Every Man Be Armed: The Evolution of a Constitutional Right* (Albuquerque: University of New Mexico Press, 1984; reprinted, Oakland, Calif.: The Independent Institute, 1994, 2000), ch. 1. See also Bernard Bailyn, *The Ideological Origins of the American Revolution* (Cambridge: Belknap Press, 1967).

4. Aristotle, *The Politics*, T. A. Sinclair trans. (New York: Penguin Books, 1962), 79.

5. Cicero, *Selected Political Speeches*, Michael Grant trans. (New York: Penguin Books, 1969), 222.

6. John Locke, *Of Civil Government: Second Treatise* (Chicago: Henry Regnery/Gateway, 1955), 114–15.

7. Algernon Sidney, *Discourses Concerning Government* (printed by the Booksellers of London and Westminster, 1698), 157.

8. Maier, *American Scripture*, 157–58.

9. Henry Onderdonk, Jr., *Revolutionary Incidents of Suffolk and Kings Counties; With an*

*Account of the Battle of Long Island, and the British Prisons and Prison-ships at New York* (New York: Leavitt & Co., 1849), 59.

10. *The Complete Writings of Thomas Paine*, Philip S. Foner ed. (New York: Citadel Press, 1969), vol. 1, at 49.

11. Ibid., 50.

12. Ibid., 54.

13. Ibid., 55–56.

14. Ibid., 56.

15. *The American Crisis II*, January 13, 1777, in Foner ed., *The Complete Writings of Thomas Paine*, vol. 1, 65.

16. Foner ed., *The Complete Writings of Thomas Paine*, vol. 1, 69.

17. *The American Crisis III*, April 19, 1777, in Foner ed., *The Complete Writings of Thomas Paine*, vol. 1, 85.

18. *Journals of the Provincial Congress, Provincial Convention, Committee of Safety and Council of Safety of the State of New-York: 1775–1776–1777* (Albany: Thurlow Weed, 1842), vol. 1, at 149–50.

19. *E.g., New York Journal*, September 7, 1775, at 3, col. 4; ibid., September 14, 1775, at 4, col. 2; and every issue thereafter.

20. *New York Journal*, October 26, 1775, at 2, col. 4.

21. *Journals of the Provincial Congress*, vol. 1, at 156.

22. *Journals of the Provincial Congress*, vol. 2, at 85.

23. Agnes Hunt, *The Provincial Committees of Safety of the American Revolution* (Cleveland: Western Reserve University, 1904; reprinted, New York: Haskell House Publishers, 1968), 65–66.

24. *Journals of the Provincial Congress*, vol. 1, at 184.

25. *Calendar of Historical Manuscripts, Relating to the War of the Revolution, in the Office of the Secretary of State, Albany, N.Y.* (Albany: Weed, Parsons and Company, Printers, 1868), vol. 1, at 201.

26. *New York Journal*, December 28, 1775, at 3, cols. 3–4.

27. *The Writings of George Washington*, John C. Fitzpatrick ed. (Washington, D.C.: U.S. Government Printing Office, 1932–1940), vol. 9, at 274–75.

28. *Journals of the Continental Congress, 1774–1779*, Worthington C. Ford ed. (Washington, D.C.: Government Printing Office, 1906), vol. 4, at 25 (January 3, 1776).

29. Ibid., 1631.

30. *Calendar of Historical Manuscripts*, vol. 1, at 218.

31. Ibid., vol. 1, at 259–60.

32. *Journals of the Continental Congress, 1774–1789*, Worthington C. Ford ed. (Washington, D.C.: Government Printing Office, 1906), vol. 4, at 204.

33. Ibid., vol. 4, at 205.

34. Hunt, *The Provincial Committees of Safety of the American Revolution*, 65–66.

35. *Calendar of Historical Manuscripts*, vol. 1, at 281–82.

36. *Laws of the Legislature of the State of New York, in Force Against the Loyalists, and Affecting the Trade of Great Britain, and British Merchants, and Others Having Property in That State* (London: H. Reynell, 1786), 110–11.

37. For summaries of test laws, laws against free speech, and other anti-loyalist enactments by the state legislatures, see appendices B and C of Claude Halstead van Tyne, *The Loyalists in the American Revolution* (New York: Bert Franklin, 1970), 318–41. See also James W. Thompson, *Anti-Loyalist Legislation During the American Revolution*, 3 Ill. L. Rev. 81 (1908); James Truslow Adams, *New England in the Republic 1776–1850* (Boston: Little, Brown & Co., 1926), 63.

38. *E.g.*, see Lester J. Cappon and Stella F. Duff, *Virginia Gazette Index, 1736–1780* (Williamsburg: The Institute of Early American History and Culture, 1950), vol. 2, which contains scores of references to such items as: "Arms, export from Great Britain prohibited . . . seized by Americans . . . seized by

British . . . seizure ordered in American colonies. . . ." Ibid., vol. 2, at 30–31. "Pistols, captured by Americans . . . export . . . to British colonies, N.Am., forbidden . . . for sale. . . ." "Pistols, pocket, for sale. . . ." Ibid., vol. 2, at 884.

39. Gage to Dartmouth, September 20, 1775, in *The Correspondence of General Thomas Gage with the Secretaries of State, and with the War Office and the Treasury, 1763–1775*, Clarence E. Carter ed. (New Haven, Conn.: Yale University Press, 1931–33), vol. 1, at 415.

40. *Virginia Gazette* (Williamsburg), September 14, 1776, at 1, cols. 1–2.

41. Ibid., October 23, 1778, at 2, col. 1.

42. *E.g.,* ibid., May 1, 1778, at 3, col. 1 ("a genteel pair of pocket pistols"); July 10, 1778, at 3, col. 3 ("three pair of four pound guns and carriages, and every other implement complete, 150 pair of pistols" for sale); February 12, 1780, at 3, col. 2 ("Blunderbusses, pistols with swivels, muskets, cutlasses").

43. *Sources of American Independence*, Howard H. Peckman ed. (Chicago: University of Chicago Press, 1978), vol. 1, at 176.

44. John W. Shy, *A People Numerous and Armed: Reflections on the Military Struggle for American Independence* (London: Oxford University Press, 1976); William F. Marina, "Revolution and Social Change: The American Revolution as a People's War," *Literature of Liberty* (April–June 1978), vol. 1, at 5, 21–27.

45. Don Higginbotham, "The American Militia: A Traditional Institution with Revolutionary Responsibilities," in Don Higginbotham ed., *Reconsiderations on the Revolutionary War* (Westport, Conn.: Greenwood Press, 1978), 103.

46. See Lawrence Delbert Cress, *Citizens in Arms: The Army and Militia in American Society to the War of 1812* (Chapel Hill: University of North Carolina Press, 1982); Don Higginbotham, "The Federalized Militia Debate: A Neglected Aspect of Second Amendment Scholarship," *The William and Mary Quarterly*, 3rd Ser., vol. 55, no. 1. (Jan. 1998), 39.

47. Henry Lee, *Memoirs of the War in the Southern Department of the United States* (New York: University Publishing Co., 1869), 90.

48. Ibid., 110. *Cf.* 167.

49. Ibid., 187.

50. Ibid.

51. Ibid., 260.

52. Ibid., 85.

53. Jefferson to Giovanni Fabbroni, June 8, 1778, Thomas Jefferson, *Writings* (New York: Literary Classics of the United States, 1984), 760.

54. Articles of Confederation, Art. II.

55. Ibid., Art. IV.

56. Ibid., Art. V.

57. Ibid., Art. VI.

58. Ibid., Art. VII.

59. Ibid., Art. IX.

60. Ibid.

61. *Journals of the Continental Congress* (October 23, 1783), 741–42.

62. Ibid.

CHAPTER 6

1. See Gordon S. Wood, *The Creation of the American Republic, 1776–1787* (Chapel Hill: University of North Carolina Press, 1998), 271–73.

2. *Extracts from the Journals of the Provincial Congress* (Charles-Town: Peter Timothy, 1776), 26–27. The committee included Charles Cotesworth Pinckney, John Rutledge, Charles Pinckney, Henry Laurens, Christopher Gadsden, Rawlins Lowndes, Arthur Middleton, Henry Middleton, Thomas Bee, Thomas Lynch, Jr., and Thomas Heyward, Jr.

3. Ibid., 82.

4. Ibid., 137–38.

5. Jonathan Elliot ed., *The Debates in the Several State Conventions on the Adoption of the Federal Constitution* (Philadelphia: J.B. Lippincott Co., 1836), vol. 4, at 316.

6. John Drayton, *Memoirs of the American Revolution . . . As Relating to South Carolina* (Charleston: A. E. Miller, 1821), vol. 1, at 378.

7. Ibid., vol. 2, at 255.

8. Ibid., vol. 2, at 266.

9. Ibid., vol. 2, at 267.

10. *The Public Laws of the State of South Carolina, from Its First Establishment as a British Province to the Year 1790, Inclusive* (Philadelphia: R. Aitken & Son, 1790), App. 13.

11. Ibid., 14.

12. Russell F. Weigley, *The Partisan War: The South Carolina Campaign of 1780–1782* (Columbia: University of South Carolina Press, 1970).

13. Drayton, *Memoirs of the American Revolution*, vol. 1, at 12.

14. *Virginia Gazette* (Williamsburg), December 1, 1774, at 2, col. 3.

15. *North Carolina Gazette* (New Bern), July 14, 1775, at 1, col. 1.

16. *Extracts from the Journals of the Provincial Congress*, 121.

17. Ibid., 54.

18. *The Public Laws of the State of South Carolina*, 174.

19. Ibid.

20. Ibid., 168. Similarly, "their using and carrying wooden swords and other mischievous and dangerous weapons" out of the plantation was prohibited, and "if he or they be armed with such offensive weapons aforesaid, him or them [white persons] to disarm, take up and whip." Ibid., 172.

21. Ibid.

22. Ibid., 205.

23. Ibid., 207.

24. George Mason, *The Papers of George Mason*, Robert A. Rutland ed. (Chapel Hill: University of North Carolina Press, 1970), vol. 1, at 210–11. On Virginia's independent voluntary companies, see E. M. Sanchez-Saavedra, *A Guide to Virginia Military Organizations in the American Revolution* (Richmond: Virginia State Library, 1978), 7 *ff.*

25. Ibid., 215–16.

26. Ibid., 229–30.

27. Ibid., 229–30.

28. *Proceedings of the Convention of Delegates* (Williamsburg, Va.: Alexander Purdue, 1776), 100–2.

29. *Virginia Gazette* (Williamsburg), October 18, November 1, and November 8, 1776, at 1.

30. Ibid., February 16, 1776, Supp. at 2.

31. Thomas Jefferson, *The Papers of Thomas Jefferson*, Julian P. Boyd ed. (Princeton, N.J.: Princeton University Press, 1950), vol. 1, at 344–45.

32. Ibid., vol. 1, at 353.

33. Ibid., vol. 1, at 347.

34. Ibid., vol. 2, at 443–44.

35. Ibid., vol. 1, at 362–63.

36. Dumas Malone, *Jefferson the Virginian*, vol. 1 of *Jefferson and His Time* (Boston: Little, Brown, & Co., 1948), 46–47.

37. Henry S. Randall, *The Life of Thomas Jefferson* (Philadelphia: J.B. Lippincott & Co., 1865), vol. 1, at 14–15.

38. *Jefferson's Memorandum Books*, James A. Bear, Jr., & Lucia C. Stanton eds. (Princeton, N.J.: Princeton University Press, 1997), 81.

39. See "Firearms" in Index and referenced text in *Jefferson's Memorandum Books*, 1550. See also

Ashley Halsey, Jr., "Jefferson's Beloved Guns," *American Rifleman* (November 1969), 17.

40. Jefferson, *The Papers of Thomas Jefferson*, vol. 1, at 377.

41. *The Commonplace Book of Thomas Jefferson: A Repertory of His Ideas on Government*, Gilbert Chinard ed. (Baltimore: Johns Hopkins University Press, 1926), vol. 4. This is a condensed version.

42. Montesquieu, *The Spirit of the Laws*, Thomas Nugent, trans. (New York: Colonial Press, 1899), vol. 1, at 36; ibid., vol. 2, at 64. In No. 797 of *The Commonplace Book* (Jefferson Papers), Jefferson copied portions of a page where Montesquieu opposed "severe punishments" for "trifling" matters. Jefferson read, but did not copy, the following: "Hence it follows, that the laws of an Italian republic [Venice], where bearing fire-arms is punished as a capital crime and where it is not more fatal to make an ill use of them than to carry them, is not agreeable to the nature of things." Montesquieu, *The Spirit of the Laws*, vol. 2, at 79–80.

43. Compare translation from Montesquieu, *The Spirit of the Laws*, vol. 1, at 57–58, with *The Commonplace Book*, Chinard ed., 261. Chinard compares this quotation with the anti-standing army provisions in Jefferson's proposed Virginia Constitution, in ibid., and with the militia clause of the Virginia Declaration of Rights, in Thomas Jefferson, *Pensées Choisies de Montesquieu tirees du Commonplace Book de Thomas Jefferson*, Gilbert Chinard ed. (Paris: Societe de Edition "Les Belles Lettres," 1925), 34.

44. *Commonplace Book*, Chinard ed., 314; Cesare Beccaria, *On Crimes and Punishments*, Henry Paolucci trans. (Englewood Cliffs, N.J.: Prentice Hall, 1963), 87–88.

45. William Eden, *Principles of Penal Law* (Dublin: John Milliken, 1772), 301.

46. Ibid., 210–11.

47. Ibid., 213–14.

48. Jefferson, *The Papers of Thomas Jefferson*, vol. 2, at 350.

49. Ibid., 251. See William W. Hening, *Statutes at Large; Being a Collection of all the Laws of Virginia from the First Session of the Legislature in the Year 1619* (Philadelphia: Thomas Desilver, 1823), vol. 9, at 267–69.

50. Act of 1757, Hening, *Statutes at Large*, vol. 7, at 95.

51. New Jersey Constitution, Art. XVIII (1776).

52. Ibid., Art. XXII.

53. Charles R. Erdman, Jr., *The New Jersey Constitution of 1776* (Princeton, N.J.: Princeton University Press, 1929), 32.

54. Ibid., 33.

55. Ibid., 36.

56. Ibid., 37.

57. William Blackstone, *Commentaries*, St. George Tucker ed. (Philadelphia: William Young Birch and Abraham Small, 1803), vol. 1, at 140–44.

58. Ibid.

59. William Griffith, *Eumenes: Being a Collection of Papers Written for the Purpose of Exhibiting Some of the More Prominent Errors and Omissions of the Constitution of New Jersey* (Trenton: G. Craft, 1799), vol. 9.

60. *Journal of the Votes and Proceedings of the Convention of New Jersey*, June 10–August 21, 1776 *passim* (Burlington: Isaac Collins, 1776). On the Constitution, see ibid., 49–51.

61. *New-York Gazette and the Weekly Mercury* (Newark, N.J.), October 5, 1776, at 2, col. 2.

62. Ibid., October 26, 1776, at 1, col. 2.

63. *Documentary History of the Ratification of the Constitution*, Merrill Jensen ed. (Madison: State Historical Society of Wisconsin, 1978), vol. 3, at 120.

64. Peter Force ed., *American Archives* (Washington D.C.: M. St. Clair Clark, 1837–1853), 5th series, vol. 1, at 1211–1212; vol. 2, at 505.

65. *New-York Gazette*, November 2, 1776, at 3, cols. 1–2.

66. *Writings of George Washington*, vol. 10, at 90.

67. *Acts of the Council and General Assembly of the State of New Jersey* (Trenton: Isaac Collins, 1784), 235.

68. Ibid., 168.

69. Ibid., 169.

70. Ibid., 180.

71. Pennsylvania Declaration of Rights, Art. XIII (1776).

72. J. Paul Selsam, *The Pennsylvania Constitution of 1776: A Study in Revolutionary Democracy* (Philadelphia: University of Pennsylvania Press, 1936), 175–76. See generally Steven Rosswurm, *Arms, Country, and Class: The Philadelphia Militia and "Lower Sort" During the American Revolution, 1775–1783* (New Brunswick, N.J.: Rutgers University Press, 1987), 94–105.

73. *Pennsylvania Gazette* (Philadelphia), June 12, 1776, at 2.

74. Selsam, *Pennsylvania Constitution of 1776*, 148.

75. *The Proceedings Relative to Calling the Conventions of 1776 and 1790* (Harrisburg, Pa.: John S. Wiestling, 1825), 48 [hereafter cited *Proceedings*].

76. Ibid., 49.

77. Richard Alan Ryerson, *The Revolution Is Now Begun: The Radical Committees of Philadelphia, 1765–1776* (Philadelphia: University of Pennsylvania Press, 1978), 117–18, 240.

78. Ibid., 113–15, 167, 241.

79. Alexander Graydon, *Memoirs of His Own Time: With Reminiscences of the Men and Events of the Revolution*, John Stockton Littell ed. (Philadelphia: Lindsay & Blakiston, 1846), 286–87.

80. John Adams, *Diary and Autobiography*, L.H. Butterfield ed. (Cambridge: Harvard University Press, 1961), 391.

81. Burton Alva Konkle, *George Bryan and the Constitution of Pennsylvania, 1731–1791* (Philadelphia: William J. Campbell, 1922), 119.

82. Ibid., 121.

83. Ibid., 117 n.1.

84. Foner ed., *The Complete Writings of Thomas Paine*, vol. 2, at 53.

85. Ibid., vol. 1, at 45.

86. Ibid., vol. 1, at 35.

87. Ibid., vol. 2, at 57.

88. Graydon, *Memoirs*, 287.

89. Ibid., 288.

90. Selsam, *Pennsylvania Constitution of 1776*, 207 n.6.

91. Pennsylvania Declaration of Rights, Art. XIII (1776); *Proceedings*, 56.

92. Compare Saul Cornell and Nathan DeDino, *A Well Regulated Right*, 73 Fordham L. Rev. 487, 496–98 (November 2004) (arguing that the Pennsylvania Declaration did not guarantee an individual right for personal protection), with *The Works of the Honourable James Wilson* (Philadelphia: Lorenzo Press, 1804), vol. 3, at 84 (noting that justifiable homicide "is expressly recognised in the constitution of Pennsylvania. 'The right of the citizens to bear arms in the defence of themselves shall not be questioned.'"). Wilson's explanation is discussed below in Chapter 13.

93. *Pennsylvania Evening Post* (Philadelphia), August 20, 1776, at 413.

94. Benjamin Franklin, *The Papers of Benjamin Franklin*, W.B. Wilcox ed. (New Haven, Conn.: Yale University Press, 1982), vol. 2, at 514 n.2, 3.

95. *Pennsylvania Evening Post*, September 26, 28, October 8, 10, 15, 17, 19, 22, 24, 1776.

96. Ibid., October 24, 1776, at 531, col. 1.

97. Ibid., col. 2.

98. Ibid., October 31, 1776, at 546.

99. *Proceedings*, 57.

100. *Pennsylvania Evening Post*, October 10, 1776, at 503.

101. *The Political Thought of Benjamin Franklin*, Ralph L. Ketcham ed. (New York: Bobbs-Merrill Co., 1965), 46.

102. Ibid., 47–8.

103. Ibid., 49.

104. Pennsylvania Constitution, Art. I, § 43 (1776); *Proceedings*, 57.

105. *Pennsylvania Evening Post*, October 10, 1776, at 503.

106. Ibid., at 527, col. 1

107. Ibid., November 5, 1776, at 554, cols. 1–2.

108. Blackstone, *Commentaries*, vol. 2, at *412.

109. Ibid., vol. 2, at *413.

110. Foner ed., *The Complete Writings of Thomas Paine*, vol. 2, at 1085.

111. Selsam, *Pennsylvania Constitution of 1776*, 178–79.

112. Virginia Declaration of Rights, Art. XIII (1776).

113. Pennsylvania Declaration of Rights, Art. XIII (1776).

114. Selsam, *Pennsylvania Constitution of 1776*, 182–83.

115. Foner ed., *The Complete Writings of Thomas Paine*, vol. 1, at 373–74.

116. Peter Force ed., *American Archives* (Washington D.C.: M. St. Clair Clark, 1837–1853), vol. 6, at 965.

117. *Acts of the General Assembly of the Commonwealth of Pennsylvania, Enacted into Laws, Since the Declaration of Independence on the Fourth Day of July, A.D. 1776*, Ch. XV, at 22 (March 17, 1777).

118. *Acts of the General Assembly of the Commonwealth of Pennsylvania* (Philadelphia: Francis Bailey, 1782), 347 (March 20, 1780).

119. *An Abridgment of the Laws of Pennsylvania, 1700–1811*, John Purdon ed. (Philadelphia: Farrand, 1811), 173.

120. Ibid., 174.

121. Ibid., 208.

122. *Documentary History of the Ratification of the Constitution*, vol. 3, at 37.

123. Ibid., vol. 3, at 37, 115.

124. Ibid., vol. 3, at 38–39.

125. *Proceedings of the Convention of the Delaware State* (Wilmington: James Adams, 1776), 12. The other members were Richard Bassett, Jacob Moore, Charles Ridgley, John Evans, Alexander Porter, James Sykes, John Jones, James Rench, and William Polk.

126. Ibid., 13.

127. Ibid., 15.

128. Konkle, *George Bryan and the Constitution of Pennsylvania*, 124 n.1.

129. Ibid., 119.

130. Ibid., 124 n.1.

131. *Pennsylvania Evening Post*, August 20, 1776, at 413.

132. *Proceedings of the Convention of the Province of Maryland* (Annapolis: Frederick Green, 1776) (August 27, 1776).

133. *Proceedings of the Convention of the Delaware State*, 16 ff.

134. *Letters to and from Caesar Rodney, 1756–1784*, George Herbert Ryden ed. (Philadelphia: University of Pennsylvania Press for the Historical Society of Delaware, 1933), 119.

135. Delaware Declaration of Rights, Art. XVIII (1776).

136. Maryland Declaration of Rights, Art. XXV (1776).

137. Virginia Declaration of Rights, Art. XIII (1776).

138. Force ed., *American Archives*, vol. 1, at 1022.

139. Delaware Declaration of Rights, Arts. XIX, XX (1776); Pennsylvania Declaration of Rights, Art. XIII (1776).

140. Pennsylvania Declaration of Rights, Art. XIII (1776).

141. *Proceedings of the Convention of the Delaware State*, 20, 40.

142. Delaware Declaration of Rights, Art. III (1776).

143. Article signed by "Philo-Alethias, Delaware," *Maryland Gazette*, October 31, 1776, at 3, col. 1.

144. *Laws of the Government of New-Castle, Kent and Sussex Upon Delaware* (Philadelphia: B. Franklin, 1741), 171.

145. *Laws of the Government of New-Castle, Kent and Sussex Upon Delaware* (Philadelphia: B. Franklin, 1763), 12.

146. *Laws of the Government* (1741), 152.

147. Ibid., 178.

148. *Proceedings of the Convention of the Delaware State*, 36.

149. Ibid., 40.

150. David C. Skaggs, *Roots of Maryland Democracy, 1753–1776* (Westport, Conn.: Greenwood Publishing Group, 1973), 220.

151. Ibid., 224.

152. Ibid., 225.

153. Ibid.

154. Ronald Hoffman, *A Spirit of Dissension: Economics, Politics, and the Revolution in Maryland* (Baltimore: Johns Hopkins University Press, 1973), 170.

155. Ibid., 171.

156. Ibid.

157. Skaggs, *Roots of Maryland Democracy*, 227–28.

158. Ibid., 190–95.

159. Ibid., 185.

160. Ibid., 191.

161. Ibid., 190–91.

162. *Proceedings of the Convention of the Province of Maryland* (Annapolis: Frederick Green, 1776), 29.

163. Ibid., 39.

164. Ibid., 49.

165. Ibid., 50–58 (October 31–November 3, 1776). The Delaware Declaration of Rights was published in the *Maryland Gazette*, October 1, 1776, at 1. Maryland's militia clause would be almost identical with that of Delaware.

166. Maryland Declaration of Rights, Art. VIII (1776).

167. Ibid., Art. XXXIII.

168. *Maryland Gazette* (Annapolis), October 13, 1768, at 2, col. 2.

169. Ibid., October 20, 1768, at 3, col. 1.

170. *Maryland Gazette*, June 22, 1775, at 1, col. 1.

171. Ibid., August 24, 1775, at 1, cols. 1–2. Local manufacture of arms was encouraged, the following advertisement being typical: "Wanted immediately, a number of hands who are acquainted in the different branches of the manufacture of firearms." Ibid., at 3, col. 1.

172. Ibid., Art. XXV.

173. Ibid., Art. XXVI. The declaration was published in the *Maryland Gazette* on November 14, 1776, at 3.

174. *Proceedings of the Convention of the Province of Maryland* (Annapolis: Frederick Green, 1775), 7.

175. *The General Public Statutory Law and Public Local Law of the State of Maryland, From the Year 1692–1839 Inclusive* (Baltimore: John D. Toy, 1840), 31.

176. *Colonial Records of North Carolina*, William L. Saunders ed. (Raleigh: Josephus Daniels, 1890), vol. 10, at 870a.

177. Ibid., vol. 10, at 870b.

178. Virginia Declaration of Rights, Art. XIII (1776).

179. Pennsylvania Declaration of Rights, Art. XIII (1776).

180. *Colonial Records of North Carolina*, vol. 10, at 918–19. The committee included "Willie Jones, Thomas Person, and Griffith Rutherford, radical leaders; Allen Jones, Thomas Jones, Samuel Ashe, and Archibald Maclaine, conservative leaders; Richard Caswell and Cornelius Harnett, who may be classed as moderates." Robert D.W. Connor, *History of North Carolina* (Chicago: Lewis Publishing Co., 1919), vol. 1, at 412.

181. *North Carolina Gazette* (New Bern), July 7, 1775, at 2, col. 3.

182. The committee was appointed on November 13 and reported the Bill of Rights on December 12, and the convention passed it on December 17, 1776. Connor, *History of North Carolina*, vol. 1, at 413. The debate took place on December 14, 16, and 17, 1776. J. Seawell Jones, *A Defense of the Revolutionary History of North Carolina from the Aspersions of Mr. Jefferson* (Raleigh: Turner and Hughes, 1834), 286.

183. *Proceedings and Debates of the Convention of North Carolina* [1835] (Raleigh: Joseph Gales and Son, 1836), 318.

184. Ibid., 391.

185. *The Papers of James Iredell*, Ron Higginbotham ed. (Raleigh: North Carolina Division of Archives & History, 1976), vol. 1, at 425.

186. *Journal of Proceedings of the Provincial Congress of North Carolina* (Newbern: James Davis, 1776), 3–4.

187. *North Carolina Gazette* (New Bern), July 7, 1775, at 2, col. 3.

188. Ibid., Art. XXV. The provision described the state boundaries, and provided that titles of individuals holding under previous laws would remain valid.

189. *Journal of Proceedings of the Provincial Congress of North Carolina* (1776), 32.

190. *Statutes of the State of North Carolina* (Edenton: Hodge and Wills, 1791), 519.

191. Ibid., 592.

192. *A Collection of the Statutes of the Parliament of England in Force in the State of North Carolina* (New Bern: Editor's Press, 1792), 6, 398.

193. See *Laws of the State of North Carolina* (Raleigh: J. Gales, 1821).

194. *Statutes of the State*, 93.


CHAPTER 7

1. Richard Price, *A Sermon Delivered to a Congregation of Protestant Dissenters* (London, 1779), 26.

2. *Documentary History of the Ratification of the Constitution*, Merrill Jensen ed. (Madison: State Historical Society of Wisconsin, 1978), vol. 3, at 201.

3. *Williamsburg Virginia Gazette*, October 27, 1774, at 2, col. 2.

4. Kenneth Coleman, *The American Revolution in Georgia, 1763–1789* (Athens: University of Georgia, 1958), 76–77.

5. Ibid., 80.

6. The Constitution of the State of Georgia (Savannah, 1777), i.

7. Committee members included: Button Gwinnett, William Belcher, Joseph Wood, Josiah Lewis, John-Adam Treutlen, Henry Jones, and George Wells. Ibid.

8. Ibid., i–ii.

9. Ibid., 1.

10. Constitution of the State of Georgia, Arts. LIX, LX, and LXI (1777).

11. Ibid., Art. XXXV.

12. Coleman, *The American Revolution in Georgia*, 87.

13. *Documentary History of the Ratification of the Constitution*, vol. 3, at 205.

14. Coleman, *The American Revolution in Georgia*, 89.

15. Ibid., 119; *Documentary History of the Ratification of the Constitution*, vol. 3, at 204.

16. Coleman, *The American Revolution in Georgia*, 94.

17. *Digest of the Laws of the State of Georgia*, Horatio Marbury & William A. Crawford eds. (Savannah: Seymour, Woolhopter, and Stebbins, 1802), 241.

18. Ibid., 241–42.

19. Ibid., 423.

20. Ibid.

21. Ibid., 424.

22. Ibid., 432.

23. Ibid., 437.

24. *New York Packet and American Advertiser*, January 4, 1776, at 1, col. 4, and at 4, col. 4.

25. Ibid., August 26, 1776, at 2, cols. 2–3.

26. *E.g.,* ibid., January 18, 1776, at 3, col. 4.

27. Ibid., April 4, 1776, at 2, col. 1.

28. Ibid., at 2, cols. 1–2.

29. Ibid., April 18, 1776, at 1, col. 4.

30. Ibid., at 2, col. 1.

31. Ibid.

32. *New York Gazette and Weekly Advertiser*, September 30, 1776 and thereafter.

33. Constitution of 1777, in *Reports of the Proceedings and Debates of the Convention of 1821*, Nathaniel H. Carter & William Stone eds. (Albany, N.Y.: F. and E. Hansford, 1821), 691–96 (hereafter cited as "Constitution of 1777").

34. Theodore Roosevelt, *Gouverneur Morris* (Boston: Houghton, Mifflin, and Co., 1898), 51.

35. *Journals of the Provincial Congress, Provincial Convention, Committee of Safety and Council of Safety of the State of New York* (Albany: T. Weed, 1842), vol. 1, at 552.

36. William Smith, William Duer, Gouverneur Morris, Robert R. Livingston, John Broome, John M. Scott, John Jay, John S. Hobart, Abraham Yates, Henry Wisner, Sr., Samuel Townsend, Charles DeWitt, and Robert Yates. Ibid. See Constitution of 1777, 692–94.

37. Constitution of 1777, 692–94.

38. For accounts of the framing of the New York Constitution, see George Dangerfield, *Chancellor Robert R. Livingston* (New York: Brace and Co., 1960), 88; George Pellew, *John Jay* (Boston: Houghton, Mifflin, 1898), 74; Henry Flanders, *The Lives and Times of the Chief Justices of the Supreme Court* (Philadelphia: J.B. Lippincott, 1869), vol. 1, at 200 *ff.*; Jared Sparks, *The Life of Gouverneur Morris* (Boston: Gray and Bowen, 1832), vol. 1, at 123; Charles Z. Lincoln, *The Constitutional History of New York* (Rochester: Lawyers Co-operative Publishing Co., 1906), 487–559. See also Edward Countryman, *A People in Revolution: The American Revolution and Political Society in New York, 1760–1790* (Baltimore: Johns Hopkins University Press, 1981).

39. Bernard Mason, *The Road to Independence: The Revolutionary Movement in New York, 1773–1777* (Lexington: University of Kentucky Press, 1966), 229.

40. Pellew, *John Jay*, 76–77.

41. *Journals of the Provincial Congress*, vol. 1, at 892.

42. New York Constitution, Art. XL (1777).

43. *New York Journal, and Dailey Patriotic Register*, June 13, 1788, at 2, cols. 1–2.

44. Pellew, *John Jay*, 87. See Douglas Greenberg, *Crime and Law Enforcement in the Colony of New York, 1691–1776* (Ithaca, N.Y.: Cornell University Press, 1974).

45. *Laws of the State of New York, Comprising the Constitution, and the Acts of the Legislature, Since the Revolution, from the First to the Fifteenth Session, Inclusive* (New York: Thomas Greenleaf, 1792), vol. 1, at 336.

46. Ibid., vol. 1, at 289, 291.

47. Ibid., vol. 1, at 491.

48. See Stephen P. Halbrook, *A Right to Bear Arms* (Westport, Conn.: Greenwood Press, Inc., 1989), 34–35, which cites references to Ira Allen, *Autobiography* (1799), in James B. Wilbur, *Ira*

*Allen: Founder of Vermont, 1751–1814* (Boston: Houghton, Mifflin, 1928); and Ira Allen, *Natural and Political History of the State of Vermont* (London: J. W. Myers, 1798), 49.

49. Allen, *Autobiography* (1799), in Wilbur, *Ira Allen: Founder of Vermont*, 40.

50. Ibid., 73–78.

51. Ibid., 85.

52. Ibid., 87.

53. *Vermont State Papers*, William Slade compl. (Middlebury: J. W. Copeland, 1823), 70.

54. Daniel Chipman, *A Memoir of Thomas Crittenden, the First Governor of Vermont* (Middlebury: D. Chipman, 1849), 27.

55. Rev. Pliny H. White, "Address on the Windsor Convention," *Vermont Historical Society Collections* (1870), vol. 1, at 63.

56. Vermont Constitution, Art. I, § 15 (1777); Pennsylvania Declaration of Rights, Art. XIII (1776).

57. Vermont Constitution, Art. XXXIX (1777); Pennsylvania Constitution, Art. I, § 43 (1776).

58. Vermont Constitution, Art. I, § 9 (1777).

59. *The Laws from the Year 1779 to 1786, Inclusive*, in *Vermont State Papers*, 307.

60. *Statutes of the State of Vermont, Passed February and March 1789* (1789), 97.

61. Ibid., 95–96.

62. Vermont Constitution, Art. I, § 18 (1787). The provision was once again readopted as *Vermont Constitution*, Art. I, § 16 (1796).

63. Massachusetts Declaration of Rights, Art. I (1780) (emphasis added).

64. Ibid., Art. XVII.

65. John Adams, *The Works of John Adams* (Boston: Little, Brown, & Co., 1851), vol. 4, at 215–16.

66. *The Writings of Samuel Adams*, Harry Alonzo Cushing ed. (New York: G. P. Putnam's Sons, 1904), vol. 2, at 102.

67. John Adams, *Legal Papers* (Cambridge: Belknap Press/Harvard University Press, 1965), vol. 1, at 137.

68. David McCullough, *John Adams* (New York: Simon & Schuster, 2001), 177.

69. *The Writings of Samuel Adams*, Harry Alonzo Cushing ed. (New York: G.P. Putnam's Sons, 1907), vol. 3, at 162–63, 172.

70. Massachusetts Declaration of Rights, Art. XIX (1780).

71. *Journal of the Convention for Framing a Constitution of Government for the State of Massachusetts Bay (1779–1780)* (Boston: Dutton & Wentworth, 1832), 41.

72. Massachusetts Declaration of Rights, Art. XVI (1780).

73. Ibid., Art. X.

74. That was not a novel concept. Sir Henry Vance the Younger defined "free Citizen[s]" as those who "have deserved to be trusted with the keeping or bearing Their own Armes in the publick defence." *The Political Works of James Harrington*, J. G. A. Pocock ed. (New York: Cambridge University Press, 1977), 109.

75. *Journal of the Convention for Framing a Constitution of Government for the State of Massachusetts Bay (1779–1780)* (Boston: Dutton & Wentworth, 1832), 41.

76. Ibid. See John Adams, *Diary and Autobiography*, L. H. Butterfield ed. (Cambridge: Harvard University Press, 1961), 401. No records of debates were kept, although in the convention of 1820–1821 some members remembered the speeches of Samuel Adams and John Adams in 1779. *Journal of Debates to Revise the Constitution of Massachusetts* (Boston: Daily Advertiser, 1853), 430, 435.

77. *The Popular Sources of Political Authority: Documents on the Massachusetts Constitution of 1780*, Oscar and Mary Handlin eds. (Cambridge: Belknap Press of Harvard University Press, 1966), 574.

78. Ibid., 624.

79. Massachusetts Declaration of Rights, Arts. I and XVII (1780).

80. John Adams, *A Defence of the Constitutions of Government of the United States of America* (London: C. Dilly, 1788), vol. 3, at 471–72.

81. William Gordon wrote the most extensive articles on the constitution in the series "To the Freemen of the Massachusetts Bay." References to Adams and the convention are included in the *Independent Chronicle*, May 4, 1780.

82. *Independent Chronicle*, June 29, 1780, at 4, col. 3.

83. Abbé de Mably, *Remarks Concerning the Government and the Laws of the United States of America: In Four Letters, Addressed to Mr. Adams* (Dublin: Moncrieffe, Jenkin, 1785), 166.

84. *The Perpetual Laws of the Commonwealth of Massachusetts, From the Establishment of Its Constitution in the Year 1780, To the End of the Year 1800* (1801), vol. 1, at 346.

85. Ibid., vol. 1, at 366.

86. "Scribble Scrabble," *Cumberland Gazette* (Portland, Me.), December 8, 1786.

87. "Senex," *Cumberland Gazette*, January 12, 1787.

88. "Scribble-Scrabble," *Cumberland Gazette*, January 26, 1787.

89. Jedidiah Morse, *The American Universal Geography* (Boston: Isaiah Thomas & Ebenezer T. Andrews, 1793), vol. 1, at 379.

90. *Commonwealth v. Blanding*, 20 Mass. (3 Pick.) 304, 314, 15 Am. Dec. 214 (1825).

91. *Sources and Documents of U.S. Constitutions*, William Finley Swindler ed. (Dobbs Ferry, N.Y.: Oceana Publications, Inc., 1973–1979), vol. 6, at 342.

92. Constitutions of New Hampshire (undated microfilm, Library of Congress), 155.

93. *An Address of the Convention . . . To the Inhabitants* (Exeter, N.H., 1782), 10.

94. Ibid., 14.

95. Robert Allen Rutland, *The Birth of the Bill of Rights* (New York: Collier Books, 1962), 81; *Documentary History of the First Federal Elections*, Merrill Jensen and Robert A. Becker eds. (Madison: University of Wisconsin, 1976), vol. 1, at 858–59.

96. *New-Hampshire Gazette and Historical Chronicle* (Portsmouth), January 6, 1775, at 1, col. 1 (Governor's Proclamation); M.L. Brown, *Firearms in Colonial America: The Impact on History and Technology, 1492–1792*, (Washington, D.C.: Smithsonian Institution, 1980), 295.

97. New Hampshire Constitution, Pt. I, Art. XIII (1784).

98. Ibid., Art. XIII.

99. Ibid., Art. VI.

100. Ibid., Art. XXX.

101. The Perpetual Laws of the State of New Hampshire (Portsmouth, 1789), 115.

102. Ibid., 116. Certain government officials and students, Quakers, Native Americans, and African Americans were excepted from the militia.

103. Ibid., 117.

104. Ibid.

105. Ibid.

106. Ibid., 184.

107. Ibid., 184–85.

108. *Documentary History of the Ratification of the Constitution*, John P. Kaminski and Gaspare J. Saladino eds. (Madison: State Historical Society of Wisconsin, 1995), vol. 18, at 188.

109. *Sources of American Independence*, Howard H. Peckham ed. (Chicago: University of Chicago Press, 1978), 150.

110. David M. Roth and Freeman Meyer, *From Revolution to Constitution: Connecticut 1763 to 1818* (Chester, Conn.: Pequot Press, 1975), 25; Melbert B. Cary, *The Connecticut Constitution* (New Haven, Conn.: The Tuttle, Morehouse and Taylor, Co., 1900), 2–3.

111. R.R. Hinman, *A General View of Connecticut at the Commencement of the Revolutionary War* (1842), in *Chronology and Documentary Handbook to the State of Connecticut*, Mary L. French ed. (Dobbs Ferry, N.Y.: Oceana, 1973), 40–50.

112. *Public Records of the Colony of Connecticut, From May 1775, to June, 1776, inclusive,* at 17, 291 (Hartford, Conn.: Brown & Parsons, n.d.). Council of Safety minutes mostly concern manufacture of gunpowder and plans of resistance. Ibid., 451 *ff.* In 1775 Connecticut had numerous gunsmiths, and a state bounty of five shillings per firearm greatly encouraged manufacture. David M. Roth, *Connecticut: A Bicentennial History* (New York: W. W. Norton, 1979), 101.

113. Ibid., 156.

114. Ibid., 22.

115. *Acts and Laws of the State of Connecticut* (Hartford: Elisha Babcock, 1784), 144.

116. Ibid., 150.

117. Ibid., 151.

118. Richard Price, *Observations on the Importance of the American Revolution* (London and Boston, 1784), 16.

119. Ibid., 58.

120. Ibid., 63.

121. Timothy Dwight, *Travels in New England and New York* (London: W. Baynes & Son, 1823), vol. 4, 335.

122. *Sources of American Independence,* Peckham ed., vol. 1, at 165.

123. Ibid., vol. 1, at 176.

124. *Newport Mercury,* March 27, 1775, at 2, col. 3.

125. David S. Lovejoy, *Rhode Island Politics and the American Revolution, 1760–1776* (Providence: Brown University Press, 1958), 173, 188.

126. *Newport Mercury,* August 14, 1775, at 3, col. 2.

127. Public Laws of the State of Rhode Island (Providence: Carter and Wilkinson, 1798), 429–30.

128. Ibid., 426.

129. Ibid., 5.

130. Ibid., 612–14.

131. Ibid., 593.

132. Ibid., 583.

133. Thomas Jefferson, *The Papers of Thomas Jefferson,* Julian P. Boyd ed. (Princeton, N.J.: Princeton University Press, 1950), vol. 2, at 444.

134. Ibid., vol. 2, at 443–44. Emphasis added.

135. Act of 1772, William W. Hening, *Statutes at Large; Being a Collection of all the Laws of Virginia from the First Session of the Legislature in the Year 1619,* vol. 8, at 593.

136. Blackstone, *Commentaries,* vol. 2, at *341.

137. Jefferson's Bill for Establishing a Manufactory of Arms, which defined "arms" as muskets, carbines, pistols, and swords, passed in 1779. Thomas Jefferson, *The Papers of Thomas Jefferson,* Julian P. Boyd ed. (Princeton, N.J.: Princeton University Press, 1951), vol. 3, at 132, 135.

138. "But one species of firearms, the pistol, is never called a gun." Noah Webster, *An American Dictionary of the English Language* (New York: S. Converse, 1828), definition of "gun."

139. Jefferson, *The Papers of Thomas Jefferson,* vol. 2, at 444.

140. Ibid.

141. The Acts of 1748 (Hening, *Statutes at Large,* vol. 6, 109–10) and 1792 (Hening, *Statutes at Large,* vol. 12, at 123) stated: "No negro or mulatto shall keep or carry any gun, powder, shot, club, or other weapon whatever [under penalty of 39 lashes] . . . *provided nonetheless,* that every free negro or mulatto, being a housekeeper, may be permitted to keep one gun, powder and shot," and a "bond or free negro" may "keep and use" a gun by license at frontier plantations.

142. Act of 1785, Hening, *Statutes at Large,* vol. 12, at 182.

143. Jefferson, *The Papers of Thomas Jefferson,* vol. 2, at 663.

CHAPTER 8

1. See generally Forrest McDonald, *Novus Ordo Seclorum: The Intellectual Origins of the Constitution* (Lawrence: University Press of Kansas, 1985).

2. *The Papers of George Mason*, Robert A. Rutland ed. (Chapel Hill: University of North Carolina Press, 1970), vol. 3, at 896–97.

3. Jonathan Elliot ed., *Debates on the Adoption of the Federal Constitution in the Convention Held at Philadelphia . . . Vol. V. Supplementary to Elliot's Debates* (Philadelphia: J.B. Lippincott, 1845), 172.

4. Ibid., 440.

5. Ibid.

6. Ibid., 443.

7. Ibid.

8. Ibid.

9. Ibid.

10. Ibid., 444.

11. Ibid.

12. Ibid.

13. Ibid.

14. Ibid., 445.

15. Ibid.

16. Ibid., 464.

17. Ibid., 464–65.

18. Ibid., 465.

19. Ibid.

20. Stephen P. Halbrook, *A Right to Bear Arms* (Westport, Conn.: Greenwood Press, Inc., 1989), 26, 32, 46.

21. Elliot, *Debates on the Adoption of the Federal Constitution in the Convention Held at Philadelphia . . . Vol. V. Supplementary to Elliot's Debates*, 466.

22. Ibid., 466–67.

23. U.S. Constitution, Art. I, § 8.

24. Ibid.

25. Ibid., Art. II, § 2.

26. Ibid., Art. I, § 10.

27. Elliot, *Debates on the Adoption of the Federal Constitution in the Convention Held at Philadelphia . . . Vol. V. Supplementary to Elliot's Debates*, 544.

28. Ibid., 545.

29. Ibid.

30. U.S. Constitution, Art. IV, § 2.

31. Ibid., Art. I, §§ 9, 10.

32. Ibid., Art. III, § 2.

33. Elliot, *Debates on the Adoption of the Federal Constitution in the Convention Held at Philadelphia . . . Vol. V. Supplementary to Elliot's Debates*, 538.

34. Ibid., 538.

35. Ibid.

36. Ibid.

37. Ibid., 545.

38. Ibid.

39. Ibid., 554.

40. Ibid., 565.

41. *Documentary History of the Ratification of the Constitution*, John P. Kaminski and Gaspare J. Saladino eds. (Madison: State Historical Society of Wisconsin, 1988), vol. 8, at 43.

42. Ibid., vol. 8, at 45.

43. Richard M. Rollins, *The Long Journey of Noah Webster* (Philadelphia: University of Pennsylvania, 1980), 52–53.

44. Ibid., 51–52.

45. *Documentary History of the Ratification of the Constitution*, John P. Kaminski & Gaspare J. Saladino eds. (Madison: State Historical Society of Wisconsin, 1981), vol. 13, at 405–6.

46. Noah Webster, *An Examination of the Leading Principles of the Federal Constitution* (Philadelphia, 1787), 43.

47. *The Federalist*, Nos. 29 (Hamilton) and 45 (Madison), in *The Federalist Papers* (New Rochelle, N.Y.: Arlington House, n.d.), 185, 299.

48. John S. Morgan, *Noah Webster* (New York: Mason/Charter Publishers Inc., 1975), 114.

49. *Documentary History of the Ratification of the Constitution*, Merrill Jensen ed. (Madison: State Historical Society of Wisconsin, 1976), vol. 2, at 128.

50. Ibid., vol. 2, at 181.

51. Tench Coxe, "An American Citizen IV" (October 21, 1787), in *Documentary History of the Ratification of the Constitution*, vol. 13, at 433.

52. Ibid., vol. 13, at 435.

53. Letter of October 21, 1787, in ibid., vol. 13, at 437.

54. Letter of October 26, 1787, in ibid.

55. *Documentary History of the Ratification of the Constitution*, vol. 2, at 166.

56. Ibid., vol. 2, at 158.

57. *Documentary History of the Ratification of the Constitution*, vol. 13, at 337–41.

58. Ibid., vol. 13, at 387.

59. Ibid., vol. 13, at 390–91. "Cincinnatus," apparently Richard Henry Lee or Arthur Lee, wrote in the *New York Journal* in November 1787 that the Grecian and Roman republics kept no standing armies and that:

> in the free Swiss Cantons, no standing army, was ever, or is now permitted; no, sir, in all these great and glorious republics, though surrounded with enemies, their military array was occasional, or at the utmost, annual; nor was there formerly, nor is there now, in the Swiss Cantons, any more appearance of strength kept up in time of peace, than their militia gives: and yet they are free and formidable.

*Documentary History of the Ratification of the Constitution*, John P. Kaminski ed. (Madison: State Historical Society of Wisconsin, 1983), vol. 14, at 127. See also ibid., vol. 14, at 186–87.

60. *Documentary History of the Ratification of the Constitution*, vol. 13, at 486, 490.

61. *Documentary History of the Ratification of the Constitution*, John P. Kaminski and Gaspare J. Saladino eds. (Madison: State Historical Society of Wisconsin, 1984), vol. 15, at 104.

62. Ibid., vol. 15, at 318.

63. Ibid.

64. William Blackstone, *Commentaries*, St. George Tucker ed. (Philadelphia: William Young Birch and Abraham Small, 1803), vol. 1, at 332.

65. *Documentary History of the Ratification of the Constitution*, vol. 15, at 319.

66. Ibid.

67. Ibid., vol. 15, at 320.

68. Ibid., vol. 15, at 479.

69. Ibid., vol. 15, at 488–89.

70. Ibid., vol. 15, at 492–93.

71. *Documentary History of the Ratification of the Constitution*, John P. Kaminski and Gaspare J. Saladino eds. (Madison: State Historical Society of Wisconsin, 1995), vol. 18, at 127.

72. Ibid., vol. 18, at 128.

73. Ibid., vol. 18, at 129–30.

74. Ibid., vol. 18, at 130.

75. Ibid.

76. Ibid., vol. 18, at 131.

77. *Documentary History of the Ratification of the Constitution*, vol. 14, at 15–18. See also Robert H. Webking, "Melancton Smith and the Letters from the Federal Farmer," *William & Mary Quarterly* (July 1987), vol. 3.44, no. 3, at 510.

78. *Documentary History of the Ratification of the Constitution*, vol. 14, at 27–28.

79. Ibid., vol. 14, at 38–39.

80. Ibid., vol. 14, at 45–46.

81. *Documentary History of the Ratification of the Constitution*, John P. Kaminski and Gaspare J. Saladino eds. (Madison: State Historical Society of Wisconsin, 1995), vol. 17, at 265–68.

82. Ibid., vol. 17, at 273.

83. Ibid., vol. 17, at 274.

84. Ibid., vol. 17, at 343.

85. Ibid., vol. 17, at 346.

86. Ibid., vol. 17, at 347–50.

87. Ibid., vol. 17, at 362. Also in *Additional Letters from the Federal Farmer to the Republican* (New York: Thomas Greenleaf, 1788), 169.

88. Ibid., vol. 17, at 363. Also in *Additional Letters from the Federal Farmer to the Republican*, 170. Emphasis added.

89. David McCullough, *John Adams* (New York: Simon & Schuster, 2001), 378.

90. *E.g.*, *Documentary History of the Ratification of the Constitution*, vol. 2, at 160.

91. John Adams, *A Defence of the Constitutions of Government of the United States of America* (London, 1787), vol. 1, at 28–30.

92. Ibid., vol. 1, at 38–39.

93. John Adams, *A Defence of the Constitutions of Government of the United States of America* (1787–88), vol. 3, at 471–72. Newspapers of the time alluded to Rome's disarming of conquered peoples. The *Massachusetts Centinel*, April 11, 1787 recalled "the old Roman Senator, who after his country subdued the commonwealth of Carthage, had made them deliver up . . . their arms . . . and rendered them unable to protect themselves. . . ." *Documentary History of the Ratification of the Constitution*, vol. 13, at 79.

94. Adams, *A Defence of the Constitutions of Government of the United States of America*, vol. 3, at 474.

95. Ibid., vol.3, at 475.

96. *Documentary History of the Ratification of the Constitution*, vol. 14, at 464–65.

97. Thomas Jefferson, *Writings*, Merrill D. Peterson ed. (New York: The Library of America, 1984), 816–17.

98. *Jefferson's Memorandum Books*, James A. Bear, Jr., and Lucia C. Stanton eds. (Princeton, N.J.: Princeton University Press, 1997), 615–16.

99. Ibid., 615 n.55; Ashley Halsey, Jr., "Jefferson's Beloved Guns," *American Rifleman* (November 1969), 17, 20; Halsey, "How Thomas Jefferson's Pistols Were Restored," *American Rifleman* (November 1969), 21.

100. *Jefferson's Memorandum Books*, 675.

101. Jefferson, *Writings*, 215.

102. Ibid., 216.

103. Ashley Halsey, Jr., "George Washington's Favorite Guns," *American Rifleman* (February 1968), 23.

CHAPTER 9

1. *Documentary History of the Ratification of the Constitution*, Merrill Jensen ed. (Madison: State Historical Society of Wisconsin, 1976), vol. 2, at 209.

2. *Documentary History of the Ratification of the Constitution*, Merrill Jensen ed. (Madison: State Historical Society of Wisconsin, 1976), vol. 3, at 41.

3. Wilson was quoted as stating about the Constitution in debate on November 24, 1787: "In its principles, it is surely democratical; for, however wide and various the firearms of power may appear, they may all be traced to one source, the people." Ibid., vol. 2, at 336. However, two longer versions of the speech use the term "streams of power," suggesting that "firearms of power" was a misprint. Ibid., vol. 2, at 349, 363.

4. Jonathan Elliot ed., *The Debates in the Several State Conventions on the Adoption of the Federal Constitution* (Philadelphia: J.B. Lippincott, 1836), vol. 2, at 435–36.

5. *Documentary History of the Ratification of the Constitution*, vol. 2, at 441.

6. Elliot ed., *Debates in the Several State Conventions on the Adoption of the Federal Constitution*, vol. 2, at 453–54.

7. *Documentary History of the Ratification of the Constitution*, vol. 2, at 508–9.

8. Elliot ed., *Debates in the Several State Conventions on the Adoption of the Federal Constitution*, vol. 2, at 495.

9. Ibid., vol. 2, at 521.

10. Ibid., vol. 2, at 522.

11. Ibid., vol. 2, at 537.

12. Ibid., vol. 2, at 540.

13. *Documentary History of the Ratification of the Constitution*, vol. 2, at 597–99.

14. Ibid., vol. 2, at 599–600.

15. Ibid., vol. 2, at 589–91, 600.

16. Ibid., vol. 2, at 617.

17. Ibid., vol. 2, at 597, 623.

18. Ibid., vol. 2, at 623–24.

19. Pennsylvania Declaration of Rights, Art. XIII (1776).

20. William Blackstone, *Commentaries*, St. George Tucker ed. (Philadelphia: William Young Birch and Abraham Small, 1803), vol. 2, at 412–13.

21. *Cf.* Paul Finkelman, *"A Well Regulated Militia": The Second Amendment in Historical Perspective* 76, Chi.–Kent L. Rev. 195, 206–09 (2000)(arguing that the differences in the Minority proposal and what became the Second Amendment indicate that the latter was not intended to protect individual rights).

22. Pennsylvania Constitution, Art. I, § 43 (1776).

23. *Documentary History of the Ratification of the Constitution*, vol. 2, at 598, 624.

24. Burton Alva Konkle, *George Bryan and the Constitution of Pennsylvania, 1731–1791* (Philadelphia: William J. Campbell, 1922), 258.

25. Ibid., 309–38.

26. Ibid., 630.

27. *Documentary History of the Ratification of the Constitution*, vol. 2, at 598, 624.

28. Ibid., vol. 2, at 638.

29. *Independent Gazetteer*, February 11, 1788, in *Documentary History of the Ratification of the Constitution*, vol. 2 (microfilm supplement), at 1695.

30. *Pennsylvania Gazette*, February 20, 1788, in *Documentary History of the Ratification of the Constitution*, vol. 2, at 439.

31. *Pennsylvania Gazette*, February 20, 1788, in *Documentary History of the Ratification of the Constitution*, vol. 2 (microfilm supplement), at 1778–1780.

32. Philadelphia *Freeman's Journal*, April 23, 1788, in *Documentary History of the Ratification of the Constitution*, John P. Kaminski and Gaspare J. Saladino eds. (Madison: State Historical Society of Wisconsin, 1995), vol. 17, at 137.

33. Montesquieu, *The Spirit of the Laws*, Thomas Nugent, trans. (1899), vol. 2, at 79–80.

34. *Documentary History of the Ratification of the Constitution*, vol. 2 (microfilm supplement), at 2483.

35. "The Government of Nature Delineated" (1788), in ibid., vol. 2 (microfilm supplement), at 2524.

36. Ibid., vol. 2, at 2526.

37. Elliot ed., *Debates in the Several State Conventions on the Adoption of the Federal Constitution*, vol. 2, at 545.

38. Ibid., vol. 2, at 545–46. For the Virginia source, see Jonathan Elliot ed., *The Debates in the Several State Conventions on the Adoption of the Federal Constitution* (Philadelphia: J. B. Lippincott, 1836), vol. 3, at 660.

39. *Documentary History of the Ratification of the Constitution*, vol. 3, at 125.

40. *Documentary History of The Ratification of the Constitution*, John P. Kaminski and Gaspare J. Saladino eds. (Madison: State Historical Society of Wisconsin, 1988), vol. 8, at 43.

41. *New Jersey Journal*, December 19, 1787, in ibid., vol. 8, at 154–55.

42. *Documentary History of the Ratification of the Constitution*, vol. 3, at 223.

43. Ibid., vol. 3, at 247.

44. *Documentary History of the Ratification of the Constitution*, vol. 3, at 389.

45. Ibid.

46. Ibid., vol. 3, at 489–90.

47. *Documentary History of the First Federal Elections, 1788–1790*, Gordon DenBoer ed. (Madison: University of Wisconsin Press, 1984), vol. 2, at 13.

48. *Documentary History of the Ratification of the Constitution*, John P. Kaminski and Gaspare J. Saladino eds. (Madison: State Historical Society of Wisconsin, 1997), vol. 4, at 90.

49. Ibid., vol. 4, at 90–91.

50. *Documentary History of the Ratification of the Constitution*, John P. Kaminski and Gaspare J. Saladino eds. (Madison: State Historical Society of Wisconsin, 1998), vol. 5, at 1035.

51. Ibid., vol. 4, at 353.

52. *The Freeman's Journal* (Philadelphia), January 16, 1788, in *The Antifederalist Papers*, Morton Borden ed. (Ann Arbor: Michigan State University, 1965), 75.

53. Ibid.

54. *Documentary History of the Ratification of the Constitution*, vol. 4, at 392, 395.

55. Ibid., vol. 5, at 514.

56. *Documentary History of the Ratification of the Constitution*, John P. Kaminski and Gaspare J. Saladino eds. (Madison: State Historical Society of Wisconsin, 2000), vol. 6, at 1310.

57. Ibid., vol. 6, at 1311.

58. Ibid., vol. 6, at 1315. Also in Elliot ed., *Debates in the Several State Conventions on the Adoption of the Federal Constitution*, vol. 2, at 78.

59. Ibid., vol. 6, at 1316–17. Also in Elliot ed., *Debates in the Several State Conventions on the Adoption of the Federal Constitution*, vol. 2, at 80.

60. Ibid., vol. 6, at 1331–32.

61. Ibid., vol. 6, at 1322–23. Also in Elliot ed., *Debates in the Several State Conventions on the Adoption of the Federal Constitution*, vol. 2, at 87.

62. Ibid., vol. 6, at 1328. Also in Elliot ed., *Debates in the Several State Conventions on the Adoption of the Federal Constitution*, vol. 2, at 93.

63. Ibid., vol. 6, at 1328. Also in Elliot ed., *Debates in the Several State Conventions on the Adoption of the Federal Constitution*, vol. 2, at 94.

64. Ibid., vol. 6, at 1337. Also in Elliot ed., *Debates in the Several State Conventions on the Adoption of the Federal Constitution*, vol. 2, at 97.

65. *Massachusetts Gazette*, January 25, 1788, in *Documentary History of the Ratification of the Constitution*, vol. 5, at 804.

66. Ibid., vol. 6, at 1381.

67. Ibid., vol. 6, at 1384–85.

68. Ibid., vol. 6, at 1395.

69. Ibid., vol. 6, at 1397.

70. Ibid.

71. Ibid., vol. 6, at 1399–1400.

72. Ibid., vol. 6, at 1400.

73. Ibid., vol. 6, at 1450.

74. Ibid.

75. Ibid., vol. 6, at 1450–51.

76. *Massachusetts Gazette*, February 5, 1788, in *Documentary History of the Ratification of the Constitution*, vol. 5, at 865–66.

77. *Documentary History of the Ratification of the Constitution*, vol. 6, at 1453.

78. Ibid., vol. 6, at 1454.

79. Ibid., vol. 6, at 1490.

80. *Documentary History of the Ratification of the Constitution*, John P. Kaminski and Gaspare J. Saladino eds. (Madison: State Historical Society of Wisconsin, 2001), vol. 7, at 1583–84.

81. Ibid.

82. Ibid., vol. 6, at 1461–62.

83. Ibid., vol. 6, at 1469.

84. *Massachusetts Gazette*, February 8, 1788, in ibid., vol. 7, at 1612.

85. Ibid., vol. 7, at 1612 n.2.

86. *Documentary History of the Ratification of the Constitution*, vol. 7, at 1597.

87. Ibid.

88. Ibid., vol. 7, at 1598.

89. *Creating the Bill of Rights: The Documentary Record from the First Federal Congress*, Helen E. Veit *et al.* eds. (Baltimore: Johns Hopkins University Press, 1991), 241.

90. *Independent Chronicle*, August 6, 1789, in *Documentary History of the Ratification of the Constitution*, vol. 6, at 1453. Also in "From the Boston Independent Chronicle," *Independent Gazetteer*, August 20, 1789, at 2, col. 2.

91. Jonathan Elliot ed., *The Debates in the Several State Conventions on the Adoption of the Federal Constitution* (Philadelphia: J. B. Lippincott, 1836), vol. 1, at 372.

92. Ibid., vol. 1, at 382.

93. Ibid., vol. 1, at 324.

94. William Paca, Samuel Chase, and Robert Goldsborough. Ibid., vol. 2, at 549.

95. Ibid., vol. 2, at 550.

96. Ibid., vol. 2, at 552.

97. Ibid., vol. 2, at 553.

98. Ibid., vol. 2, at 555. On the above proceedings, see also *Documentary History of the Ratification of the Constitution*, vol. 17, at 241–46.

99. Jonathan Elliot ed., *The Debates in the Several State Conventions on the Adoption of the Federal Constitution* (Philadelphia: J. B. Lippincott, 1836), vol. 4, at 313.

100. Ibid., vol. 4, at 315.

101. Ibid., vol. 4, at 316.

102. Ibid.

103. Ibid., vol. 4, at 319.

104. Ibid., vol. 4, at 320.

105. Ibid., vol. 4, at 337.

106. Ibid., vol. 4, at 338.

107. Ibid., vol. 4, at 341.

108. *Documentary History of the Ratification of the Constitution*, John P. Kaminski and Gaspare

J. Saladino eds. (Madison: State Historical Society of Wisconsin, 1986), vol. 16, at 179.

109. Besides Sullivan, the federalists on the committee included John Langdon, Bartlett (Josiah or Thomas), Benjamin Bellows, Samuel Livermore, Benjamin West, Francis Worcester, and John Pickering. Antifederalists were Atherton, Joseph Badger, Thomas Dow, Smith (Ebenezer or Jonathan), Abel Parker, William Hooper, and Charles Barrett. Ibid., vol. 16, at 79. See also Joseph B. Walker, *A History of the New Hampshire Convention* (Boston: Cupples & Hurd, 1888), 40.

110. *Documentary History of the Ratification of the Constitution*, John P. Kaminski and Gaspare J. Saladino eds. (Madison: State Historical Society of Wisconsin, 1995), vol. 18, at 187.

111. Ibid., vol. 18, at 188; Elliot ed., *Debates in the Several State Conventions on the Adoption of the Federal Constitution*, vol. 1, at 326. "The right to bear arms, going back to the English Bill of Rights, received recognition in the Second Amendment to the Constitution. . . . Counting this article, seven out of twelve of New Hampshire's proposals were ultimately accepted." Edward Dumbauld, *The Bill of Rights and What It Means Today* (Norman: University of Oklahoma Press, 1957), 21 n.37.

112. *New-Hampshire Mercury* (Portsmouth), September 27, 1786, reprinted as "An account of the insurrection in New-Hampshire in 1786," *Collections of the New Hampshire Historical Society* (Concord: Jacob B. Moore, 1832), vol. 2, 117.

113. *Cf.* Paul Finkelman, *"A Well Regulated Militia": The Second Amendment in Historical Perspective*, 195, 229 (arguing that "Congress shall never disarm any Citizen" actually meant that "Congress cannot disarm the militias").

114. Walker, *A History of the New Hampshire Convention*, 40.

115. Ibid., 41.

116. Ibid., 42.

117. "Remarks," No. II, *Federal Gazette* (Philadelphia), October 24, 1788.

118. No. IV, *Fayetteville Gazette* (North Carolina), October 12, 1789, at 1, cols. 2–3 and 2, cols. 1–2.

119. No. VIII, *Federal Gazette*, November 14, 1788.

120. Ibid.

121. No. XI, *Federal Gazette*, November 28, 1788.

122. Ibid.

123. No. XII, ibid., December 2, 1788, and No. XXVIII, ibid., February 16, 1789.

124. *Documentary History of the First Federal Elections*, Merrill Jensen and Robert A. Becker eds. (Madison: University of Wisconsin, 1976), vol. 1, at 839–40. However, the federalists too supported an armed population. The *New Hampshire Spy*, March 10, 1789, reported that the state was "engaged in organising her militia, which is by far the best disciplined in the United States." Ibid., vol. 1, at 840.

CHAPTER 10

1. *The Documentary History of the Ratification of the Constitution*, John P. Kaminski and Gaspare J. Saladino eds. (Madison: State Historical Society of Wisconsin, 1988), vol. 8, at 401–2.

2. *Winchester Gazette* (Virginia), February 22, 1788, in ibid., vol. 8, at 404.

3. Ibid.

4. Ibid., vol. 8, at 404–5.

5. *The Documentary History of the Ratification of the Constitution*, vol. 8, at 250–51.

6. Spencer to Madison, letter dated February 28, 1788, ibid., vol. 8, at 425.

7. Ibid., vol. 8, at 427 n.4.

8. A Native of Virginia: Observations upon the Proposed Plan of Federal Government, 2 April 1788, in *The Documentary History of the Ratification of the Constitution*, John P. Kaminski and Gaspare J. Saladino eds. (Madison: State Historical Society of Wisconsin, 1990), vol. 9, at 658.

9. Ibid., vol. 9, at 714.

10. Ibid., vol. 9, at 773–74.

11. Ibid., vol. 9, at 859.

12. Ibid., vol. 9, at 883.

13. Ibid., vol. 9, at 878–79.

14. Jonathan Elliot ed., *The Debates in the Several State Conventions on the Adoption of the Federal Constitution* (Philadelphia: J. B. Lippincott, 1836), vol. 3, at 37.

15. Ibid., vol. 3, at 45.

16. Ibid., vol. 3, at 51.

17. Ibid., vol. 3, at 51–52.

18. Ibid., vol. 3, at 52 (quoting U.S. Constitution, Art. 1, § 8, cl. 16).

19. Ibid., vol. 3, at 76–77; *The Documentary History of the Ratification of the Constitution*, vol. 9, at 981.

20. Elliot ed., *Debates in the Several State Conventions on the Adoption of the Federal Constitution*, vol. 3, at 90.

21. Ibid., vol. 3, at 112.

22. Ibid., vol. 3, at 137; *The Documentary History of the Ratification of the Constitution* (Madison: State Historical Society of Wisconsin, 1990), vol. 9, at 1036.

23. Elliot ed., *Debates in the Several State Conventions on the Adoption of the Federal Constitution*, vol. 3, at 149.

24. Ibid., vol. 3, at 150; *The Documentary History of the Ratification of the Constitution*, vol. 9, at 1046–47.

25. *The Documentary History of The Ratification of the Constitution*, vol. 9, at 817.

26. Ibid., vol. 9, at 819.

27. Ibid., vol. 9, at 821.

28. Frank Monaghan, *Heritage of Freedom: The History & Significance of the Basic Documents of American Liberty* (Princeton, N.J.: Princeton University Press, 1947), 58.

29. *The Documentary History of the Ratification of the Constitution*, vol. 9, at 821.

30. Ibid., vol. 9, at 823.

31. U.S. Constitution, Art. I, § 8, cl. 17.

32. Elliot ed., *Debates in the Several State Conventions on the Adoption of the Federal Constitution*, vol. 3, at 168–69 (referring to Art. 1, § 8, cl. 17); *The Documentary History of the Ratification of the Constitution*, vol. 9, at 1065.

33. Elliot ed., *Debates in the Several State Conventions on the Adoption of the Federal Constitution*, vol. 3, at 169 (referring to Art. 1, § 8, cl. 18); *The Documentary History of the Ratification of the Constitution*, vol. 9, at 1066.

34. Elliot ed., *Debates in the Several State Conventions on the Adoption of the Federal Constitution*, vol. 3, at 171; *The Documentary History of the Ratification of the Constitution*, vol. 9, at 1068.

35. See Ch. 5 of this work and Henry Lee, *Memoirs of the War in the Southern Department of the United States* (New York: University Publishing Co., 1869).

36. Elliot ed., *Debates in the Several State Conventions on the Adoption of the Federal Constitution*, vol. 3, at 178; *The Documentary History of the Ratification of the Constitution*, vol. 9, at 1074.

37. Elliot ed., *Debates in the Several State Conventions on the Adoption of the Federal Constitution*, vol. 3, at 191; *The Documentary History of the Ratification of the Constitution*, vol. 9, at 1085.

38. Elliot ed., *Debates in the Several State Conventions on the Adoption of the Federal Constitution*, vol. 3, at 246–47; *The Documentary History of the Ratification of the Constitution*, vol. 9, at 1135–36.

39. Elliot ed., *Debates in the Several State Conventions on the Adoption of the Federal Constitution*, vol. 3, at 206.

40. *Virginia Independent Chronicle*, June 11, 1788, in *The Documentary History of the Ratification of the Constitution*, John P. Kaminski and Gaspare J. Saladino eds. (Madison: State Historical Society of Wisconsin, 1993), vol. 10, at 1604.

41. Elliot ed., *Debates in the Several State Conventions on the Adoption of the Federal Constitution*, vol. 3, at 379.

42. Ibid., vol. 3, at 380.

43. Ibid.

44. Sir William Keith, *A Collection of Papers and Other Tracts* (London: J. Mechell, 1740), 180.

45. Ibid., 170.

46. Ibid., 175.

47. Sir William Keith, *Two Papers on the Subject of Taxing the British Colonies in America* (London: J. Almon, 1767), 9.

48. Ibid., 8.

49. Elliot ed., *Debates in the Several State Conventions on the Adoption of the Federal Constitution*, vol. 3, at 381.

50. Ibid., vol. 3, at 386.

51. Ibid., vol. 3, at 391.

52. Ibid., vol. 3, at 418.

53. Ibid., vol. 3, at 419–20.

54. Ibid., vol. 3, at 421.

55. Elliot ed., *Debates in the Several State Conventions on the Adoption of the Federal Constitution*, vol. 3, at 425–26.

56. Ibid., vol. 3, at 428.

57. Ibid., vol. 3, at 430.

58. Ibid., vol. 3, at 440.

59. U.S. Constitution, Art. IV, § 4.

60. Elliot ed., *Debates in the Several State Conventions on the Adoption of the Federal Constitution*, vol. 3, at 441; *The Documentary History of the Ratification of the Constitution*, vol. 10, at 1325.

61. James Madison to Ambrose Madison, June 24, 1788, in *The Papers of James Madison*, Robert Rutland *et al.* eds. (Charlottesville: University of Virginia Press, 1977), vol. 11, at 170.

62. Elliot ed., *Debates in the Several State Conventions on the Adoption of the Federal Constitution*, vol. 3, at 587.

63. Ibid., vol. 3, at 653.

64. Ibid., vol. 3, at 587.

65. Ibid., vol. 3, at 588; *The Documentary History of the Ratification of the Constitution*, vol. 10, at 1475–9.

66. Elliot ed., *Debates in the Several State Conventions on the Adoption of the Federal Constitution*, vol. 3, at 593.

67. Ibid.

68. Ibid., vol. 3, at 594; *The Documentary History of the Ratification of the Constitution*, vol. 10, at 1475–9.

69. Elliot ed., *Debates in the Several State Conventions on the Adoption of the Federal Constitution*, vol. 3, at 600.

70. Ibid., vol. 3, at 659.

71. Ibid., vol. 3, at 660.

72. Ibid., vol. 3, at 602.

73. Ibid., vol. 3, at 610.

74. Ibid., vol. 3, at 618.

75. Ibid., vol. 3, at 620.

76. Ibid., vol. 3, at 625.

77. Ibid., vol. 3, at 626–27.

78. Ibid., vol. 3, at 627.

79. Ibid., vol. 3, at 628.

80. Ibid., vol. 3, at 629–30.

81. Ibid., vol. 3, at 630.

82. Ibid., vol. 3, at 646.

83. Ibid., vol. 3, at 647–48.

84. Ibid., vol. 3, at 650.

85. Ibid., vol. 3, at 653.

86. Ibid.

87. Ibid., vol. 3, at 653–54.

88. Ibid., vol. 3, at 656.

89. Ibid.

90. Ibid., vol. 3, at 657.

91. Ibid., vol. 3, at 658–59.

92. *The Papers of George Mason*, Robert A. Rutland ed. (Chapel Hill: University of North Carolina Press, 1970), vol. 3, at 1068–71.

93. *The Documentary History of the Ratification of the Constitution*, vol. 9, at 821.

94. Elliot ed., *Debates in the Several State Conventions on the Adoption of the Federal Constitution*, vol. 3, at 659.

95. Ibid.

96. Ibid., vol. 3, at 660.

97. This proposal and its ultimate failure is not mentioned by supporters of the view that the Second Amendment only protects essentially what this proposal embodied. *E.g.*, Finkelman, *"A Well Regulated Militia": The Second Amendment in Historical Perspective*, 76 Chi.–Kent. L. Rev. 195, 201 (2000).

98. *The Documentary History of the Ratification of the Constitution*, vol. 9, at 821–23.

99. Ibid., vol. 10, at 1336.

100. Elliot ed., *Debates in the Several State Conventions on the Adoption of the Federal Constitution*, vol. 3, at 661–62.

CHAPTER 11

1. *Documentary History of the Ratification of the Constitution*, John P. Kaminski *et al.* eds. (Madison: Wisconsin Historical Society Press, 2003), vol. 19, at 157.

2. "From the Wilmington Centinel, To the People of North Carolina," *New York Journal and Daily Patriotic Register*, April 21, 1788, at 2, col. 2. This is the same newspaper as was previously called the *New York Journal and Daily Advertiser.*

3. *The Documentary History of the Ratification of the Constitution*, John P. Kaminski and Gaspare J. Saladino eds. (Madison: State Historical Society of Wisconsin, 1984), vol. 15, at 319.

4. *The Antifederalist Papers*, Morton Borden ed. (Ann Arbor: Michigan State University, 1965), 75.

5. *The Documentary History of the Ratification of the Constitution*, John P. Kaminski and Gaspare J. Saladino eds. (Madison: State Historical Society of Wisconsin, 1990), vol. 9, at 813.

6. Ibid., vol. 9, at 825.

7. Jonathan Elliot ed., *The Debates in the Several State Conventions on the Adoption of the Federal Constitution* (Philadelphia: J. B. Lippincott, 1836), vol. 2, at 214.

8. *The Documentary History of the Ratification of the Constitution*, John P. Kaminski and Gaspare J. Saladino eds. (Madison: State Historical Society of Wisconsin, 1993), vol. 10, at 1510 n.28.

9. Elliot ed., *Debates in the Several State Conventions on the Adoption of the Federal Constitution*, vol. 2, at 220.

10. Ibid., vol. 2, at 338.

11. Ibid., vol. 2, at 384.

12. Ibid., vol. 2, at 398.

13. Ibid., vol. 2, at 399.

14. Ibid., vol. 2, at 402.

15. Ibid., vol. 2, at 401.

16. Ibid., vol. 2, at 403.

17. Ibid., vol. 2, at 404.

18. Ibid., vol. 2, at 397.

19. Ibid., vol. 2, at 406.

20. Ibid.

21. Ibid., vol. 2, at 410.

22. Ibid.

23. Ibid., vol. 2, 411–12.

24. Ibid., vol. 2, at 413–14.

25. Jonathan Elliot ed., *The Debates in the Several State Conventions on the Adoption of the Federal Constitution* (Philadelphia: J. B. Lippincott, 1836), vol. 1, at 327.

26. Ibid., vol. 1, at 328. Also in *The Documentary History of the Ratification of the Constitution*, John P. Kaminski and Gaspare J. Saladino eds. (Madison: State Historical Society of Wisconsin, 1995), vol. 18, at 298.

27. Jonathan Elliot ed., *The Debates in the Several State Conventions on the Adoption of the Federal Constitution* (Philadelphia: J. B. Lippincott, 1836), vol. 3, at 658–59.

28. Elliot ed., *Debates in the Several State Conventions on the Adoption of the Federal Constitution*, vol. 1, at 328.

29. Ibid.

30. Ibid.

31. Ibid.

32. Ibid., vol. 1, at 329.

33. Ibid. Also in *The Documentary History of the Ratification of the Constitution*, vol. 18, at 300.

34. Elliot ed., *The Debates in the Several State Conventions on the Adoption of the Federal Constitution,* vol. 1, at 329.

35. Ibid., vol. 1, at 330.

36. Ibid., vol. 1, at 331. Also in *The Documentary History of the Ratification of the Constitution*, vol. 18, at 305.

37. See also the *New York Journal*, August 14, 1788, at 2, col. 4 ("the people will resist arbitrary power").

38. "From the Wilmington Centinel, To the People of North Carolina," *New York Journal*, April 21, 1788, at 2, col. 2. This issue of the *Wilmington Centinel* is not extant. *Documentary History of the Ratification of the Constitution*, John P. Kaminski *et al.* eds. (Madison: Wisconsin Historical Society Press, 2004), vol. 20, at 1185, App. of "Antifederalist Newspaper Articles."

39. North Carolina Declaration of Rights, XVII (1776).

40. R. D. W. Conner, *History of North Carolina: The Colonial and Revolutionary Periods, 1584–1783* (Chicago: Lewis Publishing Co., 1919), vol. 2, at 34.

41. Ibid., vol. 2, at 33.

42. Jonathan Elliot ed., *The Debates in the Several State Conventions on the Adoption of the Federal Constitution* (Philadelphia: J. B. Lippincott, 1836), vol. 4, at 9.

43. Ibid., vol. 4, at 64.

44. Ibid. The debates fail to specify whether the speaker was Archibald Maclaine or William Maclaine.

45. Ibid., vol. 4, at 137.

46. Ibid., vol. 4, at 138.

47. Ibid., vol. 4, at 141.

48. Ibid., vol. 4, at 142.

49. Ibid., vol. 4, at 148.

50. Ibid., vol. 4, at 149.

51. *The Papers of James Iredell*, Don Higginbotham ed. (Raleigh: North Carolina Division of Archives and History, 1976), vol. 1, at 79.

52. Elliot ed., *Debates in the Several State Conventions on the Adoption of the Federal Constitution*, vol. 4, at 153–54.

53. Ibid., vol. 4, at 161.

54. Ibid., vol. 4, at 166–67.

55. Ibid., vol. 4, at 167–68. The debates fail to specify whether the speaker was Timothy Bloodworth or James Bloodworth.

56. Ibid., vol. 4, at 168.

57. Ibid., vol. 4, at 200.

58. Ibid., vol. 4, at 185.

59. Ibid., vol. 4, at 201–2.

60. Ibid., vol. 4, at 203.

61. Ibid., vol. 4, at 208.

62. Ibid., vol. 4, at 209.

63. Ibid., vol. 4, at 210.

64. Ibid., vol. 4, at 216.

65. Ibid., vol. 4, at 219.

66. Ibid., vol. 4, at 222–23.

67. Ibid., vol. 4, at 225.

68. Ibid., vol. 4, at 226.

69. Ibid., vol. 4, at 233.

70. Ibid., vol. 4, at 240.

71. Ibid., vol. 4, at 241.

72. Ibid., vol. 4, at 242.

73. Ibid., vol. 4, at 243.

74. Ibid., vol. 4, at 244. This is identical to the Virginia provision. Elliot ed., *Debates in the Several State Conventions on the Adoption of the Federal Constitution*, vol. 3, at 659. Also in *The Documentary History of the Ratification of the Constitution*, vol. 18, at 316.

75. Elliot ed., *Debates in the Several State Conventions on the Adoption of the Federal Constitution*, vol. 4, at 244.

76. Ibid.

77. Ibid., vol. 4, at 245. This, too, is identical with the Virginia proposal. Elliot ed., *Debates in the Several State Conventions on the Adoption of the Federal Constitution*, vol. 3, at 660. Also in *The Documentary History of the Ratification of the Constitution*, vol. 18, at 318.

78. Elliot ed., *Debates in the Several State Conventions on the Adoption of the Federal Constitution*, vol. 4, at 247.

79. Ibid., vol. 4, at 248–49.

80. Ibid., vol. 4, at 251.

81. *The Documentary History of the Ratification of the Constitution*, vol. 18, at 130.

82. *The Papers of James Madison*, Robert Rutland *et al.* eds. (Charlottesville: University of Virginia Press, 1977), vol. 11, at 297–98.

83. Ibid., vol. 11, at 307.

84. *The Papers of James Madison*, Charles F. Hobson *et al.* eds. (Charlottesville: University of Virginia Press, 1979), vol. 12, at 211.

85. Elliot ed., *Debates in the Several State Conventions on the Adoption of the Federal Constitution*, vol. 1, at 333.

CHAPTER 12

1. Robert Allen Rutland, *The Birth of the Bill of Rights* (New York: Collier Books, 1962), 196.

2. James Monroe Papers, New York Public Library, Miscellaneous Papers and Undated Letters.

3. Robert Allen Rutland, *James Madison: The Founding Father* (New York: Macmillan, 1987), 59–60.

4. Madison, Notes for Speech in Congress, June 8, 1789, *The Papers of James Madison*, Charles F. Hobson *et al.* eds. (Charlottesville: University Press of Virginia, 1979), vol. 12, at 193.

5. Ibid., vol. 12, at 193–94.

6. An Act Declaring the Rights and Liberties of the Subject, 1 W. & M., Sess. 2, cl. 2 (1689).

7. *Documentary History of the First Federal Congress of the United States of America*, Charlene Bangs Bickford ed. (Baltimore: Johns Hopkins University Press, 1986), vol. 4, at 9–10.

8. Ibid., vol. 4, at 10.

9. Ibid.

10. Ibid.

11. Ibid.

12. *Documentary History of the Ratification of the Constitution*, John P. Kaminski and Gaspare J. Saladino eds. (Madison: State Historical Society of Wisconsin, 1984), vol. 15, at 318.

13. Bickford ed., *Documentary History of the First Federal Congress of the United States of America*, vol. 4, at 11.

14. Ibid.

15. Ibid.

16. Ibid., vol. 4, at 12.

17. Russell L. Caplan, "The History and Meaning of the Ninth Amendment," in *The Rights Retained By the People: The History and Meaning of the Ninth Amendment*, Randy E. Barnett ed. (Lanham, Md.: University Publishing Associates, Inc., 1989), 278–79 and n.142, observes:

> Madison's distinction between powers and rights assumed a sharply definable boundary between governmental and individual discretion. For Madison, a power was a delegated capacity allowing the government to perform certain kinds of acts. . . . It is Madison's consistent usage, which eliminated the ambiguous concept of state rights as referring to both governmental and personal rights, replacing it with the clearer power/right dichotomy, that was adopted with the Bill of Rights.

18. *Documentary History of the First Federal Congress of the United States of America*, Charlene Bangs Bickford *et al.* eds. (Baltimore: Johns Hopkins University Press, 1992), vol. 11, at 819–20.

19. Ibid., vol. 11, at 821.

20. Ibid., vol. 11, at 822. Also in *Annals of Congress* (Washington, D.C.: Gales and Seaton, 1834), vol. 1, at 436–37.

21. Bickford *et al.* eds., *Documentary History of the First Federal Congress of the United States of America*, vol. 11, at 828. Also in *Annals of Congress*, vol. 1, at 442.

22. Bickford *et al.* eds., *Documentary History of the First Federal Congress of the United States of America*, vol. 11, at 824. Also in *Annals of Congress*, vol. 1, at 438.

23. Jonathan Elliot ed., *The Debates in the Several State Conventions on the Adoption of the Federal Constitution* (Philadelphia: J. B. Lippincott, 1836), vol. 3, at 660 (Virginia); vol. 4, at 245 (North Carolina); vol. 2, at 545–46 (Harrisburg). See also *Documentary History of the Ratification of the Constitution*, Merrill Jensen ed. (Madison: State Historical Society of Wisconsin, 1976), vol. 2, at 624 (Pennsylvania "Dissent of Minority").

24. Ames to Thomas Dwight, June 11, 1789, *Works of Fisher Ames*, Seth Ames ed. (New York 1854), vol. 1, at 52–53.

25. Ames to F. R. Minoe, June 12, 1789, ibid., vol. 1, at 53–54.

26. *Creating the Bill of Rights: The Documentary Record from the First Federal Congress*, Helen E. Veit *et al.* eds. (Baltimore: Johns Hopkins University Press, 1991), 249.

27. Ibid., 253. Also in Hobson *et al.* eds., *The Papers of James Madison*, vol. 12, at 258.

28. *Federal Gazette*, June 18, 1789, at 2, col. 1. Madison's proposals had been published two days before in the same paper. *Federal Gazette*, June 16, 1789, at 2, cols. 2–3.

29. Coxe to Madison, June 18, 1789, Hobson *et al.* eds., *The Papers of James Madison*, vol. 12, at 239–40.

30. Madison to Coxe, June 24, 1789, ibid., vol. 12, at 257.

31. *New York Packet*, June 23, 1789 at 2, cols. 1–2.

32. Madison to Coxe, June 24, 1789, Hobson *et al.* eds., *The Papers of James Madison*, vol. 12, at 257.

33. *Massachusetts Centinel* (Boston), July 4, 1789, at 1, col. 2.

34. Jack N. Rakove, *The Second Amendment: The Highest Stage of Originalism,* 76 Chi.–Kent L. Rev., 103, 115 n.30, 123 n.48 (2000).

35. *Federal Gazette*, June 30, 1789, at 2, cols. 1–2.

36. *Federal Gazette*, July 2, 1789, at 2, col. 1.

37. Veit *et al.* eds., *Creating the Bill of Rights*, 260–61. Spelling and punctuation corrected. For Nasson's earlier correspondence with Thatcher, see ibid., 251.

38. Ibid., 261. Spelling and punctuation corrected.

39. Ibid., 241.

40. *Documentary History of the Ratification of the Constitution*, John P. Kaminski and Gaspare J. Saladino eds. (Madison: State Historical Society of Wisconsin, 2000, 2001), vol. 6, at 1490; vol. 7, at 1583–84, 1597–98.

41. Hobson *et al.* eds., *The Papers of James Madison*, vol. 12, at 363–64.

42. Thomas Jefferson, *The Papers of Thomas Jefferson*, Julian P. Boyd *et al.* eds. (Princeton, N.J.: Princeton University Press, 1951), vol. 1, at 344–45.

43. The other members included Abraham Baldwin, Aedanus Burke, Nicolas Gilman, George Clymer, Egbert Benson, Benjamin Goodhue, Elias Boudinot, and George Gale. Bickford ed., *Documentary History of the First Federal Congress of the United States of America*, vol. 4, at 4. See also Bickford *et al.* eds., *Documentary History of the First Federal Congress of the United States of America* (Baltimore: Johns Hopkins University Press, 1992), vol. 11, at 1157–63 (debate on motion to commit to committee).

44. James C. Hutson, "The Bill of Rights: The Roger Sherman Draft," *This Constitution*, no. 18, at 36 (Spring/Summer 1988). The draft was discovered in 1987.

45. Ibid.

46. Letter dated August 8, 1789. Veit *et al.* eds., *Creating the Bill of Rights*, 272.

47. *Pennsylvania Packet*, December 21, 1790, in *Documentary History of the First Federal Congress*, William Charles DiGiacomantonio *et al.* eds. (Baltimore: Johns Hopkins University Press, 1995), vol. 14, at 92–93.

48. Bickford ed., *Documentary History of the First Federal Congress of the United States of America*, vol. 4, at 28.

49. Elliot ed., *Debates in the Several State Conventions on the Adoption of the Federal Constitution*, vol. 3, at 658–59 (Virginia); vol. 4, at 244 (North Carolina).

50. Bickford ed., *Documentary History of the First Federal Congress of the United States of America*, vol. 4, at 10–11, 28–29.

51. Ibid., vol. 4, at 28.

52. Ibid., vol. 4, at 29.

53. *Independent Chronicle*, August 6, 1789, in *Documentary History of the Ratification of the Constitution*, vol. 6, at 1453. Reprinted in "From the Boston Independent Chronicle," *Independent Gazetteer*, August 20, 1789, at 2, col. 2.

54. *The Writings of Samuel Adams*, Harry Alonzo Cushing ed. (New York: G.P. Putnam's Sons, 1908), vol. 4, at 334.

55. Letter dated April 22, 1789, ibid., vol. 4, at 326–27.

56. Veit *et al.* eds., *Creating the Bill of Rights*, 272–73.

57. Hutson, "The Bill of Rights," *This Constitution*, no. 18, at 36 (Spring/Summer 1988).

58. Bickford *et al.* eds., *Documentary History of the First Federal Congress of the United States of America*, vol. 11, at 1221–22.

59. Ibid., vol. 11, at 1230.

60. Ibid., vol. 11, at 1240. Also in *Annals of Congress*, vol. 1, at 717–18.

61. Bickford *et al.* eds., *Documentary History of the First Federal Congress of the United States of America*, vol. 11, at 1242.

62. Ibid., vol. 11, at 1253–54.

63. Jonathan Elliot ed., *The Debates on the Adoption of the Federal Constitution in the Convention Held at Philadelphia . . . Vol. V. Supplementary to Elliot's Debates* (Philadelphia: J. B. Lippincott, 1845), 538.

64. *Documentary History of the First Federal Congress of the United States of America*, vol. 11, at 1261. Also in *Annals of Congress*, vol. 1, at 729–30.

65. *Documentary History of the First Federal Congress of the United States of America*, vol. 11, at 1261. Also in *Annals of Congress*, vol. 1, at 730.

66. *Documentary History of the First Federal Congress of the United States of America*, vol. 11, at 1262.

67. Ibid., vol. 11, at 1263.

68. *Documentary History of the Ratification of the Constitution*, vol. 6, at 1337. Also in Elliot ed., *Debates in the Several State Conventions on the Adoption of the Federal Constitution*, vol. 2, at 97.

69. Bickford *et al.* eds., *Documentary History of the First Federal Congress of the United States of America*, vol. 11, at 1270.

70. Ibid., vol. 11, at 1280.

71. Ibid., vol. 11, at 1285–86. Also in *Annals of Congress*, vol. 1, at 749–50.

72. Bickford *et al.* eds., *Documentary History of the First Federal Congress of the United States of America*, vol. 11, at 1286. Also in *Annals of Congress*, vol. 1, at 750.

73. Bickford *et al.* eds., *Documentary History of the First Federal Congress of the United States of America*, vol. 11, at 1286.

74. Ibid., vol. 11, at 1286–87.

75. Ibid., vol. 11, at 1287.

76. Ibid., vol. 11, at 1287–88. Also in *Annals of Congress*, vol. 1, at 750–51.

77. Bickford *et al.* eds., *Documentary History of the First Federal Congress of the United States of America*, vol. 11, at 1288. Also in *Annals of Congress*, vol. 1, at 751.

78. Bickford *et al.* eds., *Documentary History of the First Federal Congress of the United States of America*, vol. 11, at 1288. Also in *Annals of Congress*, vol. 1, at 752.

79. Bickford *et al.* eds., *Documentary History of the First Federal Congress of the United States of America*, vol. 11, at 1288–91.

80. Ibid., vol. 11, at 1291–2.

81. Ibid., vol. 11, at 1292–93.

82. Ibid., vol. 11, at 1300–1.

83. Ibid., vol. 11, at 1297.

84. Muhlenberg to Rush, August 18, 1789, in Veit *et al.* eds., *Creating the Bill of Rights,* 280.

85. Ibid., 309.

86. Ibid., 280.

87. *Documentary History of the Ratification of the Constitution*, Merrill Jensen ed. (Madison: State Historical Society of Wisconsin, 1976), vol. 2, 623–24.

88. *Documentary History of the First Federal Congress of the United States of America*, vol. 11, at 1308.

89. Letter of August 24, 1789, in Hobson *et al.* eds., *The Papers of James Madison*, vol. 12, at 352.

90. Bickford *et al.* eds., *Documentary History of the First Federal Congress of the United States of*

*America*, vol. 11, at 1309. See also version in *Annals of Congress*, vol. 1, at 766–67.

91.  Bickford *et al.* eds., *Documentary History of the First Federal Congress of the United States of America*, vol. 11, at 1309. See also version in *Annals of Congress*, vol. 1, at 767.

92.  Bickford *et al.* eds., *Documentary History of the First Federal Congress of the United States of America*, vol. 11, at 1310.

93.  Ibid., vol. 11, at 1319.

94.  Ibid., vol. 11, at 1319–23.

95.  Hobson *et al.* eds., *The Papers of James Madison*, vol. 12, at 348.

96.  Edmund Randolph to James Madison, August 18, 1789, ibid., vol. 12, at 345.

97.  Veit *et al.* eds., *Creating the Bill of Rights*, 289.

98.  Richard Henry Lee to Charles Lee, August 28, 1789, *Letters of Richard Henry Lee* (New York: Macmillan, 1914), vol. 2, at 499.

99.  "Political Maxims," *New York Daily Advertiser*, August 15, 1789, at 2, col. 1.

100.  *Independent Gazetteer* (Philadelphia), August 18, 1789, at 3, col. 1.

101.  Centinel Revived, no. xxix, *Independent Gazetteer*, September 9, 1789, at 2, col. 2.

102.  *Documentary History of the Ratification of the Constitution*, vol. 2, at 617.

103.  Elliot ed., *Debates in the Several State Conventions on the Adoption of the Federal Constitution*, vol. 3, at 660 (Virginia); vol. 4, at 245 (North Carolina); vol. 2, at 545–46 (Harrisburg convention). See also *Documentary History of the Ratification of the Constitution*, vol. 2, at 624 (Pennsylvania Dissent of Minority).

104.  Veit *et al.* eds., *Creating the Bill of Rights*, 300.

105.  *The Diary of William Maclay and Other Notes on Senate Debates: 4 March 1789–3 March 1791*, Kenneth R. Bowling and Helen E. Veit eds. (Baltimore: Johns Hopkins University Press, 1988), 133.

106.  *Journal of the First Session of the Senate of the United States of America* (Washington, D.C.: Gales & Seaton, 1820), 70.

107.  Ibid., 71.

108.  Ibid.

109.  Letter dated September 9, 1789 (spelling corrected). Veit *et al.* eds., *Creating the Bill of Rights*, 293.

110.  Those voting against the clauses included Senators Carroll, Dalton, Ellsworth, Elmer, Johnson, King, Paterson, Read, and Schuyler. *Journal of the First Session of the Senate of the United States of America*, 71.

111.  Ibid.

112.  See Jack N. Rakove, *The Second Amendment: The Highest Stage of Originalism*, 76 Chi.–Kent L. Rev., 103, 124-25 (2000).

113.  Bickford *et al.* eds., *Documentary History of the First Federal Congress of the United States of America*, vol. 11, at 1285–86. Also in *Annals of Congress*, vol. 1, at 749–50.

114.  *Journal of the First Session of the Senate of the United States of America*, 72.

115.  Ibid., 73.

116.  Bickford ed., *Documentary History of the First Federal Congress of the United States of America*, vol. 4, at 31 n.34.

117.  *Journal of the First Session of the Senate of the United States of America*, 74.

118.  Ibid., 75.

119.  Ibid.

120.  John Randolph to St. George Tucker, September 11, 1789. Veit *et al.* eds., *Creating the Bill of Rights*, 293. Attribution of this information to Lee is suggested in Kenneth Russell Bowling, *"A Tub to the Whale": The Founding Fathers and Adoption of the Federal Bill of Rights* (Virginia Commission on the Bicentennial of the U.S. Constitution, n.d.), 12.

121.  *Journal of the First Session of the Senate of the United States of America*, 77.

122.  Ibid. While the minutes do not reflect the makers of motions, and no recorded vote was

taken on the above, a recorded vote on another matter the same day reveals the following senators present: Bassett, Carroll, Dalton, Ellsworth, Grayson, Gunn, Henry, Johnson, Izard, King, Lee, Morris, Paterson, Read, Schuyler, and Wingate.

123. Ibid., 71.

124. Ibid., 77.

125. Bickford *et al.* eds., *Documentary History of the First Federal Congress of the United States of America*, vol. 11, at 1287–88. Also in *Annals of Congress*, vol. 1, at 751.

126. *Journal of the First Session of the Senate of the United States of America*, 77.

127. Ibid., 77–78.

128. Bickford ed., *Documentary History of the First Federal Congress of the United States of America*, vol. 4, at 8.

129. Ibid., vol. 4, at 43.

130. Ibid., vol. 4, at 45.


CHAPTER 13

1. Ratification by the following three-fourths of the states made the Bill of Rights effective:

| | |
|---|---|
| New Jersey | November 20, 1789 |
| New York | February 24, 1790 |
| Maryland | December 19, 1789 |
| Pennsylvania | March 10, 1790 |
| North Carolina | December 22, 1789 |
| Rhode Island | June 7, 1790 |
| South Carolina | January 19, 1790 |
| Vermont | November 3, 1791 |
| New Hampshire | January 25, 1790 |
| Virginia | December 15, 1791 |
| Delaware | January 28, 1790 |

The first ten amendments would be later ratified in *1939*, obviously as a symbolic gesture, by Massachusetts, Georgia, and Connecticut.

2. *Gazette of the United States*, October 14, 1789, at 211, col. 2.

3. "An Idea of a Constitution," *Independent Gazetteer*, December 28, 1789, at 3, col. 3.

4. David Ramsay, *The History of the American Revolution* (Philadelphia: R. Aitken, 1789; reprinted, Indianapolis: Liberty Classics, 1990), vol. 1, at 176–77. See Peter C. Messer, "From a Revolutionary History to a History of Revolution: David Ramsay and the American Revolution," *Journal of the Early Republic* (2002), vol. 22, no. 2, 205; Arthur Shaffer, *To Be an American: David Ramsay and the Making of the American Consciousness* (Columbia: University of South Carolina Press, 1991), 90, 105.

5. *The Papers of James Madison*, Charles F. Hobson *et al.* eds. (Charlottesville: University of Virginia Press, 1979), vol. 12, at 460.

6. Ibid., vol. 12, at 454–55.

7. http://www.usdoj.gov/jmd/ls/agbiographies.htm (accessed December 14, 2007).

8. Hobson *et al.* eds., *The Papers of James Madison*, vol. 12, at 456.

9. Ibid., vol. 12, at 460.

10. *Journal of the Senate* [Virginia], December 12, 1789, 61–65.

11. Ibid., 62–63.

12. Ibid., 63.

13. Ibid.

14. Jonathan Elliot ed., *The Debates in the Several State Conventions on the Adoption of the Federal Constitution* (Philadelphia, J. B. Lippincott, 1836), vol. 3, at 661.

15. *Journal of the Senate* [Virginia], December 12, 1789, 63–64.

16. Elliot ed., *Debates in the Several State Conventions on the Adoption of the Federal Constitution*, vol. 3, at 659.

17. *Journal of the Senate* [Virginia], December 12, 1789, 64.

18. Elliot ed., *Debates in the Several State Conventions on the Adoption of the Federal Constitution*, vol. 3, at 660.

19. *Journal of the Senate* [Virginia], December 12, 1789, 64.

20. Hobson *et al.* eds., *The Papers of James Madison*, vol. 12, at 464–65.

21. March 19, 1790. William Wirt, *Patrick Henry: Life, Correspondence and Speeches* (New York: Scribner's, 1891; reprinted 1951), vol. 3, at 417–18.

22. *E.g.,* "Summary of the principal Amendments proposed to the [Constitution of the United States] which appear more immediately proper to be adopted," post May 29, 1790 MSS, College of William & Mary, Tucker-Coleman Collection, Box 39b notebooks, Notebook VI, at 214.

23. *Federal Gazette,* January 5, 1790, at 2, col. 3.

24. *Federal Gazette,* January 15, 1790, at 3, col. 3.

25. Denys P. Myers, *Massachusetts and the First Ten Amendments* (Washington, D.C.: U.S. Government, 1936), 10.

26. Ibid., 11.

27. Ibid., 11–13.

28. William Blackstone, *Commentaries,* St. George Tucker ed. (Philadelphia: William Young Birch and Abraham Small, 1803), vol. 1, at 332.

29. Myers, *Massachusetts and the First Ten Amendments,* 28.

30. Ibid., 11–12.

31. *Providence Gazette & Country Journal,* January 30, 1790, at 1.

32. *Minutes of the Convention Held at South Kingstown, Rhode Island, in March 1790, which Failed to Adopt the Constitution of the United States,* Theodore Foster ed. (Providence, Rhode-Island Historical Society, 1929), 58.

33. Ibid.

34. Ibid.

35. Ibid., 60.

36. Ibid., n.77.

37. Ibid., 61.

38. Ibid., 95.

39. Ibid.

40. Ibid., 62.

41. Ibid., 77.

42. Ibid., 78.

43. Ibid., 23.

44. John P. Kaminski, "'Outcast' Rhode Island – The Absent State," *This Constitution,* no. 15, at 36–37 (Summer 1987). See Frank Green Bates, *Rhode Island and the Formation of the Union* (New York: Columbia University, 1898), 149–200.

45. *The Diary of William Maclay and Other Notes on Senate Debates: 4 March 1789–3 March 1791,* Kenneth R. Bowling and Helen E. Veit eds. (Baltimore and London: Johns Hopkins University Press, 1988), 271.

46. Foster ed., *Minutes of the Convention Held at South Kingstown, Rhode Island, in March 1790, which Failed to Adopt the Constitution of the United States,* 25.

47. Elliot ed., *Debates in the Several State Conventions on the Adoption of the Federal Constitution,* vol. 1, at 334.

48. Ibid., vol. 1, at 335.

49. Ibid., vol. 1, at 336–37.

50. Ibid., vol. 1, at 336.

51. Foster ed., *Minutes of the Convention Held at South Kingstown, Rhode Island, in March 1790, which Failed to Adopt the Constitution of the United States*, 26.

52. *Independent Gazetteer*, January 29, 1791, at 2, col. 3.

53. Manuscript in New York Historical Society, Albert Gallatin Papers.

54. *The Proceedings Relative to Calling the Conventions of 1776 and 1790* (Harrisburg, Pa.: John S. Wiestling, 1825), 152.

55. Ibid., 153–54. Members included William Findley, Edmond Hand, Henry Miller, James Wilson, William Irvine, William Lewis, James Ross, Charles Smith, and Alexander Addison. Biographical information on Findley, Wilson, Lewis, Ross, and Addison may be found in Alexander Graydon, *Memoirs of His Own Time* (Philadelphia: Lindsay & Blakiston, 1846), 351–56.

56. Annals of Congress, vol. 1, at 434 (June 8, 1789); *Federal Gazette* (Philadelphia), June 16, 1789, at 2, col. 2.

57. *Federal Gazette*, June 18, 1789, at 2, col. 1.

58. *The Proceedings Relative to Calling the Conventions of 1776 and 1790*, 163. Also in *Pennsylvania Gazette*, December 30, 1789.

59. E.g., *Providence Gazette & Country Journal*, January 30, 1790, at 1.

60. *The Proceedings Relative to Calling the Conventions of 1776 and 1790*, 380.

61. On their role at the state convention, *see* Graydon, *Memoirs of His Own Time*, 355–56.

62. *The Proceedings Relative to Calling the Conventions of 1776 and 1790*, 173, 175.

63. Ibid., 258.

64. Ibid., 225, 263.

65. Ibid., 270–71.

66. Ibid., 274.

67. Pennsylvania Declaration of Rights, Art. XXI; *The Proceedings Relative to Calling the Conventions of 1776 and 1790*, 305.

68. Pennsylvania Declaration of Rights, Art. VI, § 2; *The Proceedings Relative to Calling the Conventions of 1776 and 1790*, 302.

69. See "Introduction" to *The Works of James Wilson*, Robert Green McCloskey ed. (Cambridge: Belknap Press, 1967), vol. 1, at 1–48.

70. *The Works of the Honourable James Wilson* (Philadelphia: Lorenzo Press, 1804), vol. 2, at 496.

71. James Otis relied on the same passage in arguing self-defense in a trial held in 1771. John Adams, *Legal Papers* (Cambridge: Belknap Press/Harvard University Press, 1965), vol. 1, at 160 n.16. The passage is quoted in William Eden, *Principles of Penal Law* (Dublin: John Milliken, 1772), 213–14, a work heavily relied on by Thomas Jefferson. *The Commonplace Book of Thomas Jefferson: A Repertory of His Ideas on Government*, Gilbert Chinard ed. (Baltimore: Johns Hopkins University Press, 1926), 324–26.

72. *The Works of the Honourable James Wilson*, vol. 2, at 496, quoting "Cic. pro Mil." (*Cicero pro Milo*) in Latin. The above translation is from Cicero, *Selected Political Speeches*, Michael Grant trans. (New York: Penguin Books, 1969), 222.

73. *The Works of the Honourable James Wilson*, vol. 2, at 496, citing "3. Bl. Com. 4."

74. Blackstone, *Commentaries*, vol. 3, at *4.

75. *The Works of the Honourable James Wilson*, vol. 3, at 84.

76. Ibid., citing "Bac. on Gov. 40."

77. Nathaniel Bacon, *An Historical and Political Discourse of the Laws and Government of England. Collected from Some Manuscript Notes of John Selden, Esq.* (London: D. Browne and A. Millar, 1760), vol. 1, at 40.

78. Ibid., vol. 1, at 192.

79. Ibid., vol. 2, at 59.

80. *The Works of the Honourable James Wilson*, vol. 3, at 84–85, citing "7. Rep. 6."

81. *The Works of the Honourable James Wilson*, vol. 3, at 84.

82. The members were Nicholas Ridgely, Richard Bassett, John Clayton, Kensey Johns, Rhoads Shankland, Charles Polk, Thomas Montgomery, Edward Roche, James Sykes, Peter Robinson, and Isaac Cooper. *Minutes of the Convention of the Delaware State* (1791), 12–13. The first five on this list were members of the 1776 convention. *Proceedings of the Convention of the Delaware State, Held at New-Castle on Tuesday the Twenty-Seventh of August, 1776* (Wilmington: J. Adams, 1776), 6.

83. *Minutes of the Convention of the Delaware State*, 18.

84. Ibid., 22 (December 17, 1791).

85. Pennsylvania Declaration of Rights, Art. XXI (1790).

86. Delaware Declaration of Rights, Art. XVIII (1776).

87. Harold B. Hancock, *The Loyalists of Revolutionary Delaware* (Newark: University of Delaware Press, 1977), 48–50.

88. *Documentary History of the Ratification of the Constitution*, Merrill Jensen ed. (Madison: State Historical Society of Wisconsin, 1976), vol. 3, at 62, 97.

89. *Minutes of the Grand Committee of the Whole Convention of the State of Delaware* (Wilmington: James Adams, 1792), 12 (December 20, 1791).

90. *Documentary History of the Ratification of the Constitution*, vol. 3, at 62, 97.

91. *Laws of the State of Delaware, 1700–1797* (New Castle: Samuel and John Adams, 1797), 968.

92. Delaware Constitution, Art. I, § 17 (1792).

93. *Minutes of the Convention of the Delaware State*, 42–43.

94. *Minutes of the Grand Committee of the Whole*, 13.

95. *Laws of the State of Delaware*, 104.

96. Ibid., 1136.

97. Kentucky Constitution, Art. XII, § 22 (1792).

98. Ibid., Art. XII, § 23.

99. Ibid., Art. VI, § 2.

## CHAPTER 14

1. Speech of January 7, 1790, *Independent Chronicle* (Boston), January 14, 1790, at 3.

2. Chapter 33 in *Statutes at Large of the United States of America* (Boston: Little & Brown, 1845), vol. 1, at 271 (May 8, 1792). See generally Richard H. Kohn, *Eagle and Sword: The Federalists and the Creation of the Military Establishment in America, 1783–1802* (New York: Free Press, 1975).

3. *Debates and Proceedings in the Congress of the United States* (January 18, 1790), vol. 2, at App. 2088.

4. Ibid., vol. 2, at 2092.

5. Ibid., vol. 2, at 2095.

6. *The Diary of William Maclay and Other Notes on Senate Debates: 4 March 1789–3 March 1791*, Kenneth R. Bowling and Helen E. Veit eds. (Baltimore and London: Johns Hopkins University Press, 1988), 240.

7. Ibid., 101 n.7.

8. Ibid., 231.

9. Ibid., 245.

10. Ibid., 246.

11. Ibid., 246–47.

12. Ibid., 250.

13. Ibid., 252.

14. Pennsylvania Declaration of Rights, Art. XIII (1776).

15. *The Proceedings Relative to Calling the Conventions of 1776 and 1790* (Harrisburg, Pa.: John S. Wiestling, 1825), 244.

16. *The Diary of William Maclay and Other Notes on Senate Debates*, 385, 395.

17. Ibid., 312.

18. Ibid.

19. "Political Maxims," *Independent Gazetteer*, July 24, 1790, at 2, col. 1.

20. Ibid., July 31, 1790, at 2, col. 2.

21. See *Documentary History of the First Federal Congress*, Charlene Bickford & Helen Veit eds. (Baltimore: Johns Hopkins University Press, 1986), vol. 5, at 1458–60.

22. Ibid., vol. 5, at 1460–61.

23. *Annals of Congress* (December 16, 1790), vol. 2, at 1804. Also in *Documentary History of the First Federal Congress: Debates in the House of Representatives*, William Charles DiGiacomantonio *et al.* eds. (Baltimore: Johns Hopkins University Press, 1995), vol. 14, at 72, from *Gazette of the United States*, December 22, 1790.

24. *Documentary History of the First Federal Congress*, vol. 5, at 1462 n.6. See also *Documentary History of the First Federal Congress: Debates in the House of Representatives*, vol. 14, at 72–74.

25. *Annals of Congress* (December 16, 1790), vol. 2, at 1805–6. Also in *Documentary History of the First Federal Congress: Debates in the House of Representatives*, vol. 14, at 72–73.

26. *Annals of Congress* (December 16, 1790), vol. 2, at 1806. Also in *Documentary History of the First Federal Congress: Debates in the House of Representatives*, vol. 14, at 73.

27. *Annals of Congress* (December 16, 1790), vol. 2, at 1806; also in *Documentary History of the First Federal Congress: Debates in the House of Representatives*, vol. 14, at 73–74.

28. *Documentary History of the First Federal Congress: Debates in the House of Representatives*, vol. 14, at 49–50, from the *General Advertiser*, December 17, 1790.

29. Ibid., vol. 14, at 50 n.13.

30. Ibid., vol. 14, at 56–57, from the *Pennsylvania Packet*, December 18, 1790.

31. Ibid., vol. 14, at 51, from the *General Advertiser*, December 17, 1790.

32. Ibid., vol. 14, at 51–52.

33. Ibid., vol. 14, at 52.

34. Ibid., vol. 14, at 60, from the *Pennsylvania Packet*, Dec. 8, 1790.

35. Jonathan Elliot ed., *Debates on the Adoption of the Federal Constitution in the Convention Held at Philadelphia . . . Vol. V. Supplementary to Elliot's Debates* (Philadelphia: J. B. Lippincott, 1845), 464–65.

36. *Documentary History of the First Federal Congress: Debates in the House of Representatives*, vol. 14, at 62, from the *Pennsylvania Packet*, December 18, 1790.

37. *Documentary History of the First Federal Congress*, vol. 5, at 1461 n.3.

38. *Documentary History of the First Federal Congress: Debates in the House of Representatives*, vol. 14, at 63–64.

39. *Annals of Congress* (December 16, 1790), vol. 2, at 1809.

40. *Documentary History of the First Federal Congress: Debates in the House of Representatives*, vol. 14, at 64.

41. *Annals of Congress* (December 22, 1790), vol. 2, at 1821–22.

42. *Documentary History of the First Federal Congress: Debates in the House of Representatives*, vol. 14, at 64, from the *Pennsylvania Packet*, December 18, 1790.

43. Ibid., vol. 14, at 81, from the *General Advertiser*, December 18, 1790.

44. Ibid., vol. 14, at 92–93, from the *Pennsylvania Packet*, December 21, 1790.

45. Ibid., vol. 14, at 95.

46. Ibid., vol. 14, at 112–13, from *Gazette of the United States*, December 25, 1790.

47. The company's website is http://www.ahacsite.org/ (visited December 15, 2007).

48. *Documentary History of the First Federal Congress: Debates in the House of Representatives*, vol. 14, at 183, from *Dunlap's American Daily Advertiser*, January 6, 1791.

49. Ibid., vol. 14, at 184.

50. Chapter 33 in *Statutes at Large*, vol. 1, at 271 (May 8, 1792).

51. § 1, ibid.

52. § 2, ibid., vol. 1, at 272.

53. § 1, ibid., vol. 1, at 271.

54. Michael A. Bellesiles, *Arming America* (New York: Alfred A. Knopf, 2000), 230, citing U.S. Statutes 1:271–74.

55. Noah Webster, *An American Dictionary of the English Language* (New York: S. Converse, 1828).

56. Ibid.

57. Ibid.

58. Ibid.

59. § 1 of Chapter 33, *Statutes at Large*, vol. 1, at 271 (May 8, 1792).

60. Ibid.

61. § 4, ibid., vol. 1, at 272.

62. § 1, ibid., vol. 1, at 272.

63. §§ 6 and 10, ibid., vol. 1, at 273.

64. Samuel Latham Mitchill, *An Oration Pronounced Before the Society of Black Friars at Their Anniversary Festival, In the City of New-York, on Monday, the 11th of November, 1793* (New York: Friar M'Lean, 1793), 27-28.

65. 14 Stat. 422, 423 (1867).

66. 32 Stat. 775, 780 (1903).

67. Ibid., at 775.

68. Cf. H. Richard Uviller and William G. Merkel, *The Militia and the Right to Arms, Or, How the Second Amendment Fell Silent* (Durham, N.C.: Duke University Press, 2002), 109–144.

## CHAPTER 15

1. Mary Haldane Coleman, *St. George Tucker: Citizen of No Mean City* (Richmond, Va.: The Dietz Press, 1938), 127.

2. See Stephen P. Halbrook, "St. George Tucker: The American Blackstone," *Virginia Bar News*, 32, at 45–50 (February 1984).

3. Coleman, *St. George Tucker*, 35, 48–58.

4. "Biography of the Judges," 4 Virginia Reports (4 Call.) xxviii (1827).

5. William Blackstone, *Commentaries,* St. George Tucker ed. (Philadelphia: William Young Birch and Abraham Small, 1803), vol. 1, at 143 n.40.

6. Ibid., App. 300.

7. See Stephen P. Halbrook, *That Every Man Be Armed: The Evolution of a Constitutional Right* (Albuquerque: University of New Mexico Press, 1984; reprinted, Oakland, Calif.: Independent Institute, 1994, 2000), 51–53.

8. Blackstone, *Commentaries*, vol. 1, App. 357.

9. Ibid., vol. 1, at 289.

10. Ibid., vol. 1, at 315–16.

11. Ibid., vol. 5, App. n.B, at 19.

12. Jonathan Elliot ed., *Debates on the Adoption of the Federal Constitution in the Convention Held at Philadelphia . . . Vol. V. Supplementary to Elliot's Debates* (Philadelphia: J. B. Lippincott, 1845), 203–05.

13. *Documentary History of the Ratification of the Constitution*, John P. Kaminski and Gaspare J. Saladino eds. (Madison: State Historical Society of Wisconsin, 1995), vol. 18, at 127.

14. *The Law Practice of Alexander Hamilton*, Julius L. Goebel Jr. ed. (New York: Columbia University Press, 1964), vol. 1, at 831.

15. Merrill Lindsay, "Pistols Shed Light on Famed Duel," *Smithsonian*, at 94 (November 1976). See also Joseph J. Ellis, *Founding Brothers* (New York: Alfred A. Knopf, 2000), 37.

16. Adams to James Lloyd, February 17, 1815, in *The Works of John Adams, Second President of the United States* (Boston: Little, Brown, & Co., 1856), vol. 10, at 124.

17. To William Branch Giles, April 20, 1807, in Thomas Jefferson, *Writings* (New York: Library of America, 1984), 1175.

18. *Federal Gazette*, June 18, 1789, at 2, col. 1.

19. See Stephen P. Halbrook and David B. Kopel, "Tench Coxe and the Right to Keep and Bear Arms, 1787–1823," 7 *William & Mary Bill of Rights Journal* (February 1999), 347.

20. *Democratic Press* (Philadelphia), January 23, 1823, at 2, col. 2.

21. Sherman [Coxe's pen name], "To the People of the United States," no. IX, apparently published in the *Democratic Press* or in the *Philadelphia Sentinel and Mercantile Advertiser* in 1823, or possibly 1824. *Papers of Tench Coxe in the Coxe Family Papers at the Historical Society of Pennsylvania* (microfilm; Philadelphia: Historical Society of Pennsylvania, 1977), Reel 113, at 716.

22. Ibid., at 717.

23. William H. Sumner, *An Inquiry into the Importance of the Militia to a Free Commonwealth in a Letter . . . To John Adams . . . With His Answer* (Boston: Cummings & Hilliard, 1823), 21.

24. Ibid., 39–40.

25. Ibid., 69–70.

26. Timothy Dwight, *Travels in New England and New York* (New Haven, Conn.: Timothy Dwight, 1821), vol. 1, at 17.

27. Ibid.

28. *The Writings of Thomas Jefferson*, Paul Leicester Ford ed. (New York: G. P. Putnam's Sons, 1892–99), vol. 7, at 84.

29. For photographs and detailed descriptions, see Ashley Halsey, Jr., "George Washington's Favorite Guns," *American Rifleman* (February 1968), 23.

30. Benjamin Ogle Tayloe, *Our Neighbors on LaFayette Square: Anecdotes and Reminiscences* (Washington, D.C.: Library of American Institute of Architects, 1872), 47.

31. The rifle is now at the Frazier Historical Arms Museum, Louisville, Kentucky. Sheldon S. Shafer, "Historic gun finds a home," *Courier-Journal*, February 16, 2004.

32. *Copies of the Wills of General George Washington... and Other Interesting Records of the County of Fairfax, Virginia* (publisher not identified), 20.

33. Eugene E. Prussing, *The Estate of George Washington, Deceased* (Boston: Little, Brown, & Co., 1927), 416, 418, 486, 441.

34. George Morgan, *The True Patrick Henry* (Philadelphia: J. B. Lippincott, 1907), 464.

35. Jefferson, *Writings*, 505.

36. Thomas Jefferson to ?, 1803, in *The Writings of Thomas Jefferson*, Andrew A. Lipscomb and Albert Ellery Bergh eds. (Washington, D.C.: Millenium Edition, 20 vols., 1903–4), vol. 10, at 365.

37. Jefferson, *Writings*, 547.

38. Thomas Jefferson to Jacob J. Brown, 1808, Lipscomb and Bergh eds., *The Writings of Thomas Jefferson*, vol. 11, at 432.

39. "Memoirs of a Monticello Slave as dictated to Charles Campbell by Issac," in *Jefferson at Monticello*, James A. Bear, Jr. ed. (Charlottesville: University Press of Virginia, 1967), 17–18.

40. See "Firearms" in Index and referenced text in *Jefferson's Memorandum Books*, James A. Bear, Jr., & Lucia C. Stanton eds. (Princeton, N.J.: Princeton University Press, 1997), 1550. See also Ashley Halsey, Jr., "Jefferson's Beloved Guns," *American Rifleman* (November 1969), 17.

41. Halsey, "Jefferson's Beloved Guns," 17, 18.

42. Jefferson, *Writings*, 1246.

43. Jefferson to Peter Minor, July 20, 1822, quoted by former Monticello archivist James A. Bear, Jr., "Guns, Exercise, and Hunting" (Charlottesville, Monticello, n.d. mimeograph), at 3.

44. Jefferson, *Writings*, 1491–92.

45. Ibid., 1493–94.

46. See will and codicil in *The Writings of Thomas Jefferson*, Andrew A. Lipscomb ed. (Washington, D.C.: Thomas Jefferson Memorial Association, 1905), vol. 19, unpaginated facsimile. The inventories and appraisals of Jefferson's estates included Monticello and the Campbell County Tufton and Lego farms. The originals are in the Albemarle County Will Books referenced as follows: 8:281–83, 9:1–2, 9:20–22.

47. Robert A. Rutland, *James Madison: The Founding Father* (New York: Macmillan, 1987), 251.

48. Madison, "James Madison's Autobiography," 2 *William & Mary Quarterly*, (1945), 191, 208.

## CHAPTER 16

1. See Jack N. Rakove, *The Second Amendment: The Highest Stage of Originalism*, 76 Chi.–Kent L. Rev., 103, 119-20 n.38 (2000).

2. U.S. Constitution, Art. I, § 8.

3. U.S. Constitution, Art. I, § 2.

4. Noah Webster, *A Compendious Dictionary of the English Language* (New Haven, Conn.: Sidney's Press, 1806), 220.

5. Noah Webster, *On Being American: Selected Writings, 1783–1828*, Homer D. Babbidge, Jr. ed. (New York: Frederick A. Praeger, 1967), 166.

6. Noah Webster, *An American Dictionary of the English Language* (New York: S. Converse, 1828) ("people," 3).

7. Ibid., ("right," 10).

8. Ibid., ("keep").

9. Ibid., ("keep," 18).

10. *Documentary History of the Ratification of the Constitution*, John P. Kaminski and Gaspare J. Saladino eds. (Madison: State Historical Society of Wisconsin, 2000), vol. 6, at 1453.

11. St. George Tucker, *A Dissertation on Slavery* (Philadelphia: Matthew Carey Pub., 1796), 20.

12. *Digest of the Laws of the State of Georgia*, Horatio Marbury and William A. Crawford eds. (Savannah: Seymour, Woolhopter, and Stebbins, 1802), 263. *Cf.* Garry Wills, *A Necessary Evil: A History of the American Distrust of Government* (New York: Simon & Schuster, 1999), 258–59 (arguing that to "keep" arms meant to hold them in a communal military arsenal).

13. Webster, *An American Dictionary of the English Language* ("bear," 2 and 3).

14. § 1 and 4, Militia Act, in Chapter 33, *Statutes at Large*, vol. 1, at 271, 272 (May 8, 1792).

15. Garry Wills, "To Keep and Bear Arms," *New York Review of Books*, *42*, 14 (September 21, 1995).

16. See Webster, *An American Dictionary of the English Language*, defining "coat" in part as: "An upper garment, of whatever material it may be made. . . . That on which ensigns armorial are portrayed; usually called a *coat of arms.*"

17. While "bearing arms" may mean in some contexts "bearing coats of arms," bearing arms "in a coat" is not one of those contexts. The College of Arms refers to knights being "recognised by the arms they bore on their shields" and to "bear[ing] arms" on a military expedition. See http://www.college-of-arms.gov.uk/About/12.htm#c (accessed December 15, 2007).

18. Webster, *An American Dictionary of the English Language* ("pistol").

19. George C. Neumann, *A History of Weapons of the American Revolution* (New York: Bonanza Books, 1967), 151.

20. Tucker, *A Dissertation on Slavery*, 93.

21. Michael C. Dorf, *What Does the Second Amendment Mean Today?*, 76 Chi.–Kent L. Rev. 291, 317 (2000).

22. Webster, *An American Dictionary of the English Language* ("arms," 1).

23. Ibid. ("arms," 4).

24. Ibid. ("arms," end).

25. Ibid. ("gun").

26. Noah Webster, *An Examination of the Leading Principles of the Federal Constitution* (Philadelphia: Prichard & Hall, 1787), 43.

27. Webster, *An American Dictionary of the English Language*.

28. Wilfrid E. Rumble, "James Madison on the Value of Bills of Rights," *Constitutionalism: Nomos XX*, J. Roland Pennock and John W. Chapman eds. (New York: New York University Press, 1979), 122, 137.

29. Virginia Declaration of Rights (1776), XIII.

30. Webster, *An American Dictionary of the English Language* ("militia").

31. Ibid. ("regulated").

32. Ibid. ("necessary," 1).

33. Ibid. ("security," 1).

34. Ibid. ("free").

35. Ibid. ("state").

36. William Blackstone, *Commentaries*, St. George Tucker ed. (Philadelphia: William Young Birch and Abraham Small, 1803), vol. 4, at 151–52.

37. *The Papers of James Madison*, Robert A. Rutland *et al.* eds. (Chicago: University of Chicago Press, 1973), vol. 8, at 298–99.

38. Earl of Middlesex, *A Treaties concerning the Militia* (London: J. Millan, 1752), 13.

39. The syllogism is symbolized as follows:

$$p \supset q$$

$$\frac{p}{\therefore q}$$

The above is explained in any standard logic text. *E.g.*, Robert J. Fogelin, *Understanding Arguments: An Introduction to Informal Logic* (New York: Harcourt Brace Jovanovich, 1978), 132.

40. See Fogelin, *Understanding Arguments*, 132. The fallacy of denying the antecedent is symbolized as follows:

$$p \supset q$$

$$\frac{\sim p}{\therefore \sim q}$$

41. U.S. Constitution, Art. I, § 8.

42. Cf. Nelson Lund, *A Primer on the Constitutional Right to Keep and Bear Arms* (Potomac Falls: Virginia Institute for Public Policy, 2002), no. 7, at 6.

43. See U.S. Constitution, Art. I, § 8 ("the Congress shall have power"); Art. II, § 1 ("the executive power"); Art. III, § 1 ("the judicial power").

44. Webster, *An American Dictionary of the English Language* ("power," 11).

45. U.S. Constitution, Art. I, § 8, cls. 12 and 13.

46. Ibid., Art. I, § 10, cl. 3.

47. Blackstone, *Commentaries*, Tucker ed., vol. 1, at App. 308.

# Index

Note: "Bill of Rights" in upper case refers to the Bill of Rights after its final ratification in 1791. Lower case "bills of rights" refers to bills of rights in general or various forms, proposals, amendments discussed and debated prior to, or during, the Bill of Rights ratification process. It also refers to state bills of rights when those bills are not named. Unless otherwise indicated, "Constitution" refers to the U.S. Constitution.

# A Note on the Author

S TEPHEN  P.  H ALBROOK  received his Ph.D. in
Philosophy from Florida State University and J.D. from
Georgetown University Law Center. An attorney in Fairfax, Virginia, he has
argued constitutional law cases in the Supreme Court, and is a research fellow
with the Independent Institute. His books include *That Every Man Be Armed:
The Evolution of a Constitutional Right*; *Freedmen, the Fourteenth Amendment,
and the Right to Bear Arms, 1866-1876*; *A Right to Bear Arms: State and Federal
Bills of Rights and Constitutional Guarantees*; *Firearms Law Deskbook: Federal
and State Criminal Practice*; *The Swiss and the Nazis: How the Alpine Republic
Survived in the Shadow of the Third Reich*; and *Target Switzerland: Swiss Armed
Neutrality in World War II* (also in German, French, Italian, and Polish). *See
also* www.stephenhalbrook.com.

# INDEPENDENT STUDIES IN POLITICAL ECONOMY

*For further information and a catalog of publications, please contact:*

THE INDEPENDENT INSTITUTE

100 Swan Way, Oakland, California 94621-1428, U.S.A.

510-632-1366 • Fax 510-568-6040 • info@independent.org • www.independent.org